CW00688791

R · U · S · H

TRIBUTE

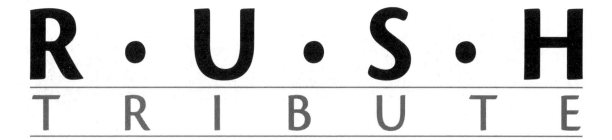

R·U·S·H TRIBUTE

MERELEY PLAYERS

Robert Telleria

QUARRY MUSIC BOOKS

R · U · S · H

Copyright © Robert Telleria, 2002. All rights reserved.

The publisher acknowledges the support of the
Government of Canada, Department of Canadian
Heritage, Book Publishing Industry Development
Program.

ISBN 1-55082-271-3

Cover, frontpiece, and color insert photos by
Brandon Klayman. All other photos and
ephemera from the collection of Robert Telleria.

Design and type by The Right Type,
Kingston, Ontario.

Printed and bound in Canada by
Transcontinental, Toronto, Ontario.

Published by Quarry Press Inc.,
P.O. Box 1061, Kingston, Ontario
K7L 4Y5 Canada.

Corrections can be e-mailed to:
Videovrtigo@aol.com for subsequent
book revisions.

·CONTENTS·

" I think we're not hip. We're basically musicians, players, and there are a lot of rock and roll purists who I don't think like us fucking around with the genre so much. When we first came out we were one of the most slagged bands in the history of rock and roll. That seems to have changed over the years as different critics have taken more time to try and understand what we were all about. "

— Geddy Lee, *Rolling Stone,* 2000

" They're good apples, squeaky clean. "

— Sam "The Record Man" Sniderman, *Maclean's,* 1991

" I think we're something apart from trends. We're neither a trendy nor a fashionable band, but our audiences are growing so it still has to be in vogue with those people. I think we appeal to a mentality, and there's still a lot of that mentality out there. "

— Geddy Lee

· I N T R O D U C T I O N ·

IN THE SUMMER OF 1999, I threw more than a decade's worth of research onto *The Rush Reference Page*,

domain: www.newworldreport.com.

The fans had a feast. It had been more than a decade since the official bio from the 'B-Man' Bill Banasiewicz and there was not even an official website for the greatest rock trio of all time. After a few months of slow but steady improvements, just days before 2000, the sheer weight of the site pulled it under. The exhaustive encyclopedia of all things Rush had capsized, presumably lost in the Cyber Sea. And the fans again had famine. They wondered if there would be another. If I had jumped ship … or worse … if the files were lost forever. Alas! I *did* recover the data and set my sights on a new course. There would be a long time before the New World Report could return, and there was still the starving fans to worry about. Technology had let me down, and I feared the information might have been stolen or replicated by pirates in the time it was down. The new land was actually old territory—the *written* word. No more scrolling, downloading, clicking … just good old fashioned *page-turning*. A book. The kind you can always carry around, always open up wherever you are. Though not official, the biggest one yet on Rush.

Biography & Chronology

First, biographical portraits for the three band members, to show that these icons are not deities but actual flesh and blood humans, with normal lives outside their profession. This section is followed by a chronology of notable career highlights, from their bluesy beginnings as a struggling bar band who played a little too loud, to the aggressive power trio with lyrical sci-fi symbolism who filled arenas. From progressive leanings to new wave explorations, with nary a hit single. To overwhelming respect for their musicianship with two decades worth of honors. They may be 'rock stars' but their history shows that they are not the sort of theatric, scandalous celebrity types identified by the masses, but low-key, soft-spoken musicians with a dream and a work ethic. Merely players. A listing of the chart positions, awards, and honors at a glance follow. A great tool for fans to use with confidence as the final word against the cynical rock purists, snobby jazz musos, or any other insecure species who unfortunately never 'got' these artists (or a break of their own). One has the right to not like them out of taste, but to dismiss their accomplishments is being the short-sighted fools they are.

Words & Music

Though not a publishing first, this section details the inspirational and intellectual poetry of Rush's lyrics (more specifically, drummer Neil Peart's lyrics). Compellingly written, philosophical, tasteful and universal, the songs are accompanied by relevant insight into the making of the song, including the musical approaches.

Instruments

For the first time in one compendium—a musician's dreambook—the instruments that Rush chose to make the music with over the years, both in the studio and on tour. And shoptalk from Rush to back up their instrumental selections and recording approaches.

Discography & Videography

Rush's albums have been released worldwide on almost every format. I have attempted to catalog it all—yes, even eight tracks count! This section will principally be of collector's interest (even though it still won't designate anal details like label color variations, test pressings, etc). Still, a casual observer just may find the list of non-commercial album singles (or radio promos) fascinating. And one look at the videography will have newer fans seeking out used copies of concerts as well as harassing the band's label for a new video compilation (which is long overdue). I did not list any bootlegs because not only are they unofficial, they are ever-growing, and they often have poor sound quality (though some are soundboard and/or professionally recorded). There are plenty of resources on the internet to find such items, however. And demos—none have reached the public to date, so don't be fooled by the home-made impostors with isolated vocals that surface from time to time. Many fans are not aware of how much Rush has participated with other artists because of little or no documentation in previous biographies. The band is always guest performing on another artist's recordings or producing a side project. Benefit recordings are listed here as well as solo projects.

Tours

Without hit singles, Rush had to tour. And tour. And tour. After that, they toured some more. And so I thought this very grueling aspect of the band's career should get its own chapter. The itinerary, or tour dates section, shows what road hogs Rush were, though it is certainly incomplete. Opening acts are listed beside the dates. Also provided is a list of songs they performed on each tour in order, for nostalgia, for the curious, and for hardcore fans to go and hunt down bootlegs to hear their favorite cuts performed live. And even more—the instruments they played on tour are listed.

Bibliography

Though they've been cruising under the mass media radar for years, members of Rush were and are not entire strangers to the press. They've had more than their share of magazine coverage and radio/TV interviews as the listings will clearly show. Listings of books and related literature close this section.

Tributes & Collectibles

This section is here to reflect the cult phenom Rush is. A collection of significant fanzines, cover bands, tribute recordings, artists who have thanked Rush in their liner notes, and the often bizarre world of Rush mentionings and references in all forms of media. Then to even more fascinating realm of Rush collectibles, from songbooks and backstage passes to pins and hats. A feast for the fans.

Rush News

To keep abreast of Rush news and to make contact with other Rush fans, try these resources.

Trust Funds:

Selena Taylor Trust Fund
c/o Anthem Entertainment
189 Carlton Street
Toronto, Ontario
Canada M5A2K7

Fanzines:

The Spirit of Rush
23 Garden Close
Chinbrook Rd, Grove Park, London UK
SE12 9TG

Since 1987, one of the best sources for Rush news via snail mail.

Official Websites:

The only official sites for members of the Rush 'family'. Geddy shares webspace with Andrew MacNaughton, who offers original photos on his site.

www.geddylee.net
www.myfavoriteheadache.com
www.andrewmacnaughtan.net

Other Websites:

www.rushbackstage.com
The Rush Backstage Club
#14-1095 Skyview Drive
Burlington, Ontario, Canada L7P 4W7

The official site. Authentic ShowTech merchandise includes t-shirts, jackets, hats, pins, sheet music, videos, more.

www.rush.com
www.rushworld.net
www.r-u-s-h.com

The Rush Interactive Network. Features a list of the most popular fan sites, updates, message boards, interviews, chats, Orbit Room info, and other such madness.

www.rushradio.net
It's not WYYZ-FM and there's no static on this frequency. All Rush, all day, all long.

www.canoe.ca
Canada's best source for rock updates with current Rush news.

www.terrybrown.net
See what Rush's old producer is up to and a list of all his work.

www.resist.demon.co.uk
Longtime fan Jim Wright's collectibles site is a good place to peruse variations in Rush singles and vinyl.

Rush Collectors Resource-
www.wellers.demon.co.uk
Another collector, Dave Wellers, and his list of singles. Except there's a nice breakdown of bootleg recordings.

http://24.93.200.44:2112 (The Digital Rush Experience)
Covers the wonderful world of bootlegs, describing the quality and setlists.

BIOGRAPHY & CHRONOLOGY

Alex Lifeson

Alex Lifeson was born Alexander Zivojinovich on August 27, 1953 in Fernie, British Columbia, Canada.

ALEX   My father Ned is Yugoslavian, and he worked in the mines in Fernie, British Columbia. When I was two, he hurt his back, and our family moved to Toronto. We all lived together in a real ethnic area of the city. Actually, it was great—there were millions of us living in this house, and no one spoke English on the street, but we all managed somehow to understand each other. (Guitar Player)

Until now, he had only practiced on a neighbor's guitar and on a viola, but in 1965 his parents bought him his first guitar.

ALEX   My mother Mellie has a beautiful voice, and she always sang to us. I can still recall her singing lullabies. But I really didn't start playing music until I was about 12, when I got a Kent classical guitar for Christmas. It was $11.00 new, right off the shelf, and the action was about 14″ above the neck. (Guitar Player)

The first thing he learned to play was the Noblesse cigarette commercial jingle. Always inventing, Alex later took the tone arm of his record player and forced the needle into the wood of his guitar body, creating his first 'amplifier'. He finally got a real amp, a small Kent, but he wanted a more-professional model so he so he taped the word 'Vox' to it. His next guitar was an electric—a Japanese-made $59 Conora electric solid-body, which he also 'modified'.

ALEX   When I got it, I painted it all psychedelic. Around that time Cream had come out, and I had to have a guitar that looked like Eric Clapton's Gibson SG. (Guitar Player)

Alex changed his last name to Lifeson because that is literally what his birth surname means in Croatian.

Geddy Lee

Geddy Lee was born Gary Lee Weinrib on July 29, 1953 in Willowdale, Ontario, Canada, with two siblings.

GEDDY My parents were in Poland at the outset of the war, and the Germans came in and every man they thought was a threat to them they took out and shot. As the war went on, they moved on to concentration camps. They were sent to Auschwitz where they survived. (Circus)

Around the time Alex picked up guitar, Gary's father passed away. He begins his musical training.

GEDDY It was your basic suburban story where you're very young and your mother thinks you should play the piano. I must have been nine or ten, and I remember going to lessons twice a week for a couple of years at the most. When I was really young, my sister took piano lessons and I was intrigued by the sounds. I was able to listen to the parts she was learning and figure them out by ear. I always trusted my ear, even when I was pretty young, and my ear has been my bread and butter. (Keyboard)

His mother Mary's thick Yiddish accent gives Gary his new name, *Geddy* among his peers and it sticks.

GEDDY When I was quite young she called me Gary, but my friends thought it sounded like Geddy so they called me Geddy. When I was about 14 or 15 and joined the Musician's Union, I joined as Geddy. (TV Guide Online)

Geddy had known Alex since their days in Fisherville Junior High. Geddy and Alex would play guitars after meeting in a history class.

GEDDY I remember the first time I ever saw that guy's mug. He was wearing a really weird paisley shirt. I remember the smarmy look on his face. (Bassics)

Neil Peart

Neil Peart was born on September 12, 1952 in Hamilton, Ontario, Canada as the first child of four, to parents of Welsh-English ancestry. Four years later they relocated from the farm country to the St. Catharines area of Southern Ontario.

NEIL In early adolescence, my hormones attached themselves to music. Mom and Dad gave me a transistor radio, and I used to lay in bed at night with it turned down low and pressed to my ear, tuned to pop stations in Toronto, Hamilton, Welland, or Buffalo. I still remember the first song that galvanized me: 'Chains', a simple pop tune by one of those girl groups, with close harmonies syncopated over a driving shuffle. No great classic or anything, but as I listened to that song on my transistor, suddenly I *understood*. This changed everything. (The Standard)

Neil discovered rhythm. His first drumset was a Japanese made Stewart 4-piece outfit in red sparkle with three Ajax cymbals.

NEIL   I just used to bang around the house on things, and pick up chop sticks and play on my sister's play pen. For my thirteenth birthday my parents paid for drum lessons. I had had piano lessons a few years before that and wasn't really that interested. But with drums, somehow I was interested. When it got to the point of being bored with lessons, I wasn't bored with playing. It was something I wanted to do everyday. So it was no sacrifice. No agony all. It was a pleasure. I'd come home everyday from school and play along with the radio. (Modern Drummer)

NEIL   Every Saturday morning, I took the bus uptown, and climbed the stairs to the Peninsula Conservatory of Music, above St. Paul Street. My teacher was Don George—someone else to whom I owe a lot. Don started me off so well: he emphasized the basics of technique (the famous 26 rudiments) and sight reading, but also showed me the flashier stuff, and was always enthusiastic and supportive. (The Standard)

Neil played with five-piece groups like Mumblin Sumpthin and The Majority.

NEIL   All the first bands I played in were blue-eyed soul bands. I played a lot of James Brown and Wilson Pickett tunes, because in the Toronto area that's what was popular at the time. All of us grew up playing "In The Midnight Hour". R&B is a part of my roots, and as a band I think we all played it and enjoyed it. (Modern Drummer)

Making his decision to drop out of Lakeport High School, Neil drummed for area bands such as J.R. Flood.

NEIL   Even by 1967, in our whole school there were only about three guys that dared to have long hair and in the hallways we endured constant verbal abuse: 'is that a girl?' 'hey sweetheart!' and other intelligent remarks. Outside it was worse—bullying threats and even beatings. All because we were freaks. (The Standard)

1968

April: As Led Zeppelin is formed by the Yardbirds' Jimmy Page on the other side of the Atlantic, in Scarborough, Ontario, 15-year old Alex Zivojinovich starts a trio called The Projection. Alex was borrowing various amps, like his friend Geddy's Traynor.

ALEX I couldn't afford a real good guitar at the time, so I used to borrow different ones from friends. We used to go to his house after school and just sit around and play, both of us plugging in to it. (Guitar Player 1980)

GEDDY We met in the eighth grade. I worked in my mother's hardware store for a while and Alex worked in a gas station. (Chronicles)

He was also borrowing guitars, like a solid-body Harmony (which looked like a Les Paul), and his other friend Lindy Young's Gibson Firebird.

ALEX My earliest influences were people such as Clapton, Jimi Hendrix, and Jimmy Page. Page was probably my greatest influence early on. Rush started just a little before the time Led Zeppelin came out, and when I heard the first album, I thought, "'They're doing just the things we want to do: They have the sound we want to have." And if we were that good, we could have played like that, too, if you know what I mean. (Guitar Player 1980)

John Rutsey, a friend of Alex's since the 4th grade and his neighbor across the street, volunteered to play drums. Playing Cream-style rock at school dances, they enlist bassist-vocalist Jeff Jones from Lactic Acid. By August, the band breaks up.

ALEX We had a repertoire of about 15 songs like "Gloria" and "Satisfaction", fairly simple numbers. It was a lot of fun, but we never played anywhere except for a few parties. If someone would have a party, we'd get one of our mothers to drive. (Guitar Player 1980)

September: Bill Rutsey, John's older brother, suggests the name 'Rush' when Alex and John begin looking for a new name for their new band. They find a replacement for Jeff Jones in their mutual classmate Gary, who plays rhythm guitar, a Conora that he also painted psychedelic.

ALEX We got a fairly regular gig at a drop-in center every Friday night. After a couple of months, we had a small name for ourselves, and eventually we tied in with the parks and recreation department of Toronto and did some outings for them. Also there were junior high school dances, for which we received about $40 a gig. So it was something; we split the money—13 bucks each. (Guitar Player 1980)

Gary and Alex write their first song together—"Losing Again", a 12-bar blues number. With the new funds, Alex buys a professional Gibson guitar.

December 25: Lindy joins Rush as keyboardist after a gig at the Coff-In with Rush in November. He actually plays a variety of instruments, including drums and guitar.

1969

January: A four-piece Rush debuts at the Coff-In covering Traffic, Willie Dixon, and Ten Years After. By February, Lindy begins singing more leads, especially on "You Don't Love Me" by John Mayall.

ALEX Right from when we started, I don't think we had any dreams about becoming the Rolling Stones or anything like that—it was just something we wanted to do; it was something that was a lot of fun. (Guitar Player 1980)

May: Gary kicked out (John thought Gary was stealing the spotlight). Joe Perna replaces him, and Rush becomes Hadrian.

Familiar with the band's frequent Coff-In shows, 16-year-old high-school dropout Ray Danniels approaches Rush at a southern Ontario school to ask if he could be their manager. They agree and he begins to book them from his own agency, Universal Sounds.

JOHN RUTSEY Ray was enthusiastic, talkative, a salesman type of guy. (Visions)

Gary forms the band Ogilvie in June but renames the group to 'Judd' in July. Alex pumps gas and works with his father Ned, a plumber. Geddy works in his mother's variety store. She calls him 'Geddy' in her thick Yiddish accent and the name sticks, with Geddy dropping Weinrib for his stage name. Alex also changed his surname to Lifeson, which is a rough translation of his Yugoslavian surname "son of life".

The Coff-In could only accommodate 150 people but twice that number were attending shows throughout November.

"Child Reborn" is one of the first Rush songs with notable time changes.

1970

September: Rush reforms to its original trio ensemble. This time they are bonded by the love of heavier blues rock (Cream, Jimi Hendrix, The Who, and Led Zeppelin). At shows, these bands' hits are covered as well as original songs, including "Number One", "Keep in Line", "Run Willie Run", "Mike's Idea", and "Tale". During the year, new songs surfaced in the set: "Sing Guitar", "Morning Star", "Marguerite", "Feel So Good", and "Love Light". Of this new batch of tunes, only "Garden Road" would be kept for a few more years.

ALEX After about five months, about a third of our repertoire was original tunes, and this held us back from playing a lot of places because people wanted to hear stuff they could relate to—songs on the AM radio stations and things like that. Some of the cover versions of songs we did, like "Fire", "Purple Haze", and "For What

It's Worth" we had our own arrangements for, so they didn't sound just like the originals. (Guitar Player 1980)

John acts as frontman introducing songs in their typical three 45-minute sets. Audience attendance varied from 200 (especially in their hometown) to just 35. Tickets for Rush gigs (in high-school auditoriums or gyms) are about $0.75 and the band is paid $350 a gig. Universal Sounds (Music Shoppe International) becomes their booking agent.

1971

February: Mitch Bossi temporarily joins Rush on rhythm guitar, making the band a quartet once again. Alex and fiancee Charlene McNicol have a son, Justin, while living together away from home. The two had been together for three years at this point. Ray urges Rush to play more covers to get more gigs. Ray's Beatles tribute band Liverpool was the most successful group that he managed at this time, helping establish good PR contacts throughout Canada and some of the U.S.A.). Rush were the least successful of all his acts, but they were the only band doing originals.

May: The Province of Ontario lowers the legal drinking age from 21 to 18, allowing Rush to play in the growing number of rock clubs. Their first gig is at the Gasworks.

ALEX After I finished high school the band really started happening. It wasn't just two gigs on weekends; it was six gigs a week, five sets a night. We got a pretty strong following after a while in Toronto, and we made lots of friends. (Guitar Player 1980)

Summer: During what the band called "The Dead Summer" (with Ray able to book only three gigs), Mitch is thrown out because he feels the band is "too serious." He told *City* magazine: "I didn't see too much future in the band. They didn't worry about security. They thought everything would turn out all right."

Fall: In their off time from their regular jobs, Geddy and Alex write extra hard rock songs like "Working Man" (about the jobs the band had when not playing bars) and "Slaughterhouse" (about animal rights). These marked the first songs the band published through CAPAC, Canada. Playing six nights (each with five sets) at Abbey Road pub (downtown Toronto) earns the band $1,000 a week.

1972

Rush begins gigs at bars like Larry's Hideaway, the Piccadilly Tube, and the Colonial, all in southern Ontario throughout 1972. Gigs in northern Ontario were more challenging.

GEDDY   We played a pub night at a local college and they kept telling us "Don't play too loud, we can't hear the beer orders." (Rolling Stone)

GEDDY   The worst was northern Ontario. They don't care what you do. They don't care if you do the greatest original material in the world if their ears haven't heard it before. They just want to get drunk and hear their favorite tunes. (Circus)

The Rush road crew was made up of just two men. For the last three years, "Major" Ian Grandy had mixed sound, and set up lights and drums. Now Liam Birt takes on some of the duties. With money earned from gigs, new gear was purchased, including Geddy's Fender Precision bass, Sunn cabinets, Alex's Marshall amps and pedals, and John's seven-piece blue Gretsch kit. All this gear is crammed in an Econoline van that the crew takes turns driving.

Geddy develops an interest in "art rock" (particularly Yes, Genesis, ELP, King Crimson, and Pink Floyd), while Alex takes six months worth of classical guitar lessons with school friend Elliot Goldner (who studied with Eli Kassner), using money earned from gigs.

ALEX   But Elliot was in a motorcycle accident, which kept him going in and out of the hospital for two years. Every week I'd go over and study with him, until he finally went back in for six months. Then the lessons stopped, and Rush started gigging more. (Guitar Player 1980)

1973

Spring: Rush books studio time with producer Bill Bryant at Rochdale College's 2-track facility called Sound Horn, but it was at Eastern Sound Studios that they recorded their first single, "Not Fade Away", a Buddy Holly cover, with "You Can't Fight It", a Lee-Rutsey original, on the B-side. They recorded on their own label, Moon Records, produced by David Stock. The logo and registered company name cost $400. Well-known distributors London Records had agreed to distribute the 1000 copies of the single, but the single received no airplay.

ALEX   Nobody wanted to pick us up; they said we were too heavy, and there was no market for the music the band was playing. So all the record companies in Canada passed on us. (Guitar Player 1980)

Summer: John Rutsey leaves the band temporarily due to illness and rejoins again.

JOHN RUTSEY   I was just going through a real struggle at the time with the band. I was just a mixed up kid and I began writing all sorts of additional lyrics because most of the lyrics we had were just what rhymed. So we made a conscious effort and I started writing some lyrics. (Visions)

Geddy later touches up the lyrics.

October 27: Rush opens for the New York Dolls at the 1200-seat Victory Burlesque Theatre on Spadina Ave in Toronto. The Dolls were a popular punk/glam band; Buster Poindexter (David Johansen) was a member of the band before becoming a well-known singer/actor.

After Rush is turned down twice by every major label in Canada, Ray Danniels sells Music Shoppe International to fund studio time for the band. With Vic Wilson, Daniels forms a new agency, S.R.O. (Standing Room Only) Management.

Debut album *Rush* on Moon Records is cut for $9000 at Toronto Sound Studios, which was owned by an Englishman named Terry Brown. He had previous mixing experience with The Who, Donovan, Procol Harum, and the Troggs, as well as Canadians April Wine and Thundermug. Little did anyone know, Terry would be Rush's co-producer for another decade.

ALEX   We were going in when the rates were a little cheaper. We'd finish a gig at 1:30, pack up, go to the studio until about 8 or 9, and the crew would take our gear back to the club, set it up, and we'd go down and play. I think we had two nights off in a row a total of three times in the course of six months. (BBC Rock Hour)

In just three days, the album is recorded and mixed, in middle-of-the-night sessions, just eight hours after gigs. "Here Again" and "Need Some Love" are redone. "Not Fade Away" is replaced by "Finding My Way". "In the Mood" is recorded at Eastern Sound. London Records distributes 3500 copies of the disc.

ALEX   Rush was very influenced by Led Zeppelin and Black Sabbath. We wanted to be as heavy as we could. But we were very proud of that first album. It will always have a special place in my heart … we had reached a certain level of success. (Hit Parader)

December: Debut release is delayed due to OPEC oil crisis (vinyl is a petroleum by-product).

1974

January: After four months of searching for an interested distributor, the first LP *Rush* is released independently in Ontario on Moon Records, mastered by Gilbert Kong. Initial sales are good considering there was no cost-friendly way to promote it other than playing live around Ontario.

Lead track "Finding My Way" is played on Toronto's CHUM-FM by DJ David Marsden, catching Alex's ear. He calls Marsden to thank him as it was the first time the band got any airplay.

ALEX Putting a record out was really a big deal, going into a studio. And I remember thinking, going into the studio: all the musicians I like, and all the bands that I like, do this. This is what they do. At one time sure, they played bars, and high schools, or whatever, but to go into a studio and record something, and make something that's permanent; that was a big deal. And then of course hearing it on the radio followed that. And again, because it was in Toronto, it meant even more to me, 'cause this was hometown. (Up Close)

May: Their second American performance to 1300 people takes place at the drive-in theater grounds in Lansing, Michigan. The reception is described as "indifferent."

WMMS-FM in Cleveland (the birthplace of rock and roll) program director Donna Halper receives a copy of *Rush* from Bob Roper, an A & M Canada rep and a friend of Ray Danniels. Halper begins playing "Working Man", thus exposing American radio to Rush for the first time. About 50 listeners phone the station, some thinking they just heard a new Led Zeppelin B-side. Roper happened to owe Ray Danniels a favor. Cliff Burnstein, a Mercury A & R rep, after receiving a copy of *Rush*, called Donna Halper, who said the record was getting a great response and that "Working Man" is the song.

CLIFF BURNSTEIN I hung up the phone, put it on, and sure enough it was a motherfucker. (Visions)

Ira Blacker's U.S. booking agency ATI (American Talent International) negotiates a booking deal with Ray and Vic. Cover artist Paul Weldon (who had designed Funkadelic's covers) played in Edward Bear, another band managed by Vic and Ray.

Rush sells 2000 copies in the U.S.A. and 3000 in Canada. The band is close to signing to Casablanca Records (same label as KISS), but negotiates a recording contract during a conference call with Chicago-based Mercury Records' president Irwin Steinberg and promotion manager Cliff Burnstein, who signed Canadians Bachman-Turner Overdrive. They receive a $75,000 advance ($25,000 towards future albums) as part of $200,000 contract for two albums. Ira Blacker, considered the band's American manager at the time, leaves ATI to form his own I-Mouse Management and would later settle out of court in an ownership dispute for $250,000. Phonogram would handle global distribution and Moon would continue as executive production company until 1991.

June 28: Ray books Rush opening for ZZ Top to an audience of 3,000 that goes over well, although Rush is denied a second encore by the Texas blues boogie trio.

ALEX We opened with 'Finding My Way' and the crowd went crazy! They obviously knew the material. We got an encore, and before we could go back up for a second encore, somebody ordered the lights turned up. (Visions)

Two weeks before the tour, John Rutsey quits the band for various reasons. As far as creative differences, Rutsey did suggest they stay as a basic rock trio, but Geddy and Alex wanted to graduate into more challenging, art-rock styles of playing.

ALEX John was not the easiest person to get along with. He was quite moody at times and I think he expected a lot from his friends … We'd already thought about getting a new drummer for the past year … We played another six weeks of gigs and strangely enough, we had the best time we'd ever had playing together. (Visions)

ALEX He gave up playing shortly after he left the band and went into bodybuilding. He competed on an amateur level for a while, doing that for a few years, and has sort of been in and out of that, but he still works out, and I work out with him a few times a week at a local gym at a Gold's, here in Toronto. (Rockline 1989)

Rush were forced to audition new drummers. On the second day of auditions, a tall, short-haired man named Neil arrives with his six-piece drumset (covered in silver wallpaper) stuffed in garbage cans. He learned the material quickly, adding an even more dynamic touch to the arrangements.

GEDDY We really didn't know how to start, so we just went with recommendations from other musicians that we knew. Someone had mentioned Neil's name to one of our managers at the time. He told us about him. We said, well, go see the guy. So he drove out to St. Catherine's where Neil was working in his father's farm equipment store. (In the Studio)

ALEX He had a very small set of Rogers [drums], I think. And he pounded the crap out of them. He really hit them hard. Incredible power and strength even back then. Of course, Geddy and him just hit it off. They, being a rhythm section, just got into a groove, and they were playing like mad. It took my ear a little longer to get a little more warmed up to Neil. But after Ged and I talked about it, we decided that this guy's *it*—he's just too good. (In the Studio)

All the great bands seemed to come from the U.K. at this time. Even fellow Canadian Pat Travers formed his band there successfully. Neil had moved to England hoping to make it there as a drummer. When he was not selling souvenirs at The Great Frog and Gear on London's Carnaby Street, he would perform in bands like Seventh Wave.

NEIL I packed up my drums and my records and moved to England when I was 18 thinking I'd just find a band. I was a big fish in a small pond, and threw myself into the biggest pond possible, musically speaking. It was all very depressing and very educational. In trying out for a band I'd discover that they were far, far over my head in technical knowledge, in their mastery of the language and also in their snobbery—I'd just go away feeling like a piece of dirt. (Musician)

July 29: Geddy's 21st birthday, and Neil officially leaves his current cover band Hush (named after the Deep Purple song but largely a Who cover quartet) and joins Rush. Hush members thought he had made a big mistake. Neil found a new artistic challenge in Rush, writing lyrics. Geddy told Alex nicknamed their new lyricist 'The Professor'.

GEDDY At the time, he had never written any lyrics … had never thought of it, I don't think. We had a date, like eight days later to play at the Pittsburgh Civic Arena opening for Uriah Heep and Manfred Mann. So that was first and foremost in our minds; we were just looking for a drummer. We never thought about lyrics or anything like that. The more we got to know Neil, the more we realized his immense knowledge of the English language and his interest in reading. He was a very different person for us—a person full of ideas and very verbose. Alex and I just looked at each other—this is the guy to solve all or problems (laughs) … (In the Studio)

NEIL I came into it by default, just because the other two guys didn't want to write lyrics. I've always liked words. I've always liked reading, so I had a go at it. I like doing it. When I'm doing it, I try to do the best I can. It's pretty secondary, I don't put that much importance on it. A lot of times you just think of a lyrical idea as a good musical vehicle. I'll think up an image, or I'll hear about a certain metaphor that's really picturesque. A good verbal image is a really good musical stimulus. If I come up with a really good picture lyrically, I can take it to the other two guys and automatically express to them a musical approach. (Modern Drummer)

GEDDY We had a pretty definite idea as to what we wanted and as soon as Neil came in and sat behind his kit, we just knew he was right. He was doing things we'd always wanted to hear behind our music—and Neil is also our man of words. (Circus)

NEIL There was a little more racket coming from the drum kit. Part of the conflict and tension with the previous drummer was that Geddy and Alex were starting to think in ways that he either couldn't or wouldn't keep up with. (Seconds 1994)

The next day, the band celebrate by purchasing new gear at Long and McQuade Music, with an advance from the record company.

NEIL It was a Babes in Toyland kind of day, total fantasy. All the way we were screaming and yelling up the highway. (Visions)

Howard Ungerleider, who had worked for ATI, joins the road crew, taking over lighting, and Dave Scace, who worked with Alex, was replaced by Jim Johnson.

August 14: As Mercury releases *Rush* to the States, the young band opens for Uriah Heep and Manfred Mann to a crowd of 11,462 in Pittsburgh, PA—their first American appearance with Neil. Their new gear is debuted on stage as well.

August 26: Simulcast on WMMS-FM, Cleveland. Donna Halper was stage announcer for the band's second appearance at the Agora Ballroom.

ALEX We got a real strong response the second time around, so we were booked two weeks later. (Visions)

August 31: The *Cincinnati Enquirer*'s Jim Knippenberg writes favorably about Rush, noting, "the only weakness with all of this has to do with the lyrics. They could use some polish. And a little variety. Perhaps some getting away from the 'love is the thing' and 'let's boogie' thing for a time. Instead, it's a more polished sound, complete with the variety you hardly ever find in heavy metal."

GEDDY I don't like [the category of] metal. We need a new name. (Cincinnati Enquirer)

GEDDY It's strange hearing this album they've released. We did it almost two years ago, and although I'm pleased with it, it's sort of old to me. I see it from a different standpoint. (Circus)

September: Rush tapes a show for King Biscuit Flower Hour and appear on Toronto show *Boogie*.

October: The album *Rush* climbs to US #105, the highest charting debut for Mercury for years.

October 9: The band appears on *Don Kirshner's Rock Concert*.

October 27: Rush supports New York Dolls in concert in Toronto.

November 28: *LA Times'* Dennis Hunt opines, "Rush's flagrantly derivative music was neither interesting nor listenable. It was amplified many decibels beyond what is comfortable for even the heartiest ears." Marc Shapiro in the *Hollywood Daily News* described Rush's gig at the Whisky a Go Go as "heavy metal tedium. The Canadian entry into the 'let's learn three chords and become the new Black Sabbath' derby relied on cliché riffs throughout its set and only twice did this reporter perceive anything resembling an imaginative riff."

Rush begins writing their sophomore album on the road, booking studio time in January. Geddy and Alex noted Neil's writing abilities and encouraged him to take charge of the lyrics.

GEDDY We had exactly 26 minutes to be onstage and offstage. We had two people on our road crew. We were traveling maybe 200 to 500 miles a night. We wrote songs in cars while moving, we wrote songs in hotel rooms, wherever we could get a minute alone. (Heart of Gold)

NEIL I never thought seriously about writing lyrics until I joined this band and it became a necessity because no one else was doing it. (Circus).

December 5: WQIV-FM radio simulcasts performance at Electric Ladyland Studios, New York. They opt to record their sophomore album there, but ultimately choose to finish touring.

December 6: Rush appears on ABC-TV's *In Concert*.

December 20: Rush Tour ends and the band enjoys the holidays. At the end of the year, 75,000 copies of *Rush* had sold in the United States alone, making it the biggest selling U.S. debut in Mercury's history.

1975

January: The album *Fly By Night* recorded and mixed in ten days. Engineered by Terry Brown, mastered by Gilbert Kong again.

February 14: Tour kicks off in Toronto.

February 15: *Fly By Night* is released in North America, and the first album is released in Britain.

NEIL Geddy had to scream in the beginning to be heard over the rest of the band because our equipment was so bad. (Chicago Tribune)

There was concern that Rush might be another 'fly by night' act marked by the tradition of winning Most Promising Group at the Juno Awards (Canada's version of the Grammy Awards) … their first award ever.

GEDDY That was a great help to us in Canada. It brought us a lot of attention from a lot of people who hadn't heard of us or people who hadn't taken us seriously. But it didn't help us much anywhere else. (Rush)

March 12: Alex marries Charlene.

Rush supports Aerosmith on tour. They rent a car in Toronto and decide to use it for stateside transportation.

ALEX We brought the car back with 11,000 miles on it. It didn't have any hubcaps left, the radio was smashed, the mirror was gone. It was ruined. They were quite surprised. (Rolling Stone)

Rush opens for Sha Na Na at a '50s music concert in Baltimore and are booed off stage halfway through their set.

GEDDY Everybody was ready to bop. We came out and just blistered their faces. (In Concert)

March 24: Juno Awards ceremony held at Queen Elizabeth Theatre in Toronto.

April 13: Rush opens for KISS at a sold out Detroit Michigan Palace audience of 4500 fans.

NEIL KISS is the only band that's never given us any trouble on the road. Lots of times it's not a band's fault that the opening act gets fucked over, and it's not worth talking about, but it does happen all the time. Kiss impose reasonable restrictions and we get along really well with them as friends and businesswise. (Circus)

Skip Gildersleeve meets the band here and replaces Jim Johnson. Liam switches from bass to guitar tech, and Ian serves as drum tech and sound man, Howard as road and lighting manager.

June 7: The stage is the San Diego Civic Center, where Rush plans a joke on KISS.

NEIL We were gonna dress up as them, put on their makeup, and go out and do our set as them, but what finally happened was an onstage pie fight in front of 6,000 screaming kids. They caught us at the end of our set by surprise, and the whole stage was covered in shaving cream and whipped cream. Then it was our turn at the end of their set. All their guitars and drums and machines were completely buried in shaving cream, so their encore sounded just great! (Circus)

June 25: Headlining Massey Hall in Toronto, Rush sells out all 2,765 seats. Labelmates (on sister company Taurus Records) Max Webster open. The critic from the *Globe and Mail* observed, "the young and fresh faced crowd seemed completely content with Rush's unsophisticated approach to rock. Pretty standard heavy metal stuff … Lee's voice sounds like the damned howling in Hades. They must be doing something right judging by the number of women who leapt onto the stage to give Lee roses and plant wet ones on his cheek."

June 29: Rush tour ends in Port Dover, Ontario, and the band begins recording again.

Also on the Moon label is the Ian Thomas band, whose keyboardist Hugh Syme shows interest in designing album art. His work earns him the Rush album cover illustrator position.

HUGH Having always been intrigued by album cover graphics as a vehicle for selling albums and because of my background in art having been, you know, forever—I basically requested to do one of Ian's albums. I've always been into painting and drawing and Anthem Records—basically, it can be said that Anthem is Rush—saw my album graphics and wanted me to do something for them. (Creem)

September: the second album, *Caress of Steel*, is disappointing commercially and the 40-date tour of dives is dubbed the 'Down the Tubes Tour'.

ALEX Our management were worried, the record company thought we were going down the tubes. We weren't making any money at all, we didn't get paid for months and we got pissed off. (Sounds)

The album stalls at #148 in the U.S. in November. S.R.O. was $325,000 in debt, Alex was using wedding money for rent, and Ray Danniels developed an ulcer during this time.

ALEX We started headlining small places on the Caress tour and we didn't do that well in the majority of the halls. (Visions)

GEDDY It was a low point for us in some ways, but it was also the time that we realized we had to be our own biggest fans and just make the music we believed in. (Hit Parader)

December: Highly pressured but undaunted, Rush begins writing their next album. As they say in the business, 'you're only as big as your current album'.

1976

January 10: The 'Down the Tubes Tour' ends in Toronto.

March: It's America's bicentennial year and Rush's next album, *2112*, is fittingly about revolution. This album was their most aggressive, energetic, ambitious, and successful recording to date, selling 100,000 copies in a week. *2112* was strongly supported by Cliff Burnstein to hopeless execs at the record company, but marketing followed the strong sales.

GEDDY It's a gratifying album to play because I think it was the first album that our sound—the *Rush* sound—came together. (Salt Lake City Tribune)

But the media largely thought otherwise. A *Billboard* reviewer commented, "Rush will need a bit more distinctive sound if they are to progress much more."

March 15: Four dates in Hollywood, CA open the two-month, 50-city tour which will be supporting Styx on the west coast, Foghat in the east, and Aerosmith in Indiana.

April: In a *Circus* interview, Dan Nooger wrote if Geddy's voice "was any higher and raspier, his audience would consist exclusively of dogs and extraterrestrials."

GEDDY If I had a nickel for every insult about my voice, I'd probably be a millionare … I've had some amazing comparisons, some of the most stupid comments. (Sounds)

While acknowledging that Bachman Tuner Overdrive opened the door for Great White Northern rockers like Rush, Alex proclaims, "our favorite Canadian band is ourselves."

May: *2112* peaks at U.S. #61, selling 160,000 copies at this point. For the band, it was time to start assembling a live compilation, to be mixed at Toronto Sound Studios.

NEIL With *2112,* we felt we had reached a first plateau. We had realized the goals we set for ourselves before the second album. Musically, it looked like a logical place to do a live album. We had four albums' worth of material honed down to a live show. And the record company was hot for a live album. (Circus)

NEIL There's a lot of anger on it because that's what we were feeling. It was a key album. If it hadn't been successful, it probably would have been our last. (LA Times)

June 11–13: Rush tapes performances of three sold-out dates at Toronto's Massey Hall (4,000 people each night). The third show was added in response to demand.

NEIL Ultimately, every city has the place that's the 'in' spot where all the hip local bands play. I used to dream about playing those places. I never thought bigger than that. For every set of goals achieved, new ones come along to replace them. After I would achieve one goal it would mean nothing. I used to think to play there [Massey Hall] would be the ultimate. But then you get there and worry about other things. (Modern Drummer)

NEIL All this angst was coming out of me during the course of the [final] night, and I was annoyed, and I figured the album was ruined because of all this. And then we listened back to those tapes and those were the ones that had all the energy, and it's true that anger can sometimes bring out the passion in the music. (Jim Ladd Innerview)

LIAM BIRT Hometown is always intense. Everyone wants to be at their best playing to a hometown audience. Add to that the pressure that we were recording a live album, it was extremely high pressure for a few days. (Visions)

July: Geddy marries Nancy Young, ex-bandmate Lindy Young's sister. After the traditional Jewish wedding, the two honeymoon in Hawaii for two weeks.

August 31: Rush garners a positive review for the band's free concert show with Head East. Ralph Baum writes in The Vidette about the Illinois State

University's auditorium show, "Rush got off to a slow start, with most of the audience not knowing how to take Geddy Lee's lead vocals. Although he sounds like a cross between Beverly Sills and Robert Plant, his vocal musicianship goes well with the versatile guitar of Alex Lifeson. With their new album, Rush offers an alternative to standard rock-ism." The Midwest would continue to be a stronghold for the band for years.

September 29: After three remixes, the double live album, *All the World's a Stage*, featuring the Toronto shows, is released. It becomes their first Billboard Top 40 album (at #40) in November.

NEIL [*All the World's a Stage*] presents our material to people who may have heard or liked a couple of our songs, but never got into all our albums. Now they can have those songs together on one album without our having to put out a 'Best of Rush' package. (Circus)

In *Sounds* magazine, Geoff Barton wrote, "Rush are probably the best undiscovered band in Britain at the moment," but the band finds little other critical favor. Neil addressed some of the harsher music critics who described Rush as being "talentless hard rock."

NEIL The music we're playing is the music we honestly want to play. I like playing hard rock; it gives me a lot of scope. There have been inferior hard rock bands and people have used it to disguise a lack of talent. There are only two ways to be successful. One is to have a hit single or a string of them. The other is to be around so much, to always be touring, so that you'll have to be noticed. (Circus)

November 29: Mercury throws a party at Carlos and Charlie's for the band to honor their LA Forum debut on December 1, where they were scheduled to open for Ted Nugent. They will play in front of 45,000 at the California dates alone. Meanwhile, tickets for a Chicago performance (scheduled two weeks later) sell out. In Indiana, Rush would open for Bob Seger.

December 22: The previous albums, *Rush* and *Caress of Steel*, are certified gold in Canada, for selling 50,000 copies each.

Rush ends 1976 with a New Year's show at the Toronto Concert Bowl. Another date is added, with 15,000 fans in combined attendance. The shows echoed the liner notes in ATWAS: "This album to us, signifies the end of the beginning, a milestone to mark the close of chapter one in the annals of Rush."

1977

January 8: The live single "Fly By Night/In the Mood" (b/w "Something For Nothing") stalls at U.S. #88.

February: The *Detroit News* continues the critical abuse: "Lead singer Geddy Lee continues to sound as though he played one football game too many without ample equipment, guitarist Alex Lifeson studies the stage charisma of the great guitarists without ever noticing their craft, and drummer Neil Peart should take a long, hard look at learning computer programming." Meanwhile in *Sounds* Geoff Barton again champions the band: "The music was suitably captivating, many faceted, Geddy Lee's now mature vocals shrieking and soaring; Alex Lifeson's guitar work resourcefully inventive; Neil Peart's drumming original and inspiring. Although a humble three piece, Rush consistently succeed in shaming other, bigger, more powerful, more successful bands. The volume geared way up, Lee's high-pitched vocals cut through you like a chilling knife edge, the Lifeson guitar is a big, beefy roar, while the bass and drums beat time, each thud a depth charge explosion."

March: Alex and Charlene have a second son named Adrian.

Marvel Comics dedicate their 45th issue of 2112-influenced *The Defenders* to each member of the band. In it, a character named Red Rajah proclaims: "Truth is false and logic lost, consult the Rajah at all cost." *2112, All the World's a Stage*, and *Caress of Steel* are released in Britain for the first time this month also.

Cliff Burnstein compiles a recording aimed at radio, entitled *Everything Your Listeners Ever Wanted to Hear By Rush ... But You Were Afraid To Play*. Jules Abramson, Phonogram marketing director explained, "We are zeroing in on the entire Rush catalog because we feel once a person sees the group or hears a recent LP, they will want other albums by the group."

As Rush continued the All the World's a Stage Tour into spring, negative reviews still proliferated.In the *Washington Post* Larry Rohter wrote: "Sunday night's show was just another self-defeating exercise in heavy metal ... a performance devoid of intelligence, feeling or anything else usually associated with music. There were occasional echoes of Led Zeppelin, both in bassist Geddy Lee's vocals and Alex Lifeson's guitar riffs, but it's impossible to cite other influences simply because Rush's music, amplified beyond the threshold of pain, is essentially characterless."

April: Max Webster's keyboard player Terry Watkinson begins to tutor Geddy on synthesizers.

GEDDY   When I was really young, my sister took piano lessons and I was intrigued by the sounds. I was able to listen to the parts she was learning and figure them out by ear. I always trusted my ear, even when I was pretty young, and my ear has been my bread and butter. (Keyboard '84)

Ray Daniels and Vic Wilson form Anthem Records with Rush members acting as associate directors. The first single on the new label is "Making Memories".

Rush add more colorful and distinctive instrumentation on stage, practicing when they could in soundchecks. These instruments were being used for a few new compositions, "Xanadu", "Closer To the Heart" (working title of the new album given to the band by their Seattle friend Peter Talbot), and an unfinished "Cygnus X-1".

ALEX   We thought we'd try and broaden the sound on stage between the three of us by having Gedd play the keyboards and bass pedals, me playing bass pedals and double neck guitar and Neil would get a few more percussion instruments in there. (Visions)

June 1: Rush tour the United Kingdom begins in Sheffield. The first seven dates are sold out. They perform "Xanadu". The band were not expecting the imported bootlegs of their albums to have reached such cult status in the U.K.

ALEX   We thought we might have a following over in Britain, having received some fan mail. But basically we just expected small to average crowds. When we realized how strong the fan level was, we were totally blown away. (Success Under Pressure 1984)

NEIL   I got a question from an English journalist: 'Is Rush a dodgy drug reference or what?' People can't reflect back to earlier times, but in the late '60s when that name was applied it kind of had that connotation, but at the same time it was more innocent. You would talk about an adrenaline rush. But words like 'bummer' have passed into our vernacular. I'm amazed to hear grandparents use the word 'bummer', and that's without any drug connotations. Sure, that's the root of the metaphor, but that's not what it's come to mean. Those things have just passed into the language in a different way. At the time the name Rush was instituted, it had a much broader range of possibilities. (Seconds 1994)

June 4: After selling out tickets six weeks prior, the trio perform at the Hammersmith Odeon for the first time.

June 13: Euro Tour ends in Liverpool. Manchester reviewer David Redshaw asks, "How can Canada, home of Gordon Lightfoot and Anne Murray, cough up anything like Rush?"

July: New album is recorded at the castle at Rockfield Studios in Monmouth, Wales and mixed at Advision Studios in west end London in August.

GEDDY   We've always looked up to the English progressive bands and it's gonna be a good opportunity to go over there and try to capture the same sort of atmosphere. But if you look at the very big bands with longevity, they've grown and progressed and their audiences have grown and progressed with them. ... Our influences are still around—that makes it a bit tougher. We're still a young band

… we're still competing with some of our very influences. We're not looking for immediate results, we're hoping to be around for years and years. (Circus)

ALEX The way we write, we have the lyric or an idea of what the song is going to be. That idea sets a mood. By changing the time signature you can change the whole effect of the song. I guess in that respect we do go off into those changes without making a conscious effort. Yet it does make the song more complex. That influence came from the British progressive movement and bands like Yes and Genesis. (Guitar)

August: Rush go on a warm-up tour with Max Webster supporting. The band now employed a full road crew with self-taught Tony Geranios (who had worked with his brother on Blue Oyster Cult's keyboards) assisting Geddy (nicknamed Dirk) and Alex (nicknamed King Lerxst) as keyboard tech. Tony (Jack Secret) devises a system of interfacing bass pedals and synthesizers which broadens Rush's live sound. Larry Allen becomes Neil's drum tech.

GEDDY Promoters say our crew is one of the most professional around. But they are also very demanding. If our crew is going to do the job right, they feel they deserve everything that's coming to them. If there is no milk at the crew breakfast, or there aren't as many stagehands as stipulated in the contract rider, they'll complain about it. Because complaining is the only way they have to let out their frustrations on the road. (Circus)

September: The first album under Anthem, *A Farewell to Kings*, is released, with Neil's lyrics delving deeper into the realm of fantasy. Previous albums are re-issued.

NEIL Consequently you just get tied up in all that and whether you believe it or not doesn't matter. It becomes an escape and as a writer fantasy is really an excellent vehicle if you want to express an idea in its purest sense. There's nothing better than creating a completely made-to-order extra-terrestrial world in order to express that idea so you're not caught up in any preconceptions. (Sounds)

September 6: Thunder Bay, Ontario is the start stop of the tour, dubbed the 'Drive Till You Die Tour' by the band. Manager Ray Danniels would explain to *Rolling Stone* why: "We went everywhere we could. My philosophy was, if you can drive to it, do it. It was the drive-till-you-die philosophy." The band was also driving 'status' cars, though they were working far too much to enjoy them.

ALEX We decided that if we ever got to the point where we could afford it, the first thing the band is gonna do is buy nice cars for everybody. I got a Jaguar—I had an XJS, Neil had a Mercedes SL, and Geddy got a Porsche Targa. We were all pretty much in the same boat, living in apartments, with all these flashy cars. Unfortunately mine was stolen [few years later] and smashed to pieces. (BBC Rock Hour)

October: With the album hitting #33 in the U.S. and making their English debut at #22, they shoot three "live-simulated" videos at Seneca College.

Village Voice's Robert Christgau calls Rush "the most obnoxious band currently making a killing on the zonked teen circuit." The punk movement had just started.

NEIL   We happened to be recording in England when the Sex Pistols first came out, and when I saw them on TV, I was so entertained. There was no denying the charisma that John Lydon had, singing, 'no future ...' At worst, it was amusing, and at best, an amazing spectacle. As the bands started to get better, when more thoughtful bands like Talking Heads came out and later the new romantics, I embraced it totally. It was an irresistable force at that point, it was just rock music that could call itself new wave. (Seconds 1994)

GEDDY   Since we were heavy into this muso vibe, punk seemed very weird to us. We couldn't take it seriously, because we were players and these guys couldn't even play. It was comedy. (Seconds 1994)

November 16: Along with the current LP, *2112* and *All the World's a Stage* are RIAA certified gold in the U.S. (for selling 500,000 copies each).

NEIL   Our strongest point is our mentality, I think. The thing I love about this band is that we're honest. We're not in it purely as a matter of economics. It's fun and enjoyable. We would like to become rich, but that's not our sole objective. We don't see the point of trying to get a hit single by appealing to the lowest common denominator. (Circus 1976)

November 26: The ballad and future live staple "Closer to the Heart" hits U.S. #77. Perhaps fitting with its memorable bell chimes, the video along with the Don Kirshner Concert was re-aired on Christmas Day.

NEIL   We've never consciously tried to become a commercial band. We're not going to say we don't enjoy selling records, but that's just a pleasant side benefit. (Hit Parader)

1978

January: Rush's first UK single already lands the Top 40 there. "Closer to the Heart/Madrigal" reaches #36.

January 23: Rush is profiled in the cover story in *Maclean's* magazine, a widely known Canadian magazine. Geddy and Alex's high-school friend Steve Shutt, now a left winger for hockey's Montreal Canadiens, observed, "You could tell even then, even before they were doing anything, that they were looking for something to pour their energies into. Then they started their band—and nothing else mattered after that."

GEDDY I think we're something apart from trends. We're neither a trendy nor fashionable band; none of us feel that music is threatening us. More importantly, our audiences are growing so it still has to be in vogue with those people. I think we appeal to a mentality, and there's still a lot of that mentality. (Melody Maker)

February 12: The next 14-date, sold-out UK tour begins in Birmingham, England. These tours did not yet include the back projection screen (and wouldn't until 1981). One of the band's favorite activities at soundchecks is racing remote controlled cars. When Rush arrive in London, they are presented with a silver disc (60,000 copies sold) for *A Farewell to Kings*. On the subsequent six-week, sold-out tour, Rush stopped in Germany, Holland, Norway, Sweden, Belgium, and Finland.

February 19: A hot-air balloon to be piloted by Mike Glue with the Rush logo on it was to be flown over Hammersmith as a Phonogram marketing stunt, but it can't get off the launching site in Battersea Park. The next day, *New Music Express* writer Miles discussed the band's lyrical philosophy with Neil. A week later the interview goes to print, branding Rush "crypto-fascists" and warning the public against their frightening virtues (something that may have interested the public in checking out Rush even more). Neil would still be miffed about this even years later.

NEIL I'm not a fascist. I'm not some extremist. I'm a capitalist and I believe in self-reliance—but not without taking care of other people. (Melody Maker)

March: Rush wins Best Group at the Juno Awards held at Harbour Castle in Toronto. Terry wins Producer of the Year award. Over a million people had seen Rush at this point with six gold and three platinum discs in Canada, awarded by to them by Sam Sniderman, founder of The Record Man music store chain in Canada.

Archives, comprised of their first three albums, is released. A marketing move by Mercury to familiarize new fans with Rush, the album only reached #121 stateside in May and did not chart overseas.

June/July: Rush spend two and a half months recording *Hemispheres* at Rockfield Studios in Wales (the longest it will take to make an album until 1984). The engineer is Pat 'Duffo' Moran. Vocals are recorded at Advision Studios in London, engineered by Declan O'Doherty when Broon Jr. realizes the sound is not up to par for some reason.

ALEX At that point, Broon was almost getting out of his mind and Terry never gets angry and he was. I've never seen him like that before or since. (Visions)

August: Terry Brown finally takes the *Hemispheres* tapes to London's Trident Studios in Soho, to mix the album. Ray Staffert masters.

GEDDY   Hemispheres was a very technical album and an exceedingly difficult one to make, maybe the most difficult record we ever made. (GuitarOne 1999)

Rush turns down $200,000 to appear in the 1st Annual Canada Jam alongside Kansas, Atlanta Rhythm Section, the Village People, Dave Mason, the Commodores, and Earth, Wind and Fire. Neil's daughter Selena is born to his wife, Jackie Taylor.

October 14: Hemispheres Tour begins in Kingston, Ontario—the first of 113 dates.

October 29: *Hemispheres* hits stores.

NEIL   Our expenses on the road are so high we can't really make much money touring. We began this tour in a lot of debt. It will take the first part of the tour to pay that off. The second part might make us break even. (LA Times)

Sounds writer Geoff Barton was among the first to the give the new album a mixed review, calling it "either a masterpiece or a terrible mistake." Barton had been the British Phonogram press officer and actually wrote the history in the tourbook (as he did before). This is the last time he works with the band (his essay in *Words and Pictures* notwithstanding). Barton would focus during the next year on metal acts as editor of *Kerrang!* and would later assist Metallica's Lars Ulrich in compiling a British metal LP. Rush shoot videos for the second side, with Martin Gleicher again directing at a simulated concert at Seneca College, Toronto.

November 12: Neil and Alex speak about fame and fortune.

NEIL   The three of us are satisfied with the level of success we have. But a lot of people would shoot me for saying that. Our manager, for instance, is certainly interested in us becoming megastars. We're not millionaires but we're comfortable and happy. We have enough money to get all the equipment we want. We sell just enough records to give Mercury Records a return on their investment and we're able to headline across the country in some fairly big halls. We're popular enough to make enough money to give us a level of freedom without making us prisoners. But we're not popular enough to have to worry about being bothered on the street. We can walk the streets and live a normal life and not be recognized. If we didn't have that personal freedom the rock life would be awful. (Los Angeles Times)

ALEX   We're not out to become millionaires or anything like that. If we happen to make a lot of money or get material success, all well and good: We're not going to not take it. That stuff is nice, but we're doing what we want to do, playing the music we want to play, and I think audiences pick up on the fact that we're happy with being performers. (Guitar Player 1980)

November 20: Geddy warns a rowdy Tucson audience to "Move back or we'll stop playing and it'll be a bummer."

December 14: Shipping gold, *Hemispheres* peaks at #47—an unexpected slip on the U.S. popularity gauge, but in the U.K. it jumps to #14.

NEIL   It was unheard of for bands in the late '70s to record a side-long composition. We thought we could create something that would stand up to repeated listenings while utilising that format. And we did. (Hit Parader)

December 28: Rush set an indoor attendance record in Toronto as they play three sold-out nights at Maple Leaf Gardens. Geddy and Alex tape an interview to be used on an upcoming Anthem picture disc just before the show.

1979

January 8: Canadian Government honors Rush as the bands members are named 'Ambassadors of Music'.

NEIL   We are not a message band.

January 15: John Rockwell, New York rock critic, reviews the Palladium show with guest Cheap Trick and notes, "Mr. Lee sings in a spare but unusual way—a brittle androgynous tenor."

January 21: Super Bowl Sunday. Rush's opening act can't make it so Blondie replaces the act and is booed off stage in Philadelphia. At this point, Rush's 15 tons of stage gear takes about 9.5 hours to be set up by the 25 man crew. There is $150,000 in sound gear alone.

March: Rush wins Best Group again at the 8th Annual Juno Awards with Alex and Geddy in attendance. Alex begins flight training.

March 25: Rush makes an attempt to see the Space Shuttle launch of Columbia, but it is postponed.

April 23: Another European tour begins in Newcastle, England.

May 15: Rush were to play in Paris but the venue burned down a few days before.

June 4: The marathon Tour of the Hemispheres ends in Galeen, Holland at the Pink Pop Festival on a bill consisting of Mick Jagger, The Police, Peter Tosh, and Dire Straits.

The band goes during the day with Alex struggling through the show with a broken finger. After 150 shows since October, Rush takes a six-week break in Canada. They are $300,000 in debt by the end of the tour. It costs $10,000 a day to keep the equipment on the road.

ALEX We travel by bus. If we have a few days off and we want to get home fast, we'll fly. But we own two busses, and they're great. You can sit down, turn on the TV, listen to tapes, or whatever. And you can relax; you don't have to hassle with airports and work around other peoples' schedules. In addition to the buses, we have a motor home and three transport trailers, and there are 25 people in our crew. I can recall when it was only six. (Guitar Player 1980)

These days Neil's influences lean toward Stewart Copeland and Billy Cobham, while Alex's are Eddie Van Halen, Steve Howe, Al DiMeola, Paco De Lucia, John McLaughlin, Allan Holdsworth, and Rory Gallagher. Geddy produces *No Static,* an album for tourmates Wireless.

Neil is endorsed by Tama drums and Zildjian cymbals. Neil's first ads for the company read: "When I first started on drums, Zildjians were my ideal and they inspired me. Fifteen years later they still do."

Neil is subscribing to the *Objectivist Forum* at this time and the ideas will reflect in his writing. The band retires their kimonos and long hair (except Geddy) for some new wave threads.

NEIL If a visitor from another planet would ask me to define Rush, I would definitely *not* say we're a power trio. A band with three members, guitar-bass-drums, is the classic power trio, but would you call The Police a power trio? Well, I like them a lot and yes, guitar-bass-drums certainly are necessary for power, and well … The Police were pretty powerful … That's exactly what I like being in a trio, that freedom to play a larger role. I like to be busy all the time and never be bored, and never have to just keep time … I think Rush is the only trio I've ever been in. (Mats Rydstrom)

August: Rush takes six weeks off, their longest break in five years, to write new material for their *Permanent Waves* album at Lakewoods Farm in Canada. On the first night, Alex and Geddy put together "Uncle Tounouse", which is recycled into "Natural Science" later. Neil wrote in an adjacent cottage. The first three tracks were finished first. Demos were laid down at Sound Kitchen Studios.

NEIL I had also been working on making a song out of a medieval epic from King Arthur's time, called *Sir Gawain and the Green Knight*. It was a real story written around the 14th century, and I was trying to transform it while retaining its original form and style. Eventually it came to seem too awkwardly out of place with the other material we were working on, so we decided to shelve that project for the time being … whether it gets used or not isn't too important to me anymore, really, having done it. It was really a challenge to me as a lyricist to take something like an eighty-page medieval poem and try to encapsulate it in a reasonably lengthed song. (In the Studio)

GEDDY The direction of the new album is a definite move not to conceptualize. There aren't any long conceptual pieces. (City TV)

GEDDY We sort of tried to get back to our original desires as songwiters. I think we wanted to become a little more concise and be able to get our ideas across in a more concise and more contemporary manner. Music was changing, rock music was changing dramatically … with the influence of reggae and white reggae, and more sort of aggressive punk music that was coming out. We very much wanted to be a part of that. We very much wanted to learn what was going on and reflect the times as opposed to being left behind. (In the Studio)

NEIL You have to say I think it feels good to be right. Other than that there's no resentment or bitterness. (CityTV)

August 17: Rush plays Davenport, Iowa (with hundred of fans throwing sod) as they tour select Midwestern areas to 'warm-up' for the studio.

August 20: Of the Chicago Jam II show at Comiskey Park where Rush performed, Lynn Van Matre writes in the *Chicago Tribune*: "Few, however, had come for the [Asbury] Jukes brand of rock with horns; the day belonged to headliner Rush and blues-rock band Foghat, both of whom performed with a great deal of energy if little subtlety and, in the case of the alternately droning and shrill Rush, even less discernible talent." The turnout was about 30,000, four times more than the previous day, when Sha Na Na, Blondie, and Beach Boys performed.

August 26: Rush plays the Dallas Cotton Bowl along with Point Blank, Billy Thorpe, and Little River Band, and during a Canada Jam with Triumph and Prism.

September 9: A review of the Cedar Rapids, Iowa show observes: "Rush is a group which tends to produce thinking man's rock. But the sound system Friday night wouldn't allow a man to hear himself think."

September 12: On the last date of the North American warm-up in Allentown, Pennsylvania, guest Pat Travers joins Rush on stage during "Working Man".

September 22: Rush fly to Stafford, England, where they debut "The Spirit of Radio" and "Freewill" to the crowd of 20,000 fans before heading back to their home country.

October: Rush heads to Le Studio, in Morin Heights (20 miles north of Montreal) with Paul Northfield to engineer the new album. Deborah Samuel debuts as band photographer.

NEIL   Le Studio is a wonderful place, nestled in a valley of the Laurentian Mountains about 60 miles north of Montreal. It is situated on 250 acres of hilly, wooded land, surrounding a private lake. At one end of the lake is the studio, with the luxurious and comfortable guest house situated at the other, about a mile away. We commuted by bicycle, rowboat, on foot, or in laziness or bad weather, by car.

November: Mixing takes place at Trident Studios, London, again with Terry Brown engineering. A solid-state logic board is installed at Le Studio … the state of the art at the time. Le Studio has been host to the Bee Gees, Chicago, Cat Stevens, and April Wine, among other artists.

1980

January 1: The first day of the new decade, and the first album released by any artist is Rush's *Permanent Waves*.

NEIL   Regardless of whether we fit in with today's trends in music or not, the vitality is still very strong. And if you've got that vitality, I don't think the stylistic form of music matters, it doesn't make any difference whether you're doing white reggae or the resurrected '50s rock that most new wave music is made up of, or an ongoing thing like we represent, a Permanent Wave that isn't affected by styles. There are many new wave groups we enjoy and respect, like Talking Heads and Elvis Costello and Joe Jackson. Really, the joke was aimed more at the press, especially the English rock press that is inclined to write off any band that was around last week and go for whatever's happening *this* week. (Chicago Tribune)

Geddy further discussed the album on a CHUM-FM interview in Toronto. Despite this public appearance, the band has already relocated from their previous residences and will begin keeping their lives and locations private, especially Geddy who was the most stalked by fans.

ALEX   He's obviously a little more recognizable, being the singer. He had a house in the city and there were people there every single day, knocking on his door, yelling over his backyard fence and things. And he ended up moving from a house that he really loved. (Sounds)

January 3: Detroit fans, who'd been waiting in freezing temperatures outside, smash the glass of six box offices while waiting for tickets. Over 20 police officers have to restore order. The 20,029 tickets were sold and no one was seriously hurt, though some were trampled. Ironically, exactly a month before at Cincinnati's Riverfront Coliseum, 11 fans had been trampled at a Who show. A clause in Rush's contract states there will be no festival seating at any of their shows to avoid these accidents.

GEDDY It's really ignorant. It's treating kids like cattle, which they're not. It's something we've fought for a long time but nobody listens to you. They need a horrible tragedy like this before they'll go 'oh yeah maybe you're right.' (Rush)

NEIL I have wanted to get rid of festival seating for several years now but before the Cincinnati incident, no one would take that request seriously. Our audiences (like The Who's) have the tendency to get very fired up. I like an enthusiastic audience, but I do not like to watch people in physical pain. Occasionally fans would charge en masse to get to our stage during a performance. I saw people pressed against the stage, or picked up and dragged by their feet. (Portland)

ALEX We've been offered a ridiculous amount of money to play festivals, but to be quite honest I'd rather stay at home in summer and go swimming with my kids, then sacrifice two months in the winter and play smaller places. The whole band feels that way. (Sounds)

February 23: The album becomes their first Top 5 album, hitting #4 in the States and #3 in the U.K. Lead off track "The Spirit of Radio" is a #13 Top 20 UK hit (with B-side "The Trees") but only charts in at US #51 (with B-side "Circumstances"). The title stemmed from a Toronto radio station slogan for CFNY-FM, whose program director at the time was David Marsden (the man who first played Rush over the radio).

ALEX There are a few stations that were behind the band and supported us in the past, and we still try to make it to those places when we tour. There are also a lot of people who, all of a sudden, are your best buddies when before they didn't want you to come down to the station. (Guitar Player)

NEIL AM doesn't play us and a lot of FM stations don't, either. FM is now moving to AOR. That's people like the Eagles, Linda Ronstadt, Foreigner and Fleetwood Mac. Their records are produced with a lot of sugar in the grooves. It's very inoffensive. Rush doesn't fit that kind of programming. We want airplay, of course, but not bad enough to compromise a lot to get it. There will always be room for backwater bands. If all the bands were mainstream, particularly the way the mainstream is loused up now, things would be very boring. (LA Times 1978)

Rush were now a bonafide phenomenon. During the week of the February 13–19, Rush makes $584, 095, with an average of $200,000 per series. The band was actually starting to make pocket money this tour. But as Rush's popularity soared, inevitably long-time fans accused the group of 'selling out'—of changing their sound and betraying their heavy metal roots.

ALEX We never considered ourselves a heavy metal group, anyway. We feel we have more to offer than that. (Circus)

ALEX We never really were that serious. You do a couple of things that may seem that way and you're labeled no matter what you do. You're always labeled as something like, 'Here's Rush, a 'heavy metal heady' type band!'. I don't know, most of the time you couldn't give a fuck, you have a good time and that's it! (Sounds)

NEIL Playing more than two hours a night takes it out of a man, and all that travelling takes it out of you physically as well. You have to be in first-class shape to be able to do it in the first place, so you can't afford to let your health run down. So you do start learning after a while to get a good meal and a good night's sleep, so there isn't plenty of partying. (Sounds 1980)

March 10: A critic in the LA Times writes: "Bearable by most standards, 38-Special was a godsend next to headliner Rush. One fan's T-shirt Friday read: Rush—God's Gift to Me. After the group's two-hour set, I leaned more toward Lord, Have Mercy. Rush isn't a critic's band. Of the trio's first seven LPs, only two received even two stars ('mediocre') in *Rolling Stone* magazine's new 'Record Guide' book. Two other albums didn't receive any stars. They were rated worthless. The only rush I had on my mind by the end of the concert was a hasty exit to the parking lot and the sanctuary of the Seger-Costello tapes."

March 17: *Permanent Waves* is RIAA certified gold, platinum in Canada (100,000 discs), and silver in Britain.

March 23: Rush take fellow Toronto synth-rockers Saga out on the road with them as they tour their mutual homeland.

April: As "Entre Nous/Different Strings" dwindles at U.S. #110, the trio's proficient playing garners them recognition for the first time by magazine polls in *Sounds* and *Melody Maker*. Alex and Neil get cover stories in *Guitar Player* and *Modern Drummer*.

NEIL I don't feel comfortable with wires and electronic things. It's not a thing for which I have a natural empathy. It's not that I don't think that they are interesting or that there aren't a lot of possibilities. But, personally I'm satisfied with traditional percussion. I have distrust for electronic and mechanical things. (Modern Drummer 1980)

NEIL We've noticed on this tour that there are a lot more weirdoes coming out of the woodwork. We could start a 'Flake of the Week' club. We get a lot of guy sending us pictures of themselves and telling us they want to 'help us out'—they don't want to *take over*, they just want to 'do us a favor' by singing backup and doing some original dance routines. And all kinds of people send us letters saying that they have a plan to save the world and all they need is our help. Or they come up to us and say they've read all our lyrics and know exactly what we're saying and they're the only ones in the world that do. People extract amazing interpretations out of things. Someone told me one of my songs was about me going to search for God and finding Him. Yeah, right. Sure. But then there's the ideal fan, the person who appreciates every move we make and knows if we make a mistake and acts as kind of a built-in judge factor. Those are the people we write our songs for. (Chicago Tribune)

Rush plays four nights (three sold out) in Chicago, four in New York, LA, and Dallas, two in Milwaukee, Seattle, San Francisco, and Detroit, three in St. Louis (these were taped for a live 12″ release, which subsequently became bootlegged). The St. Louis tour dates are taped by NBC *The Source* for later broadcast on radio. The critic from the *Detroit News* comments: "Rush is obviously in its natural element when it the concert environment, and the band is composed of three consummately talented musicians. But Rush imprisons its music in such wearisome heavy metal conventions that its skills rarely have the opportunity to come forth. For the uninitiated, it's difficult to determine when one Rush song ends and another begins."

Whenever possible, after the show, Rush and their road crew spend late nights at a nearby ice hockey rink for a game, complete with real sticks and uniforms contributed by Montreal Canadien Steve Shutt. Backstage fan meetings are growing rarer.

NEIL I like meeting people. One of my favorite subjects to think and write about is the human race. So I'm not any kind of a misanthrope—a person who hates human beings. I'm not reclusive to that extent. But I am a private person and I'm basically shy with people I don't know, especially when I can't meet them on equal terms. If I can meet someone's friend, or even a stranger, person to person, I get a kick out of that and I enjoy it. But I feel differently when somebody comes up to me with an attitude that I'm something special, or thinks that they know something about me or that—as I read so often in letters—"You and I have a lot in common." How do *you* know? I struggled a long time to figure out why it bothered me so much. When I first joined the band, nobody knew who I was because I wasn't on the first album. There'd be kids hanging around backstage to see Alex and Geddy and not paying any attention to me. It's not any kind of a situation you can base a friendship on. When I'm home I'll write 15 to 20 postcards usually and answer the mail which I mostly get forwarded from *Modern Drummer*. (Modern Drummer 1984)

GEDDY Where do the fan and artist really meet? Through music. Everything we do, all our emotions and things we want to say, we put into our music … and when we're in the concert hall together, and we're playing and they're responding, and it's one of those nights where everything is going well, that should be communication enough. (Circus 1982)

May: A film crew tapes footage from the sold-out Buffalo show for use on TV. It was the closest they came to their hometown of Toronto on this tour. During four dates at the Palladium, Cliff Burnstein suggests Rush keep writing as he notices their creative juices flowing.

May 23: Uniondale, New York is the last stop of the U.S. Waves Tour. Rush comes out for the encore wearing New York Islanders jerseys predicting they would win the NHL Stanley Cup. And they did.

June 1: A date in Southampton opens yet another hugely successful U.K. tour, this time with five sold-out shows at London's Hammersmith Odeon. All of the shows are taped for the live album project they intended on releasing in the fall.

June 24: Rush plays Brighton, England before returning home.

July 28: Rush records "Battle Scar" with tour mates Max Webster for their album *Universal Juveniles*, in one take in Phase One Studios in Scarborough.

GEDDY We set up both bands live and producer Jack Richardson standing in the middle with a baton, sort of conducting us. (Visions)

There Pye Dubois, lyricist for the Websters, presents lyrics to "Louis the Warrior," which Neil will adapt for Rush's "Tom Sawyer". This song will be identified as the quintessential Rush song.

NEIL I think that a lot of the values and standards that we have in Rush are the same as the values that people stood for in the late '60s—being true to the idea that, when you write a song, you don't worry about whether it's suitable for airplay or commercial enough … we're at the point where we can say 'Shut up, it's none of your business' to people who would try to tell us how to work. For a long time, though, we had to fight like hell. (Chicago Tribune 1980)

August 31: Demos begin for the new Rush album at Phase One Studios.

GEDDY I think it was … actually [Canadian rockabilly star whose back-up band The Hawks went on to become The Band] Ronnie Hawkins' farm that we had rented. He had a nice farm; and there was a farmhouse and the barn was soundproof because I think he used to rehearse with his bands in there. We set up in the same fashion. We would just hack it out there. (In the Studio)

September 11: "Tom Sawyer" (still in demo form and played in its original faster tempo) and "Limelight" are debuted in Hampton Coliseum, Virginia on two-week warm-up tour before more studio time begins.

September 25: The Rush tourbus is broken into in Philadelphia.

October 2: After wrapping up the short tour in Maine the day before, the band begins recording their *Moving Pictures* album in Le Studio at Morin Heights, once again. Neil scraps a song based Thomas Hardy's Wessex Tales.

GEDDY It's a place that we love very much. It's a really comfortable place. You feel like you're recording in your own home. (CHUM FM)

Videos are shot (taking three hours each) in Le Studio for "Limelight", "Tom Sawyer", and "Vital Signs", each directed by Bruce Gowers, whose previously worked with Rod Stewart, the Bee Gees, and the Jacksons and went on to work with Queen and John Cougar. These are not shot during the actual recording of the songs but during breaks.

NEIL We've never videotaped recording sessions. Why would we want to bore our fans? (Post 1994)

Geddy has son Julian with wife Nancy Young, who would own Zapata, a designer clothes company in Toronto.

1981

January: The band is forced to finance the $9,500 album cover because of a mixing glitch that sets the band's budget/schedule back.

NEIL In a massive electronic freak-out revolution, the digital mastering machine, the mixdown computer and one of our multi-track machines gave up their collective ghosts one after the other, driving poor Broon to distraction, and setting us two weeks behind in the end. (A Rush Newsreel)

Alex gets his pilots license.

ALEX I fly whenever I get a chance. That's something I really lovedoing. I have a shower and have a nice breakfast, and I get to the airport and think airplanes all day. It's nice to have that escape. (BBC Rock Hour)

February 7: Rush's first digitally mixed/mastered album, *Moving Pictures*, is finally released.

GEDDY It was a culmination of so many things for us, so many of the experiments musically and the discussions and the honing of our craft, I guess. I think it opened the way for us to be accepted more readily on radio. There was just sort of a permanence and legitimacy that came along with the success of that album. (In the Studio)

February 20: The six-month tour begins in Kalamazoo's Wings Stadium, Michigan, with a $40,000 stage show and Max Webster guesting. Sold-out cities included Louisville, Dayton, and Binghamton.

February 25: *2112* is RIAA certified platinum (the first Rush LP to sell a million copies).

March: *Moving Pictures* becomes their biggest success thus far, reaching #3 in the U.S., holding on the charts for four weeks. And it reaches #3 in Britain as well. Rush's Mercury contract was based on anticipated sales of 2.6 million copies for each of the last four albums.

ALEX I mean we re-negotiated our record deal on the strength of that record. So that automatically added on to our longevity. We knew that we had the budget for so many albums, for the next 8 or 10 years or whatever. So in that way it guaranteed us that freedom to make whatever records we wanted to make. And to, I guess, instill some confidence in the record company that we were capable of making records that they could be commercially happy with—which is not a big priority with us, believe me. The artistic end of the album is what's most important. (In the Studio)

March 4: *All the World's a Stage* is RIAA certified platinum. New fans were definitely discovering the older Rush gems.

March 14: Though Ray Danniels had higher expectations, "Limelight/YYZ" rings in at #55 stateside as "Vital Signs" (oddly coupled with "In the Mood") just misses being a U.K. Top 40 hit (#41). In concert, Rush was injecting their old standard "Working Man" with a little reggae rejuvenation.

GEDDY I know that we are the white man and can't play reggae, it's just something that comes naturally to black people, especially people that are brought up with that kind of music, maybe that's why it's such a fascination for us. (Sounds)

GEDDY It's a real positive thing, especially the way its been melded into rock music by groups like The Police. Anytime any kind of music excites us, it variably creeps it way in our music. (CHUM FM).

Geddy would also pay tribute in their new wave contemporaries frequently wearing his Devo pin.(Incidentally, The Police recorded their hit "Every Little Thing She Does Is Magic" in Le Studio this year.)

March: At the Juno Awards, *Permanent Waves* is nominated for Album of the Year but loses to Prism.

March 24: A *Toronto Sun* concert review aptly describes the current live atmosphere: "The show was filled out by a boggling array of colored spotlights, (which were all very impressive, but ultimately gave the group the aura of Niagara Falls on an August night) back-projected slides and cartoons, fire pots and dry ice. Nice touches all, but not exactly crucial to the overall effect. Rush played with enough flashy power to hold the stage all by itself." The same reviewer noticed that Alex "sported a new look, with a nice, neat page-boy haircut that would make him welcome at any doting mother's home, and a flashy red suit, tie and shoes that gave him a certain innocent Elvis Costello appearance."

NEIL   We put everything back into our roadshow because we know how important it is to keep up the excitement of a live show. The back [screen] projection is just another way of keeping up that excitement along with the lights and all that.

March 27: Anticipating the forthcoming live album follow-up to *All the World's a Stage,* a concert film is shot at the Montreal Forum. Even while at the top of their game, Rush were still critically ill-received in some quarters. John Griffin of the *Montreal Gazette* described Geddy as sounding like "a guinea pig with an amphetamine habit" and Lifeson as "ordinary at best." He went on to say Rush was "one of the most tedious rock bands working the arena circuit today."

NEIL   We've always believed that everyone is entitled to their opinion. The only time it bothers us is when the critiques become personal vendettas instead of music reviews. If people don't like us personally, that's their business. But it shouldn't affect their attitudes towards the music. (Hit Parader)

April 12: After the Space Shuttle Columbia launch is canceled on the 10th (a day off for the band), with Texas dates thereafter, they fulfill their wish to witness the spectacle at Kennedy Space Center in Florida (this experience will inspire a song on their next LP). Neil would note the name of the VIP guest area—Red Sector A (used for another song). They go on and play Fort Worth that night.

May: Rush get a minor mention on the cover of *Rolling Stone* magazine.

GEDDY   You'd have to be a fool to ignore constructive criticism. We've changed things in our music that were pointed out to us some years ago, things about feel or a tendency to sometimes sound forced. But a lot of critics believe they are the resident experts and they make the decision on what's valid and what isn't. I think that's horse shit. (Rolling Stone)

May 19: Comedian Robert Klein interviews the band for a radio broadcast as the vintage compilation album *Rush Through Time* is released by Mercury to familiarize newcomer fans in Britain—without Rush's knowledge.

NEIL   [The album] was released entirely without our knowledge or consent (not that they need it), and certainly contains nothing of any interest—not even the cover, and certainly not that title. We wouldn't do that. Have you noticed that everyone puns with our name except us? (Backstage Club Newsletter 1988)

June 6: "Tom Sawyer/Witch Hunt", though on 100 Top 40 radio playlists, just misses being a Top 40 hit in the States, stalling at #44.

June 12: Steve Pond describes the 29,392 sold-out Forum show for the *LA Times:* "Understandably elated that their band had finally overcome critical barbs and radio apathy to perch comfortably in the Top Ten, the band's fans unleashed a loud, foolhardy barrage of firepower: a string of firecrackers, a smoke bomb, two skyrockets and three huge explosions. All that before the band had been on stage for 15 minutes. In addition to their poor placement, the short songs sounded muddy and plodding … one of the most leaden, bottom-heavy sounds in rock … Rush seemingly writes songs by jamming loose bits and pieces together with abrupt transitions; it's a style that spells boredom, not momentum." Geddy also wasn't amused by the welcoming firecrackers as he directed a comment to the celebraters: "firecrackers are not only dangerous but stupid."

Creem writer J. Kordosh, once beaten up by Ray Davies of The Kinks, conducts an infamous interview with Neil who was miffed at a satire recently printed in the magazine with a character named 'Geddy Lee Roth'.

NEIL   It was insulting—the things that were put into his mouth were things he would never say, in a way that he would never say them. And no one in their right minds would be compared to [Van Halen singer] David Lee Roth. But no! The magazine slandered Geddy. …You see, you're dealing with cynical, jaded critics here, who in a lot of cases, are frustrated musicians. The people who have given us the `humorless' tag are the frustrated, jaded people … cynical … who think that the only thing that's good is what's funny and off-color. The Stones? You don't think they're good? You can't say they're good musicians … astute? clever marketing strategists.…I think it's safe to say that Paul McCartney does not have a lot of artistic integrity … he's a prostitute. Which is not an evil thing. (Creem)

Kordosh responds by pouring on own diatribe: "It's safe to say that Paul McCartney cannot only play the bass better than Geddy Lee (I won't mention the vocals), but that he can also play guitar better than Alex Lifeson, play drums better than Neil Peart, and write about 80,000 times better than Rush and the National Hockey League put together. I mean, if you think "Mary Had a Little Lamb" and "Someone's Knocking" were outright drivel, I invite you to listen the "The Temples of Syrinx" or "Cygnus X-1 Book II" by Neil & Co. …I was later able to infer that Rush have some sort of collective paranoia about making mistakes during a live performance. Of course, this is intrinsically impossible, as their material is one gigantic mistake unto itself. Rush's last two albums aren't all that much different than their earlier Alpo. I mean, how many levels of pretentious boredom can there be? Neil Peart can hide behind every triangle, gong, bell, empty paint can, and any other percussion instrument he can think of— adults will prefer one good wallop from {Rolling Stones} Charlie Watts from now until 2112. Wait a minute, I forgot that Geddy Lee is also the group's vocalist. At least, I wanted to."

The Young National Front's magazine *Bulldog* calls Rush "Nazi rock … aryans and fascists who aren't afraid to admit it." Neil would comment that the viewpoint is "very very sad." Equally misunderstood were the band's religious/philosophical views and as Rush's popularity grew, they became a target by other foolish groups.

July 5: The band wraps up the Moving Pictures Tour in East Troy, Wisconsin, after playing 79 concerts for 905,000 fans, raking in excess of $4 million. The next move for the band: the second live album. Weeding through 50 reels of recorded concert tape begins in Toronto. The Permanent Waves Tour yields a remarkably choral performance of "Closer to the Heart" (Rush would dub the Glasgow, Scotland audience the Glaswegian Chorus on the liner notes).

GEDDY At the end of a tour you always have that kind of bittersweet feeling. You are tired and you want to go home and part of you wants to keep going. (Visions)

July 19: *The Daily Texan* runs an article about the Longhorn Christian Fellowship group's seminar "No One Here Gets Out Alive" which brands a few heavy metal acts, including Rush with their pentagram-like symbol, as satanic rockers. And as they did with KISS, people invent acronyms out of the name Rush such as "Runners Under Satan's Honor" or "Royal Ushers in Satan's House." As a side note, the word *Rush* was linked to satanism in an old German folktale about a friar (the Devil in disguise) who enters a monastery to tempt monks.

August: Another frustrated musician, Steve Weitzman, criticizes the popular trio in *Circus:* "But after seven years and 11 Mercury albums, they still can't be taken seriously as instrumentalists when compared to recent powerhouses like the Mahavishnu Orchestra or Return to Forever. They're not a true rock & roll band, as their music is all stiffly calculated and pre-planned. Though you wouldn't know it from the crowd's reaction, the band's lyrics are even weaker than the music. They've gone from utter cosmic fluff (on previous albums) to inane drivel on *Moving Pictures*. The last laugh is had by drummer Neil Peart. He gets to write this caca and doesn't even have to sing it."

September: While the forthcoming live album, *Exit … Stage Left,* is produced by Terry Brown, Rush create studio overdubs (which would generate suspicions).

NEIL We made a few repairs to the record. A part here and there would ruin an otherwise perfect song, so we patched up the odd bit. Sometimes we had hit the wrong thing or gone suddenly out of tune. When the two worlds of concerts and studios collide, it creates a real pressure zone for us. It would be so much easier if we were perfect! (Circus)

Two songs refer to their beloved producer, including the intro to "Jacob's Ladder" and the eloquent classical guitar intro to "The Trees" that Alex dubbed 'Broon's Bane'.

Neil began keeping what he called 'The Drummer's Diary', which he intended to release at some point in the future but never did. Geddy and Alex continued work on the music to "Digital Man" and "Subdivisions" using a Teac 244 Porta-studio. While renovating a set of Hayman drums in Le Studio's basement, Neil started thinking about the liveliness and resonance of thin shells versus thicker shells like the set of Tama drums he'd been using. Noticing the Hayman's musicality and thin shells, he had arrangements made for the prototype thin shelled Tama kit.

The band records an unreleased track called "Tough Break" with synth tech Tony Jack Secret' Geranios and Skip 'Slider' Gildersleeve.

October: *Exit … Stage Left* is released: 40,000 copies are preordered before its release in Britain. Alex dedicated the strains of the classical intro "Broon's Bane" to his teacher pal Eliott Goldner. Tourmates and friends Max Webster had broken up; thus the obituary in the liner notes. The members of Rush were getting noticed by even-non musicians, which prompted this statement to be printed in *Exit's* liner notes: "For reasons beyond our comprehension, we have become increasingly more popular, and hence stretched ever more thinly among ever more people. If we sometimes can't give the time they deserve to our friends and loved ones, we hope that they will understand and forgive us. After all, we didn't change, everybody else did!"

The idea of making live albums was not popular with Rush.

GEDDY They're very painful to do because there's nothing really creative about them. You play the gigs and invariably you stiffen up and it's not the same. In some ways I'm almost sorry we did *Exit*. (Success Under Pressure)

NEIL There's no denying that Rush fans are a little different from your average rock and roller … they're willing to absorb some of our lyrical ideas. The new album was designed expressly for those fans. (Hit Parader)

ALEX We were already geared up for another record. I think that had something to do with the fact we don't go crazy over live records. I don't know if you'll ever hear another live album from Rush. We enjoy the studio recordings better than the live ones.

Geddy works on audio production for the upcoming concert film video release.

October 25: A promotional and warm up tour takes off in Stafford, England. "Subdivisions" premieres live in London the same month.

November 5: At Wembley Arena in a rare instance, fans are rounded up by Kevin Flewitt (personal assistant) so Geddy, Alex, and Neil can sign autographs for each of them.

November 8: A couple thousand fans gather outside trying to get into the capacity crowd Royal Highland Exhibition Centre in Scotland as Rush is escorted by police away from fans waiting at the airport landing strip.

November: The live "Tom Sawyer/A Passage To Bangkok" single is a U.K. Top 40 hit at #25. The album hits U.K. #6 but only U.S. #10.

Geddy is asked to perform on the upcoming McKenzie Brothers (Rick Moranis and Dave Thomas from SCTV) comedy album. Thomas is a former school-mate of Geddy and brother of Ian Thomas. After 45 minutes his comments and vocals are done, and Geddy is paid for his contribution. "Ten bucks is ten bucks" would be become a familiar phrase to Rush fans. Ironically, only Alex would appear at the press party the following year.

November 28: U.S.A. promotional tour starts. An hour after guest Riot ends set, police use tear gas to stop a real riot at the Hollywood Sportatorium in Florida. Neil was late from a trip to the Virgin Islands. John Erickson tapes soundchecks and "Chemistry" is written out of one such jam.

GEDDY We've been starting to hear some very interesting soundchecks lately. When the jams start to get interesting it's a sign that your brain is getting ready to start working on some new material. (Visions)

December: *2112, Moving Pictures,* and the two live albums go platinum. Rush is the only band to have four releases achieve this in 1981.

Neil is now part of the advisory board of his favorite magazine, *Modern Drummer.*

NEIL There's something to learn in every issue of MD … it's one magazine I read from cover to cover. I'm always glad to find it in my mailbox. (Modern Drummer)

Meanwhile, Neil's editorial on Satanism and Rock Music entitled "Rock Groups Hardly Satanistic" is published:

NEIL I am writing in response to an article which was written by your reporter Jim Hankins in your issue of July 19, 'Group seeks to show rock 'n' roll Satanic.' It was awhile ago, but the article was sent to me through several intermediary steps. Besides, it's never too late to discuss a matter like this, and as I happen to be a member of one of the groups mentioned, perhaps I can interject a little rational-ity and truth into such a hysterical exercise in propaganda.

Satanism. Now here is a word that should be kept away from some people the way you should keep matches from children and guns from jealous husbands!

There is a certain trait evident in human nature which some people seem to possess in greater degrees. It derives from a state of insecurity and low self-esteem and shows itself in the actions of those who wish to make themselves look good by making others look bad. You see it everywhere once you start to look for it. People who can't gain respect for their own merits feel obliged to try and tear down those who do. We see it in the failures who try to prove their aloofness by criticizing the actions of those who actually do something, or in cases like this one where the weak and pusillanimous prove their righteousness by trying to punish the 'less-righteous.'

A big advantage to such an attitude is that it keeps them so involved in other peoples' lives that they need not examine their own. So these are the grim-faced hypocrites who are stirring around in the dark places of life hoping to find something—anything—dirtier than their own reflection. And if they can't find anything—no problem—they'll just make something up!

And here they are accusing rock musicians of being sincere and dedicated satanists attempting to poison the souls of America's youth with subliminal messages of devil-worship. You know that's almost a very good joke! Almost.

As one who knows many of these 'demonic figures' personally, especially some of those mentioned in the article, the idea of some of these sold-out, burnt-out, cynical, strutting peacocks being so deeply and religiously committed to anything (save their 'image' and chart numbers) is also a bit of a joke. And a pretty lame one at that!

These nameless mercenaries don't even demonstrate that kind of commitment in their music. Why on earth would they be bothered to go to all that trouble to put anything else into it? All they need (and care) to do is find a kind of lowest common denominator of commercial 'acceptability.' Yes, you Christian crypto-fascists, it is a joke! The only problem is—you're not laughing.

I'm not laughing anymore, either. I've started to receive too many questions and letters from confused and impressionable young people wanting to know if it's true that we worship the devil. Who is it that is corrupting the minds of young Americans?

Let us not for one minute forget that this is the same self-righteous mentality that has put itself to work persecuting witches, Christians, Jews, Quakers, Indians, Catholics, Negroes, Communists, hippies and capitalists down through the ages. There's always somebody to kick you when you're down. It seems like every group has taken its turn at one end of the stick or the other. From the bitter oppressed to the righteous oppressor is a very short step.

Speaking for myself, as lyricist and drummer for 'Rush', and one of those accused of this heinous crime, I must object, Your Honors. Far from being a closet Satanist, I confess crudely, I don't even believe in the old bastard! I wonder if that's better or worse in your eyes, Grand Inquisitor?

I can certainly assure you that my lyrics contain no 'demonic' secret messages or cleverly concealed mystical commercials. Nothing like that, I'm afraid. It is not only absurd and pathetic, but it is also totally incompatible with my philosophy, my work and my beliefs.

I get all kinds of letters from people like this whose perceptions are narrowed and distorted by pre-set values and ideas, telling me the most fantastic things that they have somehow "discovered" in my words! As is ever true—they find what they want to find. Fair enough. I know what I put in there. It isn't that, and it isn't this either. Period.

I don't wish to offend anyone's genuine beliefs, as it is a fundamental tenet in my philosophy that people should believe what they choose to believe. It must be stated, though, that when you've 'got' religion, like Siddhartha, you find it everywhere you look. And when you've got evil, you'll find it everywhere you look, too.

Ah! It's the old 'recorded backwards' trick again, is it Watson? Ha! I'm sure you could play 'The Star Spangled Banner' backwards and find a secret message there too. Wouldn't Francis Scott Key be surprised at your cleverness! How do you suppose he knew what it said in 1812?

Don't you think something as vague as this is rather like a Rorschach ink-blot, or cloud shapes? Interpretation is based on the perceiver's state of mind—not on any objective reality. An ink-blot is a cloud is a song—frontwards or backwards. One finds what one wishes to find.

Yes, there's something subliminal at work here all right. The subliminal and poisonous sickness that dwells in the minds of these fearful and pompous so-called Christians. And they even call themselves a 'Fellowship.' Think about that for a minute. Then think about what this paper and others have accomplished by giving innocent ink and paper over to this kind of drivel. You readers don't know that I would never even use the kind of grammar that these people have attributed to me, let alone the insipid and valueless supposed message. Listen to this: 'Oh Satan, you, you are the one who is shining. Walls of Satan, walls of sacrifice; I know it's you are the one I love.' That's disgusting. I mean really. You just know these people have to be sick. If you don't believe me, ask my Mom! (Modern Drummer)

Neil also is compelled to respond to a statement made by Sandy Slavin, drummer of the group Riot, who had opened for Rush during the Exit … Stage Left Tour. Sandy told a *Modern Drummer* reader that Rush *liked* Riot a lot so they chose them as a tour guest.

NEIL Now I really have no wish to cause anyone any embarrassment, least of all Sandy as he is a fine drummer, and I am sure that this is the story that he was told by some well-meaning but unprincipled merchant of hype; but it just isn't true. … The truth of this matter is that we usually request a particular group if there is one available that we like musically and/or personally, as when we have worked with Pat Travers, UFO, Max Webster, FM and others. In a situation where no one like this is available, we will leave it in the hands of the booking agency to get someone that they feel deserves an opportunity to play for our audience. … I sincerely have no wish to cause any bad feelings, and I thought long and hard about whether I should even mention it at all, but first of all, I hate untruths, and secondly I think it's a good example of the kind of thing that a serious musician has to watch out for. Pardon my lapse of taste. (Modern Drummer)

GEDDY Rock and roll's in pretty sorry shape right now. That's not to say there isn't some very good, daring and entertaining music around, but there's also a lot of crap. So many groups have no idea where to go with their music. That's one problem we've never had in this band. We just do what we do and we do it better than anyone else. That's a claim not too many other bands can make. (Hit Parader)

December 2: Live single "Closer To The Heart/Freewill" chimes in again for Christmas time at US #69.

During December, Geddy toys with ideas for new songs "The Weapon" and a new live intro for "Vital Signs". On the schooner Orianda, in the British Virgin Islands once again, Neil writes "The Analog Kid". Work on the music to "The Weapon" lasts through January.

1982

January 5: RIAA certifies *Exit ... Stage Left* gold.

February 13: MTV premieres the sixty-minute concert *Exit ... Stage Left* with an FM simulcast to hundreds of stations around the country. The dark, moody live footage satisfies most fans with its blend of old ("Xanadu", "By-Tor and the Snow Dog") and new ("Tom Sawyer", "Freewill") but the omission of the best Rush drum solo to date disappoints the growing number of Neil Peart drum disciples. The individual videos from the film will be rotated heavily throughout the spring and summer as it hits home video markets. It is directed by Martin Kahan, who went on to direct videos for Loverboy, Bon Jovi, and KISS, as well as country artists like Alan Jackson in the '90s.

The first biography on the band, with primarily 1970s photos throughout, is published. Titled simply *Rush*, it is the work of Brian Harrigan, U.K. press officer and *Melody Maker* journalist. "I, like hundreds of thousands of others, had become a believer. But then Rush aren't a bad choice of a band to believe in."

March: Both 1981 Rush albums vie for Best Album at the 11th Annual Juno Awards in Canada. Neither win. Rush meet to discuss new material in The Grange at Muskoka Lakes, Ontario.

GEDDY When we do lose some of those things it is a disappointment. After a while you kind of expect it. Just like bad reviews. At an early age you kind of learn to ignore it. (Visions)

March 15: SCTV's Bob and Doug McKenzie's *The Great White North* album is released on Mercury (Anthem Records in Canada), goes gold, hitting #8 in U.S.

and the single "Take Off" hits #16. Geddy's shrieking maybe identifiable to the majority of the public, but it was probably the last they'd ever hear of the old banshee wail of the '70s.

April 1:Little Rock, AR is the first date of the Spring Training Tour, or Tour of the Nadars, as in 'tornado country.'

April 12: Rush play St. Petersburg, Florida to end their warm-up tour.

GEDDY   That's a conscious decision, because I want to use my voice more. I want to sing more, and it's real hard to sing when you're using all your energy to stay two octaves above mortal man. It's a lot of work to keep punching your voice up. (Keyboard)

Alex planned on working on a solo album as did Geddy at this time.

ALEX   There's just not enough time. I thought I would get some work done on it in the summer because we initially planned on having at least two months, maybe two and a half months, off. It was really hectic getting everything together again, so there was no chance to work on it then. (Harmonix)

GEDDY   I'm not a big believer in guys who do solo albums just to strut their personal stuff. The only reason I'll do a 'solo' album would be to use my position to make record with musicians that I know and respect and would love to play with but don't get the chance. Mostly friends of mine at home, like Ben Mink, or Hugh Syme. (Keyboard)

Geddy discusses touring Canadian rock acts like Saga and April Wine in an HBO Intermission 'featurette' entitled *Heart of Gold*, narrated by Canadian-born actor Donald Sutherland.

GEDDY   The Canadian hard rock sound isn't as brash as American hard rock and it isn't as complex as a lot of British hard rock so there is sort of a meeting place in Canada. For a long time April Wine were really the only major Canadian band. Saga are an example of a band that chose to go a different route. They went to Puerto Rico to get some exposure, they went Germany, they went to places that accepted them first.

Sutherland closed the profile with these words: "At the fore front of heavy metal/progressive rock, Rush has led the way for a Canadian sound that dominates the world."

Alex starts building a studio in his basement. Warren Cromartie, Montreal Expos baseball player, asks Geddy, a great fan of baseball, if he can meet Rush as they record in Le Studio on their eigth album. Warren would remain friends with the band and even inspire imagery for the album design.

ALEX   Warren Cromartie, oddly enough, was really into the band and through some friends in Montreal called and asked if we'd mind much if he came up to the studio while we were recording. So he came up and we met him. He was really into the band and we were really into the Expos. Geddy's a baseball nut and he was well aware of Warren. … He's a pretty good drummer. Neil, of course, is a great influence. He came out on the road with us for a few days in Chicago and St. Louis and we've become good friends. (Harmonix)

Baseball themes would surface in the liner notes of the *Signals* album. Rush frequent The Commons, the only bar in Morin Heights.

ALEX   They have a girls softball team so when we got up there they challenged us to a game. Everybody got baseball gloves. We played …and beat them. When we were doing the credits, we thought we'd put in everybody's position from that game. (Harmonix)

Ben Mink, temporarily of synth-band FM, is asked to guest perform on "Losing It" with his electric violin.

NEIL   We had talked for a while about getting Ben Mink to play electric violin somewhere on this album, and this seemed like the perfect track. Once we got into the studio, we developed the jazzy solo section, recorded the basic track, and gave Ben a call. Fortunately he was able to get away from his group 'FM' for a couple of days, and bring his unique instrument up to play his heart out for us. … We worked him hard, squeezed him dry, and threw him away. He just stood there in front of the console, taking it and giving it, fueled by occasional sips from a bottle of C.C. Not only the monumentally fantastic solo did we demand, but we had him multiple-tracking an entire string section as well. That'll teach him to be our friend! (Stories From Signals)

Dedicated to astronauts John Young and Robert Crippen, the NASA audio excerpts in "Countdown" (as well as the footage in the video promo) are provided by Gerry Griffin, a director at NASA at the time.

ALEX   They've been very cooperative and quite friendly. It's not easy getting that kind of footage. I know Carl Sagan had a problem looking for some footage. (Harmonix)

July 15: Work commences on *Signals*, with its more synth-based melodies and less power chords. It was the first eight-song LP since *Fly By Night*.

GEDDY   Basically we didn't want to go in and make another *Moving Pictures* because that's kind of against everything we've ever done. We made a conscious effort not to play it safe and try to experiment in order to change our sound. It was time to inject some fresh blood. (Success Under Pressure)

GEDDY   We have a desire to write simpler songs but songs that stand up better. (Heart of Gold)

September: Neil gives away his first set of Tama drums through a *Modern Drummer* magazine essay contest which ended in June. He received 4,625 letters.

NEIL   Whose idea was this anyway? Why didn't someone tell me how long it takes to read 4,625 letters, not to mention choosing one winner? I'm sure I'll never be the same. There were letters from every corner of the U.S., Alaska and Hawaii, every province of Canada, England, Ireland, Scotland, Wales, Sweden, Norway, Finland, France, Germany, Australia, Hong Kong, Singapore, Indonesia, Puerto Rico, Mexico, and even a girl from Borneo! I mean, a lot of people wanted my drums! I still have my black Slingerland kit at home for practice and I can't imagine a person needing to have more than two sets. So ... I got this bright idea. I called the folks at MD and told them what I proposed to do. But a contest of drumming skill didn't seem right. There are plenty of jerks out there with talent, and all the talent in the world won't get someone out of their basement if no one can stand to deal with them. I knew I wanted it based on personality as much as anything, so the essay seemed the only way to go. My long-suffering wife Jackie was assigned the task of opening and counting letters whenever she had time to spare. It's so glamorous being married to a successful musician! So what was I looking for? Well, let me tell you what I was not looking for: People who didn't play drums but they 'thought they'd like to try'; people looking for a Rush souvenir; people who couldn't afford new drums because they were busy paying for a van, a house or other secondary interest; loads of embarrassing praise and flattery; people who would rather have something else but would take because they were free; quotes from the Bible; people who wanted to play my drums in church; people who said they couldn't get in a band because their set was too small-Jeez!-I joined Rush with an old, six-piece Rogers set finished in silver wallpaper, and two small cymbals. I wasn't born with this drum kit, ya know! Another thing that figured into my judgement was spelling, literacy and neatness. What does that have to do with drumming? Well, it tells me a lot about the attention to detail, and communication skills that will be reflected in a musician's attitude toward his music and his instrument. Another interesting thing I learned was the number of sincere and intelligent female drummers out there striving with dedication and determination. This is a nice reflection on the social changes of the last ten years or so. Guys-watch out! So what was I looking for, you ask again? I decided to look for the one that best reflected myself as an aspiring teenage drummer. I wanted to see the same, almost fanatical devotion to drums and music that excluded everything else from my life. A quiet religion, that didn't have to shout about it, brag about it, apologize for it, or even think about it-it just is. One who doesn't need discipline or will power to practice, simply because there's nothing else they'd rather do. Some wanted my drums to make them more interested, to practice more, or to make them more popular with their friends. My winner couldn't be more interested, couldn't practice more, and cares nothing about being more popular. Nor is he one of the thousands who claim the crown of 'your biggest fan.' He's just a dedicated young drummer who cares about nothing else. ... He has agreed to pass his present set to my second choice, Tom Wolf, who shares the same hopeful dedication on only three mismatched old drums. Maybe we'll start a chain reaction here. Somebody is going to end up with some coffee cans and pot lids though. I would like to thank everyone who entered. Excuse me, I've got to go see my eye doctor! (Modern Drummer)

The winner remembers getting the surprise call from Neil in the summer, then having a three-hour conversation. Then he waited for Larry Allen personally to deliver and set-up the kit. "I was only just out of high school ... I had to change my phone number just to get away from the people wanting to get to know me now they knew I had met Neil and had his drums. I used to lay in bed, look at the poster, dream about walking up to them if only to touch a cymbal ... my buddies would try to see how far I would go for Neil's drums, stuff like 'would you jump off the bridge for Neil's drums?' Money comes and goes but some things come around only once. I feel like I am obligated to take care of these things. It's a responsibility to think about when I move. Every time "Tom Sawyer" comes on the radio, I think I have those drums at home. It's up to me to keep this legacy. Just for that reason alone is worth it. There's still something magical about those drums." He also received tickets to see Rush and meet up with them backstage for a few years after this event.

Although prominently showing the trio playing on a dimlit stage, Rush's first conceptual videos are shot, directed by Grant Lough (producer of the *Exit ... Stage Left* video) and produced by Nelvana Productions.

September 3: New World Tour starts in Green Bay, Wisconsin with the Three Stooges theme song as the band's new intro music.

NEIL   We don't take ourselves seriously at all but we take our work very seriously. When we walk on stage we're professionals but offstage we're just as goofy as any other bunch of guys in a band. (Albany Times)

GEDDY   On our last tour we played too many shows, too tight, too mechanical, a lot of the spontaneity had gone out of us. I found myself going on stage thinking about baseball rather than the night's show! (Sounds)

September 6: A one-hour laser show set to the music of the new LP begins in planetariums across North America (New York, Pittsburgh, Los Angeles, Seattle, Louisville, Denver, Toronto, St. Louis) and in London, England. Running for three weeks, it is the first time an entire Laserium show features one group's music. The show is very successful.

September 9: *Signals* is released with new musical and lyrical directions.

GEDDY   Signals is definitely the direction that we've wanted to go in for a long time. It's something that comes from maturity and having been through the whole techno side of things. We've played in all those weird times and made all those big points that we've wanted to make. Now it seems that there's a bigger concern for communication and that's what this album is all about. (Sounds 1982)

NEIL   When I first started I got interested in really simple things and went back to mythology, for example, the early Greek and Anglo-Saxon tales. I then worked my way up to the Victorian writers, people like Flaubert, Dickens, and Hardy. Now I find myself reading the North and South American writers of this century. I really like John Steinbeck, F. Scott Fitzgerald and Gabriel Garcia Marquez. (Visions)

September 18: Though written and recorded in two days to fill the album, "New World Man" is Rush's first and only U.S. Billboard Top 40 hit, reaching #21. In England, the single stalls at #42. Both releases featured the live "Vital Signs" on the flipside, recorded for but omitted from the *Exit … Stage Left* album.

October: The album peaks at U.S. #10 but hits #3 in the U.K.

November: "Subdivisions/Red Barchetta (live)" peaks at U.K. #53. Canadian band Boys Brigade and Geddy discuss a future project together at an after show party.

GEDDY   Aside from the fact that I love the band and they're a great bunch of young musicians, the main reason for accepting the project was to put myself in a position I'm not expected to be in. I don't want to be restricted to producing just heavy rock groups. (Hit Parader)

Proceeds from Rush's third date in Toronto go to UNICEF. The band speaks openly about their increasingly strange fan mail.

GEDDY   Some of it's pretty weird … religious connotations, messages from God; all these things we're supposed to be saying. 'Hello, sports fans, here's a message … On the other hand there are the other letters from people who just want to say thank you. They're really gratifying. (Circus 1982)

ALEX   It's not as glamorous or exciting as some people like to believe it is. But it's an illusion that they want to have, so that's fine. Let them have it. (Guitar Player)

November 10: *Signals* is certified by RIAA for gold and platinum sales.

Rush declines an offer for an MTV Contest shortly after the tour begins. The current hard rock scene disappointed them.

GEDDY   It all sounds the same now. At one point it all came charging back and had a lot of energy, but it hasn't really gone anywhere. It's just become a commercial thing, all pasteurized and homogenized. Anyone can pick up a book and say, 'Hey, let's learn how to be a heavy-metal band: a) Get lots of amps b) Have lots of explosions c) Dress up and d) Let's use these four chords … I think it's gotten really terrible. (Circus)

Even veteran acts had fallen apart or burned out but Rush kept moving.

GEDDY   We've avoided burning out so far, because there's been too many bad, sad examples around us—people who've become junkies, lost contact with reality. There are bands like Kiss, Aerosmith and all, bands who were getting real big and leading a rock and roll lifestyle. Some of them go up, some of them go down. Some of them lose their minds and turn into junkies. It's scary watching that. I think the three of us have a desire to keep it alive and keep it working. (Sounds)

1983

Le Studio became more popular with recording artists. Asia and Police recorded there at the start of 1983. Rush remains committed to producer Terry Brown.

GEDDY   We've built up such a great relationship. We have to work with somebody who's flexible and whose opinion we respect. Terry Brown fits that category and we have very high regard for his objectivity and creativity behind the desk. One day we might decide to go for a change but if we did it wouldn't be through any lack of respect for Terry. It would be merely a case of time and change. But I really don't know if that'll ever happen. (Melody Maker)

March: But backstage at the Hollywood Sportatorium in Florida, it's decided that Rush will have to look for a new producer. The band feels the 'objective ear' of Terry Brown is just not there after nearly a decade and the much-criticized production of *Signals*. Paul Northfield would stay with Rush, although he was keeping busy engineering Honeymoon Suite and Men Without Hats through the '80s.

ALEX   I guess we got to a point where we knew each other too well and there was no mystery left. We all knew how Terry worked and Terry knew how we worked and everything just became too stable. We wanted to shake things up a bit. (Circus)

GEDDY   It was really a necessary thing, not out of any disrespect to him or any problem in communicating with each other, but a matter of our band falling into a dangerous rut. We could anticipate his input and structure our music around that. The making of Signals was very difficult. At the time, we wondered if some songs could not have been better if they were treated in a different way, but we were confused as to what our direction should be. We were so close to Terry, he was IN the band almost, and he wasn't objective anymore. We wanted to put ourselves in a kind of 'shock treatment', some kind of outside attitude to make us less insular and maybe help us learn more about what we were doing. We needed someone with new ideas and a new point of view to point out things in our music that weren't growing as rapidly as we'd like, ways of writing songs that maybe we hadn't thought of using. We felt like we weren't getting that, because our relationship had gotten too comfortable. (Only Music)

Rush agree to take French lessons while on tour.

NEIL I'm the only one still goin', but we have worked so much in Quebec, and come to like the language, and made friends there who were predominantly francophone people, and who had to struggle in English to communicate with us, well, it started to seem so one-sided and plus the communication was limited, and so we decided we were gonna take it on, so we hooked up with the Berlitz School and started having a teacher sent out to our concerts and, and uh, after sound check and before the show we would just have an hour, hour and a half of French school. (Off the Record 1984)

Tom Berry of Anthem Records accepts the LaBatt Music Express Award in Montreal for Top Group and Top Live Group on behalf of the band while Rush tours. On video, all three members thank the viewers.

GEDDY We want to thank you very much for this award … and all the people who sent in ballots and voted for us, the greatest baseball players of the world.

April 9: North American Tour ends in Montreal.

May 3: Another return to Europe as Rush play Rotterdam. "Countdown/New World Man" is a U.K. Top 40 hit at #36, outdoing even "Subdivisions". *Kerrang!* publishes exclusive photos by renowned photographer Ross Halfin, with a commentary by Malcolm Dome: "Rush may now have little in common with their Metallic past, but they certainly have much to offer to anyone with an interest in modern rock music. Definitely, New World Men …." Longtime supporter Geoff Barton reports in *Sounds* during May that he's "still struggling to come to terms with Signals" and tells Geddy that the show ranged from "utterly brilliant to the totally boring."

May 25: Edinburgh, Scotland marks the last date of the Signals Tours.

July 23: Geddy and Alex play at Celebrity Tennis Jam at New York City's Pier 84. Alex guitar 'dueled' with Buddy Guy, joined by famed tennis players John McEnroe and Vitas Gerulaitis. And Geddy was introduced by Clarence

Clemons (the sax player from Bruce Springsteen) for a cover of Otis Redding's "Sitting On The Dock Of The Bay".

GEDDY We're all pretty active. It gives you a better attitude about our work. I play tennis, and Alex is a tennis freak as well. (Rush Hour)

By summer's end the Rush Backstage Club boasts 10,000 members.

August: Alex's absorption of current guitar trends shows on new songs "Afterimage", "Kid Gloves", and "Between the Wheels". These and others are written in three weeks in rough form.

September 18–23: Five sold-out dates at the Radio City Music Hall (41,000 seats), a first for any rock band, warms up Rush for the studio. They debut "Kid Gloves" and "Body Electric" and "Red Sector A".

NEIL We rehearsed for a week up north, and then went straight to New York City and right onto the stage and played three brand new songs and the show that we'd never played before, with quite a bit of new equipment that we were using also. So it was fairly risky, but I think it worked out very well. I think that the days went by for us in kind of a blur, because we were concentrating so much on all these things, and wanting the shows to be good, and there was, of course when you play a city like New York, there's so much hoopla surrounding everything that all that was going on. (Off the Record)

GEDDY It was something that sounded interesting. We were able to preview a few of our new songs and get the show down before we went to Europe. Radio City has wonderful acoustics and it's a place we've always wanted to play. (Hit Parader)

In the audience on some dates were Bono and Adam Clayton from U2, and members of former '70s tourmates Foghat, Blue Oyster Cult, and Utopia.

November: A 10-inch action figure belonging to Geddy's son Julian is employed as producer and referred to as "Roger Kneebend" (which would turn up as a name in the liner notes of their new album). In actuality, the band had been rejected in their hunt for a 'hot' producer, such as Steve Lillywhite (U2, Big Country, Peter Gabriel, XTC, the Psychedelic Furs, etc.), who mentioned in the December 1984 issue of *Sounds* magazine, "Someone should explain to Geddy Lee that you must be a good *songwriter* to get an 'odd-time-signatured' tune across pop radio. Listen to " All You Need Is Love" by The Beatles or "Money" by Pink Floyd and there are prime examples."

December: Rush is preparing to produce the next record, *Grace Under Pressure*, themselves when Peter Henderson enters the scene. His biggest success had been with British group Supertramp, but he is the only producer who responds after Rupert Hine (The Fixx, Howard Jones, Saga, Tina Turner) backs down. The group head to Le Studio to begin the recording.

1984

January: The basic tracks, bass, drums already recorded, Alex begins guitar overdubs, working sixteen hours each time over three days. "Afterimage" is dedicated to Robbie Whelan, engineer Paul Northfield's assistant, who was killed near the studio in an auto accident.

GEDDY Henderson was very helpful, a very hard worker. His input made it possible for us to feel that we were taking control for the very first time. The bottom line was that *Grace Under Pressure* was more of a Rush produced album because the responsibility weighed on our shoulders. (Scene)

March: Videos are shot in England. "Distant Early Warning" by David Mallet (Blondie, Queen, Peter Gabriel, Def Leppard, AC/DC, Iron Maiden). Tim Pope, known for his work with Men Without Hats, Hall and Oates, The Cars, Talk Talk, and The Cure, directs the moody "Afterimage" set in Victorian Britain and following a child who loses his mother. The video is saved for a home video exclusive. "The Body Electric" and "The Enemy Within" are similarly shot by Cucumber Productions (who put together the animated portions of the Rush live show). Rocky Morton directed (Tom Tom Club).

April 12: *Grace Under Pressure* is Rush's 10th studio LP in ten years and their darkest to date, addressing topics such as war and death. To celebrate this milestone, the band decides to use a back cover portrait (the first since *2112*). They choose Yousuf Karsh, who has photographed Churchill, Picasso, Einstein, and other luminaries. The shoot is completed in an Ottawa hotel room.

NEIL It was an inspiring and elevating experience to sit before the lens of the portrayer of kings, queens, presidents, popes, astronauts, authors, scientists, and film stars. And there he was taking an album cover photo for bums like us! It was wonderful to see, at his seventy-five years of age, his tremendous energy, creativity and swift changes of mood. (Pressure Release)

GEDDY I think the picture brings out our personalities quite nicely. But it also looks a little like a bar mitzvah photo, doesn't it? (St. Paul Pioneer Press)

GEDDY I wasn't happy with Grace Under Pressure. But it was a no-win situation in that case because that album was extremely difficult to make. We went through tremendous turmoil and pressure making it, and I don't think I *could* have liked it given the circumstances. As soon as the record was done, I wanted to get away from it—and I've rarely listened to it since, because it's attached to too many difficult memories. (Bass Player '93)

"Distant Early Warning" does well as their first ambitious concept MTV video, borrowing concepts from the Stanley Kubrick film *Dr. Strangelove or How I Learned To Stop Worrying and Love the Bomb*.

GEDDY David [Mallet] shot the thing and made it believable. We saw it as being this big production. He would say look guys, leave it to me—it may not be realistic, but I can promise you it will be surrealistic. It's not like we're filming Superman. In terms of impact, it was probably our most successful video. (Rush Hour)

NEIL I don't have a strong relation to video or film as a medium. I don't get any satisfaction out of making a video. We'll film ourselves playing the song and then we might add some other images. MTV has become another avenue of exposure for some bands but their videos were interesting. MTV has the same flaws as radio in terms of being too programmed. (Modern Drummer)

The video will set the trend for future Rush videos as it debuts at #11 on the MTV Video Countdown. Geddy is interviewed.

GEDDY I don't want to give people the impression that I hate anything that has a big power chord in it because I don't, and we use that music a lot, it's a great kind of music. I just don't like the bands that abuse that. I don't like the bands that pick up the book according to the rules and say this will make me a big group because I have all those ingredients. Good heavy metal transcends heavy metal and becomes good rock. Period. (to MTV's Mark Goodman)

Kurt Loder, who would later become Mr MTV News in the late 1980s, calls Rush's playing on *Grace Under Pressure,* "Unemotional."

May: "The Body Electric/The Analog Kid" reaches U.K. #56 with the album reaching U.S. #10, doing slightly better in the U.K. at #5. Rush now sells an average of 1.2 million copies per album.

GEDDY If we can do something in five minutes that is as effective as something that takes us 20 minutes to do, and has stronger melodies and that maybe doesn't change its time signature every minute. We always underestimated the value of that and the difficulty of that. It's not so easy to write a good four or five minute song. (MTV)

Rush were a bit more accessible for interviews this year after an almost reclusive few years in their height of popularity.

GEDDY It was necessary. *Moving Pictures* became a very big record. We felt a need to protect ourselves. A lot of people and things were coming into our view and they were distracting us from what our top priorities were, which were playing well and being happy and basically enjoying what we do. Our lives were getting very confused. So we had to get a little more insular. We had, I guess, a midlife crisis. … At one time I had a house in Toronto and it became a nightmare. I had people yelling in my windows and looking through the windows. My family is important to me. My work is important to me. And baseball is very important to me (laughs). (New Music)

May 31: *LA Times*' Duncan Strauss reviews the Forum show: "At times, the trio locked into pulsing, Police-like instrumental passages. Rush produced some orchestral maneuvers that recalled '70s progressive rock. Very skillful, very boring. Perhaps this show would have been more involving if Lee's whiny vocals were less irritating. Sure, his singing has improved in the last few years, but he still sounds as though he once inhaled some helium and never quite recovered. Guitarist Gary Moore opened the show with a solid set of ringing, feisty hard rock. Moore, who has logged time with such bands as Colosseum II and Thin Lizzy, immediately won over the partisan audience with his inspired fret-grinding. "

NEIL   There's a bad thing going on with some bands, however, that I find hard to handle. We've had a lot of different bands open for us on this tour. But so many don't even care about being good. I often sit by the side of the stage, and it's great to see a good band before we play. It's inspiring and can contribute to our performance. But sometimes all they care about is the clothes, the pose and the party. What goes through their heads? (Circus)

NEIL   We are limited by who's available on the road at the moment; who has a record so their record company will pay their expenses, because an opening act doesn't make any money … as we well know the mechanism, because that's how we came up, as an opening act, and it's one reason why we still continue to have them … we'll get a big pile of CDs and videos and go through them, and see who seems to be the most interesting and the most suitable for the band. It's a complicated series of choices, I guess, but ultimately it is our choice. (Aquarian Weekly)

Over the years, members of Rush's opening acts went on to achieve greater success as solo artists or in other bands: Hawkwind (Lemmy of Morohead), Montrose (Sammy Hagar), UFO (Michael Schenker), Runaways (Joan Jett and Lita Ford), The Babys (John Waite and Journey's keyboard player Jonathan Cain, and later together in Bad English).

June: It's tennis for Geddy and Alex in their off-time recreation, and Neil is heavily into bicycling.

NEIL   For temperamental reasons I guess I prefer more non-competitive sports. I'm more solitary, too, so I really enjoy, uh, bicycling, I'm carrying a bike with me on the road this year, which I really like. (Off the Record)

June 8: Rush headline Budweiser's 7th Annual Texxas Music Festival with Ozzy Osbourne, Bryan Adams, and Gary Moore, in Dallas and Houston in 60,000 seat capacity stadiums. Due to the electronic drum set-up, "Witch Hunt", previously a studio piece on *Moving Pictures,* can now be performed live.

July 9: Geddy guest DJ's at WNEW-FM, New York.

Alex logs his 171st hour of flight (renting a Cessna while on tour).

After a decade, touring was taking its toll on the band finally, prompting half-hearted playing and breakup rumors.

ALEX   After three months you begin feeling run-down and can end up doing shows that you don't really enjoy. Sometimes you find yourself sitting in a dressing room before going on stage and all you really want to do is sleep or go and vegetate in front of the TV. (Success Under Pressure)

GEDDY   It's getting to the point where you start thinking about going on to other things, but somehow you come back to this. The tours are getting shorter every year. There's so much else in life that you want to live and do.(Pittsburgh Press)

June 26: *Grace Under Pressure* is certified gold and platinum by RIAA.

Despite continuing breakup rumors, the band's next album is to be produced by Peter Collins, who was contacted by Gary Moore.

GEDDY   Peter was a left field choice. He hadn't done anything vaguely resembling our music—Nik Kershaw, Musical Youth … but he also had done Gary Moore who was on tour with us at the time and I remember Gary raving about how good Peter was. (Circus)

ALEX   Who would have thought we'd be working with the producer for Air Supply?

August 31: Much Music goes on the air for the first time: "The Enemy Within" is the first video they broadcast. Geddy is featured in its TV spots.

September: Paul Siegel proposes an instructional drum video project to Neil but he declines. Rush's second home video, "Through the Camera Eye", is released, without the band's approval, covering recent videos and the exclusive "Afterimage" video.

September 20–21: After Red Rider warms the crowd up, video concert is taped at Toronto's Maple Leaf Gardens, engineered by Terry Brown, which surprises those who thought the group had a fallout with 'Broon'.

Melody Maker journalist Steve Gett, now 23 years old, releases his Rush biography, *Success Under Pressure,* which features exclusive photos from the collection of British photographer Fin Costello who has worked with Rush since the '70s as well as other major acts like Rolling Stones and Aerosmith.

October 12: *Moving Pictures* is RIAA certified double platinum.

November 9: Rush ends North American trek in New Haven, Connecticut.

November 16: First-ever tour of the Orient and Hawaii starts at Nagoya, Japan. The theaters were typically 3,000-seaters, except the 16,000-seat Budokan hall in Tokyo.

ALEX It's different to go over and blow a couple hundred dollars doing a week's worth of dates there. (Harmonix)

Geddy and Alex are interviewed on Japanese television about their album, and the current state of music.

GEDDY Most of the music right now is very pop oriented, very singles oriented. It's a very weak time for rock music.

Howard Ungerleider starts to do lights for Metallica's shows.

While in the Orient, Rush visits Hong Kong, and Neil takes a bicycle tour of The People's Republic of China.

NEIL We're a receptive audience for our contemporaries' music, which keeps us fresh and satisfied when we create our own. We'll never be pushed into doing solo albums because everything we like goes into Rush. (Boston Globe 1985)

1985

February 10: Geddy is asked to sing with Northern Lights on "Tears Are Not Enough", written by Bryan Adams and Jim Vallance, produced by David Foster. The Ethiopian famine benefit recording is the Canadian Artists Against Hunger's answer to Band Aid (U.K.) and U.S.A. For Africa. Other 'Lights' include Burton Cummings (The Guess Who), Neil Young, Anne Murray, Mike Reno (Loverboy), Joni Mitchell, Gordon Lightfoot, Corey Hart, and Platinum Blonde, among other celebrities like John Candy. Geddy sings proud and passionate that his country does care (the Canadians, in fact, donated more than their U.S. or U.K. counterparts). Geddy's line, "Ohhh you know that we'll be there," is finished in one take.

GEDDY This is the strangest day I've had in a long time. To see all these personalities, people from every style of music. There's no way this would have ever worked unless it was for this reason. It's like fifty lead singers pretending they're a chorus. We're an extremely fortunate civilization, North America. We don't know how good we have it especially people in the music business. These struggles aren't really struggles. The struggle that people are having in Ethiopia are the most real struggles there is. The struggle to exist. As a human being it's your obligation to give. Whatever it is. This is what we do. So this is what we give. (CBC's *Northern Lights* documentary)

Late in the month, Rush meet in Ontario where they complete composing "Mystic Rhythms", "Marathon", "The Big Money" and "Middletown Dreams".

ALEX While I was home, I didn't really play that much. I had just spent six months playing almost every day, and I was tired of the guitar and needed to get away from it. Otherwise, it would really be a boring thing for me. When I got home, I really didn't do anything for a month. I just relaxed and hung around the house. (Guitar Player 1986)

March 10: While on a four-date Spring Training Tour in Florida debuting "The Big Money" and "Middletown Dreams" live with "Marathon" and "Mystic Rhythms" played in soundchecks, Geddy finds time to watch his baseball team at their spring training grounds. Baseball players like Bryn Smith and Bill Gullickson go to a show. Steve Morse (of the Dixie Dregs and later Kansas) meets Alex, and Morse is secured a guest spot on the next tour.

ALEX He's one of the nicest guys I've ever met in my life. He's very sincere and straightforward. There's nothing pretentious about him at all. All the guys in the Steve Morse Band are great, actually. When we come in for soundcheck at 4:00, Steve's walking around playing his unplugged guitar. Then, when we go on after his set, he's still playing his guitar while he watches our show. He's constantly playing, and it shows. He's an incredible guitarist. The audience reaction is good, and it's usually tough for our opening act. People who come to see us, come to see *us*. It's never been that important who's been the opening act, because it's mostly our audience. So it's a bonus for them to get a good opening act like the Steve Morse Band. (Guitar Player 1986)

After the dates, Neil is asked to come to San Francisco to play on two tracks on jazz fusion bassist Jeff Berlin's album "Champion" with a rental kit.

NEIL I got to play together with Steve Smith (Journey). Steve actually did most of the playing. I just came in on the choruses for that thunderous double drum effect. (Modern Drummer)

Old tourmate Ronnie Montrose produces. Alex is asked to appear on Canadian 'hair' rockers Platinum Blonde's "Alien Shores" playing guitar on two tracks. Their album would go quintuple platinum in Canada.

May: *We Are the World* album released with aforementioned Northern Lights performance. Geddy is sought by Metallica, looking for a producer for their third album, *Master of Puppets.*

July 13: Live Aid ends, the famine relief concert created by Bob Geldof of the Boomtown Rats.

NEIL It's a '60s mentality, it had no action then and has no action now. Rush weren't invited to participate in Live Aid mainly because if you look at the guest list, it was very much an 'in crowd' situation. We didn't refuse to take part because of any principles mind you. Those artists should have shut up and just given their money over if they were genuine. I recall that Tears For Fears who made a decision to pull out of the concert were subsequently accused of killing children in Africa—what a shockingly irresponsible and stupid attitude to take towards the band. But I have nothing bad to say about Bob Geldof. He sacrificed everything for something he believed in. (Metal Hammer)

Andrew MacNaughtan, who runs the Rush Backstage Club in Toronto, founds a local music magazine in which he publishes his own concert photographs of Rush. He also turns up at Geddy's house, and after showing him his portfolio, Geddy is sufficiently impressed.

Part of the album is recorded in the Montserrat studio AIR studios where band favorite The Police had recorded earlier. Rush also decided to record in England again (first time since 1978!). Manor Studios is in a 1000-year old structure mentioned in the Domesday Book. U.K. session artist Andy Richards (and ex-Strawbs member, who played on many Trevor Horn-produced albums) would handle keyboard programming every time after this. Prior to Rush, Andy had worked on Frankie Goes to Hollywood. Rush will not record as an ensemble for quite some time: Nicknamed 'Mr. Big' after the brand of cigars he smokes, diminutive Peter Collins' unique approach is recording every member *separately* using a bed track from which to build on.

GEDDY   We talked to so many people who were looking for that magical person with all the answers who simply didn't exist. Working with Terry spoiled us because he was a very honest and responsible person and we were running into all these people who were horrible. We ended up doing the record with Peter Henderson and we were sort of compromising, because we really hadn't found what we were looking for, but we couldn't wait any longer and had to get on with the record. Peter worked really hard and gave 150 percent, but at the end we were left feeling cheated. We went through this wrenching experience and felt that we still hadn't found what we were looking for, but I think we found him in Peter Collins. (Only Music)

GEDDY   Peter Collins introduced this technique to us, that is by far, from Neil's point of view, the best way to record Neil. He works much better under pressure, and he's so prepared that it's a lot more concentrated to be able to just focus on him. Give him the track, and nine times out of ten, he does it on one take. (Guitar)

ALEX   He had his own engineer, Jimbo Barton, who is a great guy, as well as a fantastic engineer. He's got a great approach to doing things, especially when it comes to guitars. He can very quickly translate a guitar sound you have in your mind to the console, so that you can actually hear it. We used four or five amps at the same time, and he set up different balances within that whole group. (Guitar Player)

August: At the famous Abbey Road Studios, the 30-piece orchestra's parts are recorded on "Manhattan Project", "Marathon", and "Middletown Dreams". Strings are arranged by Anne Dudley of The Art of Noise (she's worked with numerous performers, including ABC, Moody Blues, New Edition, Phil Collins, Five Star, among others). A 25-voice choir is recorded at Angel Studios for the ending of "Marathon". The sessions cost $325,000 total with $80,000 for travel expenses to England and Montserrat.

GEDDY With our album *Grace Under Pressure*, we were there in the studio for four and a half months in the dead of winter. It was very cold. We had cabin fever by the end. You get to a dangerous state, you want to finish the record because you want to get out of there. And sometimes that kind of pressure is the wrong kind of pressure. You want to make it great and not in a hurry. Going to a different place every three weeks … that keeps you fresh. It's a really nice way to work. (Rush Hour)

September: Geddy supervises the mastering of the disc by Bob Ludwig in New York and rejects two test pressings.

GEDDY On *Signals* there was a lot of synth; the guitar sort of disappeared. On *Grace* it was almost the opposite—the guitar came roaring back to the forefront, but it crushed all the dynamics out of the synthesizers. This time we got a very satisfying balance. (Circus)

Videos are shot the same month. Geddy's brother Allan Weinrib produces "The Big Money" video for Champagne Pictures, with Robert Quartly directing the group as they jam on a giant monopoly game board with an art deco style city in the backdrop.

Neil and a group of friends cycled the Alps from Munich, Germany to Venice, Italy.

October 29: *Power Windows* is released. Alex is questioned when on the Grey Whistle Test when Rush are expected to tour the U.K. His reply, "I would imagine spring of next year. April or May." Geddy tells MTV viewers Rush didn't 'sell out'. The Omega Concern is mentioned in the liner notes, and would be on subsequent albums represented only by its Greek letter.

NEIL The Omega Concern is Alex's non-profit organization for Musical Scientists, devoted to the discovery of wonderful inventions. The Omega Stand, on which he plays his acoustic guitar, is one such, another is the stand which holds my rhyming dictionary when I'm lyric-writing, or the backlit lyric stand which

Geddy uses in the studio to hold those lyrics. And, of course, not to forget the wonderful Album-Order-Deciding-Device. (Backstage Club Newsletter 1990)

ALEX I'm developing another thing … it's short term wine storage. I'm into wines. You can open a bottle of wine without it spoiling … (Rush Hour)

Rush lyrics to songs on their latest LP are taught in some schools in the northeast in a short program in an effort to get kids to take more interest in reading. As reported in *Billboard* under the heading "Rush To Creativity," "This program created by Lifetime Learning Systems Inc. in conjunction with Polyfgram Records, offers a unique opportunity to enhance creative thinking, poetry writing skills and also encourages social awareness … by using Rush as a prototype." Rush are avid readers on the road.

ALEX I love the way [James] Michener starts his books. In the beginning, the lions and zebras roamed the veldt. It's just funny how he has to include everything that happens. (Circus 1986)

ALEX The biggest problem I find after 11 years of touring is being bored. Once you get bored, it's easy to depend on something else, whether it's drinking a lot or dope or whatever. It's really easy to fall into those things, and ultimately they go absolutely nowhere. Everybody likes to have a good time, but when it ends up taking over all your time, then that's a real problem. Geddy and I like to get up early and play racquetball or tennis. Exercise wakes you up and makes you feel a little healthier. Maybe you can go down for a swim, work out once or twice a week if the hotel has a gym, or go out to movies. I have watercolors with me, and I get into painting on the road. Neil rides his bike like mad when the weather's good. So, there are all sorts of things to do that keep your mind active and stimulated. I got *'Shogun'*—not because I wanted to read the book, but because it was long. I thought that it would keep me busy for a few weeks. Unfortunately, I got so into reading it, I'd get three hours of sleep and wake up at 7:00 in the morning to read. I finished it in a week, which is quite fast for me, so I just picked up *Noble House*. It's always a search for something to do. I'm terrified of being bored. (Guitar Player '86)

Rush decline for the second time an MTV sponsored contest. Their MTV exposure will wain in the ensuing months.

GEDDY We don't live in a very 'music business' environment. The main reason why we aren't seen around is due to time. We keep getting offered a lot of stuff, but we made a decision … that time that wasn't Rush time, was our own time. It would be no holiday coming out of a Rush project and bouncing straight into another one with other people. I need time for family, for personal travel, all kinds of interests outside of music. I don't know if that means we're less obsessed about music than most musicians or that we just get enough of our ya-yas out in Rush. But, like most things Rush, that's just the way it is. (Raw)

November 26: "The Big Money/Territories" reaches U.K. #46.

December: For the "Mystic Rhythms" video, they enlist Gerald V. Casale, who has directed Cars videos previously. The group has a press photo shoot the same day for each video shoot.

GEDDY Very interesting person to work with … Gerald Casale of Devo. Everything he said it was gonna be, it ended up being which very rarely happens. All these shots he would describe … I think he must have an acute photographic memory. He found some weird toys in this shop in London … I think he did a great job. (Rush Hour)

The Body Electric animated feature, presented by Atkinson-Arts Film, airs in Canada with a radio simulcast. The cartoon depicts a futuristic society circa 2112 with two rebel characters. Various Rush songs provide the soundtrack, such as "Cygnus X-1", "Jacob's Ladder", "Red Barchetta", and "Marathon".

December 18: RIAA certifies *Power Windows* gold.

1986

January 11: "The Big Money/Red Sector A (live)" reaches U.S. #45 and is simultaneously released with the exclusive full video on the video concert for Grace Under Pressure Tour.

NEIL The last thing I'm interested in is going back. I think that's a terrible thing. To get nostalgic about other people's music, or even about your own, makes a terrible statement about the condition of your life and your prospects for the future. I have no patience with that kind of attitude, whether it's on radio or among friends. For instance, I think that anyone who thinks that 1970 was the best year in the world has a problem. For me, the older stuff just doesn't have that nostalgic appeal at all. I never have that feeling of `gee, I wish we could recapture those magic moments,' because those magic moments weren't all that magic, if the truth be known. (Canadian Composer)

ALEX There are enough bands who sing about getting laid and partying without us getting involved (Circus)

NEIL The mid-'80s were difficult because music was moving so far away from our values. Musicianship suddenly didn't count. We had no respect from the critics and everyone else considered us kind of irrelevant. (Network '93)

January 27: *Power Windows* is RIAA certified platinum.

Rush are now ranked among the few artists of the '80s, namely, Elvis Costello, Prince, Kenny Rogers, and Pat Benatar, with the greatest number of platinum or gold albums as reported by *Rolling Stone* magazine.

February 3: Rush's PA system fails during "Marathon" at their San Diego show due to a short circuit.

February 19: At over 40,000 copies sold, *Exit … Stage Left* video goes gold.

February 28: With the audio problems of the early shows remedied, reviews continued to be favorable. Buffalo's Steve Hewitt noted in his review that "during a Rush show there is no pretentious rock star glitter, no phony playing to the audience … all attention was drawn to the stage and there Rush made no mistakes. Their show was tight, precise and perfectly executed. The intensity of the two hour show was phenomenal. With hard, honest work and innovative use of the effects Rush didn't have to hide behind the stage visuals."

March 10: The Maritime provinces of Canada, particularly Nova Scotia, rally to get Rush to play there (which they hadn't so since the '70s).

On the second LA date, Neil does his first drum clinic for Percussion Institute of Technology in Hollywood on the stage of the Great Western Forum for 90 minutes to a class of 50 PIT students. He does more clinics during May, with another at the Percussion Center in Fort Wayne in the summer.

NEIL   I've been asked to do clinics, which I'm interested in, but fearful of. But I would like to get into doing that, relating to people on that level. I like to talk about drums. I like to talk about things I'm interested in. For me to talk about things I'm honestly interested in, and obviously drums is one of them, is foremost. (Modern Drummer 1980)

Late March: Confident of the state of the sound they've achieved, Rush record shows at the Meadowlands, Long Island and Philadelphia for use on the next live album.

April 13: In the 1970s Rush opened for Blue Oyster Cult, now they return the favor by having them open for the crowd in Binghamton, New York. Metallica's credit to all three members of Rush arouses curiosity, and fans wonder if the trio had anything to do with the band (they had Cliff Burnstein managing).

NEIL   Honestly, I'm not exactly sure, though it was very nice of them. Geddy talked to them a bit about the music biz in general I think, and I talked to Lars once on the phone about his drum kit. I dunno. But it was nice of them. (Backstage Club 1990)

Other thrash groups such as Anthrax and Megadeth cite Rush as an influence.

ALEX The whole heavy metal movement doesn't really appeal to me right now. Not as it currently is, no. I think maybe in the earlier stages of our career we considered ourselves as a heavy metal band but that was back in the days of Zeppelin and Purple. But that's not to say I think any of it's garbage or anything. Many of these bands are really sincere about their music and care very much about what they're doing. I know Metallica does, it's very important to them what they're doing. And that's great. In fact I saw a lot of things in them that I saw in Rush ten or fifteen years ago. Particularly that youthful energy. (Metal Hammer)

May 26: With the tour closing in Costa Mesa, California, Rush spend summer with their families. Geddy plays at a charity tennis tournament sponsored by Le Coq Sportif. Alex had just relocated to a two-acre estate in Stoufville, Ontario, and Neil planned a trip to Switzerland with brother Dan. Neil, looking to change drums, tries out various kits and settles on Ludwig.

NEIL We went to Larry Yager's farmhouse and I spent the whole day tuning and comparing the different kits. Playing the kits side by side, and sometimes two simultaneously, I was trying to detect the subtle differences between them. (Modern Drummer)

Producers of NBC show "1986" ask to utilize "Mystic Rhythms" as their theme music.

NEIL I don't know how they came to hear the song but the show approached us and asked if they could use it. Of course, they didn't pay us anything, but they said they'd give us a credit. How did we feel about it? We thought it was nice. (Backstage Club Newsletter 1990)

Geddy and Neil begin writing music on new 'Mark of the Unicorn Performer' software from Macintosh, which changes their previous approach to compositions.

GEDDY Neil used it quite a lot, he wrote all his lyrics, or, some of his lyrics for this album on the Mac; he used one as well and he finds it easy because he can then play with words in the same way, you know, cut and paste and drop them out and look at it this way and print it out and look at it and see what works and what doesn't work. I found it difficult when he was starting to give me lyrics that were printed out of his computer because I'm so used to his little hand-written lyric sheets that he gives me, 'cause they're always so cool and he draws these little pictures on the top of them and stuff, you know, he has, for like, you know, thirteen years now; so, I think, I can't remember the song, I think it was "Prime Mover" or "Lock & Key" on this album was the first one he actually handed me this, you know, this print-out of the lyrics and it was so weird, it felt so cold to me, it's like, "I feel uncomfortable with this" and I think he just looked around for different fonts until he found, found one that was a little warmer and it was more attractive to me. Makes his job much easier. (Off the Record)

December 14: With the idea of the next record having two extra tracks, a tenth song is 'forced'. "Force Ten" is written in three hours on this, the last day of pre-production at Elora Sound with engineer Jon Erickson. Pye Dubois contributed some of the lyrics, something he hadn't done since 1981. Incidentally, Terry Brown kept producing; a notable act he worked for was Cutting Crew, who had a #1 hit with "I Just Died In Your Arms Tonight" the following year.

Jeff Berlin dedicates a song to his pals in Rush on his album *Pump It*.

1987

January 5: Rush enters The Manor, a studio in Oxfordshire, England, to begin recording *Hold Your Fire*.

February 2: Rush enters Ridge Farm Studios in Surrey, England.

March 1: Overdubs begun at Air Studios once again, in Montserrat located in Leeward Islands in the West Indies. Two weeks later, Rush were back in Toronto. Collins opens Rush up to the idea of using a female voice on some tracks. Chrissy Hynde and Cyndi Lauper both reject the offer, but Aimee Mann from 'til tuesday ("Voices Carry") agrees and is flown in to sing on "Time Stand Still", "Open Secrets", and "Tai Shan" at McClear Place (a popular studio where Paul Northfield previously worked with Glass Tiger).

GEDDY We just looked until we found a voice, that was suitable. In listening to Aimee's last record, we loved the way she sang, so we just asked her. (Only Music 1987)

That month, Steve Margoshes arranges the orchestral parts for "High Water", "Second Nature", and "Mission". They are then performed by the William Faery Engineering Brass Band, arranged and conducted by Andrew Jackman, and recorded at Mirage Studio in Oldham, England.

Neil's other kits are given away through a Spring 1987 contest in *Modern Drummer* magazine as he judges two-minute drum solos on tapes. The first prize is the red Tama set (used 1982–86), second prize is the black Slingerlands (used 1977–79), and third the silver Slingerlands (used 1974–76). Fourth prize winner gets a set of Zildjians like Neil's. 1,767 submissions are narrowed down to 30 by the magazine staff, from which Neil picks his favorites.

April 24: A gospel choir record parts to "Prime Mover" and "Mission".

May 7: Mixing begins at Guillaume Tell Studio in Paris, France.

GEDDY Its what you do so you don't wanna just go 'I'm going to work and then I'll live,' you know, you wanna do it all at the same time. You know, it's gotta be all one thing and that's the necessity for saying, 'Well, I could either mix at home or I can mix in this cheap studio around the corner; or I can go to Paris, spend a few extra dollars and have a wonderful new experience mixing,' so I vote for the latter, you know? Let's have some fun. (Off the Record)

Neil and Geddy's wives are flown in this month, as well as Neil's brother Dan. The two cycle in the Pyrenees from Barcelona, Spain to Bordeaux, France. Alex heads back to his new home in Ontario—'Graceland North' as he calls it, complete with a tennis court for him and Geddy and a swimming pool for his family. Neil's *Modern Drummer* sound supplement, "Pieces of Eight", is recorded in one day at Elora Sound with Jon Erickson engineering. Notice the "Natural Science"-like rhythm in the track.

July: Alex contributes sound supplements to magazines, while Geddy once again oversees the album mastering by Bob Ludwig at Masterdisk in New York City. Neil personally writes the winners of the drum giveaway with Larry Allen driving to each of their homes to help set-up the kits. Only the third prize winner attempts to sell the silver Slingerlands—for $10,000 in *Modern Drummer*'s next issue.

August: Video for "Time Stand Still", directed by Zbigniew Rybczynski (who previously worked with Missing Persons, Art of Noise, Simple Minds, Pet Shop Boys), features Aimee Mann struggling to capture the 'flying' trio on a teleprompter in a TV studio. Mick Burnett starts *The Spirit of Rush* in the UK, which would prove to be the longest running Rush fanzine.

September 8: *Hold Your Fire* is released; fan and biographer Bill Banasiewicz airs the album on Philadelphia radio unauthorized.

GEDDY   We had no reason to think anybody even wanted us out there because we hadn't played there in so long. I can't remember the last time we were out there, eight or nine years ago and I don't think the shows did that well. So when your memory of a concert is that you figure well there's obviously not that much interest. That's why we were determined this time to start the tour there. That would be a great way of getting to know that part of the country again. (Rush Hour)

NEIL   We believe that every album is gonna be the one that's gonna die on us. Something like *Power Windows* was an especial risk … we threw open a lot of barriers and over produced it like crazy. *Hold Your Fire* wasn't something we felt about. (Metal Hammer)

October: For the first time, a Rush single—"Time Stand Still/High Water"— fails to break the U.S. Billboard Top 100 and will be the last 45 single in the U.S.; it charts in at U.K. #42 with "Force Ten" as a B-side. Alex plays keyboard for the first time on tour on the track's chorus section.

GEDDY   I'd love to sell a zillion singles but I don't know if we know how. To sit down and calculate how to make a single, it would take such balls. I don't believe there's ever singles on Rush records. The powers that be always say 'You guys know how big you'd be if you had a hit single?' Every time we finish a record I think there are singles on it. It just shows you I don't have a clue. (Circus)

The album reaches U.S. #13 and U.K. #10. Rush's popularity undeniably shows decline. The songs got shorter, and fans wondered why longer epic length songs weren't being written.

GEDDY   They just became too easy to do, a little boring. We felt like we were just doing the same song over again, just changing the words. It's real hard to write a good song, and that seems to be of more interest to us than writing a 10 or 15 minute piece with movements all strung together. That comes to us too easily, therefore we're drawn away from it. Anything you can do too easily isn't that much of a challenge. I think one of the reasons we got away from doing long concept pieces was it started to be so didactic, we were preaching. (Only Music 12–87)

October 29: Hold Your Fire Tour kicks off in St. Johns, Newfoundland in response to the 1986 eastern Canadian Maritime provinces' 20,000-day fan petition.

November: MuchMusic airs "Rush Hour", which gets closer to the band and crew than any video interview ever before, although Neil does not take part.

November 9: *Permanent Waves* and *Exit … Stage Left* are RIAA certified platinum, while *Hold Your Fire* goes gold.

December 17: As "Lock and Key," directed by Tony Vanden Ende (Art of Noise, Simply Red), gets limited video play (the live footage spliced in from a New Haven, Connecticut show with scenes clipped from a 1932 prison drama "The Last Mile"), MTV airs their last broadcast of a Rush concert (P/G Tour). Subject arises whether another live release will see the light of day.

GEDDY   We haven't made a 100 percent commitment to it, but I think it's very possible. We recorded about eight shows on the last tour and we'll probably do the same this time. (Only Music)

1988

February: The tour is reviewed by Duncan Strauss in the *LA Times:* "Maybe the threesome recognizes that the music itself is far from bracing, which would explain why they checked in with this season's second-most impressive and/or silliest visual presentation (after Pink Floyd)." Promoters for Monsters of Rock (an annual event at England's Castle Donnington) offer Rush a spot but the band turns it down.

NEIL One of our roadcrew (Howard Ungerleider) freelanced for a band (Metallica) at Donnington last year and he was telling us about the screens erected to stop missiles being hurled onstage. Why put yourself through that? We are happiest in arenas, that's our forte. (Metal Hammer)

ALEX We've been offered a ridiculous amount of money to play festivals, but to be quite honest I'd rather stay at home in summer and go swimming with my kids, then sacrifice two months in the winter and play smaller places. The whole band feels that way. (Sounds)

April 10: "Prime Mover/Tai Shan" hits U.K. #43 as the North American tour stops in Dayton, Ohio. Like Van Halen's "no brown M&Ms" policy, the press publicizes Rush's own backstage catering quirk: Coca Cola only if its bottled old fashioned.

April 21–23: As the first European tour in five years starts in Birmingham, England, performances are taped for the upcoming live album *A Show of Hands* (with primarily long shots on the second day), directed by Larry Jordan. Howard Ungerleider uses white spotlights for the occasions as red light translates harder to film.

GEDDY We had 10 cameras around the stage, big cranes, guys all trying to be discreet, but in no way being discreet. Talk about being uptight! Worried about the recording? Forget it! You got cameras stuck in your face. (Canadian Musician 1989)

A few years earlier Alex had commented on the acoustics of U.K. venues.

ALEX We figured that if people wanted to see us, then we'll play the bigger halls, although I didn't know all these U.K. halls are as bad as they are. (Success Under Pressure)

The effort, this time, was trying to capture a looser performance than the previous concert videos, despite Geddy's responsibility for even more musical roles.

ALEX Sometimes I don't know how Geddy does it. He's whacking notes with one hand on his bass, he's singing, he's got another hand on the keyboard, he's playing one set of bass pedals and he's triggering something else with his other foot. He's got everything going! There's not much—well, maybe one thing—left that he can use! (Sounds)

May 5: Tour ends in Stuttgart, Germany.

Visions: The Official Biography, by Bill Banasiewicz, a project co-ordinated by Anthem's Pegi Cecconi, is finally in bookstores. It is the first bio on the band to be authorized (written by their friend who followed them since 1977 on the road) and features many photos from Geddy's scrapbooks. Geddy convinces

Anthem Records to release long-time friend and artist Mendelson Joe's *Born To Cuddle*. He also lends voice to a Japanese music release produced by Yomiuri Giants, the baseball team for which Warren Cromartie played for after his Montreal career.

During the summer, though exhausted from the tour, Alex finds time to contribute guitar work to "Hands Of Man" from *The Big Picture: Dream On the Horizon Olympics* tribute album and an album by Brian Greenway (ex-guitarist for the fellow Canadian rockers Aldo Nova and April Wine). He also makes his production debut with the Toronto band Clean Slate, showing his support for unsigned and struggling bands on "Rush Hour":

ALEX Bands get signed and they have a couple of EPs out, and you never hear from them again. That's the way a lot of record companies look at signing new talent. They don't give any consideration to developing a band whereas we were afforded that. We were given a chance to develop over a series of records and over years, over tours. That doesn't exist anymore. It's a different world than it was ten years ago. (Rush Hour)

Neil privately publishes *Radiance Over the Rockies*, his personal account of biking from Calgary to Vancouver.

NEIL It's faster than walking, but still slow enough that you're intimately connected to your surroundings. And people are much more friendly to cyclists than to either pedestrians or motorists. A cyclist is obviously a harmless eccentric. (Network)

Neil also cycles through West Africa.

NEIL I was bicycling around Togo and Ghana, and the Ivory Coast, and I got to sit in with a troupe of Togolese drummers. (Boston Globe)

Bill Banasiewicz, who had aired HYF tracks early over Philadelphia airwaves to the band's dismay, now airs ASOH tracks. This time the band turns the cold shoulder on him.

November: Though ready for release, the double live set is produced by Rush (engineered by Paul Northfield) but delayed.

NEIL The approach to sound was a difficult balance too. In retrospect we always felt that *All The World's A Stage* was a little too raw, and that *Exit ... Stage Left* was a little too refined, so we were trying to find the right balance somewhere in between. We're pleased with what we've got, and hope you will be too. We wanted it to sound *good*, but we wanted it to sound *live* too, and it's difficult to find the right meeting point sometimes. (Backstage Club)

Geddy becomes the first cover feature of *Bass Player* magazine's premiere issue:

GEDDY You can bluff a song, but not for very long. In the end you can't make a career of it. A lot of people can have one great hit record, but it's very hard to bluff a career. (Bass Player '88)

GEDDY I know my name pops up in these keyboard polls from time to time, and it's really unfair, because I really am not a good keyboard player. I'm really strictly a synthesist and sort of an orchestrator. I am learning how to play keyboards better every day, and I am presently studying piano. (Bass Player)

GEDDY I have to tell you, it's really boring. I'm supposed to start each day by practicing the Hanon exercises, doing scales in contrary motion, and that kind of thing. But it's already helping me. The other day, as I was working with a friend on one of his projects, I noticed that my fingers were subconsciously falling onto the right keys for a change. (Keyboard 1989)

November 11: Geddy and Alex appear at the 2nd Annual Toronto Music Awards to present an award simulcast on Q107 FM. They win Group of the Year.

Originally SRO VP Val Azzoli's plan was to limited the release of the concert film to repertory theaters in North America. This time the drum solo, though truncated near the end, is included. Though they have a six-month break, Rush switches to Atlantic Records for a three-album contract as a retrospective CD set is in the works at Mercury (where their contract expired).

GEDDY We switched labels because we didn't have any feel for who was at our old company anymore and I kind of objected to being inherited and transferred from one president to another. We are NOT a typical band. We're regarded as difficult because we have low key life styles. We went to Atlantic because they are more music orientated. We just needed a fresh start! (Rock World 1993)

NEIL We started to feel a little taken for granted. We are not a record company's dream. Atlantic, our new label, is convinced that they can do better for us. We're not saying, 'Sign us because we'll sell more records with you.' They're saying, 'Sign with us because we'll sell more records.' It's a pretty simple thing. When you go in with the blank slate and begin the whole process of coming up with a record, it's a fearsome thing. (Modern Drummer 1989)

Val Azzoli tells *Canadian Musician,* "They've discovered they don't much like what they're hearing on the radio in their spare time. This is the first time Ged's been home for six months straight in 20 years. That's a long time. I dunno what this new album, which will be due out at the end of the year, will be like, but Ged's saying stuff like, 'God is this radio now? Come on! No one's kicking ass anymore!'"

1989

January 10: *A Show of Hands* is released, accompanied by a platinum-selling video a few months later.

NEIL   Geddy is very interested in visual arts, and he's a big film buff. He was very influential with our live concert video because it was a way for him to apply an interest. (Modern Drummer)

After the last album, the thought of calling it quits inevitably came up again.

GEDDY   There's something in our nature that wants to stay together. There's something that tells us this is too good a chemistry, the relationship musically, to throw away. (MuchMusic)

GEDDY   I don't know if we ever talked about splitting up but individually we all thought about it. It never actually came out of our mouths. The time around *Hold Your Fire,* that tour was a very difficult tour for me personally. I was getting ill a lot on the road, and I wasn't very healthy and the tour seemed to go on forever. I don't think we were enjoying ourselves. Following that I think we had kind of a dark period. (Musique Plus)

Neil contacts author Kevin Anderson about his *Grace Under Pressure*-inspired sci-fi novel, *Resurrection Inc.* The two become friends and will collaborate on future writings.

March: Pre-production on a new album begins at Chalet Studio, overlooking Lake Ontario and adjacent to Reaction Studios.

GEDDY   There was no great master plan and there's never been. It's like we're starting to write this coming Monday, and none of us know what the hell we're gonna write. We just get together and everybody's a little anxious and something comes out. I kind of like it, it's a natural kind of way to write. Whatever musician or person you are at the time sort of gets captured at that moment; they're kind of like time capsules in a way. I guess we got a lot of time capsules lying around (laughs). (MuchMusic 1990)

NEIL   It's like starting drumming over. At the beginning, improvement and progression come so rapidly, whereas after 20-odd years of drumming, I've reached the point of such small return that I know I'm at my potential. Without false humility or unworthy pride, I can say that I'm as good as I can be. And that's a difficult thing to face. (Network)

March 9: *A Show of Hands* is RIAA certified gold. The video ships gold in a week.

June: Back to Le Studio once again, Rush team up with Rupert Hine and engineer Stephen W. Tayler. Hine, who also plays keyboards, contributes a new dimension to Rush's new material for *Presto*—background vocals. Geddy's friend Jason Sniderman is brought in for additional keyboards. Sniderman, VP of the 100-store Sam the Record Man record chain, would ask *Billboard*, "Tell me a band that Rush can be compared to. Nobody. There's not another band that plays like this. It's not heavy metal, they're not a dinosaur band. It's progressive, but not progressive like Marillion or Genesis."

GEDDY   Very early in the writing, Rupert pointed out a few tendencies we had as writers which later proved to be important. Because we're players—when we record we tend to go after perfect performances. I was getting sick and tired of working with computers and synthesizers. Fortunately, so was Rupert. We were united in our rebellion, and decided to use a more organic approach. We made a pact to stay away from strings, pianos and organs—to stay away from digital technology. (Canadian Musician)

GEDDY   It's funny, progressive rock is kind of an old expression. When Rupert Hine first came to work with us he was scratching his head, it just isn't right to call it progressive rock anymore. Maybe we should call it post-progressive rock or PPRock (laughs). (MuchMusic)

GEDDY   Well I certainly identify with progressive rock and I certainly don't mind Rush being labeled as a progressive rock group. I have always felt I was more accurately a hard rock musician. I don't know if such a thing as progressive rock exists anymore. If it does, it's being reinvented by bands like Radiohead and artists like that who are pushing the envelope a little bit. So it's a somewhat dated phrase but I don't think it's an objectionable phrase. (Global Bass Online '00)

Neil is interviewed by William Miller for his third cover story *in Modern Drummer*, talking about everything from touring to ear plugs.

NEIL   I think it's an ill-understood thing, the effects of loud sounds on the ears. I've read a lot about it, and most of the information is conflicting. The band has a serious ear check every year before we begin recording an album. By the way, I really object to ear protection. When I see bands that play ridiculously loud and wear ear plugs, I think it's a stupid thing. If you're not going to accept it, why should you bludgeon your audience with it? I love loud music and always have, and I think there's a certain forcefulness about it that's irreplaceable and part of the energy of rock that I like. However, I think you're losing touch with your instrument with ear plugs, and if you need them to get through a performance, then maybe the music is too loud. (Modern Drummer '89)

GEDDY   I have experienced some loss. My doctor tells me that my hearing is perfect except for a dip around 4khz. I blame that on a particular monitor guy I had for many years. One too many feedback bursts. (Guitar Player)

June 9: The recent concert video is RIAA certified gold and platinum. Fans raise questions about the censored section where Alex takes the microphone in "La Villa Strangiato".

NEIL   I'm afraid it's a non-story—he wasn't censored or anything like that. His vocalizing was impromptu and unexpected, and his microphone wasn't turned on! Yep, as simple and dull as that. As for what he was saying, it was something like this: "La la la la la la." (Backstage Club Newsletter 1990)

"A Show of Hands" video hits #2 on the Video Sales charts after 13 weeks, right under mega-seller "Moonwalker" by Michael Jackson.

July: Recalling the 1981 Texas controversy, The John Ankerberg Show attacks Rush's "Anthem" and "2112" for being satanic music with backward messages.

September: While mixing at Metropolis in London, Alex is asked by Gary Langdon (engineer for Art of Noise), who is in a studio next door, to play with Richie Blackmore of Deep Purple and Rainbow fame, Robert Plant of Led Zeppelin fame, Ian Gillan of Black Sabbath fame, Brian May of Queen, and Bruce Dickinson of Iron Maiden, among others, on Life Aid Armenia's "Smoke on the Water" (U.K. #39 single). Neil was also invited over to participate in the supersession but declined. The album was to benefit the Armenian earthquake survivors. Rush also contribute a song to *After the Hurricane* for Montserrat storm survivors.

CBS-Sony now distribute Rush in Canada through an agreement with Anthem Entertainment. Geddy adopts the little circular, tinted specs from this point on.

GEDDY   I get mistaken for John Lennon. And once in a while for … Bono [U2 singer]. (Rolling Stone)

GEDDY   We're taken so seriously, even by kids. They over-amplify everything you say, they don't when you're joking. They think that there's some heavy thing that's being done. You know, what did that mean when you went up to Alex and grabbed his nose? (MuchMusic Spotlight '87)

Andrew MacNaughtan makes his debut as not only personal assistant to the band but official band photographer, represented by the album sleeve's stylish, black and white portraits.

GEDDY   He fits very well into our organization pretty easily. And I think he's got a great eye. Photographs are something that we make a priority shall we say. He makes it very painless for us. (MuchMusic)

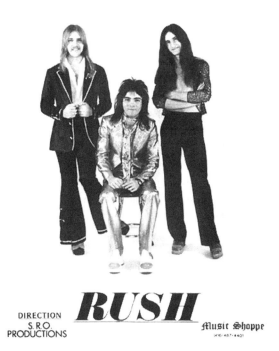

DIRECTION
S.R.O.
PRODUCTIONS

RUSH

Music Shoppe
(416) 487-1601

Early publicity photos: Rush in 1973 with original drummer John Rutsey (Music Shoppe), with a moustached Neil Peart in 1975 (Mercury Records).

1974 debut album and first 7" single 1973, both on Rush's independent Moon label.

Dutch 7" single for "Fly By Night/Best I Can" (first picture sleeve for Rush); Canadian black cover variant of "Archives"; UK 12" for "Closer To the Heart", their first UK single.

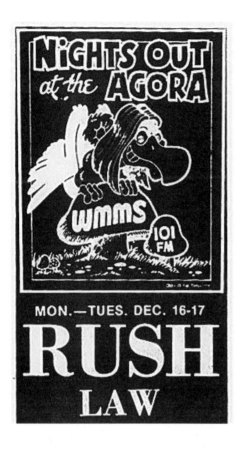

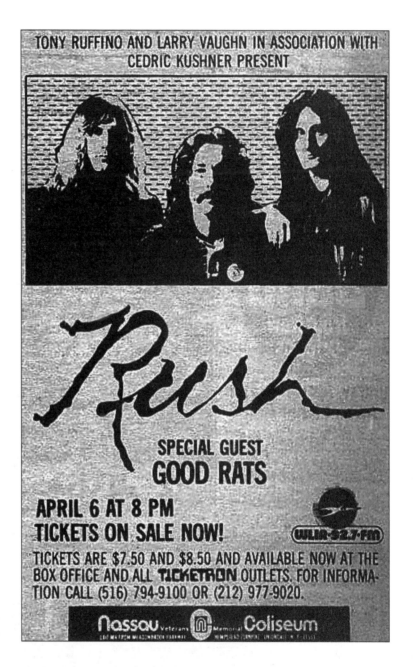

Rush concert ads from the 1970s.

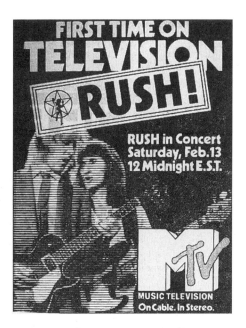

Clockwise from left (all from 1981): "Rush Through Time" German ad; MTV ad for "Exit Stage Left" broadcast; roadies Liam Birt, Howard Ungerleider and Nick Kotos backstage. Alex in a NY backstage meeting with Atlantic reps.

After completing a sold-out two-night stand at Madison Square Garden, **Rush** pose backstage with (l-r): Atlantic VP/Promo **Danny Buch**; Atlantic President **Danny Goldberg**; Atlantic Group Co-Chairman/Co-CEO **Doug Morris**; Atlantic Exec. VP/GM **Val Azzoli**; **Alex Lifeson**, Rush; Rush's manager **Ray Danniels**; Atlantic Group Vice Chairman **Mel Lewinter**.

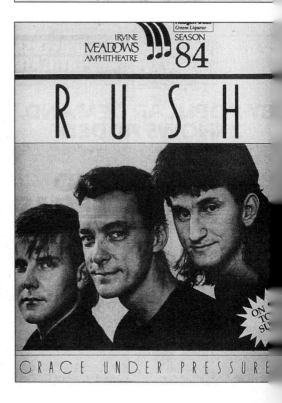

Rush tour ads in the 1980s and
a thank you from the band for
the 1990 Toronto Music Awards.

A commercial MIDI Rush collection; a sample of Rush feature stories in trade magazines.

An Anthem Records promotional photo of Rush during "Roll the Bones" video shoot, later used for "Counterparts" publicity. Photograph by Andrew MacNaughtan.

November 9: National 'Midnight Star' computer bulletin board started by fan Jimmy Lang.

November 14: *Presto* is released and fans begin to notice the return to catchier and more organic songs.

GEDDY *Presto* is kind of a renewal to me. It's a renewal of energy and a positive outlook, in musical terms and in personal terms, both in my place in the band and my feeling about recording. (Canadian Musician 1990)

NEIL With this album, we started out with a couple of basic underlying ideas to work from. We discussed the idea of letting the music grow from our basic unit, which is guitar, bass, and drums. On past albums we tended to write a lot with keyboards and then apply the other instruments afterwards. We thought it would be more interesting to be a bit more linear and do the writing around the guitar framework, and thinking of it as an ensemble as guitar, bass, and drums. (Modern Drummer)

"Show Don't Tell" is a #1 radio single for a few weeks on AOR. The director of the video, Doug Freel, previously did videos for Anthrax, Alannah Myles, The Cult, Def Leppard, and Poison. The young man in the video is not Alex's son, though some rumors persist by fans. Geddy records "Get Ready" for an all-star musical tribute to Motown bass legend James Jamerson.

November 18: Geddy appears for the final time on MTV.

December: *Presto* (their last U.S. vinyl release) peaks at U.S. #16. In the U.K. no commercial singles are released and the album stalls at #27.

1990

January 11: *Presto* is RIAA certified gold.

With the tour getting ready to start, so does the idea of adding a fourth member again.

GEDDY Rush is like a young boys club. We don't want any other members to join! We make it work with the three of us and we don't have another opinion to deal with, and another personality to wrestle with on the road. We are afraid of tampering with the chemistry. (Rock World 11/93)

January: CAPAC (Composers, Authors, Performers Association of Canada) merges with PROCAN (Performing Rights Organization of Canada) to form SOCAN (Society of Composers, Authors and Music Publishers of Canada).

KISS's Paul Stanley introduces "The Pass" on MTV's Hard 30 videoshow, depicting Rush in a schoolyard in New York City, directed by Matt Mahurin, who would re-use the visual for Metallica's "Unforgiven" video.

February 17: A 'Canned Food Rush' nonperishable food drive starts in Greenville, South Carolina as the six-month tour begins.

GEDDY   I don't see there being any reason to stop. I think the age barrier in rock 'n' roll has gone. I think the bottom line is whether or not you sell records. If you stop selling, that can hasten the demise of any creative outfit. (Canadian Musician 1990)

April: Rush shoot a simulated concert video for radio single "Superconductor" in New York City with an open call for extras, Gerald V. Casale once again directing. Robert Scovill, who worked with Def Leppard's concerts, handles Rush now.

April 4: In the LA Times, the tour is reviewed again, this time positively:"New metal bands such as King's X and even Voivod ape Rushisms, Rush's albums still sell millions, and the elements of Rush songs so reviled by rock 'n' roll intellectuals—turgid meandering, sections that don't seem to have anything to do with each other, dopey, slightly mystical lyrics, sterility of execution—could just as well apply to critics' faves Metallica. Rush, which played the Pacific Amphitheatre on Saturday, has never been racist or sexist; they've never been on rock 'n' roll power trips; their quiet on-stage smugness is almost refreshing compared to the obnoxious braggadocio of a Skid Row or a Motley Crue."

May 1: In Atlanta, members of Mr. Big come out to sing with Geddy on "In The Mood" following an incident where their guitarist got a power drill stuck in his hair during some guitar stunt.

May 12: In the *Boston Globe,* the concert reviewer writes, "Opener Mr. Big sunk in the folly of vanity, and even moster bassist Billy Sheehan couldn't save face. The title to the song "Addicted to That Rush" was just a funny coincidence. This band lacked Rush's smarts."

May 16/17: Rush raises $200,000 for the United Way Foundation in Toronto's Maple Leaf Gardens. Voivod opens up for the band.

NEIL   Playing hometown is a nightmare. Everybody wants a piece of your time. Friends you haven't seen for years come out of the woodwork and want tickets. It gets so hectic that at the office the staff made t-shirts with the slogan 'I Survived Rush Playing Toronto'. (Hamilton Chronicle)

June 29: After this last night of the 70-date tour in Irvine, California, Rush will have earned $16 million (approximately $4 million in merchandise).

ALEX   Before *Presto,* we were pretty exhausted. We were kind of burned out from touring. We took a good break and got back into that record with a lot of enthusiasm. And the tour that followed was probably one of the best tours we've ever done, it was paced well and we went to really good parts of America. Not *all* the good parts mind you, just *some* of the good parts! (Much Music)

August: Alex contributes to Lawrence Gowan's "Lost Brotherhood" album with friends /ex-tour guest Red Rider guitarist Ken Greer, Tony Levin on bass, and Jerry Marotta on drums.

September 4: Mercury finally releases *Chronicles,* a 28-track compilation after a litigation trial to rights when Rush switched labels. Rush removes "Battle Scar" and "Take Off" and replace it with "Show Don't Tell" to stop Mercury's treatment of the band as has-beens. Journalist John Swenson (who'd supported Rush and wrote of their skill in *Guitar World* and *Circus* since the early 80s) wrote the essay inside the double album.

September 15: Alex and Geddy appear at the Malibu Tennis and Music Fest in Saddlerock Ranch with members of Saga, Survivor, and REO Speedwagon's Kevin Cronin and Eddie Money. They perform "In The Mood" with Mr. Big drummer Pat Torpey. Kansas does "Carry On Wayward Son", performed with Alex, and their drummer performed on "Closer to the Heart".

October 13: *Chronicles* peaks at U.S. #51 and U.K. #42.

November 6: *Chronicles* 12-track video compilation released, omitting "A Farewell to Kings".

November 13; Canadian Academy of Recording Arts and Sciences (CARAS) honors Rush as Artists of the Decade at a gala awards ceremony in Toronto's Grand Sheraton Centre. Sam "The Record Man" Sniderman presents the award (recalling how he first met them in 1977 Junos): "I was impressed enough to remember how mature they were. In an industry that has been known to be able to destroy all human elements if you let it, they are a shining example of what can be achieved in fame and fortune, through talent and discipline, and still remain the same nice people they started out as."

NEIL   We appreciate it very much. For a group, I guess this is really a tribute to endurance. It's no small achievement for a band even to stay together for a decade, never mind *sixteen* years. And no one is more amazed than we are. Most of all we thank our families, for if we have endured, they have endured the most. (Acceptance Speech)

GEDDY   It's a terrific honor. We had trouble figuring out which decade at first (laughs). (MuchMusic Spotlight 1990)

ALEX   We've been quite successful through the '80s… I guess we *do* deserve this award! (MuchMusic Spotlight 1990)

December 5: At Superstars, Mississauga, Ontario, Geddy and Neil receive the Q107 Toronto Music Awards for Best Bass Player and Drummer, respectively; Alex loses to blind guitar great Jeff Healey. Presenter Sebastian Bach (Canadian singer for the metal band Skid Row) displayed his great love of the band as he tried to get the audience to chant with him "Rush!" as they opened up the winners' names.

At the Toronto City Hall, the Mayor Art Eggleton announces, "I am pleased to declare today to be Toronto's Musicians Day as a recognition of not only them but also a recognition of all the fine talent we have in our city. This award goes for the second time to these three gentleman who have sold in excess of 30 million records worldwide and who have contributed a great deal to music here in Toronto and in Canada and all over the world. And also contributed to the community. What they have done for the United Way and what they have done to the quality of life in Toronto is equally important to all of the massive contributions that they have made in music. So I am particularly proud to recognize them today. Geddy, Neil and Alec [sic] …"

During December, Rush begin pre-production at Chalet Studio (or as the band refers to it, "Shallow Studio") for *Roll the Bones* using CL Notator software and an Atari computer.

ALEX   Everyone's up around 9 o'clock. Breakfast, watch the war for a little bit. (Guitar Player)

GEDDY   Alex would have to finish lifting weights. I'd get half the stuff written before he came in. We write on and off all day, break for dinner and go back in the evening. Usually that's when Neil gets involved. He'll offer opinions on what we've done. (Guitar Player)

1991

February: Rush begins recording at Le Studio, Morin Heights, with additional studio time at McClear Place, Toronto.

April 5: Neil appears at the Buddy Rich Memorial Scholarship concert to play jazz numbers like "Cotton Tail" and "One O'Clock Jump".

NEIL   I realized that year that I had been playing drums for twenty-five years, so I felt I should do it for myself to mark the occasion. I wanted to honor him by playing as much like him as I could. I even tried to figure out the stickings he used, as much as possible. I did have a few problems with the event. I was the last drummer to rehearse with the band on the rehearsal day, and since it was late in the day a few of the guys in the band had to leave to play gigs. Steve Marcus, Buddy's long-time tenor sax player, had to leave. The pianist had to leave early, so that was a drag. The Basie and Ellington songs I performed were both founded on piano/bass/drums trio, and to not be able to fully rehearse with the piano made it difficult. The setup on the day of the concert wasn't well-planned either. I was far away from the band, and it was very tough for me to hear them. The horns were inaudible to me! when I watch the video of my performance I can see myself *straining* to hear them. It's hard to play under those conditions. (Modern Drummer)

May: Alex makes the *Guitar* magazine Hall of Fame as work ends on Rush's 14th studio effort.

July: Mixing of the album takes place at Nomis Studios, London, produced once again by Rupert Hine.

GEDDY   We had a very pleasant experience on *Presto* working with Rupert. He and his engineer Stephen W. Taylor are professional, very congenial, extremely musical and we found things went very smoothly and very quickly. It was probably the fastest we've made a record in some time. We say we made the record in 8 weeks, but we spent 10 weeks rehearsing and writing so the recording time was quick—that's good because that's usually the painful part. Our intent was to express ourselves in a kind of looser, more hard rockin' way, so I guess we were fairly exuberant during our writing. (Canadian Musician)

GEDDY   Our engineer has a great idea for slotting frequencies. We realized something we didn't a few records ago. Just cause you can overdub a thousand great ideas doesn't mean you should. (Guitar Player)

September 3: *Roll the Bones* is a U.S. #3 hit and U.K. #10, held off by Metallica's commercialized black album.

NEIL   Every time we put a record and it does well we think, 'Yes! We've gotten away with it again.' We never take anything for granted, we constantly feel as though we have to live up to expectations. Perhaps that's why our fans are so loyal. Whether we're playing in Omaha or New York, we always go out there with the idea of doing our best, and I think we've built up a reputation for integrity because of that. (Chicago Tribune)

Record sales were now being calculated by SoundScan, instead of projected sales by how many copies leave the label factory. SoundScan is more accurate, showing Rush's popularity may have dipped but not as drastically as previously thought. It hadn't been possible for Rush to crack the Top 5 through a decade and *Presto*'s disappointing sales had worried Atlantic about taking chances with this album, so the executive production was all Tour Manager Liam Birt's hands.

October: Throughout the month, the radio singles, the first three tracks, all hit #1. One of the reasons why *Roll the Bones* feels like a rejuvenation to the band and some fans is because they made sure to deal with youthfulness again more overtly thematically. And the songs were designed to be catchier, with their most obvious commercial stab ever.

GEDDY   Our last tour was a lot of fun. When it came time to do this record, I think we found ourselves, you know … fired up. (Rush Spotlight)

NEIL   The bottom line, that they know that when it comes even to the album cover, or our T-shirts and tourbooks, down to the music and the lyrics and the production, every aspect of it, we take personal care about. (Up Close 1994)

October: Rehearsals begin for the largest Rush tour yet with 100 stops on the itinerary.

GEDDY   After years of saying we're touring less and less and less, we recklessly extended this tour. So we're just gonna tour until June and see if we're still standing at the end. (MuchMusic)

GEDDY   The first couple of days are usually hilarious. You think you know a song but you start playing it, and it sounds terrible. The first day of rehearsal we sound like a lame garage band trying to play Rush songs. After a couple of days we start sounding like a Rush clone band, and then in the second week or so we start sounding like us. (Guitar School)

Howard Ungerleider is busy working Metallica and Queensryche shows, so he cannot work with on the upcoming tour. Shawn Richardson replaces Howard this time. Europe would be visited for the first time in four years.

October 25: As the new album is RIAA certified gold, Rush embark on the Roll the Bones tour in Hamilton, Ontario, Neil's birthplace, to and audience of 13,000 fans.

November: The title track comes in at #49 in the U.K. Directed by Chris Painter, the video, featuring an animated rapping skeleton and an elaborate set modeled after the album's front cover, receives light airplay afternoons and late nights on MTV stateside. Painter's video experience was based in heavy metal acts like Motley Crue, Tesla, Queensryche, Cinderella, and Chrissy Steele. He explained why he took on Rush. "Unlike a lot of other rock and rock bands, the lyrics are very, very intelligent in a Rush song but yet the music is still very hard rocking. And that's what I look for as a video director. I want lyrics that are more than just your typical nonsense, throwaway lyrics *and* I want a band that can really rock and roll. Rush are both those things."

GEDDY   We created a monster. (Circus)

GEDDY Well, I don't think I ever considered us real rock 'n' roll in the first place. We may have rocked, but we didn't always roll. As other forms of heavy rock have developed over the years, in context, I don't think we're really that hard. (Sacramento News and Review 11/20/96)

Michael Vander Veldt, the boy kicking the skull on the cover, also stars in the clip, and though young, he showed a little Rush wisdom, admitting he didn't believe in fate, chance, or destiny either.

The question of why Rush seemed to have few female fans inevitably popped up.

GEDDY The trend has always been mostly male. I think that's because we attract sort of a young musician type audience. When we did *Signals* we started to getting more girl fans. Sometimes we'd come out and there'd be girls screaming. Things got back to normal the next tour. (Rush Hour '87)

ALEX We've noticed especially on this tour there are a lot more female fans coming to our shows. And they know them music, they know the lyrics. They're not just being dragged with their boyfriends. And you see them in the front rows." Asked if it's because Rush are getting cuter, Alex replied, "You know I get mistaken for Richard Gere all the time and I don't know why." (MuchMusic 1992)

ALEX I don't get hounded the way Geddy does, because I look like a regular guy. But Geddy has such a distinctive appearance that people can really pick him out in a crowd … me, I can take the kids to school or do the grocery shopping, no problem. It's very normal. (Macleans 1991)

December 2: Neil makes his first Rockline appearance.

December 6: In New York, Rush is presented with the Gold Ticket Award (100,000th ticket sale) by Madison Square Garden's Ron Delsener and Bruce Moran.

December 16: Rush plays a sell-out crowd in Toronto with Canadian guests The Tragically Hip. Seven dollars of each of the 11,906 tickets go to the United Way. Canned food is requested again by the band, resulting in 15,000 lbs. for Toronto's Daily Bread food bank. Eventually the donations raised by Rush would reach $1 million. Local reviews were pleasing as per usual but as one *Toronto Sun* reporter put it, "it was those giant inflatable bunnies, frugging away to Lee's thumping bass as 'Superconductor' grooved into 'Tom Sawyer', that really made the evening."

1992

January: Neil thanks the readers of *Modern Drummer* in a letter, for yet another award—Best Recorded Drum Performance, what he calls his "hardest won" yet.

NEIL Even after 25 years of playing drums—and the good fortune to have been appreciated for it—I remain humble before all the master drummers of the past, present, and future. And though I've learned a little bit about drumming, there's still so much more to know. We can all be inspired by those masters to work toward more knowledge, greater accomplishment, and true excellence. And certainly my own quest for excellence continues. While fully aware of all my faults, in music and in life, the eternal consolation is: 'Hey, at least I'm getting better!' I happily remain a 'work in progress'.

January 8: *Chronicles* video is certified gold by RIAA.

January 23: Rush is honored with a Lifetime Achievement award by the Musician's Institute of Technology in Los Angeles, CA ; Geddy and Alex attend. San Francisco based trio Primus are optioned by Atlantic as an opening act with their appeal to a younger crowd, who've already accepted their eclectic, offbeat funk-metal style. Each member proudly and publicly make no apologies about their great admiration for Rush. "It was momentous when I first shook Geddy's hand," Les Claypool, Primus's bassist-vocalist, announced on the MTV '"Headbangers Ball" program.

GEDDY We got quite close with them. We used to jam with them every day for an hour and a half before they went on. We got a whole assortment of instruments that we couldn't play—accordion, clarinet, flute—and we had so much fun just trying to make music that it planted a seed that that's what it's all about. All of these bands on the West Coast were doing really interesting things, and to us it was a real positive explosion. The five or six years previous were such a dull, boring time for rock music. But this was a kind of rock music we could relate to because some of it is so weird and unconventional. It had an inspiring effect on us. (Chicago Sun Times 1994)

ALEX We listened to their material … and thought it was great. The first show, I fell in love with them. They have a youthfulness and an energy that was new and fresh. We've become very, very close friends. (German TV Interview)

January 30: Proceeds from the Oakland gig go to pediatric AIDS research organization, AmFar.

GEDDY All of us are interested in what's happening in AIDS. We tried to think what was the most effective way of helping. To our mind it was in research. We want to help stop the disease. (New Music)

January 31: A music critic for *The San Francisco Chronicle* writes, "It may, in fact, be the band's refusal to allow any outside influences to shape the band—punk, new wave, post-modernism have all come and gone without making a dent on Rush—that is responsible for the enormous loyalty the band commands." Life on the road has its consolations beyond acts of fan loyalty.

NEIL Within the last 10 years, our lives have gotten so much bigger that suddenly we can take advantage of being on the road. If we're in a city for a day or two, we can go to an art museum or we can play tennis or golf or go for a bike ride. (Orlando Sentinel)

March: David Foster and Celine Dion via satellite in Los Angeles announce that Rush are Juno Award winners for Best Rock Group and Best Album Cover (Hugh Syme). Ironically, they lose their Grammy Rock Instrumental nomination for "Where's My Thing?" nomination to their own tour guest, guitarist extraordinaire, Eric Johnson ("Cliffs of Dover")! Meanwhile, Terry Brown produces Montreal trio Voivod (recent Rush tourmate). *Spin* magazine's Bob Mack interviews Neil, who makes a reference to Rush's music as anti-suicidal and inspiring in a reference to major league baseball player/Rush fan Randy Johnson.

NEIL Who's that guy in Seattle that pitched a no hitter? He'd played his drums that day and when he was out there he was thinking of Rush songs. (Spin)

April: Rush becomes the second top donator in pop (under Madonna) to raise $100,000 to AmFar. "Ghost of a Chance" is a significant rock radio hit. Neil guest performs on three tracks by Rheostatics, an eclectic college-radio band also out of Canada. Curiously, one of their songs is called "California Dreamline". Longtime friend Joe Mendelson forms Artists Against Racism, and Neil is the second person to join the campaign. Rush seems at last to be receiving widespread respect from the media, for instance in *Circus:* "That's what's impressive about Rush—that three can sound like ten without posing, pandering to idiots, or relying on the sort of tattoo-powered stage tantrums that can send an audience home with an angry taste in their mouths."

April 10: Rush embarks on European tour, including two nights at Wembley Arena, a Paris date, and a week of shows in Germany. "Roll the Bones/Show Don't Tell" charts in at UK #49.

NEIL Primus was opening for us, and Herb Alexander and I would have jams in the tune-up room before the show. He had a PureCussion drumset in there, and I had some hand drums. We'd be jamming, and members of their band and our band would drift in and out of the room and join us in making some impromptu music. For the most part people would be using instruments that they don't normally play. Someone would pick up an accordion, and someone else would pick up a flute—that was primo! Somebody would be playing bass, and somebody would be playing on anything we could find to hit. (Modern Drummer)

April 13: RIAA certifies *Chronicles* gold and platinum.

May: An ABC-TV filmcrew records footage from the German dates for use in an "In Concert" profile hosted by Latin rocker Carlos Santana. They also use

Detroit Palacevision footage and interviews from last year. A caller on Rockline tells guest Geddy Lee that he has named his son after him. Geddy replies, "I hope he doesn't resent that!"

June 28: Rush ends the highly successful tour with a stop in Chicago, Illinois. They will be the sixth top grossing road act at the end of the year.

August: Skid Row covers a Rush tune (the ATWAS version of "What You're Doing") on their *all-covers* EP, making them the first major act to do a Rush tribute. The instrumental "Where's My Thing?" is allowed to be used in a promotional video by the Canadian Air Force 417th TAC Squadron. In Cold Lake, Alberta, Alex is given the chance to fly in a CF-5A jet (piloted by Gordon Cooper) and is given his own flight suit (originally reading 'Captain Lerxst'), about which he remarks, "we might need a larger suit." The story was published in the defunct military journal *Sentinel*.

ALEX   I lived as a child very close to the airbase in Toronto and I remember the airplanes used to go overhead there and as a child it was really exciting to see, and it's something that always stays with you. (MuchMusic)

When asked to describe the four hour flight, Alex jokes "it's like sex, but not as messy." In addition to using the track free of charge, Anthem gave 419 Squadron a Canadian platinum certification for *Roll The Bones,* which was mounted onto the 419's "we love us" wall.

October: Neil bicycles through Mali, Senegal, and The Gambia. Mobile Fidelity begins releasing 24-kt. discs of Rush albums, mastered from original recordings, starting with *Moving Pictures.*

1993

March: Neil Peart is the first representative of a musical group to sign on to the Artists Against Racism poster campaign. AAR was founded by Mendelson Joe and Lisa Cherniak to remind everyone, especially youth, that "we are all one people… from different places". Canada has the largest "hate-rock" music label in North America, and AAR was partly a reaction to that sad fact. Other artists aboard include Aerosmith, Paul Newman, Bush, Dan Aykroyd, Martin Short, BB King, and dozens more. Album preproduction for *Counterparts* begins at Chalet Studios.

ALEX   Before we started this record, I spent a month messing with ProTools and Cubase [music software], and I finished a couple of cassettes of ideas and fairly complete songs. It was nice to go into the writing stage with that material. (Guitar School)

April: Rush enters Studio Morin Heights (Le Studio). John Webster guest performs on keyboards.

GEDDY   Alex is very reactionary. He must have said 10,000 times that he didn't want any keyboards on the album, so when I brought my keyboards into the studio there was an immediate atmosphere. He kept looking at them like they were really threatening. (Raw)

May 8: Rush attends a Musicians of the Millenium evening party in Cambridge, Massachusetts. A shot of the three at a table will be used for their subsequent album. Next day, world's oldest humor magazine, the 117-year old *Harvard Lampoon,* honors Rush as the Musicians of the Millenium for their "artistic achievement, sense of humor and coolness." For years critics called the band "too serious," Steve Lookner, an ex-member of the executive board, explains to the press. "They're very literate—one of the few bands that actually puts some humor into its lyrics and tries to make jokes once in a while. When there's a band that tries to be funny in an industry which doesn't have a lot of humor in it, we respect that." Previous awards had been given to Natalie Wood, Winston Churchill, George Foreman, Robin Williams, John Cleese, and Bill Cosby. Fans come from as far south as Florida, just to catch a glimpse of their heroes for the 7th annual ceremony, where Lampoon staff dressed in various costumes—as past winners, as monks chanting "Tom Sawyer", as impersonators, including a disgruntled John Rutsey, as Michael McDonald singing "Red Barchetta", as Rush's parents, as a head of the fanclub, as a grateful Mark Twain, as a caveman promoting *Power Windows,* as an unauthorized biographer, as a Freddie Mercury singing "Subdivisions", as an alien (future winner), as Conan O'Brien.

GEDDY   I guess there is a serious side to us, but it was a great relief to us to have the opportunity to go to the Lampoon and for them to recognize a lot of these stupid things we put in our songs. Here's this generation of young bright lights who will be making their way into comic writing and positions of leadership in the future and they got the jokes. (Network)

GEDDY   I'm also grateful that after the partying with them last night that I'm still alive. (Acceptance Speech)

ALEX   College kids, what do you know about life? What do you know about lying in a hotel room ordering room service? Sitting around, not being responsible for yourself. Party last night? I thought they could drink. Big Al could show them a few things! Anyway thanks for your hospitality. (Acceptance Speech)

NEIL   We laughed, we cried, we drank. (Acceptance Speech)

RAY DANNIELS Rush are like three athletes. Every season they've showed up to play. They've never retired to tried to come back, or released a record and not toured. (Billboard)

Rush refused to do autographs as they were mobbed getting into the limo to go back home. Alex would later joke to MuchMusic: "They told us we were supposed to get degrees!" But instead the band each got pizza from Tommy's Pizzeria. CNN (Cable News Network) even acknowledged this achievement.

June: Peter Collins is again recruited to do Rush's next few albums because the band felt it was time to get heavy and organic-sounding again.

GEDDY Peter's responsible for making sure that everything's under control. That allows us to be simply the musicians. I think it's really important when you are playing to be a *player*, without always having to switch back and forth to be the guy who's judging it. (Canadian Musician)

GEDDY We enjoyed working with Peter before. Since then he's been working with a large number of heavy bands whose music has more to do with ours, so we were intrigued. We've always kept in touch and were looking for an opportunity to work together, and we decided to try it this time. I'm glad we did. Since we had a certain sound in mind for the record, Peter helped us to go on a search for the right engineer. We listened to hundreds of tapes trying to find the right guy. And, for the first time, we used one engineer to do the recording and another to do the mixing. The recording engineer ended up being a South African named Kevin 'The Caveman' Shirley. His name says it all; we were after bold and organic sounds, and he was the man for the job—he has brilliant miking technique and a great ear for natural recording. (Bass Player)

ALEX We wanted to be that energetic three-piece band we were in the past. We decide to strip down our approach and bring up my guitar. (Guitar Player)

GEDDY There are moments that are heavier than anything we have ever done in a long time. But even if we became really heavy again it wouldn't be like the way we were on *2112*. Those records were made in a certain time and place and the only way we'd be able to recreate it would be accidentally. If we did it on purpose, it would sound like bullshit. (Raw 1993)

July 13: Geddy fulfills his dream of singing the Canadian Anthem, "O Canada", at the 64th Annual All-Star Major League Baseball Game at Camden Field, Baltimore.

GEDDY It was a tremendous thrill. And I'd never do it again. I was far too nervous beforehand and it's so hard to hear yourself sing through the echoing of the stadium. I think it was the slowest version of 'O Canada' every performed. (TV Guide Online)

Peter Zezel (hockey player for the Toronto Maple Leafs at this time) drops by the studio to see his cousin Alex during the recording of Rush's 15th studio album. Michael Kamen, noted film composer (*Pink Floyd The Wall, Lethal Weapon, Brazil, The Dead Zone, Robin Hood,* among others) conducts the orchestra on one track ("Nobody's Hero").

August: Tracks mixed at McClear Place, Toronto.

NEIL Michael Letho was brought in to mix the tracks and he constructed some beautiful mixes with instruments coming in and out, perfectly complementing each other. He brought a certain amount of refinement to the proceedings. If we had just used Michael, the record might have been too refined. Had we just used the Caveman, it would have been too raw. So we had the best combination of influences. (Modern Drummer)

GEDDY We're at that period in our lives where we're starting to question our relationships with each other. You start to ask, 'Why am I still hanging around with these guys?' To some extent *Counterparts* is a recognition of how the three of us have grown in different ways of the past few years. There were certainly a lot more fights during these sessions. Almost every Monday morning Alex and I would have a full-blown, in-your-face argument. It was probably a good thing. (Raw 1993)

August 24: A radio station in Cleveland, Ohio makes an announcement that Neil is dying of colon cancer. Fans flood the phones at *Modern Drummer*.

NEIL You don't know how many times I've heard that rumor. Strangers have come up to me and asked, 'Is it true? Are you dying of cancer?' If it were true, imagine the insensitivity of someone asking you point blank if you're dying. Be that as it may, let me put an end to all of these rumors. I'm absolutely fine, and as far as I know I plan on living a long and happy life. Even my daughter said I looked like a chemotherapy patient! But those bandanas did an excellent job keeping the sweat out of my eyes. (Modern Drummer)

September: Rush awarded Best Group at the Toronto Music Awards. After receiving the Harold Moon SOCAN Music Award, The Arts Foundation of Greater Toronto bestows the 'Best Artist' award on Rush. CityTV/Muchmusic program director Denise Donlon was part of the board jury 30 million records and six million concert tickets (a record 22 dates at Toronto's Maple Leaf Gardens). Maurizio Belli, an award-winning cinematographer, and Stuart Clarefield film the band and their parents for a TV profile. Alex is scuba diving with past-Prime Minister Pierre Trudeau, and only Geddy and Neil appear to accept at the ceremony.

NEIL It is very special for us indeed to receive an award that has A-R-T in it. Fair enough. It keeps us humble. When I look at the names of some of the other people who have received the award, I feel humbler still. Thanks in due go to our manager Ray Danniels for practicing the A-R-T of business … equally we have to thank our wives and children who make many of the same sacrifices for A-R-T that we do, without being able to call themselves *artists*. (Acceptance Speech)

Rush contributes their $5,000 award to an AIDS hospice. Geddy, Alex, and Neil as well as Ray Danniels each match the prize to donate $20,000 to Casey House.

September 5: Alex plays on the Kumbaya (musical fundraiser for AIDS) telethon at the Ontario Place Forum around 8:30 p.m. alongside of friend Tom Cochrane (who toured with Rush while singing for Red Rider in 1984) and Molly Johnson. Alex jammed on Tom's hit from the previous year, "Life is a Highway", as well as participating in blues numbers.

ALEX Andrew MacNaughton called me and told me that Kumbaya was putting on this thing and asked me if I would be available to play and I said, of course I would. It was as easy as that! … We're all giving our time here … helping this very worthy cause.

Geddy also is asked to appear in a Canadian public service announcement TV spot for Kumbaya Festival. In the commercial, the serene guitar outro to "Ghost of a Chance" plays as Geddy speaks, standing in a lonely sea of gravestones.

September 26: The entire album is aired. The new sound could be described as Pearl Jam meets Rush, and it was exactly what they had been looking for.

GEDDY One of our main goals of this record was to have a drier, bigger sound, especially the rhythmic side of the record. We have been learning in the past few years, how to become more groove oriented, which is tough for white Canadian musicians! Neil and I have been trying to perfect a lot of new rhythmic things. There seem to be more bands blending rhythmic stuff with hard rock, and I think it's a great marriage. It's one of those bandwagons we are quite happy to jump onto. We like Fishbone and the Red Hot Chili Peppers who have such eclectic influences, and their rhythm sections have that American groove thing going which is very appealing to us. (Rock World)

ALEX Pearl Jam and Alice in Chains—I've been really getting off on 'Dirt'. And I love Eric Johnson's playing. (Guitar Player 1993)

GEDDY I think that there's some great bands out there now, bands who are weird as hell. There was a real hole in the American rock scene at one time, there were all these glam metal bands coming out of L.A., but there really didn't seem to be anything happening. There's a lot of musicians here and a lot of the music is very explorative—bands like Primus, Fishbone, Soundgarden—these are bands I feel are really doing interesting things. They're helping to create another generation of musicians who will keep exploring what you can do with rock. Pop bands like the Chili Peppers, and Nirvana, to a certain degree, although they're a little over-cooked right now, at least it's good stuff. To me, Nirvana aren't any different from The Police. They're just The Police with a grungier sound, it's good pop, nothing wrong with it. But I don't know what made us cool suddenly. I guess this is what happens when you hang around for a long time. (Seconds 1994)

GEDDY   Musically I think we are living in a very healthy time. There was a real hole in the music scene five years ago … What happens is that because most people in the music business don't know anything about music, they accidentally sign some bands that are pretty good. In the wake of Nirvana's success, a lot a bands who are better musically, have come to light. A lot of A&R people don't want to take any chances because their jobs depend on it. I supposes it's understandable, but unfortunate. (Rock World 11/93)

NEIL   Grunge became really tired really fast because it was all there was in the hip universe; where in healthier times before and after big waves like that, things tend to be the most satisfying because there's so much music to choose from, and even the charts will reflect a broad stylistic input. (Seconds)

October 19: *Counterparts* is released and debuts at #2, becoming their highest charting album ever (though it didn't stay there longer than a week). In the U.K., it charts in at #14. Rush had made a point to play there on the last tour, but there was no denying their popularity had slipped. "Stick It Out", a radio-aimed rocker, was prepared after the rest of the album was completed. The song does better than any Rush radio track in the previous seven years, staying at #1 for weeks. It also is aided by a music video directed by Samuel Bayer (videos for Nirvana, Cracker, Candlebox, Blind Melon).

November: Neil interviews the Liberal Jean Chretien, running for Prime Minister, for a 10 minute "Intimate and Interactive: A Concert of Politics" special on Muchmusic.

NEIL   I'd like us to stay together. I'd like Canadians to be prosperous and healthy. And I'd like Canada to play an effective role on the world's stage.

Neil, still undecided after reading Chretien's book, asks about the number of jobs and taxes his programs will create, agrees that handguns should be banned, and is sure to ask if Chretien supports AIDS funding. Chretien is elected a few days later.

NEIL   People should do what they want and not hurt me. Left-wing libertarian is what I call myself, because I do believe in the safety-net aspect of society. I expect that to be voluntary, but unfortunately my experience with human nature has led me to be somewhat skeptical of that. I've decided that as a libertarian benevolent dictator I would institute social programs. (Seconds)

December: Geddy appears on the cover of *Bass Player* for the first time in five years. Rush declines offers to play Woodstock '94 and what would be their first appearance on "Saturday Night Live". Alex talks about his wife's black '83 Mercedes in *Car Stereo Review* magazine, whose editor Mike Mettler will rave about many a Rush album in future publications.

December 1: *2112* is RIAA certified double platinum, *Hemispheres* and *A Farewell To Kings* each platinum, *Fly By Night* gold and platinum, *Caress of Steel* gold. The vintage Rush albums, while not shameful to members of the band, are nonetheless somewhat embarrassing.

GEDDY   I have fond memories of them. Nowadays, to me, they sound a little dated, extremely naïve … but that's ok. (Sounds)

NEIL   Those are like your fridge paintings when you were a child—only your mom doesn't keep dragging those out for everyone to see and compare your present work to. (Albany Times)

December 7: *Counterparts* is RIAA certified gold.

1994

January: *Seconds* magazine sums up the trio's ageless appeal. "Rush shows the MTV-driven caravan of Johnny-come-lately, faux-gnarly-dude franchise bands like Bland Lemon and the Stone Gossard Pilots a thing or two about dexterity, sincerity and bombast. Imagine King's X or Alice In Chains abandoned at a Canadian Star Trek convention, or Super Dave Osborne In Utero, and you've got a good feel for the latest din emanating from these forty-something men of steel. These low-profile album-rock tycoons deserve their just due as the Led Zep of Generation X, the ELP for Reagan's kidz, and the reason punk rock has survived since Johnny Rotten first wet his bondage pants seemingly ages ago."

In the age of CD box sets, eventually fans start to wonder if any work from Rush has been left out from their catalog.

GEDDY   What we write is what you get on a Rush album. We don't … we don't ever write extra songs. If a song isn't worthy to be on a record, we usually don't finish it, so it gets kinda tossed in the garbage. So, we may be the only band with a 20-year existence that has no material in the can, 'cause everything we've written has gone on record. So, you know, we're a great disappointment after … if we all get killed in a car crash, or something like that, it would be a great disappointment to our record company. (Up Close)

GEDDY   If a song's not good enough to be on a record, then throw it away. Why have substandard stuff laying around? I think it just waters down your standards. If it wasn't good enough to make your record, it's an inferior song. If it's inferior in your eyes, why give it to the public? (Guitar 1996)

ALEX   We've always had a policy that we only wrote and worked on songs that were going to be on the records. We never wrote any more music or recorded any unreleased material ever. We've done a few things in the recording sessions, but they would definitely get an X-rating. (Calgary Sun 1998)

NEIL   Every song we write, if we like it enough to go to all the trouble of writing it, we put it on the record. We don't have unreleased tracks which some people can't understand. (St. Petersburg Times 1996)

January 22: In 1984 Alex had said in the *Milwaukee Journal,* "I really *really* doubt if we will be touring like this when we're 40 years old," but the *Counterparts* Tour nevertheless begins in Pensacola, Florida with guest Candlebox. This time, pyrotechnics would replace the lasers and no 1984 material would be played at all. Rush were even considering touring again after the current six-month jaunt.

ALEX   The tentative plan is to go out in January of '95 and do a 20th anniversary coinciding with the 20th album release. We've talked about some ideas that we've had. One idea that we had was to do 'An Evening with'. Break it up between the two decades of the history of the band, and have a little bit of a film presentation in between during a short intermission, and do a set that's made up of songs from the first album right through to the last album in chronological order. Just make it kind of a special presentation. (Rockline)

GEDDY   Well, in terms of instructional videos, I'm too busy watching them to have any time to do one myself. (Rockline)

February: Neil has been wearing African tam hats (to replace last year's bandanas) to all shows, his new trademark. "Drumbeats" reflects more of his Afro-centric fascination. The song is a short story conceived and written by Kevin J. Anderson (with input and polishes by Neil) written for the horror anthology, *Shock Rock II.* The tale is about a rock drummer who goes to Africa and discovers villagers who are using human skins for drums:

NEIL   Bicycling through Africa was about the furthest thing from a rock concert tour that Danny could imagine—which was why he'd done it, after promoting the latest Blitzkrieg album and performing each song until the tracks were worn smooth in his head. This cleared his mind, gave him a sense of balance, perspective.

In the studio, he had messed around with drum synthesizers and reverbs and the new technology designed to turn computer hackers into musicians. But this drum sounded different, solid and pure, and it hooked him through the heart, hypnotizing him.'

Though he experimented with writing short fiction, Neil has no plans on returning to writing sci-fi epics such as "2112" or "Cygnus X-1".

NEIL   Ironically, I'm less and less interested in fiction … there's plenty of good material out there just in what people do everyday and why." (Aquarian Weekly)

February 10: *The Sacramento Bee* covered the tour: "Opening the show with a film projected on a stage-wide screen, the band lampooned the often-pompus openings of shows such as theirs with a terrific takeoff on '2001: A Space Odyssey'. Using imagery from its latest album, with 'Thus Spake Zarathustra' on the sound system, a giant bolt swept through deep space for a rendezvous with a giant nut, a promising sign that the band doesn't take its grand gestures entirely seriously. In the same vein were other attempts at levity, as when the normally silent guitarist Alex Lifeson took the microphone to introduce the band members with their names juxtaposed, introducing himself as Alec Baldwin."

March 20: At the O'Keefe Center, Toronto Rush is honored during the Juno Awards with an induction into the Canadian Music Hall of Fame, joining such notable artists as Anne Murray, Gordon Lightfoot, Neil Young, Joni Mitchell, and The Band. Tom Cochrane hosted the segment. "Tonight we're here to blow the lid off our three friends. To salute a 20-year-old career that defines commitment, artistic integrity and spectacular achievement." Guest appearances by members of fellow Canadian Mike Myers (of Wayne's World), The Tragically Hip, and Barenaked Ladies, as well as Ben Mink, Sebastian Bach, Max Webster's Kim Mitchell, Joe Carter and Paul Molitor of the Toronto Blue Jays, Sam Sniderman, and Alex's son Justin. American bands Living Colour and Soundgarden also offered salutations. "Rush are the guys to listen to," Larry LaLonde of Primus urged young musicians. Ray Danniels proudly confessed, "I know of no other rock group that's released 18 or 19 records and toured for every one of them. It's very much been like a sports team. You show up every season. You may not win the World Series or Stanley Cup every time, but you sure as hell make the playoffs." Peter Collins remarked, "The dynamics between the three are extraordinary. There's a brotherly love, there's an instinct and intuition that works in a miraculous way."

In accepting the award Neil thanked the bus drivers and fans.

NEIL   We may provide the music, but they provide the audience. Nietzsche said without music life can be a mistake. More unnerving for us, is that without music we would have to get a life. And without an audience, we would have to get a job!

Alex (realizing his speech was misplaced): Three dozen eggs. Two liters of milk. 150 Valiums. That's kinda what's it been like!

March 23: Michael Norman bashes Rush in the *Cleveland Plain Dealer:* "I have never experienced anything quite as excruciating as the Rush concert Wednesday night at the Coliseum. Going to a Rush show is sort of like joining Mr. Peabody for a bad trip in the Wabac Machine. Making matters worse, you've heard most of the songs a thousand times before because the idiots who program your town's radio stations play them all the time. "Tom Sawyer." "Limelight." "Spirit of Radio." "Closer to the Heart." And so on, ad nauseum. There are a couple of new tunes from the latest Rush release, "Counterparts," the 19th album of the band's 20-year recording career. But the lyrics that seem profound to the drunk sitting next to you strike your sober mind as sophomoric and stupid. Ditto the music, which, for the most part, seems slick, bombastic and soulless. Lee's nasal monotone is as annoying as ever. The same goes for Lifeson's unimaginative, ride-the-scales riffing."

ALEX When we finish this tour I'm going to have a big chunk of time so I'm starting to toy with the idea of a solo project. The last few times I've committed myself to just messing around, I've liked the results. They're quite different from what we do in the band which in the past wasn't the case. (Guitar School)

April 1: Primus joins Rush on tour again. The tour is another grand success as Rush is counted among the top ten draws throughout the season.

May 7: Rush plays Toronto on their last tour stop. They also set the record for most performances Maple Leaf Gardens, 22.

May 15: Birth of Geddy's daughter, Kyla Avril Weinrib.

June 24: Neil's autobiographical essay "A Port Boy's Story" is published by a St. Catherine's area newspaper *The Standard*. The editor Brian Collins was in the band Hush that Neil left to join Rush in the early '70s.

September 3: Alex appears on MuchMusic in a very amusing afternoon appearance on "MuchLive" plugging Kumbaya with Tom Cochrane, Bill Bell, Molly Johnson, and Larry Gowan, reminiscing about the past 10 years of the music channel.

ALEX We actually broke up you know? I decided to start another band and I figured Geddy and Neil would like to play in it and they said yeah. (MuchMusic)

During the next day's Kumbaya activities, Pye Dubois recited the actual poem "Between Sun and Moon" was based on, "There is Lake Between Sun and Moon." At night, Alex and the others got together for a rendition of Jimi Hendrix's "All Along the Watchtower". Alex would also play alongside John Cody and Mae Moore at Kumbaya.

September 29: Geddy at Canadian Music Video Awards presents Best Metal Video Award.

October 4: Twenty-one drummers appear on the Neil-produced CD *Burning For Buddy: A Tribute to the Music of Buddy Rich* recorded at Bearsville Studios, in New York's Catskill Mountains area. The disc is received well on radio, and tops the Jazz charts. A month later Neil is given the Buddy Rich Lifetime Achievement Award.

NEIL My roots do come from jazz. I grew up listening to big band jazz, which my father loved—Glenn Miller, Duke Ellington, Count Basie, and the great drummers who played with them. Frank Sinatra and Tony Bennett always had great musicians. (Modern Drummer)

Signals is released on Mobile Fidelity 24-kt and ultradisc this month also. Many fans are curious why a verse is missing in "The Weapon". Mo Fi's comment on this: "The master tapes, which were provided to us directly from the Rush offices in Canada, did not include these vocals. Apparently, these vocals were edited in at a later time." Alex and friends Tim Notter and Pam Fenton open 100-seat Orbit Room on College Aveenue in Toronto this month as well.

November 3: Neil appears on U.S. cable tv show "Politically Incorrect" hosted by Bill Maher. Alan Zweibel ("Saturday Night Live" comedy writer), comedian Franklin Ajaye, and Elizabeth Wurtzel (author of *Prozac Nation*) are part of the roundtable discussion of media matters. Neil questions Maher's belief that movies should supplement the literature they're based on. "So you should read Shakespeare and not see the play?" Neil asks before Maher dumbly replies, "Um…what are you saying?" He also admits he has watched the wildly popular "Beavis and Butthead" (even wears a B&B shirt in his new CD). The MTV animated show about two juvenile ignorami watching videos all day actually used "Stick It Out" in an episode around this time. The characters are disappointed upon learning that the "cool guitar" riff is Rush, at which point they make fun of Geddy's high vocals in "Spirit of Radio". Butthead agrees the guitar is cool "if you happen to be a wuss," but that the idea of "a dude in dreadlocks strapped to a chair on a pole was a good idea for a video."

Ray Danniels is now managing Van Halen and Queensryche, who lost their manager Ed Leffler to cancer. Alex Van Halen's wife is Ray's sister (who will divorce in 1998.)

1995

January 27: *Moving Pictures* is RIAA certified quadruple platinum. February issue of *Modern Drummer* magazine has Neil and Buddy Rich on the cover together. Neil starts consulting drum teacher Freddie Gruber after Journey drummer Steve Smith recommended him.

February 1: *Rush* is RIAA certified gold.

February 3: *Archives* is RIAA certified gold and platinum.

April 3: Neil's "Into Africa" article is published in *Macleans* magazine.

NEIL   Traveling in West Africa, all you worry about is keep moving and finding water. And for most of us in life we never have to worry about finding water, so I find it refreshing to have my life brought down to that basic level where I'm worrying about finding some rice to eat and finding some water to drink. It's a really healthy set of values to get in touch with, I think more people could do it, getting in touch with real life and how hard it can be sometimes. (Mats Rydstrom Q and A 1997)

June: Alex begins work on his self-produced solo debut. He also appears as "Big Al" Dexter at The Orbit Room with The Dexters—Lou Pomanti (vocals), Peter Cardinali (bass), Bernie LaBarge (guitar), and Mike Sloski (drums)—for the recording of the privately-released CD, "Hip To The Tip". The enhanced disk also includes a video tour of the Orbit Room among other features. Geddy spends some time on the internet playing fantasy rotisserie baseball with his league the Flying Hamisches.

September 2: Alex appears at the Kumbaya Festival at the Molson Amphitheatre once again to play with The Boomers, formerly The Ian Thomas Band. In free time from working on the second volume to "Burning For Buddy", Neil contributes to the first disc of "Drum Lessons with the Greats Volume 2" (which also features also featured Primus drummer Tim Alexander). Geddy co-presents an award for Best Metal Video on the Muchmusic Awards to I Mother Earth.

September: The recording hiatus would soon be over as Rush prepares to return to the studio.

GEDDY   I needed to get away from Rush, I needed to get away from music period, and just re-examine my life and make sure I was living the kind of life I wanted to live, and enjoying all the domestic things that a lot of people take for granted every day. But when you live on the road, and when you're constantly touring, you miss that stuff. It was great for me, but about a year through it I started feeling like there was this hole in my life, and that was the need for me to express myself musically. I was very ready to go back to work after 18 months. (T4E Premiere)

Neil writes of the new approach to drumming he's taken under Freddie Gruber's tutorage.

NEIL   After playing for 30 years, I decided to take a year away from performing in order to devote some time to some serious study. Under the guidance of master teacher Fred Gruber, I ended up basically starting over, 'reinventing' myself, and changing absolutely everything about the way I approach the drums, both physically and mentally. As part of the process, I began to desire an instrument, a 'voice' which reflected this 'new/old' me. A voice which could be both traditional and innovative, with unparalleled tone and response. I found this 'new/old' vision exemplified in the drums and the people of Drum Workshop. (DW Advertisement)

NEIL At 70 years old, he's been a teacher for about 40 years, and has evolved a real understanding how the body works in relation to hitting things with sticks, which is the elements of what we do. I got together with him, and basically restarted everything—changed completely the way I set up the drums, completely the way I sit at them, the way I hold the sticks, the ends of the sticks that I hold, everything was completely rebuilt. I sat down in my basement day after day practicing every day like a little kid, rebuilding these things because I was really eager to take this challenge. Despite what it might bring in terms of results I thought, 'This is great, start all over!' Thirty years, throw it all away. I certainly feel that I came to understand a lot of things that I didn't understand before, and I certainly feel as if I knew nothing before. I guess that's some element of progress. (T4E Premiere)

GEDDY He wasn't happy with the way he was grooving, he wanted a little more snap to his playing. It just has a bit more bounce and if you listen to his work, particularly on the high hats, there's a great groove thing happening. Of course, he's still thunderous and his parts are still as mental as they ever were. He hasn't really lost the bombast, he's just added some more swing to the whole thing. (Bassics 1997)

NEIL When Rush joined Atlantic, Ahmet Ertegun told me, we got to get you playing jazz. (Billboard)

In time for the studio, Neil's new Drum Workshop kit arrives in a custom Blood Red Sparkle that nostalgically "echoes" his childhood set.

November 17: *2112* is RIAA certified triple platinum.

November 21: *Chronicles* is RIAA certified double platinum.

December: Clif Norrell (Faith No More, REM, Catharine Wheel) comes on board as recording engineer for the new Rush album. Around Christmas, Sebastian Bach visits Alex who's working his song "Promise" and records a vocal.

ALEX As things developed and as I wrote the rest of the—one single male voice. So, when I talked to Edwin about working on the record and we got focused on all the songs, I decided to go with him. The take that Sebastian did on the song was really, really great, and Sebastian is a fabulous singer. Talk about energy! The whole studio at home was shaking when he was out there jumping around, bouncing off the walls doing it. I really felt really badly about not using him on the record, because I know that it meant something to him, and he really enjoyed working on it. (Rockline)

1996

January: Rush heads back to the familiar surroundings of Chalet studio for pre-production on "Boys Camp", relying on the basic tracks laid down on Macintosh Power Tools for their next album, *Test For Echo*.

GEDDY   It's an old farm house, a country kitchen, all the views of the house are quite beautiful; quite an expanse of what used to be farmland, and on the border of this particular property there are still some farms, and a lot of trees. Way off in the distance you can see the nuclear reactors. A number of bedrooms, and attached to the farmhouse is I guess what used to be a barn, or something like that, but it's a big glass-windowed environment that Alex and I set up our gear in—it's a studio—and Neil has his drums in one corner, there's a control room upstairs. We create our own comfortable writing environment there, Alex and I. (T4E Premiere)

ALEX: The first few days we didn't do any work. Ged and I sat outside, drank coffee and talked about where we wanted to go as people. We talked a time about the band and all of that, but mostly about ourselves and the kinds of things that we had gone through over this two-year period we had off. It was great, because we made a connection. (Canadian Musician 1996)

GEDDY   This time I didn't have to stay overnight at the Chalet for it to be productive. I didn't have to sleep in the same house with them. I commuted. The drive up let me clear my head and I got to listen to tapes of the last day, think about arrangements and stuff. I was happier because I got to sleep in my own bed, see my wife and kids and my life wasn't disrupted. By the time I got to work, I was just so vibed up and ready. (Canadian Musician 1996)

GEDDY   *Counterparts* was not what I'd consider to be a tension-free record. There was a lot of pressure. We were using other computers … It was a nightmare. (Bassics 1997)

Recording on the drums begins at Bearsville Studios.

ALEX   Peter had been bugging us to go there and do drum tracks, and we avoided it for a number of reasons. Where we usually do drums, Le Studio, in Morin Heights, Quebec, is really close to where Neil lives. But the room at Bearsville is an enormous wooden room with high ceilings. It's like a hangar, it's about three stories high—Neil's drums sounded particularly amazing in there. (Canadian Musician 1996)

Val Azzoli is promoted to co-CEO by CEO Ahmet Ertegun. "The reason we went after him," Ertegun explained, "was that we were very impressed with him in his previous role involving Rush." (Billboard)

January 9: Alex's side project *Victor* (US #99) released with guests bassist Peter Cardinali of the Dexters, bassist Les Claypool of Primus, Tom Cochrane, guitarist Bill Bell, and even Alex's youngest son Adrian, who co-wrote "The Big Dance" and "At the End", as well as contributing synth programming.

ALEX   Adrian writes a lot of electronica, I would almost call it transient … not really dance music, it's a little tougher sounding than that. We're actually in the process of putting some mixes together so we can seek a deal for him. (Mackietone News 2000)

Alex speaks on the album on the title track. "Victor" is not only a song based on the Auden poem, but collectively the name of the group on the album. On the first track "Don't Care", Alex actually wrote in a vulgar phrase which is a first for any member of Rush on a recording.

ALEX   What people probably expected from me for this album was guitar doodling. I really didn't want to do that. I don't particularly like records like that. They don't last very long. You're impressed by the ability of the player but after a couple of listens it's 'So big deal!' (Rag)

February–March: Guitars are recorded at Reaction Studios whose clients previously included Geddy's nephew Rob Higgins' band Change Of Heart, Rheostatics, Barenaked Ladies, and Anne Murray.

ALEX   What we wanted was somewhere private. We had worked a lot at McClear Pathe, and they have three very busy studios, so you're sharing the lounge with everyone else that worked there. That's fine for corporate stuff and commercial works. But for us, we wanted to have a place that was all our own. And there aren't too many studios anymore that are like that, who could accommodate us, with the kind of sounds we wanted and the size of the room. So we went to Reaction. It worked out great. The people there, like Ormond Jobin, were great and everyone was really nice, so it was a great vibe. (Canadian Musician 1996)

ALEX   You do have to know when to stop. Otherwise, you'll spend years working on something and, I think, Def Leppard is an example of that. Their records certainly have sounded incredible, incredibly produced, well-produced. But they've spent, two, three years making a record; they get to the guitars and they decide they want to redo the drums and then they decide they want to redo the guitars, and then the vocals. I think if you've captured initial energy and excitement of the song and you've gotten them to a point that you're happy with, then you have to move away from it. (Up Close 1994)

April: Final mixing at McClear Place with engineer Andy Wallace (Nirvana, Rage Against the Machine, Faith No More, Sonic Youth, Bad Religion, Alice in Chains, Smashing Pumpkins).

GEDDY   He had to adjust to a band that mixes the bass so loud. We always have to break these guys in, but his first mix was surprisingly in a direction that we wanted in the first place. He's got brilliant engineer chops. He brought out a lot of extra dynamics and things that I didn't even know were there. I think the record sounds very different for us as a result. (Canadian Musician)

Alex appears on CDs by Tom Cochrane and I Mother Earth. Neil's article "Chasing Some Midnight Rays" is published in *Cycle World Canada*.

June: While Rush finishes work on their 16th studio outing, manager Ray Danniels is busy firing singer Sammy Hagar from Van Halen, and getting David Lee Roth back for an MTV publicity move. Ray enlists Gary Cherone of SRO's other acts, Extreme, as the new singer.

July: An unauthorized tribute album is released, mixed by Terry Brown and featuring '90s art metal quartets like Dream Theater and Fates Warning as well as members from '80s hair-rockers Mr. Big, Dokken, Slaughter, Great White and Skid Row plus Steve Morse, Ozzy Osbourne alumni, Deen Castronovo and Jake E. Lee, and Joe Satriani bassist Stu Hamm. Rush fans were mixed about the unofficial tribute, some displeased with the performances. Did the band like it?

NEIL   Oh, God no. Just imagine if there was someone going around doing impersonations of you in front of people. I mean, it is a tribute in the true sense of the word, and bless their hearts and all that, but I would never want to hear it. (Aquarian Weekly)

NEIL   It's not a tribute album at all, and I don't care about it, I don't wanna fight it, I don't wanna help it. These people just keep putting out these cover albums, and the only reason they do it is to make money. Tribute albums have completely changed in the last couple of years to where they aren't tributes anymore, they're just people cashing in on other people's work. And they're just a bunch of bar-bands doing them, right? (Mats Rydstrom Q&A 1997)

GEDDY   It's embarrassing, this tribute stuff. (Rolling Stone)

GEDDY   We were approached about it—well after the record was under way—we wanted to know who was doing it, who was involved and what the record label was that was putting it out. And it came to us that the label was in the quote-unquote business of doing tribute records. That felt a little fishy to me. It felt like some guy was getting some musicians together, regurgitating some material and exploiting our fans' support. Fans were on the Net talking about why we were so insulted that these musicians were trying to do our songs. To them, it was great that someone was recognizing our band. So it got taken really in a weird way, and there was all this talk that we were going to sue them and have an injunction to try and stop the record, which of course was not true at all. (Westworld Magazine)

GEDDY   I like and respect a lot of the musicians that were involved in that album and I sincerely appreciate what they were trying to accomplish with that. But, I believe our legal people and our management, misrepresented us a little bit in that situation in an overprotective way. (Canoe Chat)

But would Rush ever do a covers album?

GEDDY   I think about covers from time to time, it would be fun. Of course, I would always choose a Who song if I was going to do that type of thing. That might be a fun thing for Rush down the road, to interpret somebody else's music. (Canoe Chat 2000)

August: Neil announces in *Modern Drummer* that he will not be answering anymore fan mail, providing some insight into his opinion on the internet explosion.

NEIL   For almost twenty years I have made the time to answer everybody who has written to me through *Modern Drummer.* A couple of times a year I would set aside a whole day and spend it reading these letters and writing out postcards in response—at first by hand and later on the keyboard—answering each letter individually and uniquely (i.e. no form letters). By now the total of those responses would number in the *thousands,* but I was always able to keep up with them at my own pace. Because I was careful never to talk about it in interviews and such, the numbers stayed under control—it remained 'our little secret'. Until now. All it took was a few people to go on the World-Wide GossipNet and start telling people that I had answered their letters through *Modern Drummer,* and the floodgates were open. These big mouths (or big *fingers*) have spoiled it for everyone. Including me. Personally, I feel terrible about this situation, for it has always given me a glow of satisfaction to spend that time on a little bit of altruism—knowing that I might bring a smile to these people's faces, or even encourage them a little bit. However, this is not something I want to devote my *life* to, and as I face the ever-growing pile of mail in the corner of my office, I know I will never again be able to keep up with it. So to any of you whose personal messages and requests reside in that pile, I offer my sincere apologies for not answering them. This unfortunate consequence of the much-vaunted Inter-thingy is a shame, and I do regret it. But hey—it was good while it lasted! (Modern Drummer)

September 5: The trio speak about the album premiere in Chicago with Jo Robinson, assistant program director and midday DJ at active rock station WRCX. "About eight months ago [PD] Dave Richards said, 'Let's start testing some old Metallica. Let's make sure it's cool to play a lot of Metallica in anticipation of their new album.' Well, when we found out about the new Rush album, we looked at each other and said, 'This is the same situation. This will be an event in Chicago the same way the Metallica album was an event. We'll make it seem uncool not to listen to Rush.'" (Billboard)

GEDDY   I was really kind of in a void making this record. I hadn't listened to the radio much. I'd kind of pulled myself out of the music scene and everything about it for about 18 months. I wonder what this record's like in the context of our past? Then I went through this period where I started listening to the radio and I kind of got the horrors: Boy, where do we fit into all this? It's kind of mild compared to other stuff. (Bassics 1997)

September 10: *Test For Echo* is released (U.S. #5, U.K. #25), produced by Peter Collins again.

GEDDY   I think Peter is the last of a dying breed—producers who are interested in nothing but producing songs. They don't want to touch the console, they are only interested in 'is this performance good? Is this song or arrangement good?' If something sounds great he doesn't feel he has to change it. No ego involved. Other times, he'll say, 'that song needs work, let's work on it', or 'you missed the point'. There may be only three or four songs on the album that he kind of tears apart totally, but it's a much better record for that. (Canadian Musician 1996)

ALEX   I think with a co-producer—such as Peter Collins cause he's such a great guy to work with, he's such a musical producer—he really draws all those things in, and adds a little cohesion to the whole thing, in terms of decision-making and where we go. Really, I would say 80% of it is us, but that 20% is a really important 20% that gels everything. (T4E Premiere)

GEDDY   I'm happy with most of it but I'm never happy with an entire album. (Smash)

The same *Smash* interviewer realized "this band's been around as long as I've been around," to which Geddy replied, "that's not funny. That's so sad."

The Test for Echo tour is groundbreaking. Rush is permitted to perform for two and a half hours every night (each one is recorded for later live compilation). This the first Rush tour solely without an opening act, truly "An Evening with Rush," as the band would call it. "2112" was revived in its entirety and "Natural Science" is played for the first time since 1980 in its entirety. The band also travels by private jet for the first time.

ALEX   People have a very glamorous vision of what it's like to be on the road. Certainly in the early years it was terrific, it was a dream come true, and it was very exciting. But after 22 years of it, it's really boring. It's exciting to get up on stage and play, to be sure, but the other 22 hours that you have to deal with can be really tough at times. (Toronto Sun)

GEDDY I'm afraid that we haven't paid enough attention to Europe. We have a lot of fans over there, and every four or five years we go over and do a token tour. But if you don't go over there like everybody else and tour every album, you're going to fall out of public consciousness—I think that's what's happened to us ... These days, getting everybody to agree to tour is a monumental feat. (All Star)

NEIL "There's only one of me and there are only 365 days of the year. It's just impossible to do everything everybody wants us to. We do what we can. I think it's just gonna be a fairly minimal tour of the States and Canada. (Mats Rydstrom 1997)

Rush decide to skip Europe again ... Dale Heslip directs a few more Rush videos, "Half the World" and "Driven", which only receive airplay on MTV-2 and Muchmusic.

GEDDY The fence represents the imaginary dividing line. The whole idea of someone's perception that the grass is always greener on the other side. (Muchmusic Spotlight)

September 19: Geddy presents Best International Video at Canadian Music Video Awards.

September 23: As a gesture of their respect for the phenomenally popular Seattle group vehemently opposed to video exposure, Rush sends a case of champagne backstage to Pearl Jam during their Toronto show.

October: Shot at Bearsville Studios during the making of the album, Neil's *A Work in Progress* video set explains his changed approach to playing drums. To promote it, a $20,000 drumkit replica giveaway is sponsored by Drum Workshop, Zildjian, and DCI Video. Entries went through *Modern Drummer* magazine.

NEIL I was still a little reluctant to do *A Work In Progress* because I didn't want to take the cap and gown of the teacher. With this record I decided the time was right to impart what I learned. (Connecticut Post)

NEIL You know the tv show "Connections?" It's on The Learning Channel. I got the impetus from that, where the guy just keeps popping up in different places around the globe and illustrating this really interesting story of how civilization came together. I also stress the apprenticeship that I'm going through, hence the title A Work in Progress. I still don't like seeing myself! I don't like the hear myself talk, I don't like to look at myself and I'll probably never watch this video [laughs]. It was definitely some of the hardest work I've ever done. To be on camera twelve hours a day, with the last couple of days being all talking, was a challenge. I had eleven chapter heads, one for each song, and I kind of drew one important illustration from each. (Modern Drummer)

October 19: The first show of the tour in Albany, New York, is reviewed *in The Sunday Gazette:* "Rush fans who feared that the Canadian rockers might be a bit rusty after their layoff had no reason to worry after the show started. Simply put, the band sounded better than ever." Two days later, the *Buffalo News* reported, "it may have been the most energized jam to take place in the arena since its opening. The jaw-dropper of the night was the brilliant "Natural Science" … this dynamic, reverberating epic left half the fans guffawing with glee and the other half quietly attentive."

October 23: *Test For Echo* is RIAA certified gold. The subject of making the cover of *Rolling Stone* arose yet again. David Fricke, *Rolling Stone's* music editor, explains: "The thing is, Rush has never really gone out of their way (for coverage) and they're not flashy guys. They're not from the Axl Rose school of getting attention. And to be quite honest, that's what newspaper editors and writers are attracted to." (Buffalo News)

ALEX   You know what? I don't know if I'd ever want to be on the cover of *Rolling Stone* to tell you the truth. They have this thing against us. I have a sense that they go out of their way to ignore us, so at least they're making some kind of effort (laughs). We've been around for 22 years with the same lineup; we haven't broken up and then regrouped. A lot of bands have cited us as influences and that's great. So I couldn't give a shit if we're ever on the cover of *Rolling Stone*. Just the fact that we haven't been is really cool so I hope that doesn't wrecked now. (Guitar)

NEIL   Geddy told me an interesting thing the other day. That when he was doing a small Q&A session for *Rolling Stone,* the writer [Jancee Dunn] let slip that we are their readers' number one most requested group for them to do a full story on. But they won't because of who they are and who we are. That's a trip, if you ask me. We're just not cool enough for them. But that's okay because they're not cool enough for us. (Houston Press 1996)

GEDDY   We've never gone out of our way to court that kind of press. And, also, we don't make ourselves available. If they want us to get together for a special photo session, well, they're not big priorities for us. Admittedly, it's not the smartest thing for promoting a record, but from our point of view we'd have to totally turn our lives upside-down, Neil would have to come down from Quebec. It would have to be a whole big thing just to have a photograph. I think we've generated some of that ourselves, just because we shy away. (Bassics 1997)

GEDDY   I'm sure there are Rush fans in the White House. Maybe one day all those closet Rush fans lurking in the shadows will come out of the woodwork. (Guitar)

October 30: *Chicago Tribune's* Greg Kot offers another pleasant concert review: "The ultimate rite-of-passage band, Rush remains a primarily testosterone-laden enterprise. At the sold-out United Center on Monday, the Canadian trio's audience was, at least, 75% male, and most of them appeared to know every lyric and anticipated every chord change with the accuracy of lifetime obsessives. Like the Grateful Dead, Rush is among the biggest cult bands in the world—reviled, misunderstood or dismissed by the uninitiated, but virtually the only band that matters within its tight circle of worshipers."

November: Neil's videos of *The Making of Burning for Buddy* are released. His book *The Masked Rider: Cycling Through West Africa* is published and available to fans during the tour.

NEIL   I would like to write a book one day, but it would probably be along the lines of a travel book, influenced by the new wave of travel writers. Because with something like that you can throw in anything you want. If you want to write a poem then that can be stuck in. If you want to write an essay, a diatribe or a vitriolic defamation of character, then they can fit in as well. This kind of amorphous style makes me feel a lot more comfortable than slots do. Sometimes even fiction can be a narrow constraint in the fact that you have to carry the plot forward. And as with music, you can get stuck in a certain style with fiction. Robert Ludlow had better never attempt an historical romance, nor Stephen King a serious work of literature! The same applies of course with most music. That's why Rush has been fortunate. From our beginnings we decided to remain amorphous. (Metal Hammer 1988)

NEIL   West Africa in the general sense is probably my nearest and dearest part of the world. I've made three trips to West Africa and one to East Africa over the years, and definitely will go back again. With a little effort and suffering you can find places that are so remote that they are as they always were, and consequently they are pure cultures, which are hard to find anywhere in the world anymore. (Aquarian Weekly)

The book offers a glimpse into Neil's mind and his views on everything from automobiles to religion. Some sections parallel his lyrics, like this excerpt which parallels their recent song "Totem":

"… it all seemed too complex to be accidental. There had to be a great Mind behind it all. This is known as the 'argument by design' I believe, but it left me confused and wondering for a long time afterward. Until now, in fact. Sure I still wonder … I'd like to believe in something larger than life, esp. for those times when life is small and mean. But after I've admired the poetry of the King James Bible, appreciated the peaceful wisdom of Buddhism, recoiled from a vengeful Allah, wondered about the secret societies of Freemasons and Illuminati, in the end I return to reality, and believe in Life. And that seems good to me. I can worship Nature and that fulfills my need for miracles and beauty. … Two epiphanies in one day had been too much for a linear-thinking agnostic like me." (The Masked Rider)

October 27: 5,100 fans in Rockford, Illinois petitioned to have Rush play there, and when they did, *The Rockford Register Star* reported, "Rush's three-hour show still rocked in a way that said, 'Take that, grunge boys!'"

November 28: The *LA Times* offers a generally good review of the tour: "Loads of instrumental noodling and plenty of lasers, strobes, video and live camera shots of the band members on a huge split screen behind them. (The only things missing were explosions and smoke.)"

Again rumors of cancer circulate during the tour.

NEIL I almost hate to dignify rumors by addressing them but it was just a whole bunch of bullshit people dreamed up. People were phoning my parents and asking, 'Is it true he's dying of cancer?' What if it were true? It gets so uncivilized when you think about the realities of it. People always forget that there are real people involved. (Houston Press)

December: *The Palm Beach Post* reviews the show: "Song after song was a rock-radio hit: 'Tom Sawyer, 'Closer to the Heart', and others that proved that Rush is a band without equal. Rush always brings something special to a concert. Sunday was no exception; they proved again that rock can be musical, mature and exciting."

December 18: Rush plays a secret concert at Club Phoenix in Toronto for 800 Molson Ice Blind Date winners. Though some fans were disappointed, expecting the act to be in fact Pearl Jam, many knew the treat they were in for. They had the once-in-a-lifetime opportunity to see the trio in an intimate setting (minus over-amplified gear, bouncing acoustics and a drum solo). The band is asked to play the day after Christmas, at the Labour of Love festival, but ultimately decide they rather spend the time with their families.

1997

January 4: Alex plays "Promise" with I Mother Earth at The Warehouse in Toronto. "Driven" and "Virtuality" alternate on radio.

February 26: Romeo LeBlanc, Governor General of Canada, presents Rush as Officers in the Order of Canada at Rideau Hall in Ottawa for their achievement and for raising charities over a million dollars.

NEIL It's certainly nice, it's an honor. Everybody in the world likes to be appreciated. We're certainly no exception.

GEDDY I'm just gonna show it off to my kids …

April: Neil talks with John Oakley on "Life On Life" on Canada's Life Network.

NEIL I've been working on a book about this tour as part of another book on adventure travel. Some musicians get worn out with performing, or worn out with the squeeze of trying to come up with new material all the time. If you can balance those out with other things—one of things that drove me to adventure travel is the necessity to get away, to step out of comfort, to step out of predictability ... so I would go out on treks through the desert, or through China or Africa, and it opened up my eyes to a whole new world.

May 6: *Retrospective I 1974–1980* is released, along with reissued Mercury CDs (remastered by Bob Ludwig and Brian Lee at Gateway Studios).

GEDDY Basically, we wanted to put [the music] back in its original form with a fresher sound, something which is long overdue. There have been so many incredible advances in mastering that it was time to update those albums, it was time to do that for the fans. It also gives us a chance to correct a couple of things that were messed up. I think it was on *Moving Pictures* [laughs]. Neil was left out of the picture. I mean, you know, we're not a duo, and this gives us a chance at correcting things like that. (Salt Lake Tribune)

May 7: The band hits the road, revisiting some of the same markets, starting with Phoenix, Arizona. In an interview in the Arizona Republic the next day, Rush is asked if they would ever do full-on jazz.

GEDDY Our touring schedule is so goofy, we decided to go out and hit some cities that were not available to us when we first went on the road.") ... There are moments, particularly in our instrumental material, that lean toward jazz from time to time. But no matter how you cut the cake, jazz fusion is not a whole lot of fun to listen to. It's great if you're a jazzier, not so great if you're a rocker. Something in the core of what we are is more akin to rock than jazz. If it starts to feel to loungey to us, we d rather turn the amps up than go jazzier. (Arizona Republic)

June 3:*Retrospective II* is released.

ALEX Listening to this retrospective, I guess I realized maybe how important Rush was and is. It's unique, in that there aren't too many bands around that have had that kind of history. (Toronto Sun)

June 11: "Speaking to the crowd," the *Pittsburgh Post-Gazette* reported, "Lee acknowledged that he believes that the band has 'played Pittsburgh more than any city in the universe,' and joked that they hoped to provide a representative sampling of '400,000 songs' or so ...The cynical may still dub Rush tech heads long on chops and short on soul. But plenty of great players come and go without making much of an impression. Rush may not be immortal, but its continued commercial viability is a testament to the band's ingenuity, integrity, and spirit. Rush's recent material sounded fresh and relevant."

June 17: The good reviews continue, this time in the *Columbus Dispatch*. "The lights went down, but just when everyone was expecting an intermission, the album cover from *2112* (a man shielding his eyes in front of a large, fiery pentagram—eat your heart out Marilyn Manson) was broadcast on the video screens onstage. You might be able to find fault with some parts of the show, but you would have to look awfully hard. All in all, it was a polished piece of work by a band that has been around long enough to know how to do it right."

July 1: In a Q107 FM radio contest, the first 107 concert fans to bring a bag of non-perishable food to Rush's Molson Amphitheatre Canada Day show (being filmed for a concert video) get a free copy of the new CD. *Toronto Sun* amusingly reports, "Lifeson gets a special fashion bravery award for wearing black leather pants in exceptionally muggy weather."

July 4: The tour ends in Ottawa, Ontario.

July 5: Alex records "Little Drummer Boy" for Steve Vai's *Merry Axemas* Christmas CD.

July 20: *Burning For Buddy II* finally arrives and hits #7 on the U.S. Jazz charts. In the summer months Neil works on a book about the touring life of a musician (something he's wanted to do since the early '80s).

NEIL I want to write about being a musician because it's never been done. People outside music who are good writers have tried to write about it … but they don't understand the essential mentality of it. If people could understand what it is like to be a musician, they would understand that a musician is someone who gets up in the morning, goes to work, finishes work and goes home—it would get rid of that alienation. (Modern Drummer)

August 10: Neil's 19-year-old daughter, Selena Taylor, dies when the Jeep she was driving left the westbound lane of Hwy. 401, and crashed near Brighton, Ontario.

August 30: Rush fans in Leceister, England hold first ever European Rush Convention.

GEDDY It's pretty gratifying—we've turned into what the Grateful Dead are, for our kind of music. It's almost a cult thing. (Network)

Rush are asked to do a Behind the Music special for VH1 but decline. Geddy sketches out song ideas on Emagic Logic software in his home studio.

September: Neil's lyrics are analyzed in libertarian journal *Liberty*.

1998

January: Fender issues a Ltd. Edition Geddy Lee Signature bass. Geddy also is heard in a R.A.D.D. (Rockers Against Drunk Driving) radio spot using "Driven" as background music.

June: Neil loses his wife to cancer. Newspapers will announce her passing a few weeks later.

SRO As per the family's wishes, it's kept very private. There's no service, or any charity, or anywhere to send flowers etc. They just want to be left alone at this very sad time.

ALEX I don't think he'll be the person he was, but I think he will cope with life again. Hopefully, eventually, he'll be able to find joy in all the things he did in life before. I got to think in my heart there are things about what we do that Neil really loves a lot and is not prepared to give up. (Calgary Sun)

June 23: *Whatever* soundtrack features "Tom Sawyer."

July 7: Geddy approves of the *Small Soldiers* soundtrack "Tom Sawyer" remix by DJ Z-Trip, though this replaces the actual Rush version on some new rock radio stations. The Artists Against Racism auction features Rush autographed items.

September: Robert Scovill transfers the best performances to his ear from a 72-track to a 48-track, then turns them in to Geddy who co-produces the upcoming live set with Paul Northfield (who also engineered and mixed the album at McClear Pathe Studios).

GEDDY It wasn't my intention to do another. I thought enough was enough with three double live albums out there already. But it also wasn't my intention to have the band keep producing records for this many years down the road. Who knew? (DS Premiere)

Bootlegs were popping up more than ever, and fans wondered if that was not ok with the band.

GEDDY One thing that really pissed me off, and I was at friend's house who had a live bootleg from our last tour. There I was drowning in tapes for our live record. And I'm listening to this tape recorded at a live concert by this guy with a tape recorder. I was just pissed that I was wasting all this time mixing the record and making it sound so good with something like that out there. (Fancast)

In his autobiography, shock rocker Marilyn Manson (Brian Warner) reveals that as an alienated teenager of the early '80s he felt *2112* was "the scariest album he'd ever heard."

November 3: The soundtrack to Adam Sandler comedy hit *The Waterboy* released with "Tom Sawyer".

GEDDY   It'd be cool if all soundtracks had Rush music. (Fancast)

November 10: The live *Different Stages* is released, featuring two discs largely comprised of Chicago T4E shows with some CP Tour tracks thrown in for good measure. Geddy writes the liner notes.

GEDDY   We have tried not to mess with these tapes very much and to present something that we think represents a fairly definitive retrospective of our live work and changing sound over that period of time.

GEDDY   Remarkably, we found a lot of the performances were coming from the same night. If you look, almost 70 per cent of the album is from Chicago. It's so ironic. You record over a hundred shows and you end up with an album that mostly came from one venue. I don't remember it being a particularly special night, but when I listened back to it, there's something about the sound of that venue that sounded like an event. There was an excitement in the air. Every time we out up the Chicago, Boston, Philadelphia, or one of the Detroit shows—even if those performances weren't quite so good as some others. (DS Premiere)

The third disc is a Hammersmith Odeon show from 2/20/78 that was engineered by Terry Brown.

GEDDY   The reason that show even exists is that we did it for some radio show. I can't remember which. I remember at the time I had a cold and my voice was really raw. During the early part of the show I had very little control vocally so I changed a lot of the phrasing that I normally sang with in order to compensate for the cold. Listening back to it at the time, it probably seemed dramatically weird to me so it never made it on the radio show and we just kept the tapes. So Alex and I went into the studio and we put them up and mixed them for fun about a year-and-a-half ago. We were amazed at the energy of the live performance. It was a particular kind of energy that's connected with the age that we were, the kind of players that we were. Playing those songs today would not have that same vibe. (DS Premiere)

ALEX   I listened to *Hemispheres* and I hadn't heard that in, oh boy, 15 years. It was really cool and a lot of fun. I heard things I hadn't heard us do in a while, like some of the harmonic ideas. Being reminded of that makes me think that some of those ideas might come back. Sometimes it's by going back that we replenish the future. (Vancouver Province)

November 15: Something of a first for the band: a SonicNet live fancast w/ Geddy and Alex. Geddy comments on the subject of eluding scandals.

GEDDY We never got too far in that area [laughs]. We failed that subject at rock 'n' roll school and we exceeded at the technical side. We were terribly inept at forming some form of acceptable, sexy image of our band. We were musicians, just trying to play and make the coolest music we could dream of making." (Vancouver Sun)

December 2: *Different Stages* is RIAA certified gold. This month the first comprehensive lyrical analysis of the band is published, Carol and Robert Price's excellent *Mystic Rhythms: The Philosophical Vision of Rush*. Official Rush merchandiser and close friend of the band, Mike McLoughlin dies, yet another loss for the Rush family. Patrick, Mike's son, picks up the business and the club relocates to Ontario from its Las Vegas location of over 20 years.

Narduwar the Human Serviette calls up Geddy for an interview: "You are Geddy Lee of Rush! You are God!" Geddy replies, "Well … that's an unusual way to describe me."

1999

January: While Neil takes a break to recoup, younger '90s rock/pop acts as diverse as Korn, Godsmack, Morbid Angel, 311, Cherry Popping Daddies, The Rentals, and New Radicals all mention in trade magazines they were influenced by Rush. Geddy and Alex are asked on Rockline if there's a chance they'd ever do an original soundtrack.

ALEX Both of us would love to get involved in something like that. It's a much freer kind of composing than what we're doing right now, and you have an image that you're writing to, so it could be quite exciting. (Rockline)

GEDDY I think we'd really like to do that at some point and we have had opportunities but unfortunately its never really worked out with our schedules. I guess we're really just waiting for the amount of time and the right script, and the right person to ask us. (Rockline)

Within a few months they would be recording a song specifically for a movie.

February–March: On their Rockshow, VH-1 airs Rush videos for "Tom Sawyer", "Limelight", and the *Different Stages* clip "Closer to the Heart", which intercuts footage from the original video as well as from the previously released concerts. VH-1 had become a more rock-oriented channel, filling the video void left by '90s MTV. Later in the year, "Subdivisions", "Red Sector A", "Distant Early Warning" and "Half the World" also receive airplay.

March 7: Geddy presents award at the Juno Awards.

April 19: In the Studio dedicates its *Signals/Grace Under Pressure* show to Neil in view of his tragedies.

May 14: Geddy appears alongside of Salman Rushdie (author of *The Satanic Verses*) and Rheostatics members on the "Pamela Wallin Show" in Canada.

May 27: Rush's star is added to the Canadian Walk of Fame during a ceremony at Roy Thompson Hall along with six other inductees. Neil decided to not go last minute. Also invited was John Rutsey, who did not attend either.

June 8: Alex appears with other rockers (Edwin, formerly of I Mother Earth, Jeff Martin of Tea Party, and Todd Kerns of Age of Electric) at the White Ribbon Campaign at Club Phoenix.

Geddy begins composing with k.d. lang writing partner Ben Mink (who's also worked with Anne Murray, Jane Siberry, Barenaked Ladies, Raffi, Prairie Oyster, Bruce Cockburn, etc) on guitars.

GEDDY   When Ben Mink and I decided to go down this road at least writing together, we thought … well we'll just start slowly. He came to Toronto, we sat down in my home studio and we worked for about ten days and threw some ideas together. So we carried that on over the next kinda year and a half. I would go out to Vancouver. We'd spend a week to ten days working on other stuff. So that progressed like that going back and forth from Vancouver to Toronto for like I said about a year and a half and so. And then finally I started getting really impatient because the songs started turning out better and better and better. And I said, 'Look we gotta make a decision on what we're doing here. Are we making a record for ourselves? Are we going to package this stuff up and send it around to other artists and maybe they'll record it?' So we decided to take five songs and send them around to a couple of people only and see if they could give us some input as to whether we should do a record or whether we should form a publishing union, that kind of thing, and it was Val Azzoli, who used to work for us at SRO Management (here and now he's running things at Atlantic Records), who called me up right away and he said, "Listen, I've been listening to the songs and I think you should go make a record. I think you've got something to say here, so go do it. (World Premiere)

June 22: *South Park's* feature length movie soundtrack (U.S. #4) features Geddy and Alex on the Canadian national anthem. On drums is Matt Stone, one of the creators of the show. The film is released June 30th and is a minor hit (being that it's R-rated yet appeals to a largely under 14 audience). It does not contain the track in the film.

GEDDY   Matt Stone is a major punter. He's a big Rush fan and he actually got a hold of us through our band photographer, Andrew MacNaughton. They bumped into each other at a party. I got a call when I was at Ben [Mink]'s house as we were laying down tracks that they wanted us to record the Canadian National Anthem for the movie. It was the whole 'Blame Canada' thing, so we called them back, had a funny conversation, agreed to do the project and Alex and I spent two days in his home studio and we put it together. (Global Bass Online 2000)

July 13: Geddy writes a song for and plays along with guitarist Ken Ramm, gospel vocalist Juliette Roberts, Art of Noise's Anne Dudley, and Roy Babbington on the electronica release "Euphoria". Geddy appears on an I Mother Earth album released the same day.

August: Kim Garner (formerly of SRO) takes over marketing at Universal Entertainment.

August 17: Jack Hess of Indianapolis, a Neil Peart drumset giveaway first prize winner, sells the 16-piece candy apple red Tama *Artstar* drumset on the online auction eBay for $26,100. Over the course of nine days, there are 56 bids total.

September: Geddy co-produces a five song EP for Rocket Science, led by his bassist nephew Rob Higgins (formerly of Change of Heart). Uncle Ged provides vocals to the song "Space Suit".

GEDDY It is rock with a kind of technical edge to it. I have a home studio and we have been working here and gone into the smaller studios around town to do some sessions now and again. It has been fun for me and I think fun for them as well. It is hard to say what will come of it, but it certainly has been a good experience for both of us. (Jam! Showbiz Online)

September 25: On this Saturday, Geddy performs alongside of Alex and the Dexters on "In the Mood" at the Orbit Room (using a Dexter's bass guitar.)

October 4: Geddy sings "Oh Canada" at Air Canada Centre before the Toronto Maple Leafs/Boston Bruins hockey game. Before he starts, the station carrying the game breaks to commercial, so unfortunately it was not televised.

October 25: After months of stagnation, The National Midnight Star webpage, the best unofficial online source of Rush information, ends.

November: In related events, ex-producer Terry Brown's first recorded voice performance since 1977 is included on Dream Theater's *Scenes From a Memory* CD. Van Halen fires Ray Danniels. SRO projects the *Different Stages* DVD is scheduled for release "after Spring 2000."

December 7: While plugging his book on a N.Y.C. radio talk show, David Wild, a *Rolling Stone* editor and a member of the induction staff at the Rock and Roll Hall of Fame in Cleveland, negatively addresses the induction of Rush: "It ain't ever gonna happen. Regardless of their success, Rush has never achieved critical acclaim and no one will ever vote for them ... with the exception of 'Tom Sawyer', most of it gives me a headache." He later added that "technical proficiency" is not considered a valid reason to induct an artist.

GEDDY   Of course it would be an honor to be included. I take the attitude that we're still such a young band that they aren't ready for us yet. They're still working on getting the old guys in there. (Canoe Chat)

December 31: Rush's popularity is secured as the *Canoe* online poll for Most Significant Canadian Performing Artist of the Millenium proved. Rush beat The Tragically Hip and The Band, among others, 22% to 19%. Geddy later commented that the polls made him grateful that the band were "still relevant."

2000

January 6: Alex appears on Canadian television with his hockey player pal since childhood, Steve Shutt.

Smashing Pumpkins' frontman does a live acoustic "Limelight" in Toronto while acknowledging that the band is "so indebted to Rush."

NEIL   And now all the cynical critics have been forced to accept us because a lot of the musicians in the alternative bands grew up listening to us. (St. Petersburg Times)

Two years since the release of *Different Stages,* and fans were asking for a DVD.

SRO   Ideally we really want to do the ultimate DVD. The main problem is technology. Just when we think we can produce something that the fans will love and the band can live with, it becomes dated and we have to start again. What we would have put out only a few years back would make everyone cringe by today's tech standards.

GEDDY   The footage from the Test For Echo tour is not edited; it's still in a raw state … I would like to put together a video of the show that we filmed in Toronto [1997] and some other videos that weren't seen. (Rockline 2000)

GEDDY   I have an accumulation from videos (early videos that have rarely seen the light of day) These are things I'd like to include on a future DVD package. As I've said before, I have ideas for a comprehensive DVD for Rush, but at the moment, the powers that be at Atlantic don't share my enthusiasm. It's just a waiting game. I would encourage you to write to Atlantic records and request that they move it along. (Canoe 12-21-00 Chat)

March: Alex produces three songs with Mississippi-based band 3 Doors Down in New Orleans ("Dangerous Game," "Dead Love," and "Wasted Me"). Alex also plays golf in his spare time with Phoenix Open pro Rocco Mediate. Drums were completed for the Geddy Lee solo effort at Studio X in Seattle with overdubs at Factory Studios in Vancouver and final production back at Reaction Studios in Toronto. Former Soundgarden drummer Matt Cameron, currently with Pearl Jam, plays on ten. He was suggested by Adam Casper, engineer for the Foo Fighters.

GEDDY   I know that there were times in his past that he probably had an association obviously with our music and some of him and his friends I think were Rush fans back in the old days, and I you know I don't think there's a drummer playing rock around that hasn't gone through the Neil Peart thing. So, every once in a while he had a little smile on his face and he was really diggin' it and this was a cool thing for him to do; but he really carried himself as a total professional and you know once … he is really a great drummer I mean … (MFH World Premiere)

GEDDY   I was more familiar with Soundgarden's music than Pearl Jam. He was chosen for the strength of his work in Soundgarden. Since then, I've had the pleasure of seeing Pearl Jam live and was incredibly impressed by what a great live rock and roll band they are and what a great rock and roll singer Eddie is. (Canoe Chat)

GEDDY   We had a weekend off, and we decided to use that time to see if we could write something fresh. We were successful. That was the song "Home of the Strange". The only person I considered was Jeremy. I contacted him. Happily he had two days before he went on tour with Our Lady Peace. (TV Guide Online)

Engineer David Leonard (Santana, Barenaked Ladies, Prince) is brought in to co-produce the CD.

GEDDY   David has been very good for us because he is so loose. (Canadian Musician)

The Napster cases cause fans to wonder what Rush thought of the whole idea of downloading artists' music for free.

GEDDY   I don't think anyone has any objection to fans swapping music when it's on a small and personal scale. But I think the threat of mass downloading of one's music put it in a whole other category. For that to happen it's ethical to seek permission of the artists involved. (TV Guide Online)

GEDDY   It's very unseemly to me to see so many artists coming out in favor of downloading simply out of fear of being considered uncool and pandering to the vox populi for street credibility. (TV Guide Online)

June 19: The White Ribbon Campaign again sought Rush support for their cause (ending violence against women). Geddy was asked to host the Second Annual Wine Tasting, Rare Wine Auction & Backyard Barbecue—in his own backyard located in Toronto's Rosedale neighborhood. When the *National Post* asked if he was a 'wine connoisseur', Geddy replied "I prefer 'wine geek'."

GEDDY   I've been interested in wine for 10 or 15 years, but I should say I've always resisted collecting a serious level. I collect so many things that I get very easily carried away with my hobbies. About 6 years ago I gave in and now I'm a complete wine geek. (TV Guide Online)

July: Militant metallers Rage Against the Machine announce "Working Man" will be covered for their upcoming covers album *Renegades,* but, alas, it is not finished or released.

August: Alex creates the theme to *Andromeda,* a Gene Roddenbury sci-fi show starring Kevin (*Hercules*) Sorbo, which would premiere in October. The show's co-executive producer, Robert Hewitt Wolfe, had revealed to former rock journalist Ethlie Ann *Vare (Hollywood Reporter, E!, ROCK magazine)* that the first band he'd approach to do a theme would be Rush. Alex, a casual sci-fi buff, exhaustively layered what he reported to be 20,000 guitars to "March of the High Guard". Band photographer Andrew MacNaughton directs a music video for pop star Aaron Carter, brother of Nick Carter of the Backstreet Boys. MacNaughton has directed videos since 1994, for groups like The Rainbow Butt Monkeys, The Gandharvas, The Skydiggers, Tom Cochran, Sandbox, and Great Big Sea, among others.

September 9: Neil remarries to photographer Carrie Nuttall in her town of Montecito, California. A larger reception is held October 8.

GEDDY It's hard to be still standing after a couple of devastating blows like that. He's gotten remarried and that's been very, very positive … He's got things on a very positive footing … and he's looking forward to going back to work. (Rockline)

October: "Tom Sawyer" marks the first song to appear in a major commercial for the 20th anniversary of the Japanese automobile Nissan Maxima, following a trend of ads using classic rock artists.

SRO This was approved by both the band and Anthem. We really don't have a problem with it as it was tastefully done. In this day and age where there's no real rock radio left and video TV only plays pop music, we are trying other directions to get the music out there. I know the whole 'corporate sell out' lines. I just don't think they're applicable any longer.

GEDDY I haven't heard it. I swear to God. I haven't seen it, but people keep asking me about it. We agreed to loan them like ten seconds of music like eight months ago, and I totally forgot about it. At the time they asked us, we were getting requests from all these independent movies and tv shows, like Futurama—all these people wanted to use Rush songs. I guess people are getting hard up for soundtrack material, so now they're even coming to us for it [laughs]. (Rolling Stone Online)

November 8: Geddy begins to make several public appearances in support of hisalbum, including in-store signings in New York, Detroit, and Los Angeles (with a signature Fender bass given out to one of the first 500 fans at every store). David Burrier, Atlantic's senior director of product development, sends press releases to 250 Rush fan web sites. "Rush has never let a camera into the studio before so having this is something really new and unique." (Billboard)

GEDDY　Over the last 15 years we have been increasingly doing more press and I think quite honestly, due to the things that have gone down in the last number of years, there is a lot more interest in covering myself and the band. I don't know whether this is the result of a 500 channel universe and all sorts of online magazines. But also because I do not have a tour forthcoming, I have so much more time to pay attention to interview requests. Where usually, I'd be heavily involved in preparing the live Rush production and rehearsing for the tour. And also it was an opportunity for me to make contact with the fans once again and I enjoyed that experience. (TV Guide Online)

November 10: Celebrating their 6th anniversary, Alex and The Orbit Room present Soul In the City 2000 at Capitol Event Theatre in Toronto. As the election recount goes on in Florida, *Esquire* magazine runs an amusing article on how Rush was 'right': "People, whom do you think Rush was trying to reach with 'if you choose not to decide you still have made a choice'?" The article went on to mention Neil's libertarianism and compared The Spirit of Radio's lyrical references to corporate greed to the ongoing Napster suit. "Maybe Libbies deserve another look if only because their convention will probably not showcase Fleetwood Mac and might even feature a Canadian power trio whose logo involves a naked guy and a pentagram."

November 14: Geddy Lee's long-awaited solo debut *My Favourite Headache* is released *(#52)* and will rank at #7 on the Top Internet Album Sales Chart after its first week. Geddy even makes his overdub guitar playing debut on the title track.

GEDDY　Quite frankly, had this hiatus from Rush not occurred, this album might not have happened. (Rolling Stone 2000)

The CD bears a special feature allowing the owner to enter Geddy's website for the album and download a video of the making of the album. He showed interest in touring clubs for the album, but admitted there wouldn't be time, much like the case with Alex and Victor.

GEDDY　Criticism can be constructive; sometimes you learn stuff about yourself, and sometimes it's just mean-spirited and you don't learn anything about yourself. I just take it as it comes. (Rolling Stone '00)

During the same week, VH-1 broadcasts the Top 100 Hard Rock Bands Of All Time (hosted by Carmen Electra). Rush charts at #28, between Motley Crue (#29) and Iggy Pop (#27)! Vinnie Paul, the drummer of '90s thrash metal band

Pantera, expressed his awe of Rush's "God on drums." Vernon Reid of Living Colour comments, "Rush have invented their own language," while Skid Row's Sebastian Bach confesses that his marriage proposal was made after hearing "Closer to the Heart". Other past-professed Rush fans, like Metallica's James Hetfield, chose to not comment as usual. On Rockline, Geddy's baseball pitcher pal Mark Langston (thanked in the liner notes of *Counterparts*) chimes in on the air.

GEDDY   I spend as much time as I can with my children and wife of course, reconnecting with my friends. I am very physically active—love to hike and bike, play tennis, and my wife and I love exotic travel. I collect wine, I love baseball. I love to read, go to films. Art. I have a lot of hobbies, I tell you! (Barnes and Noble online chat)

Geddy does a signing at CD World in Menlo Park, New Jersey. The first 300 people online to purchase MFH receive a laminate guaranteeing a chance to meet Geddy as well.

GEDDY   And then to know there is 800, 900, 1,000 people waiting for you to sign, it's like, holy shit! And as people came by one-by-one, with a few minutes to talk, it has seemed so important to them to let me know how important Rush has been to them and how much they enjoy this piece of work. You can't help but be thankful and grateful. (Canoe Jam!)

November 18: Geddy makes his first U.S. tv appearance in eleven years by talking live with NYC DJ Cane on VH1's Rush-friendly Rockshow. Geddy's album is released worldwide. His second single is "Grace To Grace". He spends a few days visiting Neil at his Santa Barbara residence, adjacent to the Oxnard Drum Workshop factory.

December 19: Geddy discusses the potential in his children for following a career in music or the arts on TV Guide Online Chat.

GEDDY   Well, unlikely for my son who's 20 already and although he loves music, he has not much interest playing. Although when he was very little he was a fine piano player till he stopped practicing. My daughter is another story altogether. She is a ham and very confident. I wouldn't be surprised at all if she did something in the arts. (TV Guide Online)

Alex agrees to produce the Pennyslvania band Driver (formerly Strangers With Candy, winners of an MTV Ultimate Cover Band contest the previous February, who would change their name to Lifer the following year). Frontman Aaron Fincke explains: "We wanted a player, rather than just a standard producer … We can only do so much with our songs, but he helped to clean up all of them." Alex helps mix the album before the end of the year.

December 21: Geddy talks live on the online Canoe chat about bootlegs.

GEDDY There's so many Rush bootlegs out there that it's unbelievable for me. I don't really have a problem with that concept seeing that they (fans) tape them anyway. I can't speak for the whole band though; it's something that could be discussed. In my record collection when I was younger, I had some bootlegs of artists I liked. So, it's hard for me to say to a fan 'don't go and pick one up'. (Canoe Chat)

Geddy enjoys the time off from doing publicity for his album by seeing films and developing new sport interest—basketball.

GEDDY I liked "The Grinch." I thought "The Grinch" was a fucking great film. I took my daughter to see it twice. We're sitting at home practising our Grinch imitations. I think Jim Carrey is such a great actor. He needs to get more recognition. I thought he got ripped off for 'The Truman Show.' It was just wrong that he didn't get more accolades. (Canoe)

2001

January: Behind Buddy Rich, Gene Krupa, Steve Gadd, and Tony Williams, Neil is #5 on the Most Influential Drummer List in the *Modern Drummer* magazine's 25 anniversary issue. He is dubbed "the most influential rock drummer of all time." Geddy's solo CD tops the online Canoe poll for Best Rock Album and takes the Canadian Radio Music Award for Best Solo Artist.

The band gathers back at Chalet Studio to record.

GEDDY This project is about so much more than us making a record. It is about us coming back together. It is about the psychological health and welfare of all the people who have gone through a very difficult time … I want it to happen, and I want it to happen in a very positive and natural way. (Jam Online)

GEDDY We're going to do the writing in Toronto but we will probably do a big chunk of the recording in L.A. because Neil's spending so much time there. (LA Weekly)

March 5: Though not nominated for any awards himself, Geddy presents a Juno award to Barenaked Ladies.

April: Along with Margaret Atwood, Atom Egoyan, Naomi Klein, and others, Geddy Lee signs the "Citizen Caged" petition sent to Prime Minister Chretien, an effort to defend the peaceful protesters at the Summit of the Americas in Quebec City, where police used tear gas and violence. The petition states another purpose, to make Canada "a model of democratic principles."

May 18–20: Rush's first North American convention is held at The Queen Elizabeth Theatre at the National Trade Center in Toronto. Rushcon 2001 is presented by the Face Up To Hunger Foundation (FUTHF) and 97.7 HTZ-FM of St. Catharines, Ontario. The proceeds from RushCon are donated to The Daily Bread Food Bank, a Toronto-based charity dedicated to fight hunger. Terry Brown and Donna Halper are guest speakers.

GEDDY   The trick to being able to stay in a band for a long period of time is to have a balance of career and home life and intellectual pursuits. These are the things that make up a happy life … not just being obsessed with music 24 hours a day. (Guitar School)

ALEX   It's almost beyond family. We've shared so many dreams, and we've shared so many good times and hard times together. And, basically, the chemistry is right between the three of us. Besides all that, we just work and live very well together. Perhaps the fact that we're a three-piece band also helps; you tend to avoid factions and differences of opinion which can turn into silly little hassles. And we don't seem to have those ego problems that other groups do, since we're not out to be stars. We're just out doing what we all like doing. (Guitar Player 1980)

NEIL   People say they made us what we are. They didn't. They weren't with me practicing for 30 years to develop ideas and abilities. Besides giving into that would be pleasing the lowest common denominator which is what we've always been resisting. (Sacramento Bee)

Rush begins self-producing their next album.

We're only immortal for a limited time.

Career Achievements

Albums

Billboard U.S. Charts

Rush has sold over 35 million albums worldwide as of 1999, tying them for 56th place with REO Speedwagon on the All-Time Sales list. They are #13 on the All Time Sales list. They have had 22 certifications as of 1999 (compare that to Aerosmith, Chicago, Rod Stewart, and Paul McCartney among others all tied at 20 certifications). For comparison, the big winners are Elvis Presley (62), Barbra Streisand (40), Beatles (38), and Rolling Stones (37).

Cert. Date RIAA	Album	Peak Chart Position/ Total Weeks on Chart	Sales
9/21/74	Rush	#105; 13 wks	Gold
3/15/75	Fly By Night	#113; 8 wks	Platinum
10/18/75	Caress of Steel	#148; 6 wks	Gold
4/10/76	2112	#61; 34 wks	Triple Platinum
10/2/76	All the World's a Stage	#40; 23 wks	Platinum
9/24/77	A Farewell To Kings	#33; 17 wks	Platinum
4/15/78	Archives	#121; 6 wks	Platinum
11/18/78	Hemispheres	#47; 21 wks	Platinum
2/2/80	Permanent Waves	#4 (15 wks); 36 wks	Platinum
3/7/81	Moving Pictures	#3 (21 wks) 68 wks	Quadruple Platinum
11/14/81	Exit … Stage Left	#10; 21 wks	Platinum Video (Platinum)
10/2/82	Signals	#10; (15 wks) 33 wks	Platinum
5/5/84	Grace Under Pressure	#10 (12 wks); 27 wks	Platinum
11/9/85	Power Windows	#10; 28 wks	Platinum
9/26/87	Hold Your Fire	#13; 30 wks	Gold
1/28/89	A Show of Hands	#21; 15 wks	Gold; Video (Platinum)
12/2/89	Presto	#16; 11 wks	Gold (Soundscan 122,478)
9/22/90	Chronicles	#51; 19 wks	Double Platinum
9/21/91	Roll the Bones	#3; 43 wks	Platinum Soundscan 1,111,138
11/6/93	Counterparts	#2; 26 wks	Gold Gold Soundscan 744,786
1/96	Victor	#99; #1 week on the Heatseeker	Silver
9/28/96	Test For Echo	#5; 15 wks	Gold, Gold Soundscan 459,409
1997	Retrospective I 1974 – 1980	(N/A)	Soundscan 101,239
1997	Retrospective II 1981 – 1987	(N/A)	Soundscan 135,678
1998	Different Stages	#35 (#12 in Canada)	Soundscan 202,811
2000	Geddy Lee	#51 (#38 in Canada)	Soundscan 107,633

Canadian Radio Charts

2/16/80	Permanent Waves	#12	
4/18/81	Moving Pictures	#2	
12/5/82	Exit...Stage Left	#7	
10/23/82	Signals	#1	(Top Ten 12 weeks)
5/14/84	Grace Under Pressure	#7	
11/9/85	Power Windows	#11	
10/10/87	Hold Your Fire	#10	
	A Show of Hands	(not a Top 10 album)	
12/11/89	Presto	#18	
	Roll the Bones	(not a Top 10 album)	
11/13/93	Counterparts	#6	
10/12/96	Test For Echo	#7	
12/12/98	Different Stages	#12	
11/28/00	My Favorite Headache	#38	

Canadian Singles

1981	Limelight	#16	
1982	New World Man	#2	(12 weeks)

U.S. Singles

1977	Fly By Night/In the Mood (live)	#88;	4 wks
1977	Closer To the Heart/Madrigal	#76;	4 wks
1980	The Spirit of Radio/Circumstances	#51;	8 wks
1980	Entre Nous/Different Strings	#110;	
1981	Limelight/YYZ	#55;	9 wks
1981	Tom Sawyer/Witch Hunt	#44;	13 wks
1981	Closer to the Heart (live)/Freewill (live)	#69;	7 wks
1982	New World Man/Vital Signs (live)	#21;	12 wks
1985	The Big Money	#45;	14 wks

U.K. Charts

2/75	Rush	N/A
4/75	Fly By Night	N/A
6/77	2112	N/A
3/77	Caress of Steel	N/A
3/77	All the World's a Stage	N/A
9/77	A Farewell To Kings	#22
5/78	Archives	N/A
11/78	Hemispheres	#14
1/80	Permanent Waves	#3
2/81	Moving Pictures	#3
5/81	Rush Through Time	N/A
10/81	Exit ... Stage Left	#6
9/82	Signals	#3
4/84	Grace Under Pressure	#5
11/85	Power Windows	#9
12/87	Hold Your Fire	#10

3/89	A Show of Hands	#12
1/90	Presto	#27
9/90	Chronicles	#42
9/91	Roll the Bones	#10
10/93	Counterparts	#14
9/96	Test For Echo	#25
1/99	Different Stages	N/A

U.K. Singles

1978	Closer To the Heart/Bastille Day	#36
1980	The Spirit of Radio/The Trees	#13
1981	Vital Signs/In the Mood	#41
1981	Tom Sawyer (live)/A Passage To Bangkok (live)	#25
1982	New World Man/Vital Signs (live)	#42
1982	Subdivisions/Red Barchetta (live)	#53
1983	Countdown/New World Man	#36
1984	The Body Elezctric/The Analog Kid	#56
1985	The Big Money/Territories	#46
1987	Time Stand Still/Force Ten	#42
1988	Prime Mover/Tai Shan	#43
1992	Roll the Bones/Show Don't Tell	#49

Awards

Juno Awards

1975 Winner, Most Promising New Group
1976 Nominee, Best Album Graphics (Fly By Night)
1977 Nominee, Group of the Year
1978 Winner, Group of the Year
1978 Nominee, Producer of the Year (A Farewell to Kings)
1979 Winner, Group of the Year
1979 Nominee, Best Selling Album (Hemispheres)
1979 Nominee, Producer of the Year (Hemispheres)
1980 Nominee, Group of the Year
1980 Nominee, Album of the Year (Hemispheres)
1980 Nominee, Group of the Year
1981 Nominee, Album of the Year (Permanent Waves)
1981 Nominee, Group of the Year
1981 Nominee, Producer of the Year
1981 Nominee, Best Album Graphics (Permanent Waves)
1982 Winner, Best Album Graphics (Moving Pictures)
1982 Nominee, Album of the Year (Moving Pictures; Exit … Stage Left)
1982 Nominee, Group of the Year
1983 Nominee, Album of the Year (Signals)
1983 Nominee, Producer of the Year
1983 Nominee, Song of the Year (New World Man)
1984 Nominee, Album of the Year (Grace Under Pressure)
1984 Nominee, Group of the Year
1984 Nominee, Best Album Graphics (Grace Under Pressure)
1986 Nominee, Album of the Year (Power Windows)

1986 Nominee, Producer of the Year (Power Windows)
1986 Nominee, Group of the Year
1986 Winner, Best Album Graphics (Power Windows)
1989 Nominee, Group of the Year
1990 Nominee, Producer of the Year (Presto)
1990 Winner, Best Album Cover (Presto)
1990 Nominee, Group of the Year
1991 Winner, Best Hard Rock/Heavy Metal Album of the Year (Presto)
1991 Nominee, Group of the Year
1992 Winner, Best Hard Rock Album (Roll the Bones)
1992 Winner, Best Album Design (Roll the Bones)
1992 Nominee, Producer of the Year (Roll the Bones)
1992 Nominee, Group of the Year
1994 Nominee, Juno Hall of Fame Inductee
1994 Nominee, Group of the Year
1997 Nominee, North Star Best Rock Album
1997 Nominee, Victor Best New Group
1999 Nominee, Best Album Design (Different Stages)

Grammy Awards (U.S.A.):

1982 Nominee, Best Rock Instrumental for "YYZ" (lost to The Police, "Behind My Camel")
1992 Nominee, Best Rock Instrumental for "Where's My Thing?" (lost to Eric Johnson, "Cliffs of Dover")

Circus Magazine

1975 Second Best New Band (under Average White Band)
1977 Best Band in the World (Sounds Rock Poll)
1982 Best Album (Signals)

Billboard Magazine

1981 #25 Top Pop Artist of 1981
1982 #39 Top Pop Artist of 1982
       #21 Top Pop Artist of 1982 (Signals)

Cashbox Magazine

1981 #87 Top 100 Albums of 1981 (Exit Stage Left)
1982 #46 Top 100 Albums of 1982 (Signals)

Group Honors

1979 Canadian Ambassadors of Music
1988 Toronto Rock Awards, Group of the Year
1990 CARAS (Canadian Academy of Recording Arts & Sciences), Group Artist of the Decade
1990 Toronto Mayor's Award
1990 Toronto Rock Awards

1991 Madison Square Gardens Gold Ticket Award
1992 Harold Moon SOCAN Award
1992 Musician's Institute of Technology Lifetime Achievement
1993 Harvard Lampoon Musicians of the Millenium Award
1993 Toronto Maple Leaf Gardens performance record (22 dates)
1993 Toronto Arts Award, Best Artist
1994 Juno Awards Hall of Fame
1997 Officers of the Royal Order of Canada
1999 Canadian Walk of Fame
2000 Canoe Online Poll, Musicians of the Century

Individual Honors

Geddy Lee

Melody Maker Best Bass Player 1980
Sounds Best Bass Player 1980
Guitar Player Bass Hall of Fame 1986
Keyboard Best New Talent 1981
Toronto Rock Awards Best Bass Player 1988, 1990
Bass Player Best Rock Bass Player 1988, 1989, 1991, 1993, 1995, 1996
Bass Player Honor Roll 1992

Alex Lifeson

Melody Maker Best Guitar Player 1980
Guitar Player 1st or 2nd Best Rock Guitar every year since '80 – 86; Best Rock Talent 1983
Toronto Rock Awards Best Guitarist Nominee 1988, 1990 (lost to Jeff Healey)
Guitar Hall of Fame 1991

Neil Peart

Melody Maker Best Drummer 1980
Sounds Best Drummer 1980
Modern Drummer:
Best Recorded Performance 1981, 1982, 1983, 1985, 1986, 1988, 1989, 1990, 1992, 1993, 1997, 1999
3rd Best Recorded Performance 1980
Labatt Music Express Best Member of a Group, 1982
Best All Around Drummer 1986
2nd Best All Around Drummer 1982, 1983, 1984
3rd Best All Around Drummer 1981
Most Promising Drummer 1980
Best Percussion 1982, 1983, 1984, 1985, 1986
Best Rock Drummer 1981, 1982, 1983, 1984, 1985, 1986, 1987,
        1988, 1989, 1990, 1991, 1992,1994, 1997, 1999
Hall of Fame 1983
Honor Roll 1986 Rock Drummer/Multi-Percussion
#5 Best Drummer of All Time 2000
Toronto Rock Awards Best Drummer 1988, 1990
Buddy Rich Lifetime Achievement 1994

The Lyrics

With the exception of the first Rush album, a few songs written by Geddy Lee, and one song by Alex Lifeson, Neil Peart has written the remaining lyrics in the Rush catalog.

NEIL In the overall view of things, I enjoy the songwriting the most. Because it's just us. We just go away together and work very closely and tightly—and live and breathe new things, new songs and new ideas and possible directions. (Canadian Composer 1986)

NEIL People think songwriting is all about mysterious inspiration, but really, it's about being on the edge of sleep, having an idea, and forcing yourself to get up and write it down. Or if you're in the middle of something and a phrase pops into your head, it's about saying, 'Well, this is inconvenient, but I'm going to write it down so it will be there in a year when I need it.' You have to save up your little inspirations and then sit for three days if you have to, until you get the song right. (Rochester Times Union 1991)

NEIL Anytime I have an idea, I'll make sure that I put it down so that when we do sit down to write an album, I don't have to dream it all out of thin air. I don't have to be creative on the spur of the moment, or spontaneously artistic. I just take advantage of whenever creativity strikes … I've learned to take advantage of spontaneity whenever and wherever it happens; even if I have to punch myself in the face to get out of bed in the middle of the night to write something down, I know at this point in life it's worth it. (Canadian Composer 1986)

NEIL Lyrics, or any kind of versified poetry, is very concentrated. You have to take things, filter them down. Every word has to be of strong value. I've seen that reflected in the best of the modern prose writers too—specifically the American writers of the '20s and '30s. My favorites of that era first, Theodore Dreiser and Sherwood Anderson. And then F. Scott Fitzgerald and William Faulkner. Hemingway is one of my very favorites and I like John Steinbeck and John Dos

Passos. It's the Golden Age of Literature as recognized by most people. I would like to emulate that someday as a prose writer. (Modern Drummer)

NEIL   A lot of people don't care about lyrics and they don't have to. What's important is that they're affected by the music. They need never pay attention to the lyrics except their sounds. When I am writing lyrics there are sounds that have to be sung and I think of them in a purely euphonious way. It just has to be a nice sounding series of syllables, and then if I can get an inter-relation of rhythm that satisfies me as a craftsman and if I can get some other symbolism in there (even if its personal) that will just make me happier with it … but when someone takes that vagueness … and possible interpretations … and takes it in such a diametrically opposed way to anything I ever even thought of, let alone intended … it's a little scary, but you have to say that's good, they were able to take what they wanted out of it. If they're a religious person or if they're a paranoid person who sees devil worship everywhere then certainly they'll see that … If they're sensitized to literary references but if they're not, they won't. (MuchMusic 1990)

NEIL   I know for myself as a young music fan, I never really paid attention to lyrics. If I liked the song, then I might notice the lyrics. But I would never dissect them or anything. So I don't expect that from a listener either. (Up Close 1994)

GEDDY   Alex and I were teenage idiots together, but we didn't know who this strange creature was. We did notice his incredible appetite for books and for reading. He also spoke English better than anyone we knew. In fact, better than anyone we had ever met. (Canadian Musician)

GEDDY   For one thing, Alex and I are lazy. Neil has done such a good job over the years, we feel as though anything we came up with would be crummy. But if we have ideas for songs we just jot them down and see if Neil can use them. (Bass Player 1993)

GEDDY   Neil's great to work with because he'll write umpteen songs, and if ten of them make it he's happy with that. He never insists that we use one song over another. And of course, since I have to sing those lyrics, I've got to feel pretty positive about them. He lets me react to them and gravitate to the songs that I feel arc stronger. During the course of a writing day, even though Neil's at the far end of the house, I'm running back and forth every half hour saying, 'Okay, I've got this pad nailed, but this pad is giving me trouble; can you think of an alternative?' Very rarely these days will he be inflexible about changes. (Canadian Musician)

The Music

ALEX The formula is usually the same. When we're writing together in the band, Neil will go off and work on the lyrics while Geddy and I sit together and throw ideas back and forth. Neil usually has one or two songs written before there are melodies to them, and that gets us started. Songwriting for me isn't like just sitting down, writing something out, and throwing it away if it isn't good. Most of the time the process is a very spontaneous one. (Guitar Player 1980)

GEDDY You take two kinds of attitudes when you're a singer, I think. The one is that you write the lyrics or you believe in the lyrics that have been written so strongly that you become the same statement. You have to understand and agree in order to sing it with conviction, I guess is the term I'm looking for. Then there's the other point of view where you look at yourself as an interpreter of someone else's thoughts, very much like an actor who takes a screenplay and goes out, and he didn't write the words, but he's, to the best of his ability, trying to convey the feelings that the person had written. So, I think those things come into play as my role in this band. (In the Studio)

ALEX If the lyrics come first, we work around them and what moods they are trying to create. If the song's a very up, positive thing, we use a lot of major chords; if it's sadder, or more thought provoking, we'll have minorish feels thrown in. Using time signatures other than 4/4 are more interesting from both the listeners' and the players' points of view. They're more difficult to master, but they're also more rewarding-especially when you're playing them every night. (Guitar Player 1980)

GEDDY We'd start writing on one tune for example, and we'd be really excited about an idea, we'd be developing it, we'd put it on tape, and we'd get it to a point, and we'd be looking for another part for that song. In the course of that, we'd find ourselves writing—'Hey, this is a great idea, but it doesn't really have anything to do with this song. Maybe this will work with this lyric.' I always like to keep Neil's lyrics spread-out in front of me in case something fits something I'm working on. (T4E Premiere)

GEDDY Alex's great strengths are his ingenious chord structures. He's very underrated because so much of what he does is one guitarist playing a two guitarists' role. I don't know if there's anybody on the planet who can play arpeggios as well as this guy; they're always so original and melodically interesting. You really have to listen to appreciate the complexity. (Guitar School 1994)

ALEX Geddy is very, very tight in the rhythm section. He's so tuned into Neil—even during soundcheck jams, they would start playing something I'd never heard and they'd be so locked in. They wouldn't even be looking at each other and they'd know where things are going. (Guitar School 1994)

GEDDY As much as we like to get heady or pseudo-intellectual, the reason we play in a band is because we like to play rock. I think that's the one thing you'd get the three of us to agree on: we don't want to be wimpy. So I guess whenever we feel like we're getting too mature, something in us rebels and wants to kick some butt! (Network)

The Albums

Rush (1974)

THEMES Written mostly by drummer John Rutsey, all the songs on *Rush* were meant to be rockers about drinking, rock 'n' rollin', women, work, and good times/bad times a la Led Zeppelin, Cream, and Jimi Hendrix.

COVER Art by Paul Weldon originally was printed bright red in Canada when it was pressed independently. When Mercury released it, the cover was changed to a hot pink. As the back of the album suggests, "for best results play this album." Rush was already showing their sense of humor.

"IN THE MOOD" Rush would adopt this as their encore for years to come. This was the first song Geddy wrote in 1970.

GEDDY Our lyrics were meaningless—they were just teenage angst words, that sort of thing. Now when I try writing lyrics, I find I have a lot of things I want to say, but they always come out sounding a little naïve. So I turn them over to the Prof and let him polish them up. (Bass Player 1993)

"WORKING MAN" The best-known song on the album and the earliest Rush track still receiving FM radio airplay, this song introduced the image of man as a robotic 'worker', and idea Neil would later expound upon when he joined the band.

Fly By Night (1975)

THEMES Road life, beginnings, endings, departures, reflecting on things left behind, roads ahead, dreams (from here on dreams are in almost every album), and freedom.

COVER An Eraldo Carugati painting with a Great Snowy Owl flying against a night sky, a Canadian bird, maybe a symbol of freedom in itself. Owls symbolized death, night, cold, and passivity in ancient literature and were witches' pets so there is a good tie-in to the sword and sorcery theme of "By-Tor and the Snow Dog" or the fantasy world of "Rivendell".

"Anthem" The title comes from Russian author Ayn Rand's 1938 novella about the individual against the collective will or power. In *Anthem*, a totalitarian state declares that there should be no individuals, no rights, no personality—even the word "I" is outlawed. Eventually, two people rebel. Neil drew inspiration from the character of Howard Roark in Rand's *The Fountainhead*. Neil also used the philosophy of *The Virtue of Selfishness* to put lyrics to this song born of his first-ever jam with Geddy and Alex.

NEIL I think everything I do has Howard Roark in it, you know, as much as anything. The person I write for is Howard Roark. I have as many quarrels toward the right wing, you know. I can't stand the whole concept of law-and-order and authority and everything, which is obviously the precept of right-wingism and you know it as well as I do. (Creem)

"Best I Can" This song announces a theme of dreaming of success which became a Rush staple over the next few albums.

"Beneath, Between and Behind" The song opens with a guitar riff like the break in Led Zeppelin's "Heartbreaker". Contrary to some fans' opinions, this is not a sexual song, but harkens to the ideas of travel, departure, immigration, and new beginnings.

"By-Tor and the Snow Dog" The names are purposely silly and are the nicknames Rush roadie Howard Ungerleider had for two dogs their manager owned. On the back cover of the album, Geddy is credited as being By-Tor and Alex is credited as Snow Dog. Eth is an Old English name probably for demonic power. Styx was a river in Hades, the underworld This song again is an 8-minuter demonstrating already the band's musical unity and prowess. The song is the first broken up in sections: Section III was originally called "The Battle".

NEIL My friend's Dad always said 'colder than the Tobes of Hell,' that's all. I don't know what it means. (Backstage Club 1990)

"Fly by Night" A short prologue was written as well:

> *airport scurry, flurry faces*
> *parade of passers-by*
> *people going many places*
> *with a smile or just a sigh*
> *waiting, waiting, pass the time*
> *another cigarette*
> *get in line, gate thirty-nine*
> *the time is not here yet …*

"Making Memories" Perhaps a reaction to the first album's "Finding My Way", it ties in the 'fly by night' theme with its mood and wanderlust.

"Rivendell"   The title comes from the name of the serene village in J.R.R. Tolkien's *The Lord of the Rings*, which was inhabited by elves and landscaped by misty mountains (mist was an ancient mystery as it was an indeterminate element). It was a paradise on Earth … Middle Earth between heaven and hell.

"In the End"   A coming home (from the road) song. Neil's original lyric sheet had the title written on a tombstone, which suggests a more serious meaning for the song.

Caress of Steel (1975)

THEMES   Freedom, aging, revolution. Lyrics and images have a Dark Ages mood about them, a precursor to the album *A Farewell to Kings*. The title refers to the sword and sorcery themes of the album (and reflect the work of other rock groups at the time). Steel represented the transcendent strength of the all-conquering spirit in ancient literature. The title also describes the mixture of Rush's sound: sometimes gentle and serene; most of the time aggressive and metallic.

COVER   Represented on the cover are looming gray clouds and the Necromancer, with his skull, prism, and a serpent by his side. The color was originally supposed to be chrome-toned like steel. Hugh Syme came on board as cover artist with this album.

HUGH SYME   They were pencil drawings, even though they don't look like it on the album. They printed them in a sort of pseudo-sepia tone. I had vignetted with an airbrush the blue area around the illustrations, which was later reinterpreted by the film strippers who were making the jackets in Chicago at the time. They took it upon themselves to cut a hard-edged mask around it. The lettering was cast, and chrome plated. (Creem)

"Terminat hora diem; terminat auctor opus" appears at the end of the lyrics in the album, which is 'rough' Latin for "as the hour ends the day so the author ends his work."

ALEX   There was a lot of pressure on us from the record company, from management, because *Caress Of Steel* wasn't a very commercial album. And yet, for us, it was a very successful album in terms of our own sense of creativity. We tried doing a number of things differently on the LP—longer songs, different melodic things—and it was a stepping stone for us. (Guitar Player 1980)

"Bastille Day"   This song features French Revolution imagery inspired by Charles Dickens' *A Tale of Two Cities*, with proud and defiant guitar riffs and tempos. Neil's first real themes of a class struggle and oppression. The opening line was what the Queen of France said: "If there's no bread, let them eat cake."

"I Think I'm Going Bald" A humorous attempt at a song about aging, this verse was to follow 'But now it must be wine':

> *Kitchen table hours*
> *Building castles in the sand*
> *(Now we've been)*

"Lakeside Park" Neil grew up in Port Dalhousie, where there was an amusement park on the lakeshore. The lyrics try to capture the feelings of being adolescent and being free on Victoria Day (May 24th). Music by Lee, Lifeson, and Peart.

NEIL In my early teens I also achieved every Port kid's dream: a summer job at Lakeside Park. In those days, it was still a thriving and exciting whirl of rides, games, music, and lights. So many ghosts haunt that vanished midway; so many memories bring it back for me. I ran the Bubble Game—calling out "Catch a bubble; prize every time!" all day—and sometimes the Ball Toss game. When it wasn't busy I would sit at the back door and watch the kids on the trampolines … I got fired. (A Port Boy's Story)

GEDDY A lot of the early stuff I'm really proud of. Some of it sounds really goofy, but some of it stands up better than I gave it credit for. As weird as my voice sounds when I listen back, I certainly dig some of the arrangements. I can't go back beyond *2112* really, because that starts to get a bit hairy for me, and if I hear "Lakeside Park" on the radio I cringe. What a lousy song! Still, I don't regret anything that I've done! (Raw 1993)

"The Necromancer" Subtitled "A Short Story by Rush", the title was from Tolkien's *Lord of the Rings*, in which the Necromancer, a wizard who either summons the dead or reduces the living into specter form, is confronted by three travelers, Sam, Frodo and Gollum. In the old tales of quests, the travelers were always restless and with a goal. So were Rush, always on tour. The reference to Willowdale is the name of the suburb in Toronto that the three members of Rush called home.

"Into Darkness" "Fording a river" was used by ancients in stories to show a decisive stage in a journey. That was the actual lyric Neil wrote, omitting "Dawn" altogether.

"Under the Shadow" "O'er" is an old Gaelic term. Another "bow" reference as in "Bastille Day" with the travelers becoming specters and locked in dungeons.

"Return of the Prince" The incarnation of oppression is later confronted by Prince By-Tor (title comes from Tolkien's *The Return of the King*). Neil is the voice in the intro. The labyrinth classically represented the quest to find the center (the start, the spirit, the center of time and space in the microcosm of a maze). By-Tor is not evil here (perhaps after his defeat by the Snow Dog?) and he battles for freedom.

"The Fountain of Lamneth"   Considered by some to be too over-ambitious, too convoluted, on the surface the lyrics are simple enough—a young man finding purpose in life. Each of the six suites describes a phase of his life from birth to death. The lyrics get increasingly enigmatic per suite.

ALEX   Ged and Neil wrote the lyrics for "The Fountain of Lamneth", and he thought it would be kind of nice to try to incorporate a very loose concept in it by having a starting point and ending point which would go from the beginning of side 2 to the end of side 2 and it would be one complete story, but broken up, so that it could be individual songs that, unless you look closely, wouldn't necessarily relate to each other. (1983)

"In The Valley"   The first song in the suite recounts the birth of the child and his bond with his mother. The 'valley' is a classical symbol of fertility and creation. The fountain represents the lifeforce of Man situated at the center of the four rivers of Paradise on earth. Carl Jung called this the "land of infancy" that arises when life is inhibited. The mountain is an ascension symbol, the place where the philosophers dwelled (hence it was a symbol of intellect). Fields of dew is a spiritual metaphor. Music by Lee, Lifeson, and Peart.

"Didacts and Narpets"   The second song in the suite is an argument between the teachers (didacts) and parents (anagram of narpets). Didacts is an anagram for addicts. The words heard on the song are Neil and Geddy yelling:

> *Stay! Go!*
> *Work! No!*
> *Think! Live!*
> *Earn! Give!*
> *Fight! Right!*

NEIL   Okay, I may have answered this before, but if not, the shouted words in that song represent an argument between Our Hero and the Didacts and Narpets—teachers and parents. I honestly can't remember what the actual words were, but they took up opposite positions like: "Work! Live! Earn! Give!" and like that. (Backstage Club 1991)

"No One At the Bridge"   The next song in the suite opens with sounds of waves as it describes the sea of alienation and the bridge to maturity. The troubled waters may be symbolic of the unconscious as well.

ALEX   Steve Hackett is so articulate and melodic, precise and flowing. I think our *Caress of Steel* period is when I was most influenced by him. There's even a solo on that album which is almost a steal from his style of playing. It's one of my favorites, called "No One at the Bridge". (Guitar Player 1984)

"Panacea" The title is Greek for "cure-all" and the song recounts the 'discovery' of the opposite sex, almost a mother figure again. Homer's navigation epic *The Odyssey* may have inspired this suite as Panacea could be a Calypso or Circe, an enchantress or siren who lured the hero Odysseus to stay with her on her island. The next lines were to follow the question, "have I left my life behind?"

> *The symmetry of snowflakes*
> *In the music of the stream*
> *A symphony of springtime*
> *In the shadow of a dream.*

Neil vetoed these and a few other stanzas before finalizing the song.

"Bacchus Plateau" The fifth song or chapter in the suite places the traveler at a crossroads on Bacchus Plateau. The traveler discovers wine as a temporary distraction or panacea. Bacchus was the Roman equivalent of the Greek god of wine and fertility, Dionysus, who would appear in future Rush songs. The cask of '43 symbolizes the futility of existence and the goblet, possibilities. Originally the chorus went: "You've something more to give / I guess it doesn't matter / You've so much more to live." Neil changed his character's outlook for the final lyrics: "There's not much more to live."

2112 (1976)

COVER/THEMES 1976 was America's bicentennial year, and *2112* was fittingly an album for a revolution. The electrifying cover and inner image of the naked man in the star led some people to associate Satanism with the band, but the star is not a pentagram (it's closer to a witch pentacle), and the man appears to be trying to ward off the star. For Rush fans this image has become a symbol of their allegiance to the band. The image of the five-pointed star originated in ancient Egypt, where it represented the spirit struggling against darkness. The image of the man in the star was first done by Agrippa of Nettesheim, who was illustrating the idea of the number five ruling man: five senses, five digits on each hand and foot, five wounds in Christ even.

NEIL   The red star symbolizes the autocratic society that was projected into the future, where giant computers controlled the whole society. The star was the symbol of their authority. In a way, it's an abstract symbol for authoritarian governments of any kind, whether they be democratic, dictatorial, or whatever. The man against it, of course, is the individual against this organized state, or anything that's larger than life, whether it be religion, government, or a creed of any kind that's supposed to be more important than a human life. In other words, the individual's life is important. (Modern Drummer)

NEIL   The inspiration behind it was … It's difficult always to trace those lines because so many things tend to coalesce, and in fact it ended up being quite similar to a book called *Anthem* by the writer Ayn Rand. But I didn't realize that while I was working on it, and then eventually as the story came together, the parallels became obvious to me and I thought, "Oh gee, I don't want to be a plagiarist here." So I did give credit to her writings in the liner notes. (Rockline 1991)

HUGH SYME   Initially, that logo didn't begin as an identity factor for the band, it just got adopted. We didn't consider it a mascot overall icon of representation for the band at the time. What I did do with that particular cover was read their lyrics, and understand that there is a good force and a bad force: the good force was music, creativity, and freedom of expression—and the bad force was anything that was contrary to that. The man is the hero of the story. That he is nude is just a classic tradition … the pureness of his person and creativity without the trappings of other elements such as clothing … the red star is the evil red star of the Federation. It never ready occurred to me, to be honest with you, that they would adopt it quite so seriously as a logo. (Creem)

"2112" With acknowledgment to Ayn Rand, Neil divided this sci-fi epic into seven suites. In Rand's literary totalitarian future, electricity is rediscovered, and Neil found a parallel in his tale. "2112" can also be seen as a combination of George Orwell's *1984* and Arthur C. Clarke's *2001*. The back cover of the LP includes the first part of the diary of the 'anonymous' citizen of this futuristic city of Megadon. Orwell described the London skyline similarly in *1984*. The Planets of the Solar Federation were probably survivors of an asteroid-induced cataclysm. The number 12 is itself classically indicative of a cosmic order or salvation, the reason that it is the standard for the clock or the calendar.

NEIL   *2112* is a cycle of songs based on a development and progression of some things I see in society. The cycle begins with an "Overture", then the discovery of the guitar and music. Guitars don't exist in the Solar Federation because the computers won't allow music—it's not logical. Then there's the "Presentation", where the hero brings his guitar to the priests in the temples of Syrinx. But the acolytes smash it up and send him away. And he has a dream about a planet, established simultaneously with the Solar Federation, where all the creative people went. He's never seen anything like it before, this alternative way of life; even the way they build their cities is totally different. And he gets more and more depressed because he realizes that his music is a part of that civilization and he can never be a part of it. But in the end he finds that the planet is real. The temples aren't destroyed, but things do change. (Circus)

NEIL   The extent of my influence by the writings of Ayn Rand should not be overestimated—I am no one's disciple. Yes, I believe the individual is paramount in matters of justice and liberty, but in philosophy, as Aristotle said long ago, the paramount good is *happiness*. My self-determination as an individual is *part* of the pursuit of happiness, of course, but there's more to it than that. (Backstage Club 1993)

ALEX   Without *Caress Of Steel* we couldn't ever have done *2112*. And the latter, for us, was like coming back with a vengeance. It was at that time we said, "Okay, everybody wants us to do nice short songs like we did on the first album. Do we do that, or do we pack it in, or do we say 'Screw you! Well do whatever we want!'" The last is what we decided to do, and we came back punching with *2112*: That album still feels like that to me when I listen to it today—I can feel the hostility hanging out. (Guitar Player 1980)

GEDDY   It's a gratifying album to play because I think it was the first album that our sound—the Rush sound—came together … It was our defining moment, to a certain degree. (Salt Lake Tribune 97)

"Overture"   The first song is an flamenco-like overture of music that is later heard in the 20 minutes of the side-long epic. One of the guitar riffs in "Overture" is from Petr Tchaikovsky's "1812 Overture". The lyrics "Blessed are the meek, for they shall inherit the Earth" are from the Bible's Book of Psalms 37:11 and Matthew 5:5.

"The Temples of Syrinx"   In Greek mythology, a syrinx is a water nymph. Temples are ascension symbols and are regarded to be closer to the gods with their height. In this song, the priests' system is computerized, a reality envisioned by Neil in the 1970s.

"Discovery"   Printed on the album were the lyrics "Chords that build high like a mountain" and Geddy sang it this way for the 1996 live album, but the original lyrics were the same way as was recorded, with the word "sounds" instead of "chords" ("sounds that build …").

NEIL   The word 'I' can sometimes make it difficult to be convincing. It's a very fantastic background, at a very far remove from reality. The passion of response felt by the character in there couldn't have been done in the third person. (Sounds)

"Presentation"   He finds a guitar and presents it to the priests (producer Terry Brown inspired Father Brown).

"Oracle: The Dream"   The Oracle at Delphi's Nike, goddess of victory, urged everyone to "just do it." And so the person of 2112 does 'it'.

"Soliloquy"   Originally entitled "Soliloquy of the Soul", this song was probably inspired by any one of Shakespeare's plays. This soliloquy sets up the suicide.

"Grand Finale"   At the end of the aggressive playing, Neil's voice as the 'Elder Race' assumes control in this apocalyptic finale originally called "Denouement".

"A Passage to Bangkok" Neil borrowed the title from E. M. Forster's novel, *A Passage to India*. The song describes a dreamlike journey around the world in search of marijuana fields, with and allusion to 'Acapulco Gold'. New Rush fans even today immediately notice that the synthesizer playing before the solo sounds like someone inhaling from a joint.

"The Twilight Zone" It is notable that Rush had already credited Rod Serling, the host of *The Twilight Zone* televison series, on their last album and would again on their next. This was the last track done for the album, another fantasy trip, this time through the fourth dimension. It's interesting to hear the vocals whispered at the same time they're sung. The Defenders 1977 comic book from Marvel dedicated their 45th issue to each member of the band. In it, a character named Red Rajah says: "Truth is false and logic lost, consult the Rajah at all cost."

"Lessons" The lyrics don't mean a whole lot but they almost sound like the Priests are still rambling … "You know we've told you before!" Words and music by Lifeson (Alex's only solo lyrics with Rush).

"Tears" Once again Geddy proves he's not just a screamer and his lyrics improved. Hugh Syme on the Mellotron keyboards.

"Something For Nothing" A song about self-reliance with the individual paving his own way. "You won't get wise with the sleep still in your eyes." Kingdom, power, glory—these themes turn up in future songs as well, and they are directly related to the ambition and work ethic of the individual.

All the World's a Stage (1976)

As William Shakespeare wrote, "All the world's a stage, and all the men and women merely players … They have their exits and entrances; and one man in his time plays many parts." —As You Like It, Act 2, Scene 7.

COVER The Starman image looms above the drums on the abandoned Massey Hall stage on the cover for this live album. Geddy shows the band's dry humor when he adds, "1,2 buckle my shoe" before the electric break in "In the End". Skip Gildersleeve intros the band.

HUGH AGI in Chicago did all of Rush's printing up until about four years ago. Albums like *Ooh La La* by the Faces, and *Physical Graffiti*—all of that was going on then, so we thought we'd go for a six panel jacket. (Creem 1983)

A Farewell To Kings (1977)

THEMES: renaissance, progress, imprisonment, compassion, hope, wonder. Rush decided to record this in an English castle after the last Euro tourdates. The album is about a new society, abandoning any kind of rule over the people. Like time-traveling minstrels, there is a definitely medieval atmosphere to this album. The working title for the album was "Closer to the Heart". Neil's pet birds provide the background atmosphere of a medieval forest on the first two tracks.

COVER A puppet king in a throne with castle ruins behind him and the Toronto skyline (including smoke stacks) in the background appear on the front cover. The back is black with an image of a puppet's strings.

HUGH   The sky and the foreground are not in the same place. The buildings and the sky are from Toronto, and the foreground was a demolished warehouse in Buffalo. I would've loved a cathedral in the same condition, or something more worthy of the pathos you were intended to feel for an old building being in that state. We also began a series of puns with that album, in that the King is a puppet King. There have been a lot of criticisms of the Throne over the past couple of decades as being a heritage that we really can't disregard, but certainly don't take as seriously as we used to. (Creem)

"A Farewell to Kings" The title is adapted from Ernest Hemingway's novel *A Farewell to Arms*. Longing for a new Renaissance era, this revolution is more 'down to earth', the new world envisioned on "2112", a timeless realm not necessarily set in the 13 or 14th century, for instance. As in "2112", the wise are again resented, and the sacred "Halls of Truth" are the churches, courthouses, and schools. The hypocrites are teachers, lawyers, and clergy. Music by Lee, Lifeson, and Peart.

"Xanadu" The Samuel Taylor Coleridge poem "Kubla Khan: A Vision in a Dream" inspired this epic, while opium induced dreams inspired his version. He wrote only 55 lines and left it unfinished. Neil's lyrics paraphrasing the poetry, which concerns the ancients' obsession with immortality and the person who seeks it in the land of Xanadu. Honey symbolizes rebirth and wisdom, while caves of ice are definite metaphors for the unconscious. The eternity the person in the lyrics is seeking becomes frozen and stagnant (like death or a coma). A precursor to "Time Stand Still".

"Closer to the Heart" This simple radio-aimed ballad has a memorable peaceful tubular bell chiming section. The title and opening line were penned by Neil's friend Peter Talbot. The song starts with "and" as if continuing the lines in the title track and offers solutions to the problems stated there. The Heart was believed to be the center of everything in the body in medieval times. The men in high places are not the kings in this case. The Blacksmith was appointed by the king and had ties to metallurgy and alchemy; he was equal to the accursed poet and despised prophet. The Philosopher is the Ploughman as "the sower sows the word" (Mark 4:14). Music by Lee, Lifeson and Peart.

"Cinderella Man" Everyone's favorite philanthropist with bipolar manic depression. Geddy wrote this song partly inspired by the film *Mr. Deeds Goes to Town*.

"Madrigal" A madrigal is a short love poem set to music (also the title of a contemporary Yes song) often with several parts sung by different voices. Dedicated to their wives, this Rush song is about the weariness felt by the band on the road ("I grow weary of the battle").

"Cygnus X-1" Another sci-fi epic, this song was inspired by a *Time* magazine article. Producer Terry Brown reads the Prologue through a voice synthesizer to this tale of a space ship journeying into a time warp in the Black Hole of Cygnus (Greek for dog), which is referred to as the Swan constellation where scientists believe there might be one (Stephen Hawking and Carl Sagan have said that life may exist there). The music can be described as a dark, wrenching, heavy metal vortex. The "Sound and Fury" allusion is to a line in Shakespeare's *MacBeth*, which William Faulkner used for the title of this most famous novel. The allusion to Rocinante is to Cervantes and Steinbeck.

NEIL *Rocinante* was Don Quixote's horse [from the Miguel de Cervantes novel], and also the name of John Steinbeck's truck in *Travels With Charley*. I just liked it, that's all. (Backstage Club 1990)

NEIL I was never a sci-fi nerd kid and didn't watch "Star Trek" or read science fiction, but then when I was in England, I was poor and couldn't afford to buy books. So, I was ransacking the closet where I lived and found a lot of sci-fi. It reintroduced me to the genre and made me realize it wasn't all about numbers and integrated circuits. It refreshed my idea of what the style was, and that led me into fantasy. It was a whole lot of reading at the time, of being young and interested in fantasy and science fiction and alternative universes. That was all in my reading, so naturally it was reflected in the lyrics. (Seconds 1994)

Archives (1978)

This reissue of the first three albums was released in one set.

COVER The man in the star image appears against a black-gray background.

HUGH I had every intention of making a look as much a part of the archives as possible-as opposed to being a rock 'n' roll cover. It's almost a library piece. (Creem)

Hemispheres (1978)

THEMES Mind, struggle, opposition, polarity, balance, equality.

COVER A naked man dances on the right brain hemisphere, while a business-man (from the late 19th century perhaps) walks on the other side.

BACK COVER Two more brains (the first time Hugh used the "three" image).

HUGH The band told me, "Go ahead, we'll see it when we get back," because they were in Wales for the whole album and all my conversations with them were over the telephone. They didn't see it until it got out. Technically, it's an abomination. Once again, it's an effort in the progressive area of punning. They talk about Apollo and Dionysus in the lyrics, so I figured that Apollo would be the severe, Magritte business man, and that Dionysus would, again, be the reinstitution of a figure. (Creem)

"Hemispheres" This side-long song is Book II to Cygnus X-1, drawing inspiration from Adam Smith's book *Powers of Mind*, but throwing in hints of Nietzche's *Birth of Tragedy*, notably the references to Apollo (reason) and Dionysius (desire) as two sides of the human psyche.

NEIL Apollo and Dionysus have been used in a lot of books to sort of characterize the rational side and the instinctive side. (Visions)

"Prelude" Like "Overture" the Prelude contains many movements to be heard later on. "The Prelude" was a poem by one of Neil's favorite writers at the time, T.S. Eliot.

"Apollo: Bringer of Wisdom" Apollo represents the left hemisphere. 'Left-brainers' are often logical thinkers, adept at math. Apollo was the Greek god of the sun and war.

"Dionysus: Bringer of Love" Dionysus was the Greek god of wine and fertility (read the right hemisphere.) He stood for uninhibited desire in Nietzsche's *Birth of Tragedy* and *Human, All Too Human* and was the extreme opposite of Apollo. 'Rightbrainers' are most common, and include people who are artistic and sensitive. Neil had read an essay by Ayn Rand that compared these two Greek figures.

"Armageddon: The Battle of Heart and Mind" A reference to the Biblical war, but in this case the song Apollo and Dionysus pull man in opposite directions, towards Order or Chaos, respectively. The debate between classical (Apollo) and romantic (Dionysus) culture is ongoing.

"Cygnus: Bringer of Balance" You can hear the left channel switch to the right for dramatic effect when Geddy sings the word 'hemispheres'.

NEIL I'm taking the setting back to the dawn of creation when there was just man not knowing who he is or why he's there. Apollo [a god] comes along and gives the people a shot at progress and offers all these benefits and they say 'sure we'd like fires to warm us in the winter'. They follow him along and build beautiful cities and get involved in science just for the sake of it. But they're bored because they don't have an emotional attachment to the things they're making. An ennui falls over everybody and they hang out, bored. They go after Dionysus [an opposing god] who tells them what he can offer and obviously it's the instinctive and artistic side of things—the music and dancing and love. They say, 'yeah, that sounds great after what we've had.' Everyone has a wonderful time and they leave the cities and just rave. But when winter comes along they've lost the skills that would keep them warm and that whole rational side of them doesn't function the way it did. So the wolves and cold get to them and that point they break into total anarchy and chaos. Eventually the whole problem is solved by the arrival of Cygnus. He points out the chaos that the struggle between Apollo and Dionysus is causing so they appoint him as a god—the bringer of balance.

"The Sphere" Jane Austen's novel *Sense and Sensibilty* may be alluded to in last few lines of the song.

"Circumstances" Written by Neil about his experience on his own at 18 years old in England, this is one the most discussed Rush songs ever written, with the central issue the question of whether our lives are shaped by fate or circumstances.

"The Trees" The forest is a mother symbol and may represent the perilous unconscious (while on the hemisphere theme). C.S. Lewis in "Screwtape Proposes a Toast" discusses how Greek tyrants leveled off tall stalks in corn fields to make them as good or bad (equal) as the rest. Also the cartoonish images may have been inspired by Dr. Seuss's book *Lorax*, published in the 1960s, where the trees are bickering about height. Incidentally, Neil's pet birds chirp away again on the tune.

NEIL Lyrically, that's a piece of doggerel. I certainly wouldn't be proud of the writing skill of that. What I would be proud of in that is taking a pure idea and creating an image for it. I was very proud of what I achieved in that sense. Although on the skill side it's zero. I wrote "The Trees" in about five minutes. It's simple rhyming and phrasing, but it illustrates a point so clearly, I wish I could do that all of the time. It was just a flash. I was working on an entirely different thing when I saw a cartoon picture of these trees carrying on like fools. I thought, "What if trees acted like people?" So I saw it as a cartoon really, and wrote it that way. I think that's the image that it conjures up to a listener or a reader. A very simple statement. (Modern Drummer 1980)

"La Villa Strangiato" Subtitled "an exercise in self-indulgence," this instrumental, done in one take, combines jazz fusion, metal, power rock, and other influences the members felt at the time. La villa means 'city' in Spanish, while Strangiato is made-up, a fusion of Spanish and Italian to mean 'strange'. The images in the suite titles were inspired by nightmares Alex was having. The fused German/Spanish title of the first suite is almost identical to a German song called "Gute Nacht, Freunde" by A. Yondrascheck, which features the same guitar classical intro. "To sleep perchance to dream" is from Shakespeare's *A Midsummer Night's Dream*. Lerxst was Alex's nickname. The Aragon was a region in medieval Spain, but here may also refer to the old Aragon ballrooms the band used to play. Danforth (Avenue) and Pape (Street) is a Toronto inter-section. The shreves were the names for the roadies. The guitarwork itself has been lifted from Warner Bros. cartoon music of the 1930s and '40s, particularly "Powerhouse" by Raymond Scott.

ALEX   "La Villa Strangiato" has two parts that were each recorded in one take: We felt it was a song that needed the feeling of spontaneity to make it work, so we spent over a week learning it before we recorded. After we were finished, none of us thought we'd ever be able to play it again. But now I can do it while watching TV. (Guitar Player 1980)

ALEX   I always enjoy playing that solo. I like the changes and it's a very emotive bluesy kind of solo. It too stays basically the same every night. The band is in the background modulating between two notes and it gives me a chance to wail. (Guitar 1984)

Permanent Waves (1980)

THEMES Trends as tides (they will always be going in and out), communication, freedom of choice, freewill, technology.

COVER Neil actually appears on the cover art, which is a black and white photo of a 1940s/50s era young woman with her dress being blown up as waves crash into the street behind her. On the billboards in the background are the last names of the members of Rush (Coca Cola didn't want the name close to the lady's thighs and Pearl beer became Peart). The band originally wanted to call the album 'Wavelength'. Originally the infamous 'Dewey Defeats Truman' headline (Truman in fact won the 1948 election) appeared on the covers of early Canadian pressings pressings but it had to be changed.

HUGH   … because anything that pertains to that headline, according to the *Chicago Tribune*, is an embarrassment, and is subject to litigation if we were to print up any facet of it. To boot, Coca-Cola asked that we strip out their billboard way off in the background because it was too close to a cotton-clad mons pubis. (Creem)

HUGH *Permanent Waves* is the result of a conversation which I had with Neil out at his home in the country. We spoke all evening about Rush growing up, and how we were going to do these EKG readings of each member as they were recording. We were going to tape their temples and chests and have real heartbeats of them while they were playing. So Permanent Waves was going to be a technical statement, and we were going to treat that with red and gold foil, and do a nice study in design—as opposed to a photographic thing. I walked out and, in the doorway, said "Wait! Let's try something with Donna Reed, with her permanent Toni hairdo, and have her walking out of a tidal wave situation. Neil gave me this blank look and said, "Get out of here." The following day, he asked me to consider doing just that because he'd discussed it with the band, and they'd all thought it was more likely for a cover than the serious approach. (Creem)

NEIL The woman on the cover is really a symbol of us. If you think that's sexist in a negative way—well, it's really looking at ourselves so I don't think it can be. The idea is her perfect imperturbability in the face of all this chaos. In that, she represents us. In the basic sense, all that cover picture means is forging on regardless, being completely uninvolved with all the chaos and ridiculous nonsense that's going on around us. Plus she represents the spirit of music and the spirit of radio, a symbol of perfect integrity and truth and beauty. (Sounds)

ALEX This era seems to be pushing New Wave, and this Wave, and that Wave. The material we're doing is just Permanent Wave—it's just music. It's the love of music and how, with everything new, it's just a continuation, like a wave coming back in from the ocean. (Guitar Player 1980)

NEIL When you're working with a 20-minute piece of music, I guess it must be what making a film or writing a novel is like. With something of that span you have so many threads that you have to keep together in your mind all the way through, and as you're recording one part you're trying to relate it to the other parts and make sure the continuity is going to be there as well as the integrity of the original parts. It takes a lot of concentration to pull something like that off. It was something we wanted to give a rest for a short while, though there are two pretty long tracks on this album, and the short ones are no shorter than five minutes. (Sounds)

"The Spirit of Radio": This song took its title from a Toronto radio station slogan.

GEDDY This station called CFNY in Toronto, their motto was 'The Spirit of Radio'. And they were totally free-form, at the time when all these big programmers were coming in, and consultants were telling all these stations, and all these station managers, how to keep their jobs. 'Play these records and you can, you'll keep your job.' So there was this one station that was playing anything; and you'd hear very abstract things, you know. You'd hear very hard things, or classical. It sort of reminded us of what it used to be like when FM just started, and guys like Murray the K were on the air, you know. And it was really great, and everybody was so into it, and you'd live by the FM radio; you'd just, you'd always have it on. So it reminded us of that, and we started thinking about well, what happened to that, those kind of ideals for radio? And you know, it was like radio is great, until people realize they can make money at it, and then it all changes. (Up Close 1994)

NEIL   It's not about a radio station or anything, it's really about the spirit of music when it comes right down to the basic theme of it. It's about musical integrity. We wanted to get across the idea of a radio station playing a wide variety of music. There are bits of reggae in the song and one or two verses has a new wave feel to it. We tried to get across all the different forms of music. There are no divisions there. The choruses are very electronic. It's just a digital sequencer with a glockenspiel and a counter guitar riff. The verse is a standard straight ahead Rush verse. One is a new wave, a couple of reggae verses, and some standard heavy riffing, and as much as we could possibly get in there without getting redundant. (Modern Drummer)

The last lines are twist on Simon and Garfunkel's *The Sounds of Silence*: "for the words of the prophets are written on the subway walls." The first verse syncopates the choked hi hat with the "s" sounds in the lyrics.

NEIL   This is where a sense of humor comes into it. I was sitting there thinking of the conclusion of the song and the parody came into my mind. And I thought, "Well, either this is very stupid or it's very great." But all it says is … salesman as artists I can see as an ideal, but they have no place telling us what to play onstage and they have no place in the recording studio telling us how to write songs … any more than a car salesman. (Creem)

"Freewill" "Kill them with kindness" is the play on words behind "kindness that can kill". Lotus eaters in Homer's *The Odyssey* became lazy when they ate them. An ancient symbol, the lotus can also stand for all forms of evolution.

NEIL   Lotus-land as it appears in 'Free Will' is simply a metaphor for an idealized background, a 'land of milk and honey.' It is sometimes also used as a pejorative name for Los Angeles, though that was not in my mind when I wrote it.

NEIL   "Freewill" is a new thing for us in terms of time signatures. I mentioned before that we experiment a lot with time signatures. We work in nearly everyone that I know of that's legitimate. All of the 5's, 7's, 9's, 11's, 13's and combinations thereof. I don't think that you have to play in 4/4 to feel comfortable. (Modern Drummer)

"Jacob's Ladder" Part heavy metal, part New Age, this song is not about the vision seen by Jacob in the Bible but rather the atmospheric phenomena that has been named after this vision. The tympani pounding parts rock like apocalyptic earthquakes. Alex plays like he's ascending the ladder in the clouds parting section.

NEIL   We built a whole song around a picture. We wanted to build a song around the phenomena called Jacob's Ladder, where the rays break through the clouds. I came up with a couple of short pieces of lyrics to set the musical parts up. And we built it all musically trying to describe it cinematically. As if our music were a film. We have a luminous sky happening and the whole stormy, gloomy atmosphere, and all of a sudden these shafts of brilliance come bursting through and we try to create that musically. (Modern Drummer)

NEIL   This song simply describes the phenomenon of the sun breaking through the clouds in visible rays, as it sometimes does after a rain or on a cloudy day. The actual name seems to be one of those traditional names for natural things which has probably been around for ages. I think Geddy actually suggested the idea to me, after hearing his mother-in-law use the name. It had a nice sound to it, and of course the event itself is a beautiful and inspiring one. (Backstage Club 1985)

"Entre Nous"   The title comes from from Ayn Rand's *The Fountainhead* meaning "between us" in French and captures the sense of rapport Neil feels for members of the audience. In some foreign pressings, the label included the English translation.

NEIL   When the lights come on behind us and I look out at the audience and see all those little circles, each of those circles is a person. Each person is a story. They have circumstances surrounding their lives that can never be repeated. All those people have a whole novel about their lives—the time they were born, how they grew up, what they did and what they wanted to do, their relationships with other people, their romances and marriages—all those things. And they ARE individuals. That's what I respond to. They're not a mob. They're not a crowd. They're not some lower class of degenerates. They're individuals. I'm always playing for an individual. I don't play for the crowd—for some faceless ideal of commerciality of some lowest common denominator. It's a person up there every night, who knows everything I'm supposed to do. If I don't do it, that person knows it. (Modern Drummer '84)

"Different Strings"   Another Geddy-penned ballad, with a reference to trends/ waves in the question, "did it go out of style?"

ALEX   I love the feel of the tune. It reminds me of soldiers sitting around a piano in a smoke-filled pub in England during the war. It's the type of solo I really enjoy playing—an emotive, bluesy sort of thing. (Guitar Player '80)

"Natural Science"   This is epic Rush. Life in a tidal pool is likened to our own little world in the big universe. The quantum leap forward seems inspired by the transitional evolution scene in the movie *2001: A Space Odyssey*. Like the synthesis or balance in "Cygnus", art needs to be balanced with science.

NEIL   Obviously the original relationship between man and nature was that he had to tame it in order to survive, and that became more and more sophisticated and out of hand, and finally it just became destruction. It's become the same thing with science where people don't understand it, and they are afraid of it. They think that you have to eradicate science in order to control it. (Jim Ladd Innerview)

NEIL   There is no doubt that working under pressure can be very rewarding, as we have found many times in the studio. It seems as if the creative mind slips into a burst of overdrive, allowing a brief, exhausting, but productive surge in the creative process. On the third day of my confinement this phenomenon arrived at last, and something new began to take shape. It was the product of a whole host of unconnected experiences, books, images, thoughts, feelings, observations, and confirmed principles, that somehow took the form of "Natural Science"… forged from some bits from "Gawain", some instrumental ideas that were still unused, and some parts newly-written. (Personal Waves)

ALEX   Once we had the guitar track down, we stuck a speaker cabinet outside—this was way up at a studio in Morin Heights, Quebec—and we recorded the natural echo off the mountains in combination with the sounds of splashing water and Geddy's voice. We didn't use any sort of synthetic echo on the water track. (Guitar Player 1980)

Moving Pictures (1981)

THEMES Fear of change, cinematic imagery, fame, motion, alienation, travel, control, freedom, rebellion.

COVER Men in red suits move paintings into a building which resembles a museum or library. The steps are more ascension symbols again.

NEIL   When Hugh Syme was developing the multitude of puns for the cover, he wanted the guys 'moving pictures' to have some 'moving pictures' to be moving past the people who were 'moved' by the 'picture'—get it? So he asked us to think of some ideas for these pictures. The 'man descending to hell' is actually a woman—Joan of Arc—being burned at the stake (as per 'Witch Hunt'), and the card-playing dogs are there because it was a funny, silly idea—one of the most cliched pictures we could think of—a different kind of 'moving picture'. (Backstage Club newsletter)

HUGH   It became pertinent to me later that the Queen's Park building in Toronto where it was shot had all the right elements: three arches, three pillars per arch; there are three members of Rush, and all of that. The one painting had to be of Joan

Of Arc as far as I was concerned—which ended up being a bit of a nightmare because I couldn't find any archival pictures or paintings which were suitable. So I ended up getting some burlap, and a pine post, two sticks and a bottle of scotch. Deborah Samuel, the photographer whom I used on that session, got wrapped up in burlap so she could make her cameo appearance. We just lit lighter fluid in pie plates in the foreground. It was basically a half hour session because we had no other alternative but to do it ourselves. (Creem '83)

GEDDY We looked at all those songs as little films, I think. We loved the play on words about moving pictures, and the fact that we were taking cinematic approach to writing that kind of rock music, which, to many people, I guess, seemed like a kind of silly notion; but to us—it worked. At the same time we were trying to make these stories that we were telling affecting and having some kind of emotional impact and be moving to the listener. (In the Studio)

"Tom Sawyer" Co-written with fellow Canadian rock band Max Webster's lyricist Pye Dubois (originally he called it "Louis the Warrior"), this song is about a detached streetwise rebel with mean, mean pride (pride is another theme in subsequent lyrics), partly inspired by Mark Twain's character. Geddy later would sing "catch the fish" instead of "spit" because of an incident on the tour: Roadies threw fish onstage and Geddy happened to be in that section when one flew by. Widely recognized as the quintessential Rush song with its familiar dynamics.

NEIL "Tom Sawyer" was a collaboration between myself and Pye Dubois, an excellent lyricist who wrote the lyrics for Max Webster. His original lyrics were kind of a portrait of a modern day rebel, a free-spirited individualist striding through the world wide-eyed and purposeful. I added the themes of reconciling the boy and man in myself, and the difference between what people are and what others perceive them to be—namely me, I guess. (Backstage Newsletter 1985)

NEIL There are parts of the song that I don't necessarily understand. But I like the arrogance implied. But it's mistaken arrogance. There are … little games you're expected to play that Tom Sawyer and myself don't have time for. (Sounds)

ALEX I remember when the opening keyboard thing, when we layered it on top, how cool it sounded, and what power and punch the opening had. And the toughness of the way Neil played in that opening where it's just basically the drums and Geddy with this synth rasping away in the background—then the rest of the band diving into it and screaming all the way through. I always thought that we had really, again, achieved what we set out to with that song, of having that real punky, kind of rebellious attitude to it. The full of a band, and I think … well obviously that's the appeal of the song. (In the Studio)

NEIL The instrumental section of "Tom Sawyer" grew from a little melody that Geddy had been using to set up his synthesizers at sound checks. (A Rush Newsreel)

Rush live circa 1977.

Alex with Gibson Cherry EDS Doubleneck, ES-355, and current PRS.

Alex with custom Fender Strat and trusty old Gibson Les Paul.

Neil playing Tama, Ludwig, and current DW kits.

Geddy with Rickenbacker 4001, Steinberger and current Fender Jazz.

Filming band's GUP tour live in Toronto.

Geddy taking a break on the Big Money set with Wal bas~

Alex performing at the Kumbaya festivals 1994 and 1998.

Alex performing at The Orbit Room
and White Ribbon Charity Concert.

Band at Harvard Lampoo
ceremony and at privat
Blind Date club shov

Geddy and Alex during Canada's Walk of Fame induction ceremonies.

NEIL   I'm playing full strength through the entire song and it took about a day and a half to record. I remember collapsing afterwards with raw, red aching hands and feet. I had been playing the bass drum so hard that my toes were all mashed together and *very* sore. Physically, this was certainly the most difficult track, and even now it takes as much energy to play properly as my solo. (Modern Drummer '83)

"Red Barchetta" Barchettas are actual body car types, and in its original Italian means "little boat." Inspired by Richard S. Foster's article "A Nice Morning Drive" which Neil read in a November 1973 *Car and Track* magazine, it is a sci-fi excursion in the vein of their early works about an age where cars were outlawed (perhaps because they represent individuality, sexuality, freedom, and cause pollution and accidents). Mass transit is now in the form of the Turbine Freight, which the narrator takes to a farm that has been abandoned but conceals a well-kept automobile from the past. So the car is to the guitar in "2112". The adrenaline-filled car chase led by one rebel is a cinematic image itself. The Eyes (authorities) have a two-lane wide alloy air-car vehicle that cannot cross the narrow bridge where the driver leaves them stranded. Even the senses seem heightened as if the air was purer as a result of the Motor Law. At the end of the song we realize that the chase may have been imaginary, in the mind of the uncle or nephew reliving a rebellious experience in a nostalgic fireside chat.

NEIL   It was the rarest of all animals (for ourselves, anyway!), a one take wonder. (A Rush Newsreel)

ALEX   That was the intention with 'Red Barchetta'—to create a song that was very vivid, so that you had a sense, if you listen to it and listen to the lyrics, of the action. It does become a movie. I think that song really worked with that in mind; it was successful with that intention. It's something that I think we've tried to carry on—become a little more visual with our music, since then. But that one in particular was very satisfying. It was always one of my favorites. I think it's probably my favorite from that album. I like the way the parts knit together. I like the changes. I like the melody of the song. I love the dynamics of it, the way it opens with the harmonics and creates a mood, then gets right into the driving, right up to the middle section where it's really screaming along, where you really feel like you're in the open car, and the music's very vibrant and moving. And then it ends as it began with that quiet dynamic, and lets you down lightly. So it picks you up for the whole thing and drops you off at your next spot. (In the Studio)

"YYZ" As heard in the intros in concert, "YYZ" is actually pronounced Y-Y-*Zed* (Canadian/British way of pronouncing "Z"). Neil smashes quarter-inch plywood against a stool for the crashing sound effect near the end. The loud synthesizer part is supposed to represent "coming home from a long trip," according to Geddy. Music by Lee and Peart.

NEIL YYZ is an identity code used by [Pearson] Toronto International Airport and the intro is taken from Morse code which is sent out by the beacon there. It is always a happy day when YYZ appears on our luggage tags! (A Rush Newsreel)

NEIL The song is loosely based on airport-associated images. Exotic destinations, painful partings, happy landings, that sort of thing. (Backstage Club 1990)

"Limelight" This is one of the first Rush songs to wrestle with their response to fame.

GEDDY "Limelight" was probably more of Neil's song than a lot of the songs on that album in the sense that his feelings about being in the limelight and his difficulty with coming to grips with fame and autograph seekers and a sudden lack of privacy and sudden demands on his time … he was having a very difficult time dealing with. I mean we all were, but I think he was having the most difficulty of the three of us adjusting; in the sense that I think he's more sensitive to more things than Alex and I are, it's harder for him to deal with those interruptions on his personal space and his desire to be alone. (In the Studio)

GEDDY It deals with the two kinds of ways you can look at success. On one hand, you can treat it as living out some sort of charade. On the other hand, it's something that's very real and it's really just a look both aspects. You certainly have to draw the line somewhere as far as when you become public property and when you're a private person. (CHUM-FM 1981)

NEIL Fame, for me, is embarrassing. It's not something I get arrogant about. I don't feel like people are bothering me. But, at the same time, I get embarrassed if strangers walk up to me on the street who think they know me. I just get embarrassed, tense and uncomfortable … They think they know me. They *don't* know me. They don't know anything about me. They're strangers. It just makes me defensive. (Modern Drummer 1984)

NEIL There were times when I had to change it from the first person, to say '*One* must put up barriers to keep oneself intact'. Whereas my original intention had been '*I* must put up barriers'. And when Geddy suggested the change of focus I realized it was right. (Sounds)

GEDDY During that year's tour, I didn't play the song exactly as it is on the record. I don't even know how I originally played it! People don't realize how much of a record is made up of fortunate accidents or spontaneous composition, like "oh he went to that cymbal over there so I'm gonna go with him." It's never a case of sitting down and writing it in stone. (Guitar School)

"The Camera Eye" The title and imagery come from a book by John Dos Passos. The sampled cinematic street sounds are from 'Metropolis' in *Superman: The Movie*. Part one is about New York and the hard realities, while part two is about London and the possibilities, the two verses linked by rain. Chase scenes in "Incident at Channel Q" used some of the faster parts in the song.

NEIL   Although a bit of a bluffer in rudiments, I have always loved the ominous, insistent delicacy of the distant marching snare. We were looking for a dramatic, soundtrack-like feel. (Modern Drummer)

"Witch Hunt" Subtitled "Part III of Fear," this song, with cinematic images of a night lit by torches held by howling mobs, may be about the Salem witch trials or any modern-day witch hunt. Metallica's lyrics for "Holier Than Thou" is a direct steal from "Witch Hunt's" final verse: "Point the finger, slow to understand / Arrogance and ignorance go hand in hand."

NEIL   The winner of the most rewritten song award. It would serve us as a sort of vehicle for experimentation and indulgence. For instance, we would be using Hugh Syme's talents on the keyboards, and my entire drum part was recorded twice (as two drummers) in one verse, while in another, a percussion section was created by recording each sound differently. We assembled a Vigilante Choir out in the snow and the sound of the haunted child at the beginning. (A Rush Newsreel)

NEIL   "Witch Hunt" dealt with that mentality of mob rule, and what happens to a bunch of people when they come together and they're afraid, and they go out and do something really stupid and really horrible. That was easy to grasp, and you see plenty of examples of that in real life as well as in fiction and in films of course, too. (Jim Ladd Innerview)

ALEX   We went outside of Le Studio and it was so cold, it was really cold; we were well into December by then, I think. We were all out there. We put a couple of mics outside. We started ranting and raving. We did a couple of tracks of that. I think we had a bottle of Scotch or something with us to keep us warm. So as the contents of the bottle became less and less, the ranting and raving took on a different flavor and you got little lines of—you remember the cartoon Roger Ramjet? What was the bad guys name? His gang of hoods, they always had these little things they would say whenever they were mumbling. We were in the control room after we had laid down about twelve tracks of mob—in hysterics. Every once in awhile you'd hear somebody say something really stupid. (In the Studio)

"Vital Signs" Keeping with the album themes, there's even a cinematic touch in the line "pause rewind replay". Geddy accidentally sings "evelate" instead of "elevate" near the end.

NEIL   We had purposefully left one song still unwritten with a view towards writing it in the studio. Eclectic in the extreme, it embraces a wide variety of stylistic influences, ranging from the sixties to the present. Lyrically, it derives from my response to the terminology of 'Technospeak', the language of electronics and computers, which often seems to parallel the human machine, in the functions and interrelationships they employ. It is interesting, if not irrelevant, to speculate as to whether we impose our nature on the machines that we build, or whether they are merely governed by the same inscrutable laws of Nature as we (perhaps Murphy's Laws?) Never mind! (A Rush Newsreel)

NEIL That song took about three tours to catch on. It was kind of a baby for us. We kept playing it and wouldn't give up. We put it in our encore last tour-putting it in the most exciting part of the set possible-and just demanded that people accept it because we believed in it. I still think that song represents a culmination-the best combination of music, lyrics, rhythm. It opens up so many musical approaches, from being very simplistic and minimal to becoming very over-played. Everything we wanted in the song is there. So that song was very special to us. But we had to wait. We had to be patient and wait for the audience to understand us. (Guitar '86)

Exit ... Stage Left (1981)

COVER This live album combines images from the studio albums on the cover. The night owl flies over the suited man (Apollo) from *Hemsipheres,* while the *Waves* girl peeks behind a curtain to the stage. The back cover continues the picture: the naked dancer (Dionysus) from *Hemsipheres*, the *2112* Starman picture, the *Caress of Steel* cover art in a frame is held by the movers of *Pictures* standing near the Puppet King from *Kings*, and an actual road case stenciled with the original *Rush* logo. On "Jacob's Ladder", Geddy's refers to Terry Brown when he says 'TC Broonsie'. "Broon's Bane", also a reference to Brown, was a leftover from 1979 recording sessions. The title is the favorite phrase of Snagglepuss (Hanna-Barbara cartoon character).

HUGH It was shot in a condemned theatre here in Toronto, which shall remain nameless. We decided to go with the girl pulling the curtain back on the front instead of the back. It was originally intended to be the other way around, so when I flipped the photograph over, I had to write "Rush" on the equipment box in the foreground, and I had to strip out the information on the Stage Door and write in the word "EXIT," because the album was called Exit … Stage Left. …[the front is a] Buffalo [concert] shot … We went out to get that, too. Believe it or not, we went to about 15 shows, trying to get the band saying "Thank you, good night," and at the same time, and walking towards the camera. Couldn't get it. (Creem)

NEIL We wanted to have Snagglepuss's tail on there. You know, 'Exit Stage Left', with a picture of just his tail. Forget it! They wanted all kinds of legal hassles and tons of money. (Canoe Online 10-16-96)

Signals (1982)

THEMES Communication, fame, dreams, youth alienation, transition/stagnation, suburbia, technology.

COVER On the front, a dalmation sniffing near a fire hydrant; on the back, a blueprint for a fictitious school and mall using the band's nicknames Lerxst, Dirk, Pratt (as well as the names of other friends like Warren Cromartie).

HUGH I was given the word "signals." It was such a broad concept that it was baffling for all of us. We really had trouble with that one, and I decided that, with such a phenomenally important word with the kind of potency it potentially had, to go with something really dumb, really inane. But something which would still tie in with songs such as "Chemistry", and the subdivision aspect of the fire hydrants, lawns, and neighborhood dogs. (Creem 1983)

GEDDY Hugh had this concept of taking the idea down to a basic human level—territorial or even sexual. So that's how the design with the dog and the fire hydrant came about. The little map on the back features make-believe subdivisions, with a lot of silly names and places. The red dots represent all the fire hydrants and basically the whole thing maps out a series of territories. (Success Under Pressure)

GEDDY We realized that one element often lacking in our music was feel. And we're finding that working in a shorter framework, which we used to think was the easy way out, isn't really easy at all. It comes down to being confident in our musicianship. (Circus 11–82)

NEIL I guess that *Signals* has more to do with writing about people and less about ideals. *Permanent Waves* was probably our first album that was in touch with reality—it was about people dealing with technology instead of people dealing with some futuristic fantasy world or using symbols for people. Now I'm trying to make those symbols into real people and real conflicts in real people's lives. I still want to write about ideals, I'm not interested in writing about the sewer of life." (Sounds '82)

GEDDY "Subdivisions", "Chemistry", and "The Weapon" were entirely written on keyboards. (Keyboard)

"Subdivisions" The song deals with growing up in suburbs—alienation, dreams, and conformity—as Alex explores more of an angular, textural guitar sound and synths take over more. Contrary to popular belief, Neil does not sing the part "Subdivisions" (nor does Alex who filled in for concerts and in the video promo). It was actually Toronto newsman Mark Dailey's voice.

NEIL I had been working on some lyrics and had come up with "Subdivisions", an exploration of the background from which all of us (and probably most of our audience) had come from … I listened closely [to the music Geddy and Alex were creating for the song], picking up the variations on 7/8 and _, the way the guitar adopts the role of rhythm section while the keyboards take the melody, returning to bass with guitar leading in the chorus, then the mini-moog taking over the again for the instrumental bridge. (Stories From Signals)

"The Analog Kid" Almost a sequel to "Subdivisions", the analog kid, dreaming of success, represents Rush growing up in the days of analog.

GEDDY I think every young musician can relate to this; you have this dream about 'making it' but don't really know what that means. You just go for this blind goal with your eyes closed, your heart wide open and let things happen from there. You've no idea what you're going for and what it'll be like when you get there. I don't think any of us realized how far Rush would go and I don't think we like to think about it either. (Success Under Pressure)

NEIL "The Analog Kid" was my first attempt at non-fiction. For the longest time I stepped into characters until I had my own confidence and technique to be able to step outside them as a writer. (Canadian Musician 1990)

"Chemistry" While some may consider this song to be a drug metaphor, it alludes to the subatomic world, the microcosmos. The invisible and intangible things and laws that exist are discussed in the first part of the song, and "emotional chemistry" is discussed in the second.

NEIL This tour for the first time our sound man, Jon [Erickson], has been taping our soundcheck meanderings, and it had proved very fruitful to us. On this particular day we will unknowingly write a whole song at once, each of us playing a different part. While Geddy plays what will become the keyboard melody for the bridge section, Alex is playing the guitar riff for the verses, and I'm playing the drum beat for the choruses. When Alex and Geddy get together to sift through the soundcheck tapes they will find a whole song written, and will arrange it and make a demo that will be very close to the finished song. Lyrically, this is the first time that all three of us have collaborated on the words to a song. Geddy and Alex together came up with the title and concept for the song, wrote out a few key phrases and words that they wanted to get in, then passed it along to me for organization and a little further development. When all of this is put together, we have what was probably the easiest song to write on the album." (Stories From Signals)

"Digital Man" The digital man refers to Peter Jenson, who did the digital mastering on *Moving Pictures* too. Babylon symbolically stands for any corrupt existence, or the material world.

NEIL   The Digital Man, the character is running faster than life, you know, in the fast lane and all of that, just moving faster than, than real time. (Jim Ladd Innerview)

NEIL   "Digital Man" was our first attempt at juggling totally disparate stylistic influences—ska, synth-pop and hard rock and at the time we ended up with three pieces of one song held together by Crazy Glue. (Metal Hammer)

"The Weapon" Part II of the Fear trilogy, the song alludes to U.S. President Franklin Delano Roosevelt's inaugural address, with the memorable line, "the only thing we have to fear is … fear itself." Once again, we have the church/kingdom/glory/power references.

NEIL   … it was dealing with how people use your fears against you, as a weapon, and that took a little longer to come to grips with, but eventually I got my thinking straightened out and the images that I wanted to use, and collected them all up, and it came out. (Jim Ladd Innerview)

NEIL   This brings the feel of the song perilously close to a (shudder) d-d-d-dance song, like, you know, disco! Treason! Treason! Kill the traitors! They wrote a song you can dance to! (Stories From Signals)

"New World Man" Recorded somewhat spontaneously, this song about an idealized political leader was also intended to describe the band's musical synthesis of their international influences.

GEDDY   It wouldn't have been on the record if we didn't have four minutes space available. I think what it really boiled down to was that we'd worked so hard getting all these slick sounds that we were all in the mood to put something down that was real spontaneous. In the end, the whole song took one day to write and record. It's good to put something together like that. (Success Under Pressure)

ALEX   It was the first single that we ever had that had a, quite a wide appeal, especially on radio, where it wasn't only those kind of stations that played harder stuff. As a musical piece it was a departure for us, it was something a little, a little more different, uh, and a little poppier, I think. (Up Close 1994)

"Losing It" The writer referred to in this song is Ernest Hemingway, not only his writings (*The Sun Also Rises*—"the sun will rise no more"—and *For Whom the Bell Tolls),* but also his physique. But the song was inspired by the film *The Turning Point.*

NEIL   It drew a bit from that film with Shirley MacLaine called *The Turning Point*. It was about two ballet dancers. One of them had continued on and was getting to be a bit of a has-been. The other one had given it up to get married and raise a family. I was a bit inspired from that … You have to respond to that kind of tragedy compassionately. It's a horrible thing. You spend all your life learning how to do a thing and then because of something beyond your control, all of a sudden you can't do it anymore. It's very sad. There's an essential dynamic to life that you have a prime, and you have something leading up to that prime. The essence was whether it was worse to lose something great or whether it was worse to have never known it. (Modern Drummer)

"Countdown" The white dragon in folklore symbolizes the moon and is a guardian of science in this song which documents a space shuttle lift off at Cape Canaveral.

ALEX   It was an amazing thing—an amazing sight to witness. I've never heard anything so loud in my life. Your pants are flapping, you could feel the ground vibrating and this was three miles away. That's the closest you could get. We decided right then that on the next album we'd like to do something. (Harmonix)

GEDDY   The only real keyboard solo I think I ever played was the Minimoog lead on "Countdown" and I don't think I'll ever do that again. I do a little improvisation on keyboards, but not much. I stick to business with the keyboards. (Keyboard)

NEIL   "Countdown" is another example of a song that didn't work at the time but led us forward. It was our first attempt at a documentary, taking real life and putting it into a song. It didn't work … (Modern Drummer)

Grace Under Pressure (1984)

THEMES Political references, war, death, anger, pressure, insecurity, environmental/economic issues.

COVER The icy cover painting suggests the subconscious with nightmarish pictures in the mountainscape (subliminal dog teeth and red eyes!) A bald-headed, gray humanoid is looking at the scene from the far left, while an egg in a C-clamp appears on the inside cover.

NEIL   I believe that the expression "grace under pressure" was actually coined by Dorothy Parker, to describe the attributes of a Hemingway hero, but I'm not sure. In any case, it seemed to describe the theme of the songs for that album, as well as life in the early 80s. (Backstage Club 1990)

"Distant Early Warning" Originally subtitled "Red Alert" to further create the sense of urgency, this song was written in a troubled time when nuclear war was threatened by US and USSR and when all rock groups were writing about nuclear disaster. The title refers to the distant early warning systems that are part of N.O.R.A.D. (national missile detection dishes across Canada.) Government disinformation, revolving door policies, absolute power and heavy water (found in nuclear reactors but here also meaning floods of acid rain) are the contemporary political references, while biblical images of doom appear in the reference to the cities of the plain—Sodom and Gomorrah (Gen. 19) were called cities of the plain—destroyed by fire and sulphur. 'Red Books' are political platforms in Canada. A young boy rides the missile in the accompanying music video that was inspired by the film *Dr. Strangelove or How I Learned to Stop Worrying and Love the Bomb*. The static-like sound in the beginning is actually a steam bubbler sound that the band used as a special effect along with the missile sounds.

NEIL It's a style of writing I've been sort of working towards over the last couple of albums that's, uh, kind of inspired by T.S. Eliot in a indirect way, but that style of pouring so much into it, so many images, and almost flooding the reader or the listener with ideas and images so that you don't seem to grasp anything out of it, but in the end of it you're left with something, and you're left with a feeling, or, uh, just an impression of it. (Off the Record)

NEIL The main theme of the song is a series of things, but that's certainly one of the ideas (our very tense world situation), and living in the … living in the modern world basically in all of its manifestations in terms of the distance from us of the threat of superpowers and the nuclear annihilation and all of that stuff, and these giant missiles pointed at each other across the ocean. There's all of that, but that tends to have a little bit of distance from people's lives, but at the same time I think it is omnipresent, you know, I think that threat does loom somewhere in everyone's subconscious, perhaps. And then it deals with the closer things in terms of relationships and how to keep a relationship in such a swift-moving world, and it has something to do with our particular lives, dealing with revolving doors, going in and out, but also I think that's generally true with people in the modern world where things for a lot of people are very difficult, and consequently, work and the mundane concerns of life tend to take precedence over the important values of relationships and of the larger world and the world of the abstract as opposed to the concrete, and dealing with all of those things with grace. And when I see a little bit of grace in someone's life. like when you drive past a horrible tenement building and you see these wonderful pink flamingos on the balcony up there, or something like, some little aspect of humanity that strikes you as a beautiful resistance if you like. (Jim Ladd Innerview)

NEIL Before I ever knew who or what Absalom was, I always loved the sound of it. I had thought perhaps it was an ancient prayer or something. There is a book by William Faulkner called *Absalom, Absalom*, which, again, I loved the sound of. I wanted to put it in the song, as a play on words with 'absolute' and 'obsolete,' but I thought I'd better find out for sure what it meant. So I called my wife and asked her to look it up in the encyclopedia. When I learned the real story, and its Biblical roots, I decided that it was still appropriate, as it was the ultimate expression of compassion, which is what the song was really about. 'Absalom, Absalom. My son, my son. Would God I had died for thee.' (Now don't anyone go reading any religion into that!)."

GEDDY "The Distant Early Warning" bass line is, to me, a prime example of the Geddy Lee concept. (Guitar School 1994)

"Afterimage" This song was written in memory of Robbie Whelan, a friend of the band's who died in a car accident not too far from the studio. Alex's guitar playing in the bridge flashes and disappears thoughtfully (the title is a photographical term).

"Red Sector A" The title is the name of the V.I.P. zone at Cape Canaveral's launching site, but here it is the name for a concentration camp in a futuristic Holocaust. Neil's electronic drums were meant to literally sound like 'smoking guns' (another double entendre lyrically).

NEIL I read a first-person account of someone who had survived the whole system of trains and work camps and Dachau and all of that, and this person, she was a young girl, like thirteen years old when she was sent into it, and lived in it for a few years, and then through first person accounts from other people who came out at the end of it, always glad to be alive, which again was the essence of grace, grace under pressure is that though all of it, these people never gave up the strong will to survive, through the utmost horror. I wanted to give it more of a timeless atmosphere too, because it's happened, of course, in more than one time and by more than one race of people … and another really important moving image that I got from a lot of these accounts was that at the end of it, these people of course had been totally isolated from the rest of the world, from their families, from any news at all, and they, in cases that I read, believed that they were the last people surviving. (Jim Ladd Innerview)

"The Enemy Within" Part one of the Fear trilogy, this song recalls the lyrics from Part Three, s "we must save us from ourselves As on "Hemispheres", the battle is with the enemies within. "We have met the enemy and he is us"— Pogo. That the trilogy was recorded in reverse order may allude to a kind of circular way of pinpointing the root—the individual.

NEIL The idea for the trilogy was suggested by an older man telling that he didn't think life was ruled by love, or reason, or money, or the pursuit of happiness— but by fear. This smart but cynical guy's position was that most people's actions are motivated by fear of being hungry, fear of being hurt, fear of being alone, fear of being robbed, etc,. and that people don't make choices based on hope that something good will happen, but in fear that something bad will happen. I reacted to this the way all of us tend to react to generalities: "Well, I'm not like that!" But then I started thinking about it more, watching the way people around me behaved, and I soon realized that there was something to this viewpoint, so I sketched out the three "theaters of fear," as I saw them: how fear works inside us ("The Enemy Within"), how fear is used against us ("The Weapon"), and how fear feeds the mob mentality ("Witch Hunt"). As it happened, the last theme was easiest to deal with, so it was written first, and consequently appeared first on record, and the other two followed in reverse order for the same reason. (Backstage Club 1994)

NEIL   The last three albums have each contained a part of that trilogy, and I started thinking about them all at the same time, but they appear in the order in which they were easiest to grasp. "The Enemy Within" was more difficult, because I wanted to look at how it affects me, but it was more than about me. I don't like to be introspective as a rule. I think I'm gonna set that down as my first rule, as "never be introspective!" But, I wanted to, at the same time I wanted to write about myself in a universal kind of way, I want to find things in myself that I think apply. (Jim Ladd Innerview)

"The Body Electric"   Whitman wrote the original poem "I Sing The Body Electric." In binary digits 1001001 is equivalent to the 73 decimal and that is the ASCII equal to the letter "I" (which was banned in the Ayn Rand book *Anthem*). The video borrows images from George Lucas' film *THX 1138* with its numbered prisoners in the future and the scene where the escapee goes up to the surface of the underground prison and sees the sun. The concept is actually from Plato's works, his well-known 'allegory of the cave' where reality as we see it is a shadow of the truth. The humanoid escapee in the song seems to have traces of humanity inside and tries to break free of its programmed existence.

NEIL   The Body Electric is a little piece of science fiction frippery … (Off the Record)

"Kid Gloves"   Written to describe the band's feelings towards the pressures of dealing with their jobs, their fans, their family, and themselves, this song is also a statement about youth.

ALEX   1983 was a tough year for us. The last tour was a grind, and everybody has been going through some changes. Before Peter, we had a couple of other people in mind we wanted to work with, but things got screwed up along the way and there was a bit of a panic. "Kid Gloves" is our response to rolling with the punches during pressure. (Circus)

"Red Lenses"   The 'National Midnight Star' was an SCTV creation, a parody of the tabloids, *The Star* and *National Enquirer*.

NEIL   This was probably the hardest song I have ever worked on … in spite of the pleasure it gave me and how much I enjoyed doing it, it went through so many rewrites and changed its title so many times, everything about it just went through constant refinement, each little image was juggled around and I just fought for the right words to put each little phrase together and to make it sound exactly right to me, so that it sounded a little bit nonsensical. I wanted to get that kind of Jabberwocky word games thing happening with it and also there's little things going on that your mind sort of catches without identifying, like a lot of poetic devices. You take the number of words that sound the same or start with the same letter or whatever, you just certainly don't start in the middle of it and go, oh that's alliteration! (Jim Ladd Innerview)

GEDDY   There are a couple of tracks on the last few records where just before the fade-out, I try to put my two cents in [laughs]. I did that on "Red Lenses." As it's fading out, I like to get loose—it's almost a reaction to being so structured through the whole song. It was the last thing we wrote for *Grace Under Pressure*. Usually the last track we write on each record is different from everything else. It's probably a reaction against working so hard, and all of a sudden you want to do something different to round-out the record, give it some more variety. (Guitar Player 1986)

"Between the Wheels"   Gertrude Stein used the term "lost generation". "Brother, can you spare a dime?" was a catch phrase during the Depression Era (it also was a documentary). The lines that segue to the next album: 'soaking up the cathode rays.'

NEIL   The idea of "Between The Wheels" was really kind of the opposite of "The Digital Man," in a way. And then there's the other side of it, where a person is in harmony with time and their life moves along … well, that's very rare. The opposite of that is the people whose life goes faster than they do, you know. That idea of being in the back water, or watching the action go by, or whatever, to where, the wheels of time—for instance that analogy—some people it picks them up and carries them forward, you know, and it seems to work for them as being mobile wheels. And other people in a real sense, without being too melodramatic, are crushed by those wheels … The wheels of change or time or circumstances or history or whatever just roll right over them … obliterate them … but in the middle, there are the people who are untouched by it and that's what I was getting at was the fact that these people were neither hurt nor helped by it, but it just rolled right by them and they were in a very sedentary position. (Jim Ladd Innerview)

GEDDY   We came into the rehearsal studio and I started playing. The whole song came out in about twenty minutes. We all started jamming and it became a song accidentally, or spontaneously, and then the lyrics were written. (Keyboard)

Power Windows (1985)

THEMES Incarnations/reflections of power in: economy, politics, society, achievement, emotions, dreams.

COVER A shirtless boy wearing pajamas is portrayed in an empty room by a slightly opened window. He is holding a remote and the window. With his remote he literally is turning on the night. Around him are three turned-off tv sets (representing Rush). On the back cover, the same boy is looking at you through binoculars.

GEDDY   The record is, hopefully, an objective look through the windows of power, in various applications. A lot of people think we don't want to talk about human things. We want to talk about technology or space. That's a bit of a misconception because humanity is inherent in some of the things that we're talking about. (MTV News)

GEDDY   It is pretty abstract. I love the scene of this sort of Billy Bibbot-like character confused as to his reality. The windows that he's looking out are in a sense very powerful windows. We are talking about different types of power and the way they affect us, and the way they affect him. The boy is a little shaken as to which way he should look and which window is his reality. (Rockline)

"The Big Money"   The music sounds like it's a game show theme; "Spinning wheels" may refer to game shows like *Wheel of Fortune*. Originally written as "big wheels," the line could refer to people in power.

NEIL   The genesis for that song was from the first book of *The U.S.A.* trilogy written by John Dos Passos in the 1920s. It dealt with the J.P. Morgan loans and the economic causes of World War I. I didn't want the song to be totally in the voice of a cynical anti-corporate reactionary, though, because things like the Ford Foundation do accomplish a lot of good. I mean the church and worthy events like Live Aid are big money, too. (Boston Globe 1985)

"Grand Designs"   The title of this song also comes from Dos Passos: *The Grand Design* is book III of *U.S.A.* Rush intended the song to be about contemporary music, which they felt was becoming increasingly image-oriented and superficial.

NEIL   Very often the guys will have worked out something musically and made a tape of it for which they have nothing particular in mind. 'Grand Designs' was done that way. They had the musical ideas laid out and just made a little tape for me with guitar, keyboards and drum machine, and I had that. (Guitar '86)

"Manhattan Project"   This title was taken from *Midcentury* by Dos Passos, which in turn was taken from the name of the project that built the atomic bomb that was dropped on Japan (the land of the rising sun).

NEIL   I wanted to write about the birth of the nuclear age. Well, easier said than done, especially when writing lyrics, you've got a couple of hundred words to say what you want to say. So each word counts, and each word had better be accurate, and so I found in the case of the Manhattan Project, I was having to go back and read histories of the time, histories of the place, biographies of all the people involved, and that's not without its own rewards, but it's a lot of work to go to write a song—having to read a dozen books and collate all your knowledge and experience just so you can write, you know, if it says the scientists were in the desert sands, well, make sure they were and why, and all that. (Profiled!)

"Marathon" "Heartbreak hill" is a runner's term describing that place in the marathon where a runner needs a second wind to finish. The play on words in the line "first you've got to last" (perfect for the space needed before the chorus starts again) came from Hemingway, who, in turn, adopted it from a motto used by one of Napoleon's marshals.

NEIL [The song] is about the triumph of time and a kind of message to myself (because I think life is too short for all the things that I want to do), there's a self-admonition saying that life is long enough. You can do a lot—just don't burn yourself out too fast trying to do everything at once. Marathon is a song about individual goals and trying to achieve them. And it's also about the old Chinese proverb: 'The journey of a thousand miles begins with one step.' (Canadian Composer)

"Territories" Inspired by the Tour of the Orient, this song brings to mind the "2112" lyric of "let the banners be unfurled," referring to Neil's belief that a person should be a citizen of the world, not a flag-toting nationalist.

NEIL The title comes from an area around Hong Kong called The New Territories. I was struck by the sound of that word, and the territorial instinct. And what with the Northwest Territories being part of Canada, it was just the right sort of word to describe what I was after. As for the opening line about the Middle Kingdom—that's still what China calls itself today. The reason for the Middle Kingdom is because it's a middle between Heaven and Earth. In other words, it's slightly below Heaven—but still above everybody on Earth. Some people look at patriotism or nationalism as being the next best thing to loyalty to your family. I don't buy it. (Canadian Composer)

NEIL I've never had a taste for beer… (Circus 1986)

"Middletown Dreams" Alex tries to create a feeling of suburban isolation here.

NEIL I used the exact thing which "Territories" warns against as a device in "Middletown". I chose `Middletown' because there is a Middletown in almost every state in the U.S. It comes from people identifying with a strong sense of neighborhood. It's a way of looking at the world with the eyeglass in reverse. The first character as based on a writer called Sherwood Anderson. Late in his life, Anderson literally walked down the railroad tracks out of a small town and went to Chicago in the early 1900s to become a very important writer of his generation. That's an example of a middle-aged man who may have been perceived by his neighbors, and by an objective onlooker, to have sort of finished his life and he could have stagnated in his little town. But he wasn't finished in his own mind. He had this big dream, and it was never too late for him, so he walked off and he did it. The painter Paul Gaugin is another example of a person who, late in life, just walked out of his environment and went away. He, too, became important and influential. He is the influence for the woman character of song. The second verse about the young boy wanting to run away and become a musician is a bit autobiographical. But it also reflects the backgrounds of most of the successful musicians I know, many of whom came from very unlikely backgrounds. Most of them had this dream that other people secretly smiled at, or openly laughed at, and they just went out and made it happen. (Canadian Composer)

"Emotion Detector" This song is the sole ballad on the album.

ALEX "Emotion Detector," which we thought would be a breeze, was the killer. It was very, very difficult to get the mood right. I'm still not really sold on that song. It never ended up sounding the way I had hoped it would. (Guitar Player 1986)

"Mystic Rhythms" Chaos theory, circadian rhythms—everything is revolving in the universe to an unknown mystic rhythm. "Canopy of stars" is a term referring to astrological beliefs, another mystic rhythm.

NEIL I don't really believe in astrology, but I don't discount it out-of-hand either. It's one of those things "Mystic Rhythms" talks about—"we suspend our disbelief, and we are entertained." As long as the *President* isn't being guided by astrologers (I know, I know) then it doesn't hurt anybody. (Backstage Club 1990)

NEIL I'm agnostic, but curious, and romantic enough to want it to be true. (1986)

Hold Your Fire (1987)

THEMES Instinct, time, the primitive, fire, drive, meditation, contemplation. Fire symbolizes spiritual strength and the energy at the heart of animal instinct. It represents the desire to annihilate time and bring the end.

COVER Almost blood red in color with three spheres (one for each member of course), this album cover has 'elemental' feeling. The CD and tape included pictures of the band, but the album sleeve included a photo of a man in a suit and hat juggling fire balls (holding his fire). In the background (a miniature set) is a building with the number 15 (15th LP), with Oxford shoes (like the *Waves* cover girl) and newspapers (turn the page). The clock says 9:12 (21:12 military time). The Chinese symbols on the restaurant mean Tai Shan; the "T" in restaurant is not lit, leaving the Latin "res aurant", which may mean "they hear/see things." There's a Statue of Liberty seen in a window (holding her fire) and a hand in the right window with a gun (holding his fire). Visible in other versions of the cover are *RUSH*-logo stenciled road cases to the far left.

NEIL   With the *Hold Your Fire* cover … we confused everything by putting the secondary image first, so that the red spheres reflect the fireballs which appear in the main image, which appears inside. I know it's confusing, but we thought it *looked* nice. The juggler—the "fire-holder"—is a character actor who appears in several films, notably *Tin Men*. (Backstage Club Newsletter 1991)

GEDDY   It's an abstraction that can be taken in so many different ways. Basically, you get a good feeling about the artwork, there's something that clicks about it. The three balls, geometrically and physically create a tension in the way they're suspended. They relate to the balls of fire, as it relates to holding your creative fires. It's all a play on those thoughts and everything associated with them. Sure, you can look at it as three people, three balls, but it's all that and more. (Only Music)

NEIL   I fixed on the idea of people's instincts and temperaments; and the anti-violent side is definitely a part of that. I'm very anti-violence, but I try to avoid the term 'pacifist' because it has too many simplistic, head-in-the-sand connotations. (Boston Globe)

NEIL   I get a lot of response about our most recent album from people who regard the lyrics as highly personal, which is a compliment, but totally untrue in many respects. I deal on the record with a lot of emotions and intimate things and a lot of relationship ideas, but they're all taken from other people. If I chose to write them from the perspective of the 'first person singular', then it was because that was the most effective way of transmitting my thoughts. (Metal Hammer)

Force Ten The tenth song 'forced' on the album refers to the Beaufort Wind Scale.

NEIL   We had written the entire album, and at the last minute we decided that we wanted a different kind of song. So on our very last day of pre-production, we wrote what became the opening song on the album. (Modern Drummer '89)

NEIL   "Force Ten" is about stripping away the barriers between people, learning to face the world without them. (Boston Globe)

Time Stand Still The drum rim clicks are metaphors for clock ticking and the smashing effect symbolizes time stopping. The band called on Aimee Mann for the female voice.

GEDDY   We thought we had the perfect part for a female voice, which I think it was. And, we listened to a lot of records, liked Aimee's a lot and asked her if she would sing on it which she graciously agreed to do." (Off the Record)

Open Secrets The line "That's not what I meant at all" is from T.S. Eliot's poem, "The Lovesong of J. Alfred Prufrock."

NEIL   One thing I particularly hate is confessional lyrics. The one where people where people reach down into their tormented souls and tell me how much they hurt. That's really selfish and petty! (Metal Hammer)

ALEX   For the solo I think it's the mood that's created by the music. I suppose in a way that makes it attached to the lyrics. But it's more the music that provides the trigger for what the solo does. If it's a dark, melancholy sound to that particular song, then the solo will reflect that. An example is "Open Secrets." It has that lonely mood to it from a musical point of view. I think the solo in that song reflects that wailing loneliness. (Guitar '88)

"**Second Nature**"   The second song finished on the album, "Second Nature" is a wiser take on "Closer to the Heart" with a strong ecological argument.

NEIL   "Second Nature" is conciliatory in its message: If we can't reach perfection in this world then let's at least settle for some degree of improvement. Sometimes we have to accept something less than total victory. It's like the difference between compromise and balance. The politician who campaigns for clean air but doesn't want to close down the stinking factory in his area because thousands of people will lose their jobs. My viewpoint is that I'll take as much as I can without hurting other people.

NEIL   To me it seems so obvious that we should wish our cities to be as nice as our forests and that people should behave in a humane fashion—yet this is also clearly a naive and laughable assumption. I want a perfect world and can be bothered to do something about it, yet I can't do it on my own. So, even if you don't want the things that I do, at least let's make a deal and go for some improvement at least. But you shouldn't just scream about it in a song. If you really care about a cause then get involved with people who are doing something about it, people who are self-actuating and are actively working to improve things. That's what I do in my own time, without any clarion call for publicity. I go out into the dirty world. (Metal Hammer)

NEIL   You want to say things in a way that is not only not preachy, but also not boring. So finding the images like 'Second Nature'—I was really fond of that analogy of saying 'we want our homes to be a second nature', you know. That was, taking a common phrase and being able to twist it to say what you want it to say. (Profiled!)

"**Prime Mover**"   This is Aristotle's term for the moving force in everything. Also referred to in *Midcentury* by Dos Passos.

"**Lock and Key**"   The song alludes to *The Heart Is a Lonely Hunter,* a novel by Carson McCullers. Live, Rush showed clips from film *The Last Mile* to illustrate its concept of the killer instinct.

"Mission" This song again addresses the notion of a professional or creative calling, one's mission in life.

GEDDY   It basically grew out of a conversation Neil and I had about the kind of people we consider ourselves to be, people who always knew what they wanted to do in their lives and always had this ambition and desire, but couldn't make a choice as to what to do. It was always very clear that we had to do what we do—whether we were a success or a failure—we knew we would always play music in some way. "Mission" also looks sadly at the people who have never really been sure what they should be doing and have never had a clear cut idea where to put their creative ability to reach a final, ultimate conclusion. (Bass Player)

GEDDY   I think it relates to the creative process, the burning desire to do something and how important it is to keep it, to keep your fire lit, you know, and to keep it going regardless of what you have to persevere, you know, regardless of circumstances I think its important to hold yourself together or stick to your guns basically. Its more relating to the personal inner flame, you know, hold it. As the beginning of the song "Mission" sort of explains. That was the intent and the concept of that particular song and the title of the album." (Off the Record)

"Turn the Page" The terms "Disengaging and enlightenment" in this song are from Buddhist philosophy.

GEDDY   On this tour, I had a major problem with "Turn The Page". It's a very busy bass part, and the vocal part doesn't really relate to it very much. Eventually I got it, but it took a lot of practice. You can do those things, but you have to practice them a lot. You have to split yourself, as they say. Split your hands. Split yourself in two really, and let your hands do something, and let your voice do the other. (Bass Player 1988)

"Tai Shan" This song is about Neil's climb to the top of the Chinese mountain where the natives believe that if you reach the top, you'll live a whole century. Chinese cymbals and Oriental textures set the atmosphere.

NEIL   It's a sampled Shakuhachi flute … I built the drum patterns around the wood-block rhythm that the Buddhist monks use for their chants. Subtle, but a nice touch of authenticity, I think …It is indeed Aimee Mann in there [near the end], only she's not exactly "singing" anything—we took her voice from one of the other songs and played it backwards, just as a nice texture which gave an eerie, pseudo-Chinese sound. And no, this is not backward-masking, or whatever those lunatics call it—there is *nothing* about the devil in there! (Backstage Club 1991)

"High Water" Orchestral arrangements, watery melodies, and synth textures over a wurbling guitar riff open this song about the most dynamic force in nature—water. Man comes from the water in a biological context (saltwater in our veins) as well as a geological and mythological context. The Flood or Great Deluge is referred in the first verse.

NEIL   I always feel comfortable when I'm near water, be it the sound of the ocean or even the refreshing feeling of a dip in the swimming pool. I remember being in the center of one of Japan's biggest cities and the noise pollution was incredible. But right in the middle was this garden with a small waterfall that ran over a bunch of stones. It was designed in such a way that if you sat by the waterfall, the sound of water would drown out all the surrounding noises. I think the Japanese understand the therapeutic nature of water better than most. (Canadian Musician)

A Show of Hands (1989)

COVER   The white, arty cover features characters called the "Rockin' Constructivists" designed by John Halfpenny. "Alternating currents force a show of hands", as the lyrics go in "Prime Mover".

NEIL   Hands perform, and hands respond. Hands gesture, and hands respond. A show of ears and eyes, a show of hearts and minds. A Show of Hands. (Video back cover)

NEIL   Choosing the material was difficult. We didn't want to use anything that had appeared on previous albums, with the exception of "Closer To the Heart", as it had that snappy "improv" bit at the end that we liked, so we decided to put it on. We had to keep the time down to around 74 minutes, and had to be fairly selective about the songs we included. (Backstage Club 1988)

ALEX   There was a feeling that the song had changed a bit. It opens up into a bit more of a ham towards the end. It probably translates better live, visually, than it does on the record. But there is an energy to it, and it's a very positive song. It's been connected with the band for over 13 years. (Guitar Player 1991)

NEIL   When we were coming down to deciding what to put on the tape, whether it be my drum solo or another song, I told them that I would prefer another song … I got a call from the office asking me if I'd like to include the drum solo after all. We only had a certain amount of time on the CD to fit it in with all of the songs we wanted to include, so I went in and killed a lot of the things in the solo that had appeared on earlier recorded solos of mine, so that the listener would have something fresh to hear. For the video, I had even less time for the solo. But I was still very happy with what was presented there, and since I got to decide where to edit it, it was no imposition. (Modern Drummer)

Presto (1989)

COVER On this cover, rabbits overpopulate a hill apparently under a stormy sky (black and white).

THEMES Illusions, dreams, masked feelings, cryptic writings, emotions, changing self-images, subconscious.

NEIL The idea was that these bunnies are taking matters into their own, um ... paws, and making themselves appear from the hat, and flying around in it. (Backstage Club Newsletter 1993)

NEIL *Presto* doesn't have a thematic message. There is no manifesto, although there are many threads and a strong motif of looking at life today and trying to act inside it. (Canadian Musician 1990)

NEIL There are songs on the new album where originally I heard the demo that Alex and Geddy had made with a drum machine. Parts of it might have been recorded to a purely off-the-cuff, moronic drum beat. When I came to work out my own parts for the song, I tried everything. My basic way to work on a song is to try everything I know and then eliminate all of the stuff that doesn't work until I pare it down to something that satisfies me. But there were some parts of some songs that demanded to be simple. And it's a reality that you just have to face. If it works best that way, it's incumbent upon you not to mess it up [laughs]. (Modern Drummer)

GEDDY From the word go, there was an emphasis on strong melodies and rich choruses. We wanted it to be more of a singer's album, and I think you'll notice that the arrangements musically support the vocal. Neil's lyrics to me are a lot more heartfelt. Presently, they're experience-oriented. I think they deal with living, and I find them inspirational because I think they're still ambitious. Whenever he's written something good, I feel it's more emotional." (Canadian Musician 1990)

"Show Don't Tell" The title is a phrase used by story editors. Neil's voice is mixed in low in the background on the lines "I will be the judge / Give the jury direction."

NEIL For "Show Don't Tell" I adopted an attitude and character. I took a stance and a good attitude and developed it. I think it's just a sense of growing power in my own confidence and ability. I hope it reflects growing technique. (Canadian Musician 1990)

"Chain Lightning" Alex is the "that's nice" voice in the end of this tune about the weather.

NEIL   I'm a weather fanatic—I really love weather, and I watch the weather and look for a good weatherman. And, one night I was watching it, and there are two incidents in that song that are synchronicity to one weather report, where the weatherman showed a picture of sun dogs, and described them, and they are just two little points of light that appear at sunset, often in the winter when the sky is clear and crystalline, and they are like little prisms, and they sit about ten degrees north and south of the setting sun, and they are just beautiful little diamonds of light, and often times there's a circle of light—one line—that connects them. So they are a really beautiful natural phenomenon, and I love the name too. 'Sun dogs' just has a great sound to it. And in that same weather forecast, the weatherman announced a meteor shower that night, and so my daughter and I went out on the lake in the middle of the night and watched this meteor shower. So the whole idea of the song was response and how people respond to things, and it's a thing I've found a lot in traveling around the world, too. It's not enough just to travel and see things. You have to respond to them—you have to feel them, and a lot of the thrust of that song is how things are transferred, like chain lightning or enthusiasm or energy or love are things that are contagious, and if someone feels them, they are easily transferable to another person, or in the case of watching a meteor shower, it's made more special if there is someone else there. "Reflected in another pair of eyes" is the idea that it's a wonderful thing already, just you and the meteor shower, but if there's someone else there with you to share it, then it multiplies, you know, it becomes exponentially a bigger experience, so response is a theme that recurs in several of the songs and was one of my probably dominant sub-themes in the writing. (Profiled!)

"The Pass"   Neil addresses teen suicide on this song.

NEIL   There was a lot I wanted to address in that song, and it's probably one of the hardest ones I've ever written. I spent a lot of time on it, refining it, and even more doing research. So with this song it was the same. I felt concerned about it, but, at the same time, I didn't want the classic thing of "Oh, life's not so bad, you know, it's worth living" and all that. I didn't want one of those pat, kind of cliched, patronizing statements, so I really worked hard to find out true stories, and among the people that I write to are people who are going to universities, to MIT, and collecting stories from them about people they had known and what they felt, and why the people had taken this desperate step and all of that and trying really hard to understand something that, fundamentally, to me is totally un-understandable. I just can't relate to it at all, but I wanted to write about it. And the facet that I most wanted to write about was to de-mythologize it—the same as with "Manhattan Project"—it de-mythologized the nuclear age, and it's the same thing with this facet—of taking the nobility out of it and saying that yes, it's sad, it's a horrible, tragic thing if someone takes their own life, but let's not pretend it's a hero's end. It's not a triumph. It's not a heroic epic. It's a tragedy, and it's a personal tragedy for them, but much more so for the people left behind, and I really started to get offended by the samurai kind of values that were attached to it, like here's a warrior that felt it was better to die with honor, and all of that kind of offended me. I can understand someone making the choice; it's their choice to make. I can't relate to it, and I could never imagine it, for myself, but still I thought it's a really important thing to try to get down. (Profiled!)

"War Paint" War paint refers to 'cosmetic makeup' and the psychological masks of youth, but the beat has a powwow kind of tribal beat to it. "The mirror always lies" is a generality and Neil has always said, "all generalities are false, including this one."

"Scars" Neil continues to explore psychological mysteries in this song and to expand his technique using paradiddles.

NEIL   I think it's part of everyone's experience that a certain record reflects a certain period of their life, and that's a pleasurable scar, you know, there's a mark left on you, a psychological fingerprint left by a very positive experience. And music is an easy one, but it translates to so many other parts of life where it's a given that, for instance, the sense of smell is one of the strongest forces in your memory, where a given smell will suddenly conjure up a whole time of your life, and again, it triggers another scar, it triggers another psychological imprint that was left by a pleasurable thing. So it was just, again, the metaphor of scars and using it to say that, as the song does, that these are positive and negative aspects of life that have both left their mark. Trying to make it universal, it's not autobiographical, and I took a whole autobiographical story of my own and made it one line, basically, but there are other things in there, parts of life that I've responded to in a sense of joy, and in a sense of compassion, and there's the exaltation of walking down a city street and feeling like you're above the pavement, and Christmas in New York is the perfect time to feel that, really, where you just get charged up by the whole energy and the positive feelings of it all. (Profiled!)

NEIL   After 20 years of playing, I've developed a lot of things that have proven valuable to me—even the rudiments. The pattern I play with my hands couldn't be played without paradiddles, because I have to have my hands accenting in certain places. Without knowing how to do a paradiddle I couldn't have done that. On this song I was playing eight different pads with my hands in a pattern, while I played snare and bass drum parts with my feet. I had to organize the different sounds on the pads correctly so they would fall in the order I wanted them to. Then I had to arrange all of that into a series of rhythmic patterns, not just one. It was more than a day's work before I even played a note. When Geddy and Alex did the demo, they put all kinds of percussion on the track, including congas, timbales, and bongos. We talked about bringing in a percussionist to play in addition to the drum pattern I might play. I wanted to bring in Alex Acuña, someone who is tremendously facile in that area, who could make the track exciting as well as interesting. I figured he could assign me the simple parts and we could do it together. But then they thought, "What if Neil did it all himself using pads?" It was very satisfying to me to come up with a part that worked by myself. There isn't an overdub on it. When we first played the tape for our producer, he thought I overdubbed the whole thing. Most listeners will probably think that when they hear the song. (Modern Drummer '89)

"Presto" Confucius once cited, "it's better to radiate light than heat."

NEIL   The song "Presto" reflects me and life as a theme, although I invented the scenario. Irony is also a tool I used on this album. Most times I was careful not to dramatize the situation. When you step into true fiction, you use the fiction to explain the truth and reality. (Canadian Musician 1990)

"Superconductor" In this song about pop music icons who target markets, orchestrate illusions, and manipulate reactions on and off stage, the reference to "That's Entertainment!" is a film on musicals.

"Anagram" All the words in this songs are anagrams (words within a word). "Image just an 'I' less game" relates to the album theme of illusion.

NEIL   Mongo is a character in *Blazing Saddles,* and in one scene Sheriff Bart delivers a bomb to him, with the line "Candygram for Mongo!" Thus, "Anagram for Mongo" seemed natural. As for "meaning," that is really the wrong word—it is, after all, a word game —think more of impressions, images, and an internal logic to each line, or each verse. What I was after in that, as in other songs like "Presto" and "Hand Over Fist", is more of a sense of "resonance": so that the listener might feel something, rather than think it with some people it works; with others, it doesn't. (Backstage Club 1991)

GEDDY   Sometimes you want it to be jarring and disjointed and nonsensical. I think it depends on what you're trying to do, and whether you've achieved it in your mind, and whether it actually worked, and "Anagram", I think, did work, even though it's a game—the whole song is a game. The choruses are quite smooth and quite interesting, and they have a nice sound to them and they kind of mock the whole song itself, so I think it was effective there. (Profiled!)

"Red Tide" A red tide occurs when oceans contain too many types of a one-celled organism that colors the water red and kills fish in many numbers. The song also refers to other ecological problems like the thinning ozone layer, the Greenhouse Effect, pollution, and deforestation. The sun and rain will no longer be blessed, the rivers will be lifetakers rather than lifegivers. In Edgar Allen Poe's "The Masque of Red Death," the rich have a masked ball as the Red Death (bubonic plague) ravages the countryside. 'endless winter night' lyric refers to a nuclear winter and may allude to the Dylan Thomas poem, "Do Not Go Gently Into That Good Night."

NEIL It's a bit of a selfish concern, really. I really love wildlife, and I spend a lot of my time in the outdoors when I'm not working, so that's important to me. One of my main hobbies is cycling, so air quality kind of becomes of critical importance. So, with 'Red Tide' it was a little more adamant, because I think the time is a little more critical, and I had to be firmer about it, but still there are ways of getting at it, and to me there are jokes in there, too, that probably no one in the world will ever get, but in the first verse, when I'm talking about 'Nature's new plague' and then 'Lovers pausing at the bedroom door to find an open store' and all that, to me that was obviously referring to AIDS, but it was the irony of modern life, you know, where spontaneous love still certainly does occur, but here are two lovers who have just met in the middle of the night, and they have to go find a store before they can consummate their new relationship, you know, and to me, when I put those things down, I have a smile, but I know that it's one that will never be shared. (Profiled!)

Roll the Bones (1991)

THEMES Chance, fate, random universe, fortune, failure. The title phrase was around for a while in Neil's notebook as he had lifted it from a short story by Fritz Leiber called "Gonna Roll the Bones" (Rockline)

COVER A young kid kicks a human skull walking down an alley paved of dirty dice. On the back cover, three wishbones hover over a sea at sunset. The inner elephant photo refers to the fact that dice is made from the ivory of elepantusks. (on the tourbook inner page's use of skulls spelling out in morse code "remember death")

NEIL The cover art reflects a style of 17th-century Dutch painting called *vanitas*, in which symbols, such as the skull (and also candles, books flowers, playing cards, etc.), were used to remind the good Netherlanders of life's brevity, and the ultimate transience of all material things and sensual pleasures. These paintings sometimes used a latin motto: *"memento mori,"* which translates as "remember death." So, as you can see, this is basically one of those lame intellecto-jokes, the kind that make your brain hurt to think about." (Rush Backstage Club Newsletter)

NEIL If you happen to be born in Chad or Ethiopia (or Bulgaria in the last hundred years), the odds become frighteningly high against you. Sometimes you can improve the odds by the choices you make. That's why "Roll the Bones" I thought was the ultimate title because it is the ultimate statement in spite of all these questionings and thinking of the contingencies and the accidents that can happen in life. You can't remain helpless facing a universe of futility. You got to do something really. You can either do something or not do something. It's both our choice. So I figure, choose the risk, choose the adventure. (MuchMusic)

"Dreamline" Neil had read a book by Kevin Anderson called *Lifeline*, then retitled *The Trinity Paradox* (inspired in part by Manhattan Project) in 1990 that provided some inspiration for this song.

NEIL   Each of us experiences a time when we feel immortal, when time is not passing and we're never going to die. But it's a limited-time offer—time does pass, and soon enough the realities of life comes crowding in on us, whether we're ready for them or not, and we have to get serious. This is called "facing the real world." (Row the Boats)

"Bravado" The inspiration her is Neil's reading of John Barth's *The Tidewater Tales*.

NEIL   We will pay the price but we will not count the cost"—a line from John Barth's *The Tidewater Tales* (1988) (he said I could use it) which echoed around inside me for a long time after I read the book. To me, it just means go for it. (Row the Boats)

GEDDY   That's a pretty emotional song for me. It's one of my favorites that I think we've ever written. Just because it's quite a change … it's quite a different song on the album. It's stands out on the record as being a different texture than most of the other tracks. That line to me says really says so much about the people, really that move the world, you know, the people that go out there and do what has to be done. And they're not worrying about what it's going to cost them personally down the road, they're doing what has to be done, and they're prepared to pay the price for it without worrying about … the payment that comes later." (CD Launch)

GEDDY   Neil's parts are complex, too. Listen to the end of "Bravado". There's an example of limb independence that rivals any drummer, anywhere. The fact that he nailed that in one take blows my mind. In only four days, Neil and I had all the drums and bass parts down. When you record that quickly, you wonder if maybe some ugliness will rear its head two weeks down the road. There were only a couple of little moments that sounded a tad unsteady over all that work; we're able to live without them. Alex did almost all the guitars in about eight days. (Guitar Player '91)

ALEX   The solos in "Ghost of a Chance", "Bravado", and "Roll the Bones" are basically one- or two-take solos played all the way through. When we're developing the arrangement in the writing stages, I toss a solo on tape so we have something to listen to. It's late at night, the lights are down low, and I'm by myself. These were supposed to be throwaway solos, but when it was time to do the "real" solos, Neil

had already adjusted his parts to fit what I'd played. So it came down to me trying to recreate everything—which doesn't work. You might improve the sound,
but even if you play exactly the same notes you'll never capture that magic feel.
The solos in "Ghost of a Chance" and "Bravado" are certainly my favorites on the
record, if not among my favorite solos ever. When I listen to them, I hear the
way I felt at that time. (Guitar Player 1991)

"Roll the Bones"   The game-show theme style is fused with folk guitar, funk,
rock, and rap in this song addressing elemental questions.

NEIL   I was driven to the elemental question of 'Why are we here?' I finally decided
that it was the wrong question … The reason why we're here is because we're
here. There was a big bang and then a universe. Then a fish crawled out of the
sea and walked on land. Then my mother and father got together, and I was
born. It seemed self-evident to me. The real question ought to be 'What can we
do about it?' There is so much tragedy in life that is just chance occurrence."
(Albany Times)

NEIL   We felt intrigued lyrically by what was going on in the better rap tunes and the
timing was right. Rap is a very valid expression of anger, repression, rebellion—
all the things that rock stands for. You see bands like Faith No More incorpo-
rating rap, the Public Enemy/Anthrax collaboration. To us, it wasn't fakery, but
a true expression of where rock has gone in the last few years." (Hamilton
Chronicle)

NEIL   Yeah, that started off as a lyrical experiment for me; I was hearing some of the
better rap writers, among whom I would include like LL Cool J or Public
Enemy, musicality apart, just as writers, it was really interesting. And it struck
me that it must be a lot of fun to do that; all those internal rhymes and all that
wordplay and everything. That's meat and potatoes for a lyricist; it's stuff you
love to do and can seldom get away with being so cute in a rock song. So I
thought, "Well, I'll give it a try," and I submitted actually I think the song "Roll
The Bones" without that section to the other guys and got them to like it, and
said, "Well, I have this other thing I've been working on, and see what you
think." You know, not knowing how they'd respond, but I'd had the fun of doing
it and I've been rejected before; my notebook's full of things that haven't made it
too, so that was the situation there. And they got excited about the idea, but then
how to treat it was the other question, and we did think of trying to get a real
rapper in to do it, and we even experimented with female voices, and ultimately
found that that treated version of Geddy's voice was the most satisfying as creating the persona that we wanted to get across, and was also the most satisfying to
listen to. And with the female voice in it, it wasn't as nice texturally going by,
where Geddy's voice treated like that became a nice low frequency sound, and
you could listen to it just as a musical passage without having to key in on the

lyrics or anything, just let the song go by you. And it was pleasant to the ear, so I think that was probably one of the big factors in choosing that. We'd even been in contact with people like Robby Robertson; we thought we'd like to try his voice on it and had contacted his office, and so on. John Cleese we thought of; we were going to do it as a joke version, get John Cleese in it: "Jack, relax." Get him to camp it up, but again from the musicality and longevity factors, that would have got tired quickly; that's the trouble with jokes. (Radio Special)

GEDDY   I guess that track is something that was influenced by more of the spoken word stuff that is going on, although I can't sit here and say I'm a fan of rap. I like some rap things, but a lot of I don't like. I think there's some of it that's really well done—there are some clever people out there. But it's also not a new influence. People are talking about rap music like it's something new—it's not new at all. It's been around for over a decade, if not always in one form. And there are songs, like "Territories", where we have used a similar kind of thing, although it was never related to rap because it wasn't the music of the moment—so we have used spoken word sections before. This one is written more from Neil's point of view. The lyrics were written very much in concert with contemporary rap music: the way the words react against each other and the structures form more in sympathy with what's going on in a contemporary rap way. To a degree we are having fun with that. We couldn't make up our minds really if we wanted to be influenced by rap or satirize it, so I think that song kind of falls between the cracks and in the end I think it came out to be neither, it came out to be something that is very much us. (Radio Special)

"Face Up"   The song title refers to the cliché of facing up to your problems and to card games where a wild card is turned up or down, ultimately a question of free will and responsibility for your own choices.

NEIL   Turn it up or turn that wild card down. The line that started it all. (Row the Boats)

"Where's My Thing?"   Subtitled Part IV of the "Gangster of Boats" trilogy in reference to a running joke with the band, this song makes no clianm to profundity. Neil has said on Rockline that if the band couldn't come up with a title, he'd call the song 'Gangster of Boats' (which first appeared in the HYF's liner notes).

NEIL   No deep meaning here. Just one of those things people say: "where's that … um … oh you know … where's my-thing?" For once, the lyrics are guaranteed politically correct! As soon as Geddy and Alex would come up with a good musical part, it would fit in with some lyrics I'd just written. This time I outsmarted them. I wouldn't give them anymore lyrics until an instrumental was done. It worked." (Row the Boats)

"The Big Wheel" The allusion here may be to visionary poet William Blake and his *Songs of Innocence and Experience.*

NEIL   It seems to be autobiographical, but it's really not. It's where I've looked for a universal of that trade-off between innocence and experience, and that song certainly addresses that. Not in the circumstances of my own life so much, or if it is, it's not important that it be autobiographical. Very much I want to find universal things that others can relate to, and that's a thing that's part of everyone's life, so I think that's probably one reason why I'm drawn to it. And then so much of it is drawn from observing people around me too, so that becomes a factor in it too; how they responded to life, and how they take to it. How they adapt to that innocence and experience thing. (Radio Special)

"Heresy" Here Neil takes on the question of the fall of the Berlin Wall and the 'end' of communism as a political ideology. Neil brings his African experience to bear upon the rhythm, while Alex introduces a twelve string guitar on the chorus.

NEIL   The deconstruction of the Eastern Bloc made some people happy. It made me mad. It was all a mistake? A heavy price to pay for someone's misguided ideology it seems to me. And that waste of life must be the ultimate heresy. (Row the Boats)

NEIL   One hot night I lay under the stars on a rooftop in Togo [Africa] and I heard the sound of drums from across the valley. Even on the edge of sleep the drumming moved me, the rhythm stayed in my head. (Row the Boats)

ALEX   Occasionally we do things that are slightly out just to give a particular character to the music. On "Heresy" I'm playing my acoustics in the chorus—especially the second chorus—to get a 12-string, Byrds kind of sound. We wanted to create the effect of a bunch of guys sitting around playing who aren't quite in tune. You can hear it in the acoustic—particularly the [Gibson] J-55 whick has a Nashville tuning. Of course you're gonna get that kind of fluctuation anyway when you're playing high up the neck, because the strings are so light." (Guitar Player 1991)

"Ghost of a Chance" One of the few love songs on the Rush catalog, even this one is written with a difference.

NEIL   This is the kind of song we always think ought to be a massive hit single but by this time we've learned that it won't because we're too weird. (Row the Boats)

NEIL   I've always shied away from love songs and even mentioning the word in songs because it's so much cliche, and until I thought that I'd found a new way to approach it, or a new nuance of it to express, I was not going to write one of those kind of songs. "Ghost of a Chance" fit right in with my overall theme of randomness and contingency and so on, but at the same time it was a chance for me to write about love in a different way; of saying, "Here are all these things that we go through in life and the people we meet, it's all by chance. And the corners we turn and the places we go and the people we meet there." All those things are so random and yet through all of that people do meet each other, and if they work at it they can make that encounter last. So I'm saying there's a ghost of a chance it can happen, and the odds are pretty much against it, but at the same time that ghost of a chance sometimes does come through and people do find each other and stay together. (Radio Special)

NEIL   It debunks a lot of the sentimental love songs in saying that love at first sight is not going to last forever and be made in heaven and all that. People drift together by accident, and if they are attracted to each other, that's the easy part. The hard part is making it last. (Orlando Sentinel)

"Neurotica"   In this song, Neil tries to come to terms with our collective neuroses.

NEIL   Some people can't deal with the world as it is, or themselves as they are, and feel powerless to change things—so they get all crazy. They waste away their lives in delusions, paranoia, aimless rage, and neuroses, and in the process they often make those around them miserable too. Strained friendships, broken couples, warped children. I think they should all stop it. (Row the Boats)

"You Bet Your Life"   This song continues the game of chance theme from the album title.

NEIL   If there's a chance, you might as well take it. So what if some parts of life are a crap shoot? Get out there and shoot the crap. We can change the odds, load the dice and roll again. (Row the Boats)

Counterparts (1993)

THEMES   Dualities, love, opposites, pairs.

COVER   This is the first Rush release that doesn't have the title on it. The diagram on the front cover of a nut and bolt going into one another is a sexual metaphor. The back cover is from a *National Geographic* magazine (11-92) article on optical illusions. Inside are pictures of various counterparts as well as familiar phrases.

NEIL   The notebook that I keep running all the time has little phrases or titles or bits from newspapers or conversations, or whatever, that happened to have sparked my interest at the time. So when I sit down to write lyrics, it is an all-day, every-day process, but with a lot of raw material from moments of inspiration. I just start to stitch it together and see what might connect to this, and the theme of dichotomy and the idea of counterparts not being enemies started to be present, but I didn't really have a theme or a title yet until the very end. Even then, *Counterparts* only came out almost as an accident. I was getting desperate for titles, having gone through tons of suggestions from the other guys and not really lighting on anything satisfactory, so I started free-associating through the lyrics and I pulled the word "counterpart" out of the song "Animate". It just stayed on the list, you know, it was okay but it didn't seem to have enough sparkle or pizzazz to be a title, but I just kept coming back to it. When I looked it up in the dictionary and saw how complex its meaning was, that it meant both an opposite and a duplicate, I thought, a-ha! That's what I'm writing about here, that's racism, culturalism, men and women, gays and straights, all of us, we're counterparts because we're the same but we're different. (Aquarian Weekly)

GEDDY The three of us together stands up as a stronger thing than the three of us as individuals … we really see that relationship … that 1 to 1 to 1 as being the total picture. (MuchMusic)

"Animate" Originally conceived as "Duality", this song takes on the role of the opening track about the male and female counterpart in everyone (anima and animus), a concept Carl Jung introduced to modern psychology. Jung's term, "ancient queen," is one of many describing groups of traits in males. Aristotle first used the term in his "De Anima (The Soul)". Neil offers a testimonial of praise for Tom Robbins' book *Skinny Legs and All*, which is about this very subject of reversed sexual roles.

NEIL "Animate" is not about two individuals but about one man addressing his anima—his feminine side, as defined by Carl Jung. Within that duality, what "a man must learn to gently dominate" is himself, his own "submissive trait," while also learning to "gently dominate" the animus—the male thing—and the hormone driven things like aggression and ambition. We dominate by not submitting, whether to brute instinct, violent rage or ruthless greed. (Wilderness of Mirrors)

NEIL (on Camille Paglia, whose research influenced on the lyrics)
Her odyssey has been much like mine. She came out of '60s feminism, so her credentials are sound. Then her study, basically 25 years of scholarship, led her to certain conclusions that people dismiss with a snap. She spends years and years studying something and then says, 'There's this and this difference between males and females,' and somebody says, 'No there isn't.' If somebody's not willing to do the homework on it, then they have no right to the opinion. (Chicago Tribune)

NEIL For "Animate", I used a basic R&B rhythm that I played back in my early days, coupled with that hypnotic effect that a lot of the British bands of the turn of the '90s had—bands like Curve and Lush. The middle section of the tune is the result of the impact African music has had on me, although it wasn't a specific African rhythm. (Modern Drummer '94)

"Stick It Out" Like other 'action' titles ("Show Don't Tell", "Face Up"), this song is quick witted in its word play.

NEIL   It's just a play on the words, really. "Stick It Out" meaning both a kind of arrogant display, "stick it out", but also the endurance thing; if you have a difficult thing to endure, stick it out and you get to the end. It was the pun on both of those, really, so again the duality in the song is a bit leaning both ways. The sense of forbearance, of holding back, and also the idea of fortitude: stick it out, you know, survive. But that was more of a piece of fun, that song I would say, both lyrically and musically it verges on parody, and that was one I think we just had fun with, and lyrically I certainly did, too. "Stick it out" and "spit it out" and all that was just a bit of word play. (Radio Special)

"Cut To the Chase" The line "ambition is the fire" is subliminally heard in the second verse of this song which recalls others from the Rush catalog. The line "Young enough to remember the future" recalls "New World Man"; "chooses an uphill climb" recalls "Marathon"; and "a bearing on Magnetic North" recalls "Prime Mover."

NEIL   Genius is the fire that lights itself. (Burning For Buddy)

"Nobody's Hero" While the song addresses questions of homosexuality and heroism, the focus comes to rest on the qualities of being human with reference again to Nietzsche's *Human, All Too Human.*

NEIL   It is very strong lyrically, about the death of two people, and our perception of heroic ideals. We seem to care for these people who appear to us on screen and in books, and yet we don't know much about them apart from this fake image we idolize. Yet we live amongst people who live heroic but quieter lives, and we don't pay much mind to them, until they are gone. It is a tragic song but we try to leave it with an uplifting feeling of hope. (Radio Special)

NEIL   If people think that discussing homosexuality is controversial, then they've been living under a rock. "Nobody's Hero" will probably polarize people, even though the AIDS issue is only a small part of the lyrical theme, and people will probably jump to conclusions. That's their problem. I don't worry about it, whether it's brave or foolish or whatever. When things affect you, you talk about them and it comes out in your music. You let it fly. I never had the slightest idea that it could be interpreted as controversial until someone pointed it out to me after we'd finished the record. I guess I've always worked in the music business, which is a very tolerant environment. (Raw)

NEIL In a world which is supposed to be so desperate for heroes, maybe it's time we stopped looking so far away. Surely we have learned by now not to hitch our wagons to a "star," not to bow to celebrity. We find no superhumans among actors, athletes, artists, or the aristocracy, as the media are so constantly revealing that our so-called heroes, from Prince Charles to Michael Jackson, are in reality, as old Fred Nietzsche put it, "human—all too human." (Port Boy's Story)

"Between Sun and Moon" This song was co-written with Pye Dubois (Neil and Pye now have Pysart Music Publishing). Dubois had written a poem "There Is a Lake Between Sun and Moon" previously. Lakes are important Egyptian symbols as they represent the occult (water was considered between life and death, formal and informal) and the lake always symbolized self-revelation in its reflective qualities. Phrasing inspired by T.S. Eliot's poem "The Hollow Men," and music inspired by The Who.

ALEX Pete Townshend can make an acoustic sound so heavy and powerful. I've always admired that. On "Between Sun And Moon" there's a musical bridge before the solo that's very Who-ish. I even throw Keith Richards in there. It's really a tribute to the '60s." (Guitar Player 1993)

"Alien Shore" Alex had appeared on the album *Alien Shores* by Platinum Blonde eight years before. The voice in the beginning is Alex holding his nostrils closed, saying "out of my nose."

NEIL Dualities like race or sex are not opposite but true counterparts—the same yet different—and not to be seen as some existential competition. Polarities are not to be resisted but reconciled. Reaching for the alien shore. (Wilderness of Mirrors)

"The Speed of Love" Neil takes another tack on writing a love song here, this time demythologizing the whole notion of a love song, with reference to Frank Zappa.

NEIL "The Speed Of Love" is kind of a mid-tempo, more sensitive rock song. That song probably took me the longest to find just the right elements I wanted to have in a drum part. What made it a challenge is that I wanted the feel and the transitions between sections to be just right. I played that song over and over, refining it until I was satisfied. I don't think a listener will hear all the work that went into that track. (Modern Drummer)

NEIL I just saw one of Frank Zappa's last interviews the other day, and he was talking about love songs, and the reason he would never write one is he thought they were essentially evil. And that they raise this imaginary ideal of a perfect relationship which doesn't exist in reality. And that's what songs like "Cold Fire" have to do with, is trying to tell a song about love—not a song of love. And "Speed of Love", actually, and "Cold Fire" are both the same that way, they're songs about love, about the subject of it. Again, demythologizing, debunking. (Up Close '94)

"Double Agent" In this song alluding to another T.S.Eliot poem, Alex cleverly plays a kind of secret agent/spy riff during the verses.

NEIL "Wilderness of mirrors" is a phrase from T.S.Eliot's "Gerontion" and was also applied by former CIA counterintelligence chief James Jesus Angleton to describe the world of espionage—hence the twist on "Double Agent", reflecting the clandestine workings of dreams and the subconcious. (Wilderness of Mirrors)

NEIL I noticed that sometimes if I had a difficult decision to make I'd be weighing up the pros and cons, and my conscious mind would be doing a lot of thinking and worrying, and then suddenly one morning I would wake up, and I would know what to do. And a friend of mine was working on a book about the secret war between the CIA and the FBI and asked me to be his reader, as it were, as he went along. So in reading that, I read a whole bunch of books on background of the CIA and the KGB, and all this stuff, and got totally into the world of espionage. So I thought of using the imagery of espionage, and the whole romance of cloak and dagger, and the third man. (Up Close)

GEDDY "Double Agent" was a complete exercise in self-indulgence, and really, it was one of the last things we wrote on the record, and we just kind of—we'd written all these songs that were heavily structured, and, you know, were crafted and meticulously worked on: this note and that note, and this is a song we just wanted to kind of get our ya-yas out and just have a bit of a rave. And really, it's one of the goofiest songs I think we've ever written, but I'm quite happy with the result. In its own way, I think it's an interesting little piece of lunacy. (Radio Special)

"Leave That Thing Alone!" This instrumental is a kind of a "Where's My Thing?" sequel.

GEDDY Alex and I record all our jams and many times those happy moments where we really start grooving get dissected and transformed into songs. Jamming is really a recess. I think the instrumental "Leave That Thing Alone" is the best thing we've ever written. (Guitar School)

ALEX Geddy had this little keyboard thing for the choruses and I had this clean verse thing kicking around from the last tour. It's a song that goes through many moods and creates nice colors. The solo was from my original Alesis ADAT version: just a solo I threw on, but it fit. It has almost a Celtic flavor. (Guitar School)

NEIL "Leave That Thing Alone" is built around R&B bass/drum interplay. But to make it original I had to change up parts. In the second verse I go into a Nigerian beat, like something you'd hear on a King Sunny Ade record. Later in the song I go into a quasi-jazz pattern, and all these things are introduced for our own entertainment as well as to make the piece more interesting." (Modern Drummer)

"Cold Fire" The contradictory title for this song is taken from *The Jitterbug Perfume* by Tom Robbins.

NEIL In "Cold Fire" I have the woman speaking to the man and *she's* smarter than he is. It was a difficult technical challenge lyrically, but those are the kind of things that now, after all these years, you start to feel you have the craft to take on. I don't mind writing about love now, where I would have avoided that in the previous years just because of the inability to get beyond cliches. (Network)

NEIL Along with Frank Zappa, I think that love songs are not only dumb, they're also actively harmful. They invent this fantasy that people expect their own relationships to live up to, and when they don't they result in divorce and low self-esteem and sense of failure and all that, so it's not healthy. Trying to express how a relationship really works, I invented characters and invented a situation and personalized it. Made it like a conversation between two people, of whom the woman is the smarter of the two, and made a complex little personal story. (Aquarian Weekly)

"Everyday Glory" This is the first reference to child abuse in Rush lyrics and is connected in theme with "Nobody's Hero".

NEIL The role models that we really need are to be found all around us, right in our own neighborhoods. Not some remote model of perfection which exists only as a fantasy, but everyday people who actually show us, by example, a way to behave that we can see is good, and sometimes even people who can show us what it is to be excellent. I have found, in all the neighborhoods of the world, that the heroes still outnumber the villains. (A Port Boy's Story)

Test For Echo (1996)

THEMES communication (tv, media, internet), barriers, time.

COVER The runes on the album are Arctic Inuit meaning "Echo … we are watching/listening for it." The cover features a stone structure resembling a human figure in the snow with three radio telescopes or satellite dishes in the back cover. The Inukshuk figure is supposed to be like the type Eskimos build as guides in the snow. The portraits inside are photos of Rush as kids (a trend in mid-'90s alternative rock albums). Brought to you by the letter R-r-r-r.

GEDDY [Neil] did a bike trip to Alaska … when he was there, he saw these Inukshuks which is the figure on the cover of the album. He locked in on it way back then and there was so much snow when we were making the record. (New Music)

NEIL Of all the titles we considered, 'Test For Echo' was the most evocative. Everybody needs some affirmation to know they're not alone, an echo. It was also a beautiful metaphor for us because we've been away for awhile, so we're saying, "Is anyone out there?" (Connecticut Post)

GEDDY Every album seems to have its own thing we lock in on. This album we locked in on stupid inspirational slogans. The key one, of course, was "Individually we are a ass, together we are a genius," which you have to take in the right light. And stuff like, "If you want something done right, just forget it. (T4E Premiere)

ALEX Geddy and I both were on such a roll that we didn't want to break it up. Every time we started writing something, we started another song. So we got four or five songs into pretty good shape and then played them for Neil. Consequently, he didn't hear anything for about a week, so he was panicking a little. We were very productive but he was wondering if we had a [writer's] block or something. (Canadian Musician 1996)

ALEX It just sounds like the guitars are in the right place—very present and quite bold but not overpowering anything. You can still hear everything clearly. (Guitar)

"Test For Echo" Co-written with Geddy, Alex, and Pye Dubois.

NEIL The lyrics to "Test For Echo" give a video-view of this wacky world of ours and offer this tacit response: "Excuse me, does anybody else think this is weird? Am I weird?" While the answer to those questions may be "Yes!', it's good to know that you're not the only one, you're not alone." (Canadian Musician 1996)

GEDDY … a kind of absurd thread that I like a lot. Nothing makes any sense. I like the fact that there's some nice melody and some confusion and a manic nature, and yet there's lots of space." (Canadian Musician 1996)

"Driven" This cautionary song about drunken driving emphasizes the theme of communication.

LEE "Driven" is just from a bass player's point of view. I wrote that song with three tracks of bass. I brought it to Alex and said, "here's the song; I did three tracks of bass but I just did it to fill in for the guitar," and he said, "let's keep it with the three basses." So I said, "I love you." (Canadian Musician 1996)

"Half the World" This song title refers to the differences between the geographical hemispheres and the attitudes of their residents.

GEDDY "Half The World" is one of our finest moments as songwriters as far as writing a concise song without being wimpy or syrupy. It's got a little bit of everything; nice melody, and yet it's still aggressive. It's hard for us to write that kind of song, really. You'd have to go back to "Closer To The Heart" to find an example of that. (Canadian Musician 1996)

"The Color of Right" The title refers to an expression used by lawyers. Alex plays a mandola in a main melody.

"Time and Motion" The "Between Sun and Moon" of this album, this song recalls the mystic rhythms ("The mighty ocean dances with the moon") and also "Chain Lightning".

"Totem" The line "Sweet chariot, swing low, come to take me home" is from a traditional gospel song.

ALEX The choruses in "Totem" are really interesting. I created a soundscape by using harmonics with a kind of Celtic melody over it that's quite distant. In the song, in terms of dynamics, it's a really beautiful shift … There's this line, "angels and demons inside my head," that was very visual to me, it's almost angelic. You can sort of see this imagery swirling around. (Canadian Musician 1996)

GEDDY I believe that the traditional concept of God is one that I'm not comfortable with. To borrow from Woody Allen—"If there is a God, he's an underachiever at best." For me, spirituality is a personal belief and I think it's up to each person to choose a road that is comfortable for them. I think it's really an individual viewpoint. Having grown up in a very religious home, I find the dogma and constrictions of organized religion not appropriate for my belief system. But, I'm not so arrogant as to believe that I have the answers to these questions. (Canoe Online Chat)

"Dog Years" The title comes from the novel of the same name by Gunther Wilhelm Grass. People look to Sirius, the Dog Star constellation named after the hunting dog of Orion in Greek mythology. The line "Every dog will have its day" originated from *Water Babies* by Charles Kingslay.

NEIL Certainly the listener is welcome to take it just as a piece of throwaway foolishness. Even the story of its writing is kind of amusing, because it was right when we got together for the first time, the three of us, after quite a long break apart. We did a little celebrating the first night and the following day I was a bit the worse for wear, and a little dull-witted, and I thought, "Gee, I don't think I'm going to get much done today, but I'm a professional, I'd better try." So I sat down all muzzy-headed like that and started trying to stitch words together— that's what I was there for, after all. "Dog Years" is what came out of that kind of mentality, and born of observations over the years too, of looking at my dog thinking, "What's going through his brain?" and I would think, "Just a low-level zzzzz static. Food. Walk." When I look at my dog that's how I see his brainwaves moving. (T4E Premiere)

"Virtuality" The verse "To the see the world in a grain of sand, and heaven in a flower, hold infinity in the palm of your hand and eternity in an hour" comes from William Blake. Alex's guitar in the chorus tries to simulate a modem initializing online.

GEDDY   Neil is quite negative about the web. For emailing and gathering information, it's great. But I think commercial exploitation is pretty bogus. Do you really want to spend twenty minutes of your life downloading a picture of sparkling water from some website from a water company or waiting twenty-five minutes to download naked shots of the girls of Texas A & M? Whose life is so empty that they spend time downloading this bullshit? (Music Revue)

GEDDY   I think he's more skeptical than cynical about the rush to embrace the benefits of the Net. I can't say that I agree with him on that front. The song "Virtuality" deals with that and, you know, in one sense I disagree with what the song says and, in the other, I kind of understand that point of view. So I can do the song even though I don't wholly agree with it. There is an aspect of it (the Net) that, like anything, can be abused, that can be a waste of time. But the benefits are tremendous—if you're researching something, it's out there. (Bassics 1997)

NEIL   I've become the Salman Rushdie of the Internet for daring to poke fun at it. I have some friends who use the Internet productively, but for the most part, it's the worldwide wank. But I think the Internet is a pale imitation, just like virtual reality is a pale imitation of reality. As compared to reading a book or what rock music is to an adolescent, these are deep things. There is no way the Internet can replicate that or come close to approximating it. (San Jose 1996)

NEIL   When I think about traveling to places … thinking how would you translate Palermo, Sicily or Abidjan, Ivory Coast to virtual reality … the first thing they'd do would be to take away the smells, the garbage, and defunkify it all, make it all Disneyfied. What happens in an email relationship or something is that imagination, of course, is called upon to make it come alive. Imagination is a wonderful thing, but it's also slightly dangerous because it invites illusions. I love the image that verse opens up with, seeing a woman's face through the window in the rain; that's a really romantic image. I've had that experience, seeing a woman driving by in a car, or if I'm driving by and see a woman in the window, it's a beautiful thing. The same experience if I'm riding my bicycle down the road and a car goes by, sometimes I'll smell a woman's perfume. Imagination, though, is a little bit of sense input, but the rest of it if you put anything more into it, it's just imagination. All I was pointing out there is here's a romantic little image that is imagined, so let's not pretend that it's real. You cannot feel the voltage from her fingertips, but you can imagine it. That's all I was trying to say. (T4E Premiere)

"Resist" Originally called "Taboo" (following "Totem" as in *Totem and Taboo* by Sigmund Freud), this song has a simple structure like "Bravado" (with piano recalling "War Paint.") The line "I can resist any thing except temptation" is from Oscar Wilde's play *Lady Windermere's Fan.*

GEDDY   "Resist" is one of the best songs we've written … I knew from the beginning that this was a special Rush song just by the kind of energy that came from all of us when we wrote and recorded it. (Canadian Musician 1996)

"Limbo" This free-form instrumental was born from outtakes that were in 'limbo'. "What ever happened to my Transylvania twist?" is sampled from Bobby "Boris" Pickett and the Crypt Keepers' "Monster Mash". These references may have been inspired by the Frankenstein-like arrangement.

GEDDY   This song is not about a dance or a fat guy … (T4E Tour intro)

ALEX   Absolutely nothing to do with Rush Limbaugh. We wouldn't write a song that had anything to do with him. We just thought it was fun, the play on words of "Rush Limbo." We had a lot of fun doing that as we always do with instrumentals, it was a last minute thing with that song, as most of our instrumentals are. It was written very late in the writing stages, we were already into pre-production, Neil was already working on all his drum parts for all the other songs when we dumped it in his lap and said, "Here's another one for you to learn!" As late as doing the rhythm tracks in the studio, we were still making arrangement changes on that song. So it was last-minute, which was kind of fun. The pressure was on, it was essential that we put it together in that given time. (T4E Premiere)

"Carve Away the Stone" The subject of idols (as in "Totem") comes up again in the line "make a graven image with some features of your own." In Greek mythology, Sisyphus was al wicked king whom the gods punished by having him push a giant rock up and down a hill in Hades—every time he'd get it to the top of the hill it would roll back down.

Retrospective (1997)

COVER   The red suit on the janitor sweeping the floor recalls the cover of *Moving Pictures* with the movers. Maybe he is inside a gallery of the fictitious museum from that album …

Different Stages (1998)

COVER The front cover is white with a tinker toy (with three wheels). The inside features an amusing backdrop of the Hammersmith Odeon with superimposed shots of Geddy scalping tickets in front, Alex being carried away in a strait jacket, and Neil peering out a window at it all.

ALEX *All the World's a Stage* certainly sounds just like the concerts did: very raw and explosive. With *Exit … Stage Left*, we got a bit fancy in the studio and made it sound more like a live studio recording. We cleaned it up so much that the recording didn't have, at least for me, the same kind of energy that a live show really does have or should have. *A Show of Hands* was a step in the right direction, but I don't think we really achieved it with that record either. When you put this record on, however, you feel like you're there. You can hear people talking in the first few rows and it's got toughness, body, bottom-end, and plenty of energy. (GuitarOne)

Solo Albums

Victor

ALEX I was pretty nervous about writing lyrics. I hadn't done it in about eighteen years, and I don't remember it being a particularly great experience. I was afraid I couldn't do it, and that it would sound a little corny, or whatever. But, once I settled on thematically what I wanted to do with it, it seemed to come fairly quickly. (Rockline)

ALEX They won't expect this kind of record from me … the lyrical content is dark and there's a real unsettling feel to the record. I'm a pretty happy, outgoing person. I want to create that kind of turnaround. I want to surprise people. (Rag 2-96)

"Shut Up Shuttin Up"

ALEX I got my wife, Charlene, and her best friend, Esther, who's a real character, in to do this little bit of nagging about the funny little habits that some of us have, and the silly little things that we argue about that end up becoming big things in the overall picture. We had them in there for about seven hours going through so many different things, and they were well lubricated with a couple bottles of wine. By the end of it, of course, we couldn't get them to shut up. (Rockline)

Geddy Lee: My Favorite Headache

GEDDY I have a little work book that I carry around, jotting things down all the time. Lyric writing is a bit of natural extension for me, because I am pretty damn opinionated … I write in bed a lot when the house is quiet and I have been thinking about stuff all day and at the end of the day there are conclusions and realizations. I look for that sudden clarity, and I put it down so when I come back later I can see if it still makes any sense. (Canadian Musician 2000)

"My Favorite Headache"

GEDDY Title was originally born out of a conversation Ben Mink was having with his father. His father made the comment about his mother that she was having trouble dealing with something and said, "By the way, she gets the favorite headache." Ben told me that story and after I stopped laughing, I realized that what an irony that was—the contradiction built into that phrase—having something that you love to do but it makes you crazy to do it! This for me describes the creative process to a T and my relationship with music, which is why I thought it an appropriate title for the album. (Barnes and Noble Online Chat)

GEDDY Sometimes its anger about philosophical differences. Sometimes its things I see in the universe that perplex me, attitudes that anger me, and things that I ponder. (Canadian Musician)

"The Angels Share"

GEDDY Me imagining what if the heavens were full of characters designed to interfere with our lives as opposed to help them? And I mean this in a playful way of course. And the chorus speaks to the frustration of that mischief. (Barnes and Noble Online Chat)

GEDDY I was thinking about the history of the concept of angels and how often the existence of angels on human life that come up in folklore. (TV Guide online)

"Runaway Train"

GEDDY "I was thinking about some of my friends who have difficult domestic situations. Sometimes you need a little nudge. They hold the key to their lives." (Rockline)

"Moving To Bohemia"

GEDDY We wanted an aggressive, sort of Russian attitude from real strings, so Ben studied the works of Russian composers before he wrote the parts. (Bass Player)

"Slipping"

GEDDY "Slipping" is a bit of an apology for things that have gone on in my life and a confession about my fallibility. And in spite of all my best intentions, sometimes,

I screw up. And I thought this was something that most people could relate to."
(TV Guide Online)

"Grace To Grace"

GEDDY   "Kind of inspired by my mom's life. She's a Holocaust survivor who along with most of members of my family came over after the war and they went through their own private hell. She's conducted her life in a completely elegant and heroic way. She had most of her dreams stolen from her as a child and there's so many people like her that have gone through tragedies or wars or whatever and they pick up and they just carry on. (Rockline)

Unlike some artists who refuse to let go of trademark instruments, Rush's instruments of choice changed as their styles and attitudes did, partly the result of the band's desire to grow and progress, partly the result of industry movements. They purchased their gear in 1974 with a record label advance, and for the most part the band was satisfied with the results they were getting for a few years. By the end of the 1970s, Rush's stage gear included analog synthesizers and concert percussion in an effort to become "the world's smallest symphony orchestra," as Geddy jokingly remarked to various magazines during that time.

The '70s fat bass lines and crunching guitar riffs were replaced by a more trebly bass sound and a more textural guitar approach in the '80s, augmented by the highest-end digital equipment and even electronic percussion. In the early 1980s at the height of the band's popularity and visibility, the band secured endorsements with various instrument companies. In the 1990s, the band returned to the heavy beginnings of their sound with synthesizers (unfortunately) kept to a minimum. As makes and models were discontinued, the band rode the wave of changes. Gear changes as fast as music trends.

Rush members still endorse some of the best names in gear, and still influence young musicians (and copycats) to purchase the same makes and models, in the quest to get that unmistakable and inimitable Rush sound.

Alex Lifeson

Alex Lifeson has admitted to admiration over the years for Steve Howe (Yes and Asia), Allan Holdsworth, David Lindley, Edge (U2), Andy Summers (Police), Edward Van Halen (Van Halen), Rory Gallagher, Soundgarden, Queensryche, Metallica, Pearl Jam, Smashing Pumpkins, Nine Inch Nails, and Alice in Chains. He has also expressed his pleasure in listening to classical guitar music.

ALEX I enjoy listening to Segovia and John Williams is, I think, my favorite. I also like Julian Bream, especially his lute music. I'm just starting to get into people like Paco de Lucia, Christopher Parkening, Liona Boyd, and Carlos Montoya. I remember seeing Montoya in concert, and I was totally blown away; his stuff is just unbelievable. I really enjoy listening to that music, but I don't consider myself to be a classical guitarist. I'd have to really concentrate on it for a long time, and I don't have the opportunity to do that now. (Guitar Player 1980)

ALEX Steve Howe [Yes, Asia], to some extent, was an influence. He's just such an incredible guitarist that I don't think you can't be influenced by him and his attitude and ability to do so many different things. Steve Hackett [Genesis] also was important to my growth; he has such a beautiful, controlled style and a feel for textures in his playing. But now Allan Holdsworth is my main man. I've only heard the stuff he's done with UK and with [ex-Yes drummer] Bill Bruford—his first two albums—and I especially like his use of the vibrato arm. It's not like the typical wang wang stuff a lot of players do. Allan uses it so tastefully, and uses it in conjunction with bending notes and moving around the fingerboard. I also like his tone; to me it sounds at times very much like a saxophone …"Win This Record" by David Lindley is a real favorite of mine. I really like listening to that. He's such a happy guitarist. I think I've assimilated a lot of styles and influences … I've tried to develop a style that combines broad arpeggios and suspended chords. (Guitar Player)

ALEX Andy Summers [The Police] has a good sense of combinations and selections of notes. His playing fits well into the context of their songs. Edge from U2 is right up front, an aggressive, straight-ahead, all-out player. Adrian Belew [King Crimson, Frank Zappa, Talking Heads] is the Carl Sagan of guitarists. With him, it's not only the selection of notes but also the selection of sounds. Midge Ure from Ultravox has a sense of feel that I like. I like the way his guitar sounds take up space. (Guitar 1984)

Alex on constructing guitar solos:

ALEX I like to play about eight or ten tracks of solos, and then I get kicked out of the control room [laughs]. Everybody sort of dives in. Geddy likes to really get into doing that. He and the engineer sit down, and Neil makes some suggestions. Of course, the producer is there, too, and they piece together a solo. I come back in after a couple of hours when they have something assembled, and if I like it, then we either stick with it or we keep that as a starting point and go for another whirl over some of the older tracks. (Guitar Player 1986)

ALEX Solos are a funny thing. Many solos I record at the demo stage make it to the final mix. I tend to be a perfectionist, but I've come to realize my best work is spontaneous. An unrehearsed solo may not be particularly in time or in tune, but it can possess an emotional quality that's very difficult to recapture. At this point, I'd rather live with some technical imperfections. (Guitar Player 1993)

On practice:

ALEX   I normally put the guitar down for a few months after finishing a record or tour. I asked Eric [Johnson] recently, "Do you ever put your guitar down for more than a day or two?" He said "man, after we finish a tour, I won't play for a month." I felt like [clenches fists] "Yes! Excellent!" (Guitar School 1994)

ALEX   When I pick it up again, I really stink. It takes me a while to get back into shape, but in the process, I start playing things I never would have thought of before. I discover different styles. My greatest enjoyment is sitting alone in my home studio, playing through my amp with a really great sound. Not working on a song, just playing. I get completely lost and the hours fly by. I still do it, after all these years. (Guitar Player 1993)

In September 1968 in the first stages of Rush, Alex bought a new tobacco sunburst Gibson ES-335 , part of the semi-hollow ES series (rosewood fingerboard and mahogany neck) to replace his psychedelic Conora guitar. He gave this guitar custom Pyramid pickups until the recording of *2112* and rewired it to mono.

ALEX   A little while later I bought a '63 Fender Stratocaster with vibrato … that guitar was sitting in a friend's closet for two or three years before I got it. It was brown, and it didn't look very nice, but it was a neat instrument. I recall taking it in to get some work done on it: when I got it back it never sounded right again, so I got rid of it. After that, the 335 was my only guitar for a long time. (Guitar Player 1980)

Adding a Marshall 50-watt head and one 4″¥12″ cabinet, he finally had a setup he stuck with. His effects included a Fuzz Face distortion, a Maestro phaser, a Crybaby wah-wah pedal, and an Echoplex. Alex used Dean Markley strings .009-.048 and Kay white nylon medium picks.

ALEX   For a while I went from a.010 on the high E to a .052 at the bottom, so it was really heavy. At one time I even had a .042 bottom E, but neither that or the .052 ever felt quite right. With the .048 it feels just perfect—I can pull the low E or A string if I want, which I do in a couple of spots in "Soliloquy Of The Soul" [from *2112*]. (Guitar Player 1980)

Alex's first home studio console in 1982 was an analog Mackie 32-8, then later upgraded to a 24E. In 1998, he got a Mackie D8B.

ALEX   It's in constant use between Adrian and I. I have to book time in advance just to mess around with it. (Mackietone News 2000)

Albums & Tours

Rush Album (1974)

GUITARS Gibson ES-335. Alex used a rented Rickenbacker 360 12-string acoustic on "Before and After".
AMPS Marshall JMP 50-watt half stack.
EFFECTS As above.

Rush Tour (1974) (w/Neil Peart)

Alex added a second Marshall amp making two stacks of 4×12″ cabinets.

ALEX We got an advance and went out and did some shopping at Long & McQuade Music [459 Bloor St. W., Toronto]. We went crazy, saying, "I'll take that guitar and those amps. He'll take those drums." It's something you dream about for years and years, and we actually got to do it. I bought a Marshall 50-watt amp and a '74 Les Paul Deluxe. About that guitar. I bought it right off the shelf and I must not have been thinking clearly because when I got it home and started to play it, it was a mess. I had it in a heat press on three different occasions, and its neck was just really screwed. That guitar didn't sound right, the intonation was never right, and it would never stay in tune. Eventually I traded the Deluxe in for a '74 cherry sunburst Les Paul Standard in Atlanta, which I still have at home. Then I got another '74 Les Paul Standard with a tobacco finish in '76, and I used it on our live album *All The World's A Stage*. (Guitar Player 1980)

Fly By Night Album and Tour (1975)
Caress of Steel Tour (1975)

GUITARS 335. Gibson Les Paul Standard (maple neck, rosewood fingerboard, pearl trapezoid inlays) for the slide part on "Making Memories", which was done using a metal lipstick container.
STUDIO GUITARS Rented black 335 in the Fly By Night videos. A borrowed Martin steel string acoustic for "Making Memories" and for the acoustic overdub on "Fly By Night". Rented Rickenbacker 360 12-string acoustic for "In the End".
STRINGS Dean Markleys in .009, .011, .014,.028,.038 and .048 light gauge.
STUDIO AMPS The Marshall and a Fender Super Reverb.
EFFECTS Alex used a Morley Volume/Echo pedal he would keep for future albums.

ALEX   While I play slide very seldom now, when we first started out I used to a lot on my 335. People such as Jimmy Page on "You Shook Me" and Jeff Beck on *Truth* influenced me the most and their styles reflect the way I like to play slide. (Guitar Player 1980)

Caress of Steel Album (1975)

GUITARS 335. Rented Fender Stratocaster on "Lakeside Park". Rented 10-string Fender pedal steel for bridging part of "The Necromancer". A borrowed classical guitar on "Panacea".
AMPS Same as on *Fly By Night*.

ALEX   I don't remember the tuning. Actually, that was the only time I've ever picked steel guitar. I don't really know how to play one. (Guitar Player 1980)

2112 Album (1976)

GUITARS 335. Les Paul Std (for lead parts). Black '76 Fender Stratocaster on "2112" (maple neck; until 1978 will have stock pickups). Alex also ordered a '76 Gibson ES-355 in cream custom finish (Maestro vibrato arm, gold hardware, occasional red sparkle pickguard and block inlays) that he wouldn't use until next studio album.
NEW ACOUSTIC GUITARS Gibson Dove 6-string in cherry sunburst (spruce top, square shoulder body, maple neck, Indian rosewood fretboard, mother-of-pearl parallelogram inlays and dove inlaid pickguard). Gibson B-45 12-string in sunburst (dot inlays).
STRINGS Augustine strings on classical guitars. Martin light-gauges on steel strings.

ALEX   It's always been hard for me to get used to playing a Stratocaster because of its neck and where the volume control is positioned. I don't have anywhere to rest my hand. With the Gibsons, especially the 335 and the 355, I can grab the facing around the rear pickup or just grab the bridge and rest my hand on the guitar while I'm playing. With the Fender I couldn't do that, and the volume control is so close to the pickup and bridge that it was really hard for me to get comfortable. In addition, the neck is a lot smaller on the Strat, and it feels alien to me especially after playing Gibsons for so long. But I eventually got a new black one a few years ago to replace my 335 as a second guitar, which sort of forced me in to getting used to it. (Guitar Player 1980)

ALEX   It drove me crazy trying to get used to the Strat's maple neck and fretboard, and there was so much lacquer on it when I bought the guitar that it was quite difficult to handle. I've had all the finish removed to where it's now bare wood, but the Stratocaster still doesn't sustain like the 355. (Guitar Player 1980)

AMPS Same but with a Fender Twin Reverb added.

2112 Tour (1976–77)

GUITARS In addition to the 355, a '74 Gibson Les Paul Standard in cherry sunburst was brought out on the road with Pyramid pickups which were later switched back to the stock pickups.

ALEX With the Pyramid pickups there was a really tough, compressed sound, which I like. The only problem with them was they were just too powerful; I couldn't get the clean sound I wanted for quieter things. (Guitar Player 1980)

All the World's a Stage Album (1976)

GUITARS Tobacco Les Paul Standard exclusively with amps and effects from previous tour.

All the World's a Stage Tour (1976–77)

GUITARS In addition to the Les Pauls, Alex added a cherry red Gibson EDS-1175 12/6-string doubleneck in 1976 while in Nashville (mahogany body/neck, rosewood fretboard, slashed-block inlays and PAF humbuckers). This would be used on "Xanadu".

A Farewell To Kings Album (1977)

GUITARS '76 Gibson ES-355 in custom cream finish, with ebony fingerboard rewired to mono, as seen in the videos for "Closer to the Heart" and "A Farewell To Kings". Gibson ES-335. Gibson EDS-1275 in Alpine White in addition to the red 1175 ("Xanadu"). Fender Stratocaster. '71 Ramirez classical. '77 Gibson J-55 jumbo-body acoustic (antique natural finish, spruce top, mahogany neck, mother-of-pearl dots). '77 Epiphone C-60 classical guitar. '77 Gibson BG-50 mandolin (on "Madrigal"). Custom-built Pyramid solid body electric (walnut and maple laminations, single-piece body and neck, ebony fingerboard, stainless steel frets, and phase and coil-splitting switches), which wouldn't actually be used until 1979 during the recording of *Permanent Waves*.

AMPS H/H (from the Heinl Music Corp., based in Ontario) 100w heads driving Marshall 4×12 bottoms with a Roland JC-120 amp used on "Madrigal".
EFFECTS Roland Boss Chorus.

ALEX   I've rewired everything to mono. In this sort of application I couldn't see using it as a stereo unit. If I was in a quieter band with more instruments, I'd use that capability more. I do, however, like the sounds you can get with the selector switch. But for most of the set I have it in the number 1 position, so everything's at full power. Last summer I put on a microswitch: I can preset the guitar's selector switch to, say, 3, and then by flicking the microswitch I can return to full power—the number 1 position—rather than having to turn the selector. (Guitar Player 1980)

ALEX   Actually, my white Gibson is relatively light for a double-neck guitar. My old cherry finish double-neck seems much heavier than my white one. (Guitar Player 1980)

A Farewell To Kings Tour (1977–78)
Archives Tour (1978)

GUITARS 355 became Alex's main guitar on stage, though the Les Paul Std. made appearances for "2112" and other songs from that album. Both double-necks were touring until the 1175 was damaged. It was rebuilt, painted black, then given to Eric Johnson as a gift in 1991 during the Roll the Bones Tour (then it was later stolen!). Alex was also touring with a black ES-345 (with white pickguard), which he got to replace the 335.

ALEX   We were doing a gig with Blue Oyster Cult at the Nassau Coliseum in Long Island, New York, a few years ago, and the double-neck cherry finish Gibson I had bought in Nashville shortly before that got injured. The rigging wasn't done properly, and a long-throw horn speaker fell right on top of it, shearing the bridges off and taking huge chunks out of the body. Not only that, but the horn also fell on my 335 and gouged its neck out. That really hurt. The 335 had been with me for ten years; the neck was worn down just right, the finish was worn down from playing thousands of bars and high school dances, and I was proud of it. After that I said, "This guitar is staying home. I'm not taking any further chances with it." (Guitar Player 1980)

AMPS (ON TOUR) Marshall 100w heads w/ 4×12″ cabinets, Fender Twin Reverb.
EFFECTS Electro-Harmonix Electric Mistress flanger and the Boss chorus.

Hemispheres Album (1978)

STUDIO GUITARS 355, 345, the Dove, the B-45, and the Ramirez classical. Another 345 is picked up without the white pickguard. Alex took the 355 to the video shoots.

AMPS Hiwatt 100w heads w/matching 4″×12″ cabinets.

EFFECTS Additions included Moog Taurus pedals and Roland GR-500 guitar synthesizer ("Hemispheres").

ALEX   The flamenco-ish beginning of "La Villa Strangiato" on *Hemispheres* was done with a pick, just to get it going a lot faster. My fingers aren't that quick, yet. (Guitar Player 1980)

ALEX   The 355 is much heavier, and it sustains more than the 335 does. The weight of the 355 also helps cut down on microphonics; with the 335, I had to stuff it with cotton to avoid feedback problems. (Guitar Player 1980)

ALEX   I have a Roland GR-500, but I don't use it much. I'm not really keen on it. At first it happened to fit for the texture we were going for. I used it in "Cygnus X-l" on *Hemispheres* because it had a Gretschy sort of sound to it. There are a lot of nice effects you can get, but I wouldn't give up playing regular electric guitar and dive into synthesizer. I also fooled around with a Zetaphon for a while, but it needed some work done soon after I got it. There are a lot of different guitar synthesizer units to fool around with, but the whole concept is not something I'm terribly interested in. (Guitar Player 1980)

Tour of the Hemispheres (1978–79)
Warm-up tour (1979)

GUITARS All of them, even the black Stratocaster. Even the 335 came along making an appearance at Pink Pop before it was finally retired. Alex still has it at home.

In late 1979, Alex did endorsement ads for the Alvarez-Yairi DY-87 acoustic doubleneck.

ALEX   I eventually gave the 345 to one of our road crew as a birthday gift and bought a black '78 345 to replace it. (Guitar Player 1980)

AMPS 3 Hiwatt heads driving four 4″×12″ cabinets and one Leslie (rotating speaker) cabinet. Also the Fender Twin was used.

EFFECTS 3 Roland Space Echo's, Maestro parametric filter, and Ashley pre-amps for the acoustic guitars. A custom-built L.B. effects board (designed by Liam Birt) and built by Steele-Power Supply. The Taurus pedals were now to remain in his setup. Alex built an acoustic guitar stand using a Tama Titan boom stand; his stand would be patented and mass-produced as the Omega Guitar Stand in the '80s.

ALEX   Moog Taurus bass pedals … have an effective range of two octaves. I use them a lot on "Xanadu" where I play harmony to Geddy's bass pedal line, and on "La Villa Strangiato". Most of the time I'll play the lower end while Geddy takes the high, melodic parts. (Guitar Player 1980)

ALEX   We use 24 tracks when we record. Bumping is when you take two different tracks and combine them into one. It saves space for other things. While I don't go by any formula, overall I like to double all my rhythm tracks at least once, and often three times if I can. (Guitar Player 1980)

Permanent Waves Album (1979)

GUITARS   The black Strat (neck lacquer removed) was installed with a Floyd Rose tremolo (without locking nut.) Powdered graphite or WD-40 was placed in the string slots to minimize detuning. A Gibson humbucker pickup was installed in the bridge position, screwed down as low as possible. This Fender was used to layer leads on "The Spirit of Radio" and "Different Strings" and was usually running direct. Back pickup on 7 or 8. Solos on full volume. Front is on 5–7. A new sunburst Gibson Howard Roberts Fusion was used on the rhythm to "Different Strings". The 355 was used on all the other songs except the leads on "Jacob's Ladder" (the Pyramid guitar.) Acoustics were the Gibson J-55 (heard in "Natural Science") and the Dove.

ALEX   There were problems with the [Gibson] bodies resonating like crazy. We filled them up with cotton and did all sorts of things to keep the feedback down. I really enjoyed playing those guitars during that period, but I found I wanted to get a little more clarity without going to a complete Fender setup. That's when I stuck a couple of humbuckers on a Strat. Though it felt alien, the guitar sounded really good: It had the warmth of my Gibsons with a Strat top end. Plus I still had a Strat pickup in the middle for any arpegios or clean stuff. (Guitar Player 1980)

ALEX   For acoustics I had my J-55 in standard tuning and my Dove in Nashville tuning. On the latter the bottom three strings—the E, A, and D were tuned to octaves, using thinner strings. On "Entre Nous" we wanted to get a 12-string sound but the B-45 that I'd been using had a crack in the body; also, the neck as giving way, and the tone just didn't seem to be happening. So we tried a combination of the standard tuning and the Nashville tuning on two Guitars

Together they approximated a single 12-string layout. And everything rang clear, so that's why we did that. I'm sure we'll do it again in the future. (Guitar Player 1980)

ALEX I do hammer in a few songs: play the note, and then hammer on the string above the left hand with my right. The first solo in "Natural Science" is that kind of hammering; I picked it up from Pat Travers. I also like harmonics, and the usual assortment of string bending and pull-offs. (Guitar Player)

AMPS Combinations of 3 Hiwatt 100-watt powering Hiwatt and Marshall cab. Marshall Mark II head with Marshall cabinet and 4″×12″ Celestions. Leslie cabinet with Hiwatt head and Mesa/Boogies driving Marshall bottoms, and also the Leslie cabinet, Fender Twin Reverb with 3 J.B. Lansing (J.B.L.) K140 speakers.

EFFECTS Now include Loft analog delays (intro to "Natural Science" and "Different Strings" solo). Maestro parametric filters, in addition to the previous tour's effects.

THESE WERE USED FOR ACOUSTICS Ashley SC-66 parametric equalizer and SC-40 pre-amps.

MICROPHONES Two close to each of the amps—one Sennheiser 421, one Electro-Voice RE-20; AKG 414s (room mikes) and Neumann 87s, 89s, and 47s.

Permanent Waves Tour (1980)

GUITARS The new and improved black Stratocaster was initially used on "The Spirit of Radio" and "By-Tor and the Snow Dog" for a few weeks, then the black Gibson 345 replaced it after it developed problems mid-way into the tour. The first black 345 with white pickguard is given to synth tech Tony Geranios for his birthday. The sunburst Les Paul makes its last appearance. Alex began experimenting with Canadian-made Pro*Star strings as well.

AMPS AND EFFECTS the same.

ALEX I liked the Maestro phaser as opposed to, say, MXR Phase 90s or 100s; it was a little more subtle than the MXR phase lines. But after I heard the Chorus, I loved it and decided to incorporate it into my music. Hemispheres and Permanent Waves have a lot of Chorus-almost every song has Chorus, since with a three-piece band it tends to widen the guitar sound. (Guitar Player 1980)

"Battle Scar" (1980)

GUITAR Black Fender Stratocaster.

Moving Pictures Album *(1980)*

GUITARS 355 on "Witch Hunt" and "Tom Sawyer" (solo played on the black 345). A Stratocaster in Olympic White (black pickguard, rosewood fingerboard) on "YYZ", "Vital Signs". A Stratocaster in a customized Candy Apple Red (mirror plate and rosewood fingerboard and matching red headstock) on "The Camera Eye". Black Stratocaster (maple neck) on "Red Barchetta" and "Limelight". The acoustic layered on "The Camera Eye" was the Gibson Dove in Nashville tuning.

STUDIO AMPS Hiwatts, and also two Marshall 4140 combo amps were used.
EFFECTS new effects included Advanced Audio digital delays, Roland RE-101 and 201 digital delays, an MXR M-104 Distortion+, and an MXR M-133 Micro-amp preamp.

Moving Pictures Tour *(1981)*
Exit ... Stage Left Tour *(1981–82)*
Spring Training Tour (of the Nadars) *(1982)*

GUITARS Fender Stratocasters in white and red (this one used for most medleys and encores near the end of the tour). Gibson Howard Roberts on "The Camera Eye", "Passage to Bangkok", "Tom Sawyer", "Closer", and medleys. Gibson EDS-1275 on "Xanadu". Gibson ES-355.
ACOUSTICS Ovation Adamas classical and steel-strings.
STRINGS Dean Markley medium light bronze strings on the classical.
AMPS AND EFFECTS The same.

Signals Album *(1982)*

GUITARS Stratocasters. Gibson Howard Roberts (fitted with a Kahler tremolo unit) on "Digital Man". The acoustics on the "Losing It" chorus were the Gibson Dove in Nashville tuning, and the Ovation Adamas layered together. On the videos for "Subdivisions" it was the black Strat with a new rosewood fretboard, and on "Countdown", the white one.
STUDIO AMPS Marshall combo amps.

EFFECT ADDITIONS Delta Lab DL-5 harmonizer (as heard on the solo for "The Analog Kid"), 2 Yamaha E1010 delays and a Mutron octave divider (the closing part of the solo on "The Weapon").

ALEX Kim Mitchell, who's with the Max Webster Band, has a couple of Strats with rosewood fingerboards, and they feel really nice. I get a good vibrato, and they seem to sustain better than the maple-neck ones. I may get a rosewood finger-board for my Strat too, in the future. (Guitar Player 1980)

Signals Tour (1982–83)

GUITARS Gibson Howard Roberts on "The Camera Eye" and "Closer To the Heart" among others.

Gibson ES-355 occasionally. White and black Fenders alternate as main guitar. Red Fender ("2112" medley). The Adamas steel-string and classical were the acoustics.
AMPS 4 Marshall 4140's.
EFFECTS The new ones with the MP Tour effects.

Radio City Music Hall Show Performance (1983)

GUITARS Same as previous tour, with the addition of a butterscotch-blond '59 Fender Telecaster '83 reissue (with black pickguard, ash body, maple neck and fretboard) was used on "Kid Gloves" and "New World Man".

ALEX I always disliked Teles, but I had a look at one and thought, "Well, this could come in handy." I spent a little time with it, and I got to really enjoy it. It's become invaluable in the studio; for all that clean, arpeggiated stuff, it's perfect. (Guitar Player 1986)

Grace Under Pressure Album (1983–84)

GUITARS The white Strat now has a Shark bolt-on neck, along with the infamous "Hentor Sportscaster" logos and Bill Lawrence L-500 pickup which can be used as single or double coil. The Tele was recorded on the rhythm track of "Kid Gloves", the first section of "the Body Electric" and parts of "Red Sector A". Alex took the red Strat out for the video for "Distant Early Warning" and the white one for "The Enemy Within" and "The Body Electric." The black one came out for "Afterimage."
AMPS AND EFFECTS The same.

ALEX I think a bolt on sounds better. The sustain works differently, the low end is different. I've tried a couple of straight through necks but they didn't seem particularly good or feel comfortable. I'm sure if I was forced at gunpoint to use them I would grow to like them. (Guitar Player)

ALEX 'Hentor' was the name that we had for Peter Henderson, the producer of Grace Under Pressure. When he wrote his name out to leave us his number, it looked like Peter Hentor instead of Peter Henderson, so we nicknamed him Hentor

The Barbarian. I got some Letraset and put it on this white Strat that I had. It has a Shark neck—these are unlabeled replacement necks—so I threw 'Hentor Sportscaster' on there. Amazing all the mail we used to get over that [laughs]: "Where can I buy a Hentor? How much does a Hentor cost?" (Guitar Player 1986)

Grace Under Pressure Tour (1984–85)
Spring Training tour (1985)

GUITARS Same as the Radio City dates, except the Gibsons are now retired.
AMPS Music Man solid state amps on Oriental Tour.
MIKES Sennheiser MD421's for all except the Beyer M201 on the Marshalls. Unmiked Yamaha 2″×12″ extension cabinet, Nady VHF700 wireless transmitter.

Power Windows Album (1985)

GUITARS tele on most songs with minor use of the black Strat ("Territories"). A sunburst Ovation Adamas 1985 Ltd. Series acoustic on "Mystic Rhythms" and overdubbed portions of other tracks like the second chorus in "Grand Designs". Black Fender Stratocaster with white pickguard borrowed for "The Big Money" video.
STUDIO AMPS Dean Markley CD-212 and CD-120 amps. On tracks like "Middletown Dreams", amps are mixed (Gallien-Krueger 100MPL driving two Celestion speakers in a Marshall cabinet.) The Roland Jazz Chorus amp from *A Farewell to Kings* is brought out again.
NEW EFFECTS Roland SRV-2000 digital reverbs and 3 SDD-3000 digital delays, 2 Loft 450 digital delays, Ibanez HD-1000 Harmonizer/Delay (heard on the intro to "Territories"), Delta Lab ADM-2048 digital delay (used as a flanger), and a TSR Scholz-Rockman on the "edge" setting for "Middletown Dreams"), Boss Super Distortion, Boss Octaver.

ALEX I've always liked using an echo more like a reverb. For years, I played that way because there weren't any valid reverb units around. Now, of course, there are millions of them, and they all sound great and they're studio-quality and fairly inexpensive. I used to use two echo units—one set at about 200 milliseconds and the other set at about 325 or 350. The combination of the two bouncing around creates a fairly realistic reverb, so it gives the guitar a little more depth and dimension. But once you add something like a chorus—which changes the real character of the guitar—to the echoes, you have a big swirling blob of sound. (Guitar Player 1986)

Power Windows Tour (1985–86)

Save for the Marshall combos for amps, gear remains the same. A Yamaha QX-1 digital sequencer controls an Emulator II synthesizer (which is also connected to the house) activated by a foot trigger. Moog Taurus pedals run straight to the house PA system as well as Korg MPK-130 MIDI bass pedals, which control another Emulator II.

ALEX When we started preparing for concert rehearsals, Geddy went in with Jim Burgess, a programmer in Toronto that we use for a lot of stuff, and he set it up so that we got a lot of the sequenced parts down on Emulator [sampling digital synthesizer]. They're constantly being programmed throughout the evening for the different songs. We put all the old synth sounds from the Oberheims and the MiniMoogs onto the Emulator. We condensed the whole keyboard setup and made it a little more sophisticated. It's really not a problem to get all that stuff back on there. We just put them on a disk and call them up as we go through the song. (Guitar Player 1986)

In mid-1986, Alex began using, then endorsing Signature guitars. Built in Vancouver, these were 'superstrat-style' solid-body guitars with single-coil Evans pickups (made in Victoria, Canada). Alex's Omega stands were being sold through Music Emporium at this point as well.

ALEX I'm using two Dean Markley CD-212s and two of my Marshall Combos. I switch back and forth between channel A and channel B. Channel A is a very clean setup on the CD-212; the volume is on about 4 1/2 or 5, with about 7 on treble, 5 on midrange, and about 7 on bass. That's the clean, crisp sound. Channel B is set up a little bit different. It has two gains: a dirty, distorted one, and a clean gain that's on a Spinal Tap setting of 11 [laughs]. The distorted gain's on about 3, with the actual gain for the distortion level on about 7, and then treble's close to 6, mid's about 4 1/2, and bass about 6. Master volume is on about 3 1/2, no reverb, and presence is on 7 or 8. And that gives me a good bit of crunch on that channel. I've also been using a Roland Dimension D [stereo imager] on this whole tour. I've been happy with it, but I'm almost afraid that I'm getting a bit of cancellation somewhere. For solos, there doesn't seem to be quite enough of the sustain that used to be there. I don't know if it's in my head or if it's because they're new amps, or what. (Guitar Player 1986)

Hold Your Fire Album (1987)

GUITARS Signature Artists, the Tele for doubling in cleaner passages. Adamas acoustics were also used. The main guitar was either the black Signature (as seen in "Time Stand Still" video) or white (as seen in "Lock and Key").

AMPS Same as previous but with Gallien-Krueger 100MPL pre-amps and previous Dean Markley amps with a Rane mixer.

ALEX   I think the guitar stands out more on Hold Your Fire. The heads were in the control room with the speakers in the studio. We had a clean, jangley sort of sound that we called Lerxst Sound, and found ourselves going back to use it a lot. (Visions)

ALEX   I've gotten rid of all my old analog delays, and I'm also using a digital reverb now. So, I'm moving away from bouncing echoes a little more. (Guitar Player 1986)

ALEX   I was very much influenced by Allan Holdsworth a number of years ago, the way he uses the whammy bar to slur notes and move around. That got me interested in using one and trying to develop a style with one. So many people use it now that it's not that unique, and actually I've started to move away from it a bit. I've gotten a bit lazy with my natural vibrato since I've been relying a lot more on the whammy bar. It's time for a change. (Guitar Player 1986)

Hold Your Fire Tour (1987–88)
A Show of Hands Album (1989)

GUITARS 5 Signature custom guitars. The main one was white with Boy Scouts Panther Patrol patch; or a black one used on "Limelight" and "Time Stand Still", but the dark green, midnight blue and a dark vermilion models rarely saw use. Acoustics, again were Adamas.
STRINGS Dean Markleys still, now at .009, .010, .016, .028, .038, .048 gauges.
AMPS Gallien-Krueger 2000CPL pre-amps, 2100SEL digital stereo power amps (200 watts).
EFFECTS essentially the same, with the addition of a Dimension D. Alex now had a Yamaha KX76 keyboard on his side of the stage for "Time Stand Still".

In 1988, Alex did ads for Carvin XV212 amps and guitars but didn't use them on stage.

Presto Album (1989)

GUITARS Signatures and the Tele (for clean passages). Adamas steel-string and Gibson J-55, now the "Nashville-tuned" acoustic. Alex replaced the four lower strings with lighter gauges and tuned them up an octave. Black 345 on "The Pass" video shoot and the 355 on "Show Don't Tell" video shoots.
AMPS Gallien-Kruegers and Rolands.

Presto Tour (1990)

GUITARS Signatures were used (including a red one), but late in the tour they went bankrupt. He began just using the white Signature for "The Big Money" and "Freewill" and had switched to brand new CE24 models built by Paul Reed Smith in Black (abalone dot inlays) and in Black Sunburst [dove inlays, both had rosewood fretboard, active Evans single coil pickups, 3-way toggle instead of standard pickup selector, maple neck backs, PRS vibrato with humbucking pickups.) This guitar was brought out a few months before the tour's end and seen in the "Superconductor" video.

STRINGS Dean Markley Cold Steel's. Adamas acoustics.

AMPS Gallien-Kruegers, GK CPL-2000 pre-amp, Crown Macro power amp, two 2″×12″ Celestion GK cabinets.

EFFECTS Roland GP-16 effects processor through another Crown amp driving offstage speaker boxes that are miked as the primary sound source. A Bob Bradshaw pedal board.

ALEX PRS's are the best guitars I've ever played and they really come out of the case playing perfect. The people who make them really have a sense of what I like now—I told them what I like in the action and the weight, so every guitar they build me gets better and better. I also always ask them to take off the pickup selector knobs and put in straight toggles. (Guitar Shop 1994)

ALEX On my Signatures, there was a lot of floating action in the tailpiece. They were very funny guitars to set up and I was never really happy. They required continual alignment and maintenance something I don't have to worry about with the PRS guitars. (Guitar Player)

Roll the Bones Album (1991)

GUITARS The previous PRS CE24 guitars plus two new 24's (a Dark Blue and a Vintage Cherry with abalone moon inlays). An Emerald Green one was given to tourmate Larry Lalonde of Primus. Black PRS EG4 (pickguard, rosewood fretboard, standard humbucker and two single-coils, 3-way switch and abalone moon inlays) as seen in "Roll the Bones". This model was used for finger picked solo on "The Big Wheel". '91 Fender Strat Elite (to warm-up with). Fender Telecaster (for "Bravado" and doubling rhythm parts). Washburn acoustic ("Roll the Bones") Gibson J-55, "Nashville tuned" guitar.

AMPS Gallien-Krueger with an occasional appearance by: 2 x Marshall 100-watt 2×12 combos and a Marshall 100-watt 4×12 half-stack. Demos were recorded on Alex's Tascam 388

Roll the Bones Tour *(1991–92)*

GUITARS PRS's exclusively (endorsement deal). The blue PRS CE24 was the main tour guitar. Ovation Adamas acoustics.

AMPS Gallien-Krueger solid-state amps were still used, Gallien-Krueger 2000 GPL pre-amps, Mesa/Boogie Series 400 II power amp, Crown Macro power amp, Celestion-GK 2×12's 75 watt G12M70 speakers (replaced by Crown), Bryston 2V "studio" pre-amp into 2 more Celestion-GK in conjunction w/ the Roland G-16 multi-effects processor.

BRADSHAW UNIT Roland DEP-5 for reverb, 2× TC electronics TC-2290 chorus pedals, TC-1210 spatial expander for chorus also, Digitech IPS-33B multi-effects unit for 12 string effects and harmonizing.

Kumbaya '93 Performance

GUITAR Sunburst PRS CE24

Counterparts Album *(1993)*

GUITARS Black PRS. Les Paul Std (the main riff to "Stick it Out"). Tele was also used on "Cold Fire", some clean parts and to thicken the sound as overdubs. Washburn, Gibson Dove, and the J-55, mixed in and out for acoustic parts, such as in "Nobody's Hero". Sunburst PRS was used in "Stick It Out" video; now it had a spider patch on the body.

AMPS Peavey 5150 and a 100-watt Marshall JCM 800—each w/a matching 4×12 cabinet. A Roland JC-120 was used for some small parts. The Gallien-Krueger was used to drive the effects which would run through the Peavey or Marshall.

ALEX For the first time in 12 years I recorded the guitars in the studio instead of the control room. I had two amps blaring at me. It took a couple f days to get used to it, but after that, man, I loved it. I could feel the wood vibrating against my body and hear the amps coming through the pickups. I got caught up in the whole energy of the sound and the room. I thought, "Where have I been, missing all this? For all the bed tracks, I plugged straight into the amps, with no effects, and cranked it up. (Guitar Player)

ALEX I have a big, sort of metallic sounding Washburn and a Gibson Dove that's soft and delicate. The two together made a very complete sound. I also used a Nashville-tuned Gibson J-55, which we mixed in and out. (Guitar Player)

ALEX I'll usually lay down the PRS first because I find it the most comfortable and it has the smoothest sound—a really nice low end, very nice mids and the high end isn't too shrill. Then I add the Les Paul to get thicker, lower mids and the Tele brightens it all up. (Guitar School)

ALEX   The big change is that we ended up taking out the Gallien-Krueger solid-state stuff and replacing them with the Marshalls. The GK's are still fine amps but the tube is where I'm at right now. I began hearing things that I'd been missing for a while, like a warmer, rounder tone. It's back to the stack—in fact, the other day I was standing in front of my amps with my pants waving back and forth from the extreme volume and I thought, "Man, I've really missed this!" I almost cried. All I need now is a really low guitar strap and it'll be the 70s all over again. (Guitar Shop 1994)

Counterparts Tour *(1994)*

GUITARS Classic Red PRS (with dot inlays). Sunburst Gibson Les Paul Std with white pickguard for "Stick It Out" . EDS-1275 for "Xanadu" and "Prelude". Ovation Classic for "Nobody's Hero", "Closer to the Heart", and "The Trees".

AMPS 2 100w Marshall JCM 800 and 50w Marshall 6300's each driving a pair of '60 Vintage 4″×12″ 25w cabinets. They were replaced by 30th Anniversary models with the 3 channel heads and MIDI.

NEW EFFECTS a Digitech TSR-24 multi-effects unit with DHP-55 harmonizer, Korg MPK-130 MIDI pedals, T.C. Electronics 1210 spatial expander, two T.C. 2290 delay units, Roland SDE-3000 multi-fx processor, Lexicon 224 delay and PCM-70 multi-fx units, Digitech pre-amp and Palmer PDI-05 speaker simulator for clean and acoustic sounds.

Kumbaya Performance 1994

Guitar: Red PRS.

Kumbaya Performance 1995

Guitar: Black PRS.

Victor Album *(1995)*

GUITARS PRS Dove McCarty Artist (sunburst with alder body, bolt-on neck, and Indian rosewood neck) in addition to other guitars, including a ten-string mandola (basically a large mandolin tuned an octave lower.)

Test For Echo Album (1996)

GUITARS Black and black sunburst PRS. Black Gibson Les Paul Custom. '63 Fender Strat Custom Shop reissue in sunburst (white pickguard and maple neck).
ACOUSTICS Martin classical, along with the J-55, the Washburn, a Larivee (the new company which took over Signature), and a Godin LGX in Transparent Blue (mahogany body, Tetrad combo pickups and rosewood fretboard). Godin Acousticaster. Mandola on "Half the World" and "The Color of Right". Alex plays the LGX, the J-55 and the sunburst PRS in the "Half the World" video.
AMPS Marshall 100w and 50w heads, Peavey 5150.
EFFECTS Same but with a Roland VG-08.

ALEX   I just wanted to try it [mandola]. So I just futzed around to get a feel for it, and it changed the whole personality of the song. I remember Ged when he first heard it was like, 'Whoa, I don't know about that.' It was so unusual for a Rush song to have that kind of texture. But it grew on him really quickly. I think it's probably his favorite part of the album. (All Star)

ALEX   Seventy per cent of the record is the Les Paul (Custom). It's really dense and sustains for weeks. (Guitar)

ALEX   The Digitech has different effects and sounds in it which I ran through the Palmer. Then I just knitted that in with amp sound. The Palmer just has really warm filters. (Canadian Musician 1996)

Test For Echo Tour — An Evening With Rush (1996 – 97)

GUITARS All of the guitars mentioned above were used except the Fender. Acoustic sounds were supplied by a piezo bridge pickup in one of the PRS guitars. New Scarlet Red PRS 24 with transducer "piezo" pickups for switching to acoustic on "Driven", "Closer to the Heart", "Nobody's Hero", "Virtuality", and "Natural Science". Black Gibson Les Paul Custom or sunburst Les on "2112", "Stick It Out", "Test For Echo", and "Tom Sawyer". Black PRS. Royal Blue Metallic PRS 24 on "The Big Money". Alex collects Godzilla figures throughout tour to pose by his pedals (in a playful response to the critical labeling of the band's 'dinosaur rock'.)
ADDITIONAL AMPS Mesa/Boogie V-Twin pre-amps, Digitech GSP 2101, and a T.C. electronics 1210.

Geddy Lee

Geddy first started out playing on an acoustic guitar with painted palm trees, and the first song he learned was "For Your Love" by Yardbirds. His first bass was a Conora model, painted to resemble the psychedelic bass of Cream's Jack Bruce. Though he owned a small amp, he would also borrow various Ace, GBX, and Silvertone amps before getting a Traynor combo amp with 2″×15″ speakers and a Bass Master head.

In early 1968 Geddy bought a Hagstrom bass, then in late 1969 he traded this bass in for a sunburst '69 Fender Precision (alder body, maple neck, rosewood fingerboard), fitted with La Bella flatwound strings, which he used until 1972, when he began favoring Rotosound Swing Bass roundwound strings (.105-.050). The bass was amplified through a Sunn 2000 S bass head with two 2″×15″ cabinets; the speakers were replaced with SRO 15″ speakers. Over the years, he has expressed his admiration for many bands and styles of music.

GEDDY The Fixx and Tears For Fears; they make really synthesized records. Almost everything in them is synthesized in some way or another. Peter Gabriel and Larry Fast have some pretty high-quality stuff that's state-of-the-art. I also listen to Simple Minds, Ultravox, Talk Talk, the Eurythmics, and Kind Sunny Ade. Lately, I've been listening to Howard Jones' *Human's Lib*. I think it's a real contemporary record, keyboard-ise and vocally. I like the new King Crimson album [*Three Of A Perfect Pair*]. (Keyboard)

GEDDY Billie Holiday, Louis Armstrong, Roy Orbison, even old country music—that have little to do with what I play. I don't analyze the snare or guitar sounds, I just enjoy the singing and songwriting. In terms of contemporary bands, I listen to the Cure, Simple Minds, Gypsy Kings, and I'm really into Talk Talk's remix CD—what a good compilation. I listen to Metallica from time to time, just to crank it up. A lot of ethnic music, too, stuff on Peter Gabriel's label [Real World]. I put the discs on and let it soak in. I recently got a compilation of Haitian music assemble by [film director] Jonathan Demme [Konbit! Burning Rhythms of Haiti, A&M]. (Guitar Player)

GEDDY I love [Jethro] Tull. *Thick As a Brick* is my all time favorite; it'd be at the top of my desert island list—*Passion Play*, too, which is not a very liked record, but I loved it! (Guitar School)

GEDDY I love the Tragically Hip. And there's an artist from Toronto named Hayden that I like a lot. I like Tricky and Massive Attack. I like this record by Tripping Daisy. (Rolling Stone 1996)

GEDDY I've enjoyed listening to Primus, the Red Hot Chili Peppers and Soundgarden—bands that have a more active rhythmic role coming from the bass ... I also like

Dean Garcia, who plays in Curve. He's got these zooming bass parts that fly around and are very interesting melodically and there's a lot of passion to his playing. I like Radiohead's Colin Greenwood; his parts are basic but melodically interesting. And I always keep an ear on the [original] players who influenced me: Jack Bruce [Cream], Jack Casady [Jefferson Airplane], John Entwhistle [The Who], Chris Squire [Yes] and Phil Lesh [Grateful Dead]. (Bass Player)

GEDDY   If I hear State of Emergency by Bjork, that really blows my mind. It's a brilliant song. She's awesome. She's not for everyone's taste but I love her. She is a real artist, deeply talented and her voice is as talented as any voice as I have ever heard.Jeff Berlin, a good friend of mine, and really the master bass player of the universe is always playing bass like he is Andres Segivia with three parts going at the same time. So his parts fascinate me. (Canadian Musician)

Geddy on style and practice:

GEDDY   I always use my fingers, but sometimes I grow my nails. Primarily [right-hand middle finger]. As a child, I was fortunate to have it almost chopped off. When the nail grew back, it was extraordinarily tough. It doesn't break if I use it as a pick. (Guitar Player)

GEDDY   After spending seven months touring, I can't even look at my bass. A lot of the musical development I do is during the course of a tour—that's the greatest opportunity to improve. There's a lot of dead time when I'm sitting around, and that's a good time to work on my chops. (Bass Player 1993)

Albums & Tours

Rush Album and Tour (1974)

BASSES Fender Precision bass.
AMPS Sunn 2000 S bass head with two 2″×15″ cabinets w/SRO speakers.

Rush Tour (1974) (w/Neil Peart)

BASSES Fender Precision (had a Rush decal slapped onto it). '72 Rickenbacker 4001 in Jetglo (run in stereo with the neck pickup going to the Ampeg and the bridge pickup going to the Sunn) with solid maple body, maple neck, 20-fret rosewood fretboard, mother of pearl sharkfin inlays and single-coil pickups, Rotosound Swing (Round Wound) strings, stock bridges, Schaller Deluxe machine heads.
AMPS Sunn 2000S. 2 Sunn speaker cabs w/SRO speakers. Ampeg SVT amp. 2 Ampeg V4B cabinets w/15″ speakers.

Fly By Night Album (1975)

BASSES 4001. A white 4001 was used in "Fly by Night" videos. The Precision was used for the "By-Tor" effects by running it through a fuzztone and a phaser. A Martin nylon string classical guitar on "Rivendell".

Fly By Night Tour (1975)
Caress of Steel Album and Tour (1975–76)
2112 Album and Tour (1976–77)

BASSES On *Caress of Steel*, the Precision was played on "I Think I'm Going Bald" and "Lakeside Park". In late 1975 the Precision was remodeled into a teardrop shape and given a Fender Jazz treble pickup in the bridge position. Then it was refinished into a lavender, and wired in stereo. It was also used on the tour and during part of the recording of *All the World's a Stage*.
NOTE Hugh Syme is playing on an ARP Odyssey synth on the intro to "2112" and a Mellotron 400 on "Tears".

All the World's a Stage Tour (1976–77)

BASSES 4001 now fitted with Badass II bridge. Rickenbacker 4080 doubleneck. 4080/6 with a 6-string guitar (white with black pickguard). One Rickenbacker 4080 doubleneck 4080/12 with a 480 12-string guitar (Jetglo, no pickguard). Both have customized humbucking pickups. These guitars are used on early version of "Xanadu". Rickenbacker 4002 in Mapleglo with white pickguard (Badass bridge, birdseye and curly maple, ebony fretboard, low impedance pickup; Schaller tuning pegs). Rickenbacker 3001 bass in sunburst. With its single low-impedance pickup he prefers not to record with it but to use it for warm-ups.
EFFECTS One set of Taurus Moog MK1 pedals (13 note pedal-board, 2 Voltage Control Oscillators, 4 presets, one of them programmable, interfaced with mini-Moog, Model D, cherry finish, 44 keys F-C/3.5 octaves, 3 oscillators) ; when a second set is added, the pedals move to front microphone area.

A Farewell To Kings Album (1977)

BASSES 4001 throughout with Rickenbacker 4080/12 on "Xanadu".
EFFECTS Same. Roland JC-120 Jazz Chorus used on "Madrigal".

A Farewell To Kings Tour (1977–78)

Archives Tour (1978)

BASSES Both black Rickenbackers and Fender Precision. The two 4080s (the white one for rare appearances) used on "Xanadu".
AMPS Same as the previous tour, except the Ampeg V4B cabinets are fitted with JBL K140 speakers. A Fender Twin Reverb amp is used for the 4080 guitars.
EFFECTS Same.

Hemispheres Album (1978)

BASSES Same as the previous album only the 4080 is not used.
SYNTHS Oberheim (8-voice) polyphonic.

GEDDY My actual ability on keyboards is somewhat limited, and I don't consider myself a keyboard player, although I do like playing the synthesizers. I look at myself as more of a melodic composer with the synthesizer. As a keyboard player I can't play a lot of complex chord changes or move through a very complex structure, but I can find lots and lots of melodies. (Keyboard 1984)

Hemispheres Tour (1978–79)
Warmup Tour (1979)

BASSES Same as the previous tour. 4080 used on "Xanadu" and "A Passage to Bangkok".
AMPS 2 Ashley SC-40 pre-amps. 2 BGW 750-B power amps. 2 Thiele Design speaker cabinets with 2″×15″ JBL speakers. 2 Ampeg V4B cabinets w/JBL speakers. Fender Twin Reverb.
EFFECTS Roland Boss Chorus (for 4080).
SYNTHS Same as previous tour with the addition of the Oberheim 8-voice interfaced with a second set of Taurus Moog pedals and a Roland 301 Space Echo, now used on the Mini-Moog.

Permanent Waves Album (1979)
'Battle Scar'

BASSES 4001 with the addition of a '72 black Fender Jazz (white pickguard, maple neck and ebony block inlays, Bakelite knobs, Fender/Schaller strap locks, solid alder body, '62 Fender Jazz single-coil passive pickups, Rotosound Swing Round Wound strings).
SYNTHS Same but with the addition of Oberheim OB-1 for sound effects (on "Natural Science") and sequencing in conjunction with an Oberheim DS-1

sequencer (on "The Spirit of Radio"), as a vocoder (vocal effect) on "Jacob's Ladder". Hugh Syme played the studio grand piano on "Different Strings".

Permanent Waves Tour (1980)

BASSES Same as previous tour with the white 4080/12 making more appearances.
AMPS Same as previous tour.
SYNTHS Same as previous tour and current studio set-up.

Moving Pictures Album (1980)

BASSES Jazz was the only bass used (the Rickenbacker 4001 in the "Tom Sawyer" studio video is for 'effect'). Strings were Rotosound Swing Bass 66 roundwound long scale strings (.45, .65, .80, .105).
SYNTHS An Oberheim OB-X synthesizer and a Roland digital sequencer are the news additions. Hugh Syme on synthesizers on "Witch Hunt".

GEDDY   We had a lot of different kinds of synthesizers at our disposal, too, which was I new thing, too; I mean we've used synthesizers on records previous, but they were making them much smaller, much more portable at that time. So there were a few we'd brought up to the farm with us that we had lying around. Oberheim was one of the ones we had, and we found this amazing, growling sound which we knew we had to write a song around; and it turned out to be that growling sound that's at the beginning of "Tom Sawyer". Really, that was almost the inspiration for the sound of that song. (In the Studio)

Moving Pictures Tour (1981)
Exit ... Stage Left Tour (1981)
Spring Training Tour (of the Nadars) 1982

BASSES Same, though the Fender Jazz makes ample appearances. Geddy takes along a red Ovation classical guitar.
AMPS Same as previous tour, except the guitar amp for the doubleneck is now a Yamaha GR-75, and the Thiele-Design cabinets now have Electro Voice EVM speakers.
SYNTHS Same with the Oberheim OB-X and the Mini-Moog now used with a Yamaha E1010 analog delay unit.
VOCAL MIC' Electro Voice DS-35.

Signals Album (1982)

BASSES Rick 4001 on all except "Losing It", which was the 4002 and the Fender Jazz on "Digital Man" and "New World Man".
SYNTHS Oberheim OB-Xa (61 keys, 120 programs) with an Oberheim DSX sequencer Roland JP-8 with a Roland TR-808 Compu-Rhythm sequencer (for "The Weapon"). Taurus pedals now interfaced with the OB-Xa

Signals Tour (1982–83)

BASSES 4001's and Fender Jazz; in the last leg, Geddy unveiled the Steinberger L2 bass (black, carbon-graphite, rosewood neck, 2 EMG pickups) which he used on "Digital Man" and "The Weapon".
SYNTHS Same as in the studio, with the mini-Moog and two of the old Taurus pedals.
AMPS Same as the previous tour.

GEDDY I think it looks like hell when those guys walk around with [remote] keyboards. That rubs me the wrong way. It looks 'Las Vegas' to me. The only guy who had one that looked pretty decent was Roger Powell from Utopia. He looked believable. He also plays like a maniac, which helps, and I like him a lot. He's real good. (Keyboard)

Radio City Music Hall Performances (1983)

BASSES Same, including the L2 bass.
SYNTH A new PPG Wave 2.2 synthesizer with Waveterm sampling option. The pulse on "Red Sector A" is the Roland JP-8 (Jupiter8) with TR-808 Compu-Rhythm arpeggiating bass connected; 2 sets of Taurus pedals. The PPG fills in the spot where the Oberheim OB-Xa is, while the OB-Xa takes over the space where the old OB-X was.

Grace Under Pressure Album (1983–84)

BASSES L2 bass (Geddy brought the 4001 in videos for "Enemy Within" and "Body Electric" for 'effect').
SYNTHS Same.

GEDDY Of all the instruments I've had, I think the PPG drives me the most to write. What I liked about the PPG was the fact that it was a digital—and—an analog synthesizer. Mind you, there's nothing like an analog synthesizer when you want a powerful sound. Analog synthesizers like the Oberheim OB-Xa and the

Roland JP-8 have an organic punch to them that I find difficult to get out of a digital synthesizer like the PPG. But they have their own unique areas where they shine. The PPG has a crystalline sound which sparkles. It has a very 'invisible' sort of sound that the guitar punches through very easily. (Keyboard 1984)

Grace Under Pressure Tour (1984–85)
Spring Training Tour (1985)

BASSES L2, with rare appearances by 4001.
SYNTHS PPG Wave 2.2, Roland JP-8 and TR-808 Compu-Rhythm, Oberheim OBX-a and DSX sequencer. Moog Taurus II pedals and Mini-Moog with digital delay from the mixing board.
AMPS 2 BGW 750-C power amps replace 750-B's. 2 Furman Sound PQ-3 pre-amps with 2× API 550-A equalizers replace the Ashleys. Ampeg SVT head. Also using 4 custom-made speaker Sunn cabinets each with 2×15″ SRO speakers. Telex wireless transmitter connected to a Boss GE-7B EQ switch.
VOCAL MIC' Nady wireless.

Power Windows Album (1985)

BASSES Geddy recorded with Peter Collins' English-made, natural walnut finished Wal bass (Steinberger in "Mystic Rhythms" video for effect.) Geddy got his own black Wal Pro II before the tour and video shoots in summer 1985 and started endorsing light top, medium bottom Superwound Funkmaster 303 or 606 strings (.30, .50, .70, .90) by Rotosound.
SYNTHS PPG Wave 2.3, an Emulator II digital sampler and a Yamaha DX-7.
NOTE Andy Richards, guest on synthesizers.

Power Windows Tour (1985–86)

BASSES The L2 is the only bass used until almost the end of the last leg when the Wal dominated and the L2 was used only for encore. A white L2 is also in his rig.
AMPS Same as the previous tour.
KEYBOARDS PPG Wave 2.3 now sitting on top of a Yamaha KX76 MIDI controller on Geddy's hand is another KX76 with the Roland Jupiter 8 on top of that. The Yamaha's control 4 Emulator II's, the Yamaha DX-7 Chroma, and a QX-1 sequencer.

GEDDY   For the tour we sampled the choir sound for Marathon and strings during Manhattan Project and other unplayable parts. Jack Secret changes the discs backstage but physically Alex and I must trigger them onstage. (Visions)

Hold Your Fire Album (1987)

BASSES The black Wal throughout with a Wal 5-string on "Lock and Key".
SYNTHS now included Akai S900 sampling modules and 2 Prophet VS synths.

GEDDY   You can get that sound out of most basses I think, but a Rickenbacker has a particular kind of top end, and bottom end as well. It has a particular kind of classic twang to it. I found that I wanted to get a little more subtlety in the sound, and I couldn't quite get it out of the Rick. I wanted to change the top end a little bit, get a little different shaped bottom end. Then I moved to a Steinberger, which really gave me a totally different sound. The top end didn't range as high and twangy, and the bottom end was quite a different shade. I liked it a lot, and used it onstage, and on the *Grace Under Pressure* album. But on *Power Windows* I got introduced to the Wal bass, made by a small company in England. Our producer, Peter Collins, had one and suggested I try it out. I used that bass on *Hold Your Fire*, and I'm very pleased with the results and its flexibility. I use a 4-string most of the time, but on "Lock And Key" it was a 5-string they made with an extra low "B". I find that low string really means more today, because we're living in the world of synthesizers that go lower than basses ever went before. (Bass Player 1988)

GEDDY   This was the first time we had an actual Mac set up, with software made by one of these companies that does music software. Software called Performer. That really turns your computer into a multi-track recording device and a sequencing device. It doesn't store sound, but basically stores notes so I can write, you know, all different keyboard parts and store them in the computer and play them back at will, screw around with them and when I wanna change the arrangement I can just cut and paste the arrangement around as opposed to playing it on tape recorder ten different ways and listening to which one I like best, I can cut and paste ten different versions. So it's very helpful, in a lot of ways. (Off the Record)

Hold Your Fire Tour (1987–88)
Presto Tour (1990)

BASSES Wals, and the white Steinberger (which was not used except for backup.)
AMPS Same, although the racks now have a Furman PL8Plus Power Conditioner and a Yamaha MFCI MIDI foot controller is used for mapper changers backup.

SYNTHS PPG Wave 2.3 with a Roland D-50 on top. Yamaha KX76 with a Prophet VS on top. One set of Taurus pedals has been replaced by a set of Korg MIDI pedals. Offstage keyboard setup includes: 2 Yamaha QX-1 sequencers; Yamaha DX-7 Chroma; Prophet VS. In one rack-mount is a MIDI mapper; JL Cooper MIDI patch bay (a MIDI patch matrix, 13 masters, 17 slaves); 3 Akai S900 samplers; Roland Super Jupiter; Roland D-550. The other rack contains 4 Akai S900 samplers; 2 MIDI mappers; 2 mixers designed by Tony Geranios.

GEDDY That's an actual 30-voice choir on `Marathon'. We didn't want to just use a tape of a choir singing, so we divided the choir up into many different samples. I play a fairly simple keyboard part, but it triggers each segment of the choir sample when we need it. It's a very long chorus at the end, with two key changes, and at each key change the arrangement changes slightly. With the first one, an orchestra joins the choir. For the last one, it's the same choir mixed with some strings. And every three bars or so I'll change a note to bring in another part of the choir. That's a lot of sampling time, so for that tune we had to use three [Akai] S900s. (Keyboard)

Presto Album (1989)

BASSES Same as previous album (Fender Jazz in "Show Don't Tell" video for effect).
SYNTHS Roland D-50, Akai S1000 samplers.
MIC' AKG C-44.

Presto Tour (1990)

BASSES Same as last tour, although the white Steinberger did come out for at least one performance (Miami) as a backup.

Roll the Bones Album (1991)

BASSES New Wal bass in cherry red with larger body used on all tracks except "Dreamline" and "Neurotica", which used the black Wal.
SYNTHS Korg Wavestation. Korg M-1. Ensoniq SD-1. Yamaha PF-80. The sounds used were then sampled onto: 4¥ Roland S-770 samplers and Akai S1000 samplers. An Eventide Ultraharmonizer on Geddy's voice for rap voice effect.

GEDDY I got a new Wal bass, a red one. When I ordered it, I didn't expect it to sound any different than my black one. The difference is fairly subtle, but it is warmer. This may be because it has a slightly bigger horn. It's a hornier bass ... it's a red, horny bass … I made a conscious decision to depart from my normal tone. I played with a little less top end and more bottom. (Guitar Player)

Roll the Bones Tour (1991–92)

BASSES Red and black 4-string Wals.

AMPS 2 Gallien-Krueger bass amps with 2 custom designed speaker cabinets w/ 2×15″ Celestion speakers.

SYNTHS 2 Yamaha KX76 controllers onstage (Korg MIDI pedals offstage). 2 racks of Akai S1000 samplers and Roland S770 samplers. Roland PS-1 line conditioner. Roland P330. 2× Roland 360 systems (AudioMatrix) 16 MIDI patch bays. 4× Roland M120 line mixers. 2× Anatek studio merges. JL Cooper 16-20's. Furman PL-8 power and light conditioner.

Counterparts Album (1993)

BASSES '72 Fender Jazz Bass not used since *Moving Pictures* recorded with a combination of direct and the new amp setup and also used a vintage Ampeg head on "Animate" and was also mixed in on "Stick It Out", "Cut To the Chase", "The Speed of Love", and "Everyday Glory". They were recorded with a Neve console.

SYNTHS Akai S1000 samplers. Hammond B-3 organ sample used on the second part to "Cut To the Chase."

GEDDY Peter first suggested it when we were discussing the record early on. We were talking about the sound we wanted, and he told me he thought it might be a good idea to try a bass without active pickups, to get a more aggressive sound. I like changing basses every couple of years anyway. Alex, who does all the engineering during the writing stage, got a great sound out of the bass and I was happy with the direction we were going with it. From then on, there was no turning back. (Bass Player)

GEDDY When I try to lock into a more repetitive, groove-like thing, I've found it's not about playing fewer notes—there are still the same number of notes per bar—but there is less of a *variety* of notes per bar. I had great fun doing the *Counterparts* bass tracks because of it; I felt like I was learning something all over again, and I was able to use things I already knew but applied in a different way. And I got a lot of support from Neil in that direction; he got right into it as well. Sometimes it's not the groove you're going for … it's more math. You have to appreciate that certain musicians get turned on by playing with the math and that's okay. But if you want to make music that comes from any other part of your body other than your head you have to serve the groove. (Bass Player)

Counterparts Tour (1994)

BASSES 3 Fender Custom Shop Jazzes in addition to the black one: '93 in red w/ a Hipshot "D" tuner on the E string (for "Stick It Out"); '93 in sunburst with red sparkle pickguard; '93 in black with red sparkle pickguard
AMPS Trace-Elliot GP12 SMX pre-amps, Trace-Elliot Quatra 4VR power amps, 2 cabinets with one 18″ speaker. 2 cabinets with four 10″ speakers.
SYNTHS Same as the previous tour. Synth tech Tony Geranios sampled the old Oberheim and Moog for the older songs.

Test For Echo Album (1996)

BASSES '72 Fender Jazz with Rotosound Swing long-scale roundwound strings.
AMPS None were used in the studio. Geddy recorded direct to the mixing board with processing through: SansAmp PSA-1 guitar unit (rack mounted); Demeter pre-amp (direct input to mixing board (this has an actual tube in it which gives it a warm sound); Palmer PDI-05 speaker simulator.
VOCAL MIC AKG 414, older Neumanns.

GEDDY   While the Wal has a bit more finesse in its sound-it has a snappier top end-it's not quote as aggressive in the midrange. It also doesn't have the same bottom-end response that the Fender has. The Fender has a warmer, slightly more crude bottom end and that's what I was after. (Guitar)

GEDDY   I know what I want to sound like, so I say 'this is what I want, now go get it for me'. As a result, I didn't use a bass amp on this record. [Engineer] Clif [Norell] got a really good bass sound using three different direct effects. It sounded more amp-like on record than my amp does. (Canadian Musician)

An Evening With Rush/Test For Echo Tour (1996–97)

BASSES Same rig as previous tour, including two new Jazz basses, one in black and one in Olympic White (both with red sparkle pickguards and rosewood necks) used sometimes on "Driven" and "Half the World". The red Fender is used now on "2112" and "Stick It Out".
SYNTHS The old Mini-Moog and one set of Taurus pedals were brought out again.

My Favorite Headache (2000)

BASSES '72 Fender Jazz and played an ebony Gibson Les Paul Junior guitar as well. Strings were changed every other song and laid down through Avalon U5 direct box, the second was from the Palmer PDI-05 Speaker Stimulator, third was either a Tech 21 SansAmp Bass Driver DI or a SansAmp PSA-1 guitar unit. **AMPS** included a Vox AC30, old Marshalls, National amps. Ben Mink used a Vega amp.

EFFECTS basic song structures were done on a Logic Audio 240bit hard disk system. A Vox wah pedal was used on some parts "Slipping" features a Virus synthesizer.

GEDDY   I brought all these basses out to test and my old Jazz just beats them all, I can't stop it from sounding awesome. (Canadian Musician)

GEDDY   Recently, I was at the Experience Music Project in Seattle. They have a really fine bass guitar collection there. I found an early 60's 4000 Rickenbacker. I have to say I was quite taken with it and I'm looking for one right now. But I say that without knowing how it will sound. It will be fun to track down anyway. (TV Guide Online Chat 2000)

GEDDY   I do love using keyboards and I love writing keyboard parts but I am not a player in the true sense of the word. I definably do not look at that instrument the same way as I do the bass guitar. I have a piano in the house and I was playing with my young daughter the other day and I realized what a lazy bastard I am. I really love the sound of the piano and it's so gratifying to sit down and play … I should really spend more time with it. (Global Bass Online 2000)

Neil Peart

Neil Peart began playing a Stewart 13″ tom, 16″ floor tom, and 5″×14″ snare with an 18″ Capri bass drum, and three Ajax cymbals, at the age of thirteen. These were Japanese budget musical instruments. He was able to afford an American-made Rogers drumkit in the late 1960s, but unhappy with the finish, he covered them in silver wallpaper. He used this set-up in bands like J.R. Flood and Hush before auditioning with them for Geddy and Alex.

His influences began with big band drummers like Gene Krupa and Buddy Rich, before he discovered rock and rollers like Keith Moon and Mitch Mitchell. Throughout the decades, Neil has tried to infuse his technique with approaches by Billy Cobham, Bill Bruford, Stewart Copeland, and other contemporary percussive innovators. Neil re-invented his technique in the 1990s after a studious sabbatical with drum guru Fred Gruber.

NEIL   I have told the story before about how I was a big Keith Moon fan as a beginning drummer. All I wanted to do was get in a band that would play some Who songs so I could wail like he did. But when I finally found a band that actually wanted to play these songs, I discovered to my chagrin that I didn't like playing like

Keith Moon. It was too chaotic, and things just weren't placed rationally. I wanted to play in a more careful, deliberate way—to think about what I played where, and not just "let it happen." I am driven by a strong organizational, perfectionist demon. (Modern Drummer 1988)

NEIL   Gene Krupa was probably my first seed of wanting to be a drummer. To me he was the first rock drummer. Keith Moon was another early drummer that I admired a lot, and he was probably the most flamboyant drummer there has been. So I think in the hands of someone who can already play, showmanship is great. For me, to toss a stick up in the air is a really dangerous thing. Who knows where it's going to come down? So it adds a certain amount of risk to the performance, and a certain amount of excitement. And I like to toss them high, so it's a challenge. It's not something you can take for granted; it's a little moment of tension for me. When I was younger, Keith Moon was my idol, and because of this I always wanted to be in a band that played Who songs. But when I finally got in a band that was playing Who songs, it was all so crazy that it didn't suit my character. My personality demanded structure and organization, and within the context of trying to play like Keith Moon in Who songs, it wasn't me. That's an important dividing point for any drummer—when you find out that the way your hero plays is not the way you should play. That was a significant turning point for me, when I found out that the way I thought I wanted to play really wasn't the way I wanted to play. (Modern Drummer)

NEIL   Bill Bruford [Yes] is one of my favorite drummers. I admire him for a whole variety of reasons. I like the stuff he plays, and the way he plays it. I like the music he plays within all the bands he's been in. I know Carl Palmer spends a lot of time on keyboard percussion and I admire him for that. He's getting quite proficient. Bill Bruford's getting amazing on keyboard percussion, because he's devoted the time and the energy that it takes to become a proper keyboard percussionist. I admire that to no end. People like Carl Palmer [ELP], Phil Collins [Genesis], Michael Giles [the first drummer for King Crimson], and of course Bill, were all influences. There's a guy named Kevin Ellman who played with Todd Rundgren's Utopia for a while. I don't know what happened to him. He was the first guy I heard lean into the concert toms. Nicky Mason from Pink Floyd has a different style. Very simplistic, yet ultra tasteful. Always the right thing in the right place. I heard concert toms from Mason first, then I heard Kevin Ellman who put all his arms into it. There's The Police and their drummer [Stewart Copeland] plays with simplicity but with such gusto. He has a new approach. You learn so many things here and there. There are a lot of drummers we work with, Tommy Aldridge from the Pat Travers Band is a very good drummer. I should keep a list of all the drummers I admire. (Modern Drummer)

NEIL Talking Heads are an interesting group ... Billy Cobham came along and changed the face of things and I learnt a great deal from his way of playing jazz. (Visions)

NEIL When you watch Terry Bozzio [Missing Persons, Frank Zappa, studio, UK] play electronic drums, it is essentially musical because he has the technique to back it up ... Simon Phillips (Pete Townshend, Jeff Beck), Andy Newmark ...Jerry Marotta. I particularly like the work that Jerry and Phil Collins have done with Peter Gabriel. I listen to a lot of reggae, and the percussion on modern African music, like King Sunny Ade..I like Rod Morgenstein (Dixie Dregs, Steve Morse) a lot; he's a good player and a lovely guy. Warren Cann from Ultravox, Steve Jansen from Japan and Chris Sharrock from The Icicle Works do some interesting things. I'd also like to add Omar Hakim (Sting), Peter Erskine (Weather Report-*Heavy Weather*) and Alex Acuna to the list. (Modern Drummer)

NEIL Manu Katche's use of Chinese and splash cymbals on the new Robbie Robertson album is great too. (Musician)

NEIL A good drummer that I like who plays simply is Phil Gould, who used to be with Level 42. He plays very simple, R&B-influenced drumming, but when he pulls a fill out it'll be a beautiful fill. And his feel is great. (Modern Drummer).

NEIL In the '80s there was no place for a drummer to play. The recent bands coming out of Seattle and from across the States are revealing some fantastic drummers. Somehow, the torch was passed. These drummers were practicing and improving throughout the '80s, preparing for the time when they'd get the chance. I honestly feel this is a very exciting time for drumming. It's so gratifying to hear it come back, and come back with such a *vengeance*. Just a few of the newer guys I've been enjoying include Dave Abbruzzese of Pearl Jam, Matt Cameron from Soundgarden and Temple Of The Dog—I love his playing—and Chad Gracey from the band Live, who plays just what you want to hear. (Modern Drummer)

Albums & Tours

Rush Tour (1974)
Fly By Night Album and Tour (1975)
Caress of Steel Album and Tour (1975)
2112 Album and Tour (1976)
All the World's a Stage Album and Tour (1976–77)

DRUMKIT '74 Slingerland in Chrome finish (5-ply, 8mm, maple shells, reinforcement rings): 2 14×22 bass drums; 9×13 tom tom; 9×13 tom tom; 10×14 tom tom; 16×16 floor tom.

ADDITIONAL DRUMS Slingerland Artist model 5.5×14 snare drum in Chrome finish (mahogany shell with reinforcement rings; eight lugs, RimShot steel hoops, tone control, Zoomatic strainer, 20-wire snares; filed down bearing edge). 6.5×13 steel timbale.

CYMBALS Avedis Zildjian (70s types with hollow logos or no logos): 13″ New Beat Hi Hats (medium top-heavy bottom); 8″ Splash; 10″ Splash; 16″ Medium-Heavy Crash; 18″ Medium-Heavy Crash; 20″ Medium Crash; 22″ Ping Ride (medium heavy weight).

NOTES The black Slingerland drumset in the "Fly by Night" videos was rented. It had two 24″ bass drums, 12″, 13″ concert toms and 16″ and 18″ floor toms.

HARDWARE Slingerland Set-O-Matic tom holder on bass, Slingerland Rocket snare stand, Slingerland Dynamo hi-hat stand, Slingerland Buddy Rich model straight stands; Rogers Swivo-matic single tom mount. Ludwig Speed King pedals with taped up medium-sized beaters. Ludwig hoop-mounted cymbal holders (2). Slingerland stands with rubber feet removed!

HEADS Remo Coated Weatherking Ambassadors originally then Clear stock heads.

BASS HEAD ART Original Rush logo.

STICKS Promark Rock 747 models (Japanese White Oak; wood tip); hit by the butt end only and with the varnish removed!

NEIL If you want a really powerful roll, there's nothing more powerful than triplets with two bass drums. I could certainly get along without two bass drums for 99% of my playing. But I would miss them for some important little things … I don't understand fundamentalists who would look at my kit and say all you need is four drums. When I look at my drums, the five piece setup is the basis of what I have. (Modern Drummer)

NEIL When I was starting out, if I broke the tips off my sticks I couldn't afford to buy new ones, so I would just turn them around and use the other end. I got used to it, and continue to use the heavy end of lighter sticks—it gives me a solid impact, but with less "dead weight" to sling around. (Backstage Club 1994)

NEIL I've always used 13's. I use a certain hi-hat punctuation that doesn't work with any other size. I've tried 14's, and every time we go into the studio our co-producer Terry Brown, wants me to use 14″ hi-hat cymbals. I've tried them. I'm an open minded guy. But it just doesn't happen for me. We work with a band a lot called Max Webster, and their drummer and I work very closely, listening to each other's drums. Webster told me not to change that hi-hat, because for any open hat work or any choke work, it's so quick and clean. It just wouldn't work with 14's. The decay is too slow. (Modern Drummer)

Caress of Steel Album and Tour (1975)
2112 Album and Tour (1976)
All the World's a Stage Album and Tour (1976–77)

DRUMKIT Same with these additions in Chrome finish (added after early 1975 tour with KISS): Slingerland 5.5×6 concert tom; 5.5×8 concert tom; 6.5×10 concert tom; 8×12 concert tom.
BASS DRUM ART Caress-style Rush logo on black.
CYMBALS Another Zildjian 16″ Medium-Heavy Crash.
PERCUSSION EFFECTS Latin percussion cowbells: 2 dry agogos; triple agogos; small, medium and large rock cowbells; L.P. cluster wind chimes, 25-bar chimes; Slingerland-Deagan H58 Heritage concert bells (glockenspiel) [2.5 octaves, G32 to C61 chromatic] were added during 2112 Tour. A tambourine was mixed into part of "Bastille Day" and "The Necromancer".

NEIL I've been using the same size drums for several years, and I just know what note that drum should produce. When you combine a certain type of head with a certain size drum I believe there is an optimum note, which will give you the most projection and the greatest amount of sustain. With the concert toms I just go for the note. I have a mental scale in my head. I know what those notes should be. By now it's instinctive. With the closed toms, I start with the bottom heads. I'll tune the bottom heads to the note that drum should produce, and then tune the top head to the bottom. (Modern Drummer 1980)

NEIL The concert toms have a special, effective sound of their own. Their attack and power make a good contrast to the warmer and more resonant sound of the closed toms. With careful tuning and playing, they can be made to blend, but my 12″ concert tom could never duplicate or replace the 12″ closed tom. Basically when I have to choose between two good things, I take both! (Modern Drummer)

NEIL A lot of times people think you start with all this equipment and figure out a place to put it. For drummers, I think as your kit changes grows, it does so by one little unit at a time. When my kit started growing from a small drumkit into a big one, it was literally one cowbell, one cymbal, one whatever, found its spot.

You find little ideas that will help you economize on space and let you squeeze something in. Putting one cymbal on top of another is a time-honored one, and getting things in close enough to you so that you can play them with conviction. Things have to be in reach and controllable. (Modern Drummer 1989)

All the World's a Stage Album (1976)

Same but bass drums were recorded open with heavy muffling.

A Farewell to Kings Album and Tour (1977)
Archives Tour (1978)

DRUMKIT '77 Slingerland in 'Blakrome' (5-ply Maple with reinforcement rings and standard triple-flanged steel hoops): 2 14×24 bass drums; 5.5×6 concert tom; 5.5×8 concert tom; 6.5×10 concert tom; 8×12 concert tom; 8×12 tom tom; 9×13 tom tom; 12×15 tom tom; 16×18 floor tom.

NOTE Neil finally settles on some tom/bass sizes and has all the drums, except the snare, treated with a fiberglass layer inside them—'vibrafibing', a process performed exclusively by the Percussion Center in Ft. Wayne where his new tech Larry Allen works out of.

ADDITIONAL DRUMS 6.5×13 and 14″ brass timbales.

ZILDJIANS 18″ Pang (6 traditional rivets). Single Crotale (one octave-low).

HARDWARE rubber feet removed; Tama clip-mount double tom stands. Pearl heavy-duty stands.

HEADS Remo Photo-Logo bass front heads with Starman in red on black.

PERCUSSION Latin Percussion (L.P.) vibra-slap. L.P. 28-bell bell tree (large bells down). Spectrasound 25-bar and 36-double row bar chimes. Slingerland-Deagan temple blocks finished in red enamel [set of five box shaped, birchwood blocks] ; Slingerland-Deagan 6.5×13 and 6.5×14 standard deluxe timbales in brass finish (later fitted with Rogers-style lug mounts) with clip-on stand. Premier Viscount chimes (standard) in chrome finish

HEADS Remo Weatherking Clear C.S. (Controlled Sound) Dots on the snare (sometimes coated) and basses. Remo Weatherking C.S. Black Dots on toms. Evans Rock Heavy Duty Looking Glass (mirror). Evans Hydraulic Blue-X (2-ply) on bottoms.

NEIL I had an awful time because there was a snare sound in my mind that I wanted to achieve. I went through all kinds of metal snares. And I still wasn't satisfied. It wasn't the sound I was after. Then my drum roadie phoned me about this wooden Slingerland snare. It was second hand. Sixty dollars. I tried it out and it was the one. Every other snare I've tried chokes somewhere. Either very quietly or if you hit it too hard it chokes. This one never chokes. You can play it very delicately or you can pound it to death. It always produces a very clean, very crisp sound. It has a lot of power, which I didn't expect from a wooden snare drum. It's a really strong drum. I tried other types of wooden snare drums. I tried the top of the line Slingerland snare drum. This one was a Slingerland but very inexpensive. I've tried other wooden snares, but this was the one, there's no other snare drum that will replace it for me. (Modern Drummer 1980)

NEIL Concert tom heads sound good when they're brand new, so they get changed a bit differently. They last through a month of serious road work. The Evans Mirror Heads are used on the tom toms and take a while to warm up. It takes a week to break them in. I don't change them much more than every six weeks or so. They do start to lose their sound after a while. You start to feel they're just not putting out the note they should be. Then you say "I hate to do it but let's change the heads." I like Black Dots when they're brand new. I used to use those on my snare, and the Clear Dots also sound good when they're brand new. But the Evans heads don't. It takes a while. I've gone through agonies with snare drums. I guess most drummers do. (Modern Drummer 1980)

NEIL The Vibra-Fibing on the inside of the shells is a very subtle thing. It consists of a very thin layer of fiberglass which doesn't change the natural warmth and tonality of the wood. It just seems to even out the inconsistencies and thus, the conflicting overtones are minimized. I think it results in a purer tone. All of the drums with the exception of the snare have a thin layer of fiberglass. I can tune the drums and when I get them to the right note I know the sound will be proper. (Modern Drummer)

Hemispheres Album and Tour (1978–79)

DRUMKIT Same.

CYMBALS Same but with these additions: Zildjian 20″ Swish; 18″ Wuhan Chinese cymbal; Zildjian Burma Bell; Crotale Bar (One octave, Low)—13 total mounted on top of the tubular bells; Ludwig 38″ symphonic gong on custom made stand.

PERCUSSION Additional Spectrasound brass bar chimes include: 50 (right), 72 double-row (a 32 and 40 bar) and 36-bar chimes (left) and wind chimes;

black (then red) Korean type temple blocks on custom stands; Premier 25″ copper timpani [ranges B flat to G]; Slingerland-Deagan triangles in 6⁷⁄₁₆″, 8.5″, 10.5″ [nickel plated steel]; 53″ cathedral organ pipe chimes.

NOTES on the August dates, Neil rented a Paiste gong and used Evans Mirror front bass heads without the starman image.

NEIL I had an awful time trying to get into Chinese cymbals. I bought an 18″ pang, just looking for the Chinese sound. It had a good sound and I found myself using it for different effects. But it's almost a whispery, electronic sound. When I listen to its sound in the studio, or on a tape it sounds like a phaser. It has a warm sort of sound, but it didn't have the attack I was looking for. So I got the Zildjian China type which had that, but also a lot of sustain. Larry picked this one up at Frank's Drum Shop. It was made in China. It's a 20″ with a little more bottom end to its sound … I don't use my bass drums for beats or anything like that. My double bass drums are basically for use with fills. I don't like them to be used in rhythms. I like them to spice up a fill or create a certain accent. Many drummers say that anything that you can do with two feet can be achieved with one. That just isn't true. I can anticipate a beat with both bass drums. That is something I learned from Tommy Aldridge of the Pat Travers Band. He has a really neat style with two bass drums. Instead of doing triplets with his tom toms first and then the bass drum, which is the conventional way, he learned how to do it the other way, so that the bass drums are anticipated. (Modern Drummer 1980)

Permanent Waves Album and Tour (1979–80)
"Battle Scar"

DRUMKIT '79 Tama Superstar in a custom rosewood stained veneer, int./exteriors done by Neal Graham and Larry Allen of the Percussion Center in Fort Wayne. 6-ply (9mm) Japanese Birch shells and reinforcement rings. Hoops are triple-flanged steel (standard); low-profile hoops on 6″ and 8″ concerts. The kit is also vibrafibed and hardware brass-plated by The Percussion Center: 2 14×24 bass drums; 5.5×6 concert tom; 5.5×8 concert tom; 6.5×10 concert tom; 8×12 concert tom; 8×12 tom tom; 9×13 tom tom; 12×15 tom tom; 16×18 floor tom.

HOLDOVERS Neil received a matching 5×14 Tama snare but chose to keep the Slingerland snare ('Old Faithful'), tympanum, and timbales.

CYMBALS A 20″ Wuhan China replaces 18″.

HARDWARE An offset Tama Universal ratchet-type tom holder from on one bass; the other still has the Rogers holder for the 12″. Tama Titan stands, feet removed (clip-mounts still and boom arms are Pearl). Tama brown throne. A special compartment is built to house a fan to keep Neil dry. This is mounted on Neil's left by his hihat. Neil's drumkey is mounted on the hoop of the right bass drum near a special ashtray attachment.

HEADS Ludwig Silver Dot Rockers on concert toms now. Evans heads as last tour. Remo Coated Weatherking Ambassadors on the timbales.

BASS DRUM ART Reddish-brown front bass heads had the outlined gold Starman logo. Painted by Geddy's wife Nancy.

PERCUSSION Slingerland-Deagan Symphony Orchestra Chimes in satin gold finish [1.5 octaves, ranges C-45 to F-42]; glockenspiel notebars refinished in

Rush "Profiled" CD with Group portrait by Andrew MacNaughtan taken in fall 1980.

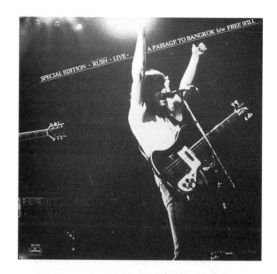
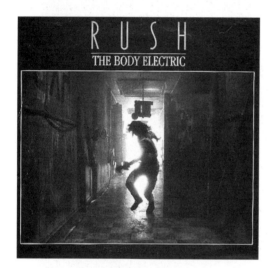

Rush vinyls: US "The Spirit of Radio" 12"; "A Passage To Bangkok (live)" 12"; Canadian "Body Electric" 7" with cover from video; US "Tom Sawyer" 7"; UK "Subdivisions" 12"; UK Power Windows album picture disc.

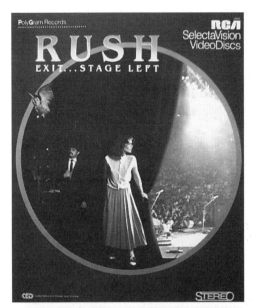

White vinyl "Prime Mover", UK "Countdown" 12", Exit Stage Left CED, "Double Agent" and "Roll the Bones" CD singles.

"Power Windows" and "Counterparts" ads.

III DISCOVERY

WHAT CAN THIS STRANGE DEVICE BE?
WHEN I TOUCH IT, IT GIVES FORTH A SOUND
IT'S GOT WIRES THAT VIBRATE, AND GIVE MUSIC
WHAT CAN THIS THING BE THAT I'VE FOUND?

SEE HOW IT SINGS LIKE A SAD HEART
AND JOYOUSLY SCREAMS OUT IT'S PAIN
SOUNDS THAT BUILD HIGH LIKE A MOUNTAIN
OR NOTES THAT FALL GENTLY LIKE RAIN

I CAN'T WAIT TO SHARE THIS NEW WONDER
THE PEOPLE WILL ALL SEE IT'S LIGHT
LET THEM ALL MAKE THEIR OWN MUSIC
THE PRIESTS PRAISE MY NAME ON THIS NIGHT

the african drum

by neil peart

V ORACLE: THE DREAM

I WANDERED HOME THROUGH SILENT STREETS
AND FELL INTO A FITFUL SLEEP
ESCAPE TO REALMS BEYOND THE NIGHT
DREAM! PLEASE CAN'T YOU SHOW ME LIGHT....

I STAND ATOP A SPIRAL STAIR
AN ORACLE CONFRONTS ME THERE
HE LEADS ME ON. LIGHT YEARS AWAY
THROUGH ASTRAL NIGHTS, GALACTIC DAYS

I SEE THE WORKS OF GIFTED HANDS
GRACE THIS STRANGE AND WONDROUS LAND
I SEE THE HAND OF MAN ARISE
WITH HUNGRY MIND, AND OPEN EYES

THEY LEFT OUR PLANETS LONG AGO
THE ELDER RACE STILL LEARN AND GROW
THEIR POWER GROWS WITH PURPOSE STRONG
TO CLAIM THE HOME, WHERE THEY BELONG

HOME TO TEAR THE TEMPLES DOWN
HOME TO CHANGE ——....

VI SOLILOQUY

THE SLEEP IS STILL IN MY EYES
THE DREAM IS STILL IN MY HEAD
I HEAVE A SIGH, AND SADLY SMILE
AND LIE AWHILE IN BED
I WISH THAT IT MIGHT COME TO PASS
NOT FADE, LIKE ALL MY DREAMS
JUST THINK OF WHAT MY LIFE MIGHT BE
IN A WORLD LIKE I HAVE SEEN
I DON'T THINK I CAN CARRY ON
THIS COLD AND EMPTY LIFE
MY SPIRITS ARE LOW IN DEPTHS OF DESPAIR
MY LIFEBLOOD..SPILLS OVER..

MUSIC BY LEE AND LIFESON
LYRICS BY PEART

Denouement

Writings by Neil Peart: exerpt from "2112" and "The African Drum" book.

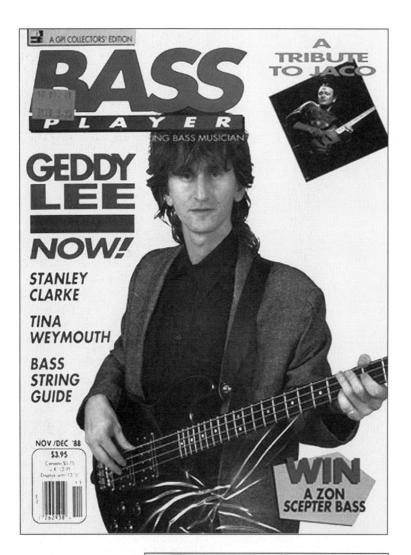

Geddy Lee in debut
Bass Player issue;
other magazines;
Victor ad.

beware the
thorns
of the black rose of
love
lest your soul they
prick

VICTOR
the band. the album.
featuring
Alex Lifeson,
guitarist of Rush,
with
Edwin of I Mother Earth
featuring
"Promise"
and
"Don't Care"
PRODUCED BY ALEX LIFESON

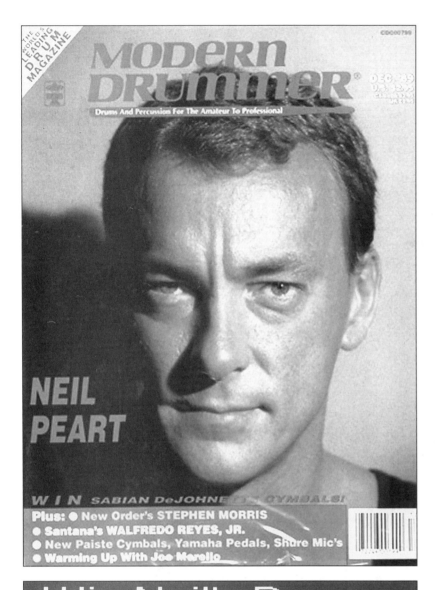

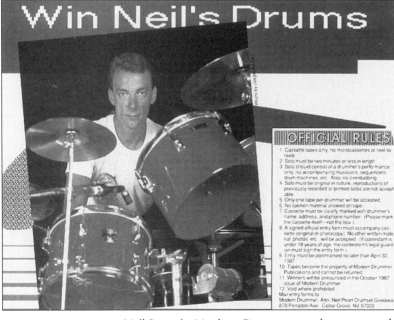

Neil Peart in Modern Drummer, endorsement ads, giveaway contests.

An Anthem Records promotional photo of Rush in early 1991. Photograph by Andrew MacNaughtan.

satin gold as well. Burma bell suspended near front by temple blocks. The chimes are in the back by the tympani now. Steel drums in "The Spirit of Radio" are played by "Erwig Chuapchuaduah". Bell tree (with large bells topside).

NEIL   The Percussion Center … I actually haven't seen their store in years. Most of our business is done by them shipping the merchandise out to us, or Neal Graham comes out from the store. He brought me my new drums a couple of weeks ago. I know he has a lot of imagination; if I want something crazy, he'll come up with it. If I want crotales on top of the tubular bells, or a temple block mounted on top of my percussion, he can do it. When you present him with an idea, he thinks of a way to achieve it. He never let me down in that respect. He built my gong stand. The gong stand mounts on the tympani and is attached to the mallet stand. (Modern Drummer 1980)

NEIL   It's a mahogany finish. The Percussion Center in Fort Wayne, where I get all my stuff, did the finish for me. I was trying to achieve a Rosewood. At home I have some Chinese Rosewood furniture, and I wanted to get that deep burgundy richness. They experimented with different kinds of inks, magic marker inks of red, blue, and black, trying to get the color. It was very difficult. (Modern Drummer 1980)

NEIL   It was the first wooden snare I ever owned. I'd always used metal ones before that and had never been totally satisfied. Then we picked up this wooden snare and it was perfect. It was THE ONE. Then I thought, "Well, if this isn't even the top-of-the-line wooden one, I must be able to get something better." So I got the top-of-the-line wooden Slingerland, and I've tried several of the wooden Tama ones. They either sound good loud or they sound good soft. None of them have the versatility that my snare has. I haven't pursued it that much because my snare makes me happy as it is. I'm not looking for something better, really. I even have the twin to that $60.00 snare behind me for the other kit. Everything's identical, but it just doesn't sound the same. I think somebody who had this snare before me did a modification on the bearing edge of the snare side. Someone filed the bearing edge where the snares go across. It's murder on the snare heads because it makes the tension very uneven, but the snare never chokes. I can play it however delicately or however hard, and it will never choke. (Modern Drummer)

NEIL   I believe in the criss-cross method of tensioning, that is, working diagonally back and forth around the drum to get an even distribution of tension. I tune the bottom [head] first and then tune the top one to it. (Modern Drummer 1987)

Moving Pictures Album and Tour (1980–81)
Exit … Stage Left/Tour (1981)

DRUMKIT remains the same but with these matching additions: '80 Tama Superstar gong bass drums (replacing the tympani); 14×20 on a Rollaway stand; 14×22 supported by shafts customized from that type of stand; '80 Tama Superstar timbales (replacing the brass timbales) 6.5×13″ and 14″ with a Stage-master stand and with regular triple-flanged tom lugs and hoops. These drums did not have reinforcement rings and were Vibrafibed also.

HEADS Remo Weatherking CS Black Dots on the concert toms. Clear Remo Ambassadors on the timbales. Evans Hydraulic tom bottoms.

MICS On "The Camera Eye" and "Vital Signs", a special PZM (Pressure Zone Microphone) was used.

NEIL   It only picks up direct sound—no reverberated signals. We used it taped onto my chest. It recreated that drummer's perspective. (Modern Drummer)

NEIL   It helped to apply that special dynamic that I hear. But still, I've never heard my drums recorded the way I hear them. (Modern Drummer 1984)

Signals Album (1982)
New World Tour (1982-83)

DRUMKIT '82 Tama Artstar prototypes with 4-ply (6mm) Japanese Birch shells in Custom Candy Apple Red with reinforcement rings and standard triple-flanged steel hoops. Hardware brass-plated and vibrafibed shells by Percussion Center once again. Superstar crest shaped badges face out. Slingerland snare was refinished to match the set after recording of album *Signals*.

HARDWARE Tama Camco pedals replace Speed Kings. Tama Titan Hi Hat stand replaces Slingerland. Two spurs on the outer side on each of the bass drums. Timbale hoops, gong bass lug casings on timbales. The bass drum tom holder is now an Omni-Sphere type (ball and socket) without Lever-Locks. The 12″ tom holder is a Tama single tom holder *welded* on the offset mount.

CYMBALS Weights on 16″ crashes change to 'Medium'.

PERCUSSION The triangles and Burma bell are retired along with the dry agogo cowbells.

CROTALES mounted on the beam holding the bar chimes above concert toms for now on.

BASS DRUM ART The same colored front bass heads as last time but with a sharper, detailed "Archives" gold Starman in opposite positions.

HEADS Evans Rock Heavy Duty Redhead tom batters (including the gong bass). Evans Tom-Tom Redhead bottoms. Remo Weatherking CS Clear Dot on the snare and bass.

NEIL   When I got the red drums, the copper started to look a bit tacky. I was afraid to get it painted because disassembling it, painting it and putting it back together might have affected it. (Modern Drummer)

NEIL   All the sound engineers in the world got together in a huge conspiracy, and convinced we drummers that the "dead" sound of big thick drums, de-tuned heads, and wads of damping was the only way to get a good sound. We were asked to take off our resonating heads, cover our batter heads with tape, get rid of those overtones, fill our bass drums with buffalo chips, oil our bass pedals, and tape our pitifully-thin wallets to the snare drums …but what if you don't like dead drums? What if you like live drums? Why shouldn't thin drum shells sound better than thick ones? And if you tuned them carefully, and made sure the inside of the shell was as perfect as wood could be? Why not? (Tama Artstar Advertisement)

Radio City Music Hall Performances (1983)

DRUMKIT the red set returns with the 20″ gong bass retired, and a new satellite kit: matching 14×18 bass drum and another red Slingerland snare (5×14).

ELECTRONIC PERCUSSION Simmons SDS-7 brain; Tom modules (4); Snare module (all whitelined); E.P.R.O.M. (Erasable Programmable Read Only Memory) Unit with ClapTrap and S.I.D. triggers between 12″ and 13″ toms; Pearl holders.

ADDITIONS A brass Tama 6½×13 timbale fitted with regular Tama tom lugs and hoop replaces wooden ones. 6″ and 8″ concert toms have high-profile rims now.

HEADS front heads are coated with reflective material.

BASS DRUM ART "P/G" from the LP label itself.

CYMBALS FOR SATELLITE KIT Avedis Zildjian: 13″ New Beat Hi Hats; 22″ Ping Ride; 16″ Medium-Thin Crash; 18″ Medium-Thin Crash; 20″ China (low-pitch thin taper) by Wuhan. A fatter taper (high-pitch) Wuhan replaced it.

PERCUSSION Bell tree, tubular bells and every bar chime, except the 25-(low by the ride) and 35-bar chimes are (below crotales on left) retired.

NEIL   When it came to adding the back kit, once I had thought of getting an acoustic bass drum and snare drum, cymbals, and then placing the electronic pads around that, it all sort of fell into place. As far as having a ride cymbal above a snare drum, I think it's great. It makes me do different things. And because of where I have that cymbal positioned, as well as the ride cymbal from my acoustic kit, I have two ride cymbals that I can reach. I have been playing patterns lately involving 16th notes between two ride cymbals that I could never do on a normal kit. (Modern Drummer 1989)

NEIL I'm a bit of a purist as, in as far as acoustic drums go, and I love them and the way they can speak, and the number of different voices I can get out of one little drum could never be equaled, I don't think, by an electronic drum, but it's more than that, it's an organic relationship with playing them and with sticking that drumstick into the drum head, the way it reacts and all of that, it's a very physical thing, but it's very satisfying, and the electronic drums don't give me that feedback at all. I use them now for about four songs out of the set, and they're just isn't near the satisfaction or the involvement with them. I feel like I'm hitting them, but I don't feel like I'm with, with them the way I do with my real drums. (Off the Record)

NEIL I didn't want to get rid of my traditional closed tom-toms because they ARE a voice. Those speak in a way that the Simmons do not. While the Simmons have a certain power and a certain dynamic quality that I like, I wasn't willing to sacrifice my acoustic drums. So I hit on the idea of having two complete drumsets. I can turn around and I have a little 18″ bass drum back there, another snare drum, another ride cymbal and the Simmons tom-toms. It doesn't interfere with the basic relationship I have with my acoustic drums, but it gives me a new avenue of expression. And I've come to realize the limitations of the Simmons as far as expression is concerned. There are certain things they *can* do and certain things they *can't*. (Modern Drummer)

Grace Under Pressure Album and Tour (1984)

HEADS snare has a Remo Weatherking C.S. Black Dot, while the 18″ satellite bass has the red Evans types with a standard in the front.

RISER a motorized octagonal riser made of red-painted oak boards now holds the bolted-in stands in position.

MIKES (bass) Beyer M88; (snare) Neumann KM3; (concerts) Calrec; (toms) Countryman Isomax II; (floor/gong) Sennheiser 421; (hihat) AKG 452; (timbales, snare underside) Shure SM57 (cymbals over head) Countryman Isomax III.

ELECTRONICS (now red backed) used on "Witch Hunt", "Closer to the Heart" and "Red Sector A". With the exception of "Closer", Neil wore headphones to play to the arpeggiator reference click. He also wore them playing "The Weapon" and "Vital Signs".

NOTES for the Oriental dates, Tama, based in Japan, made Neil a copy set with red wooden timbales. He is also given a Camco snare.

Power Windows Tour (1985–86)
A Show of Hands (recorded live tracks "Mystic Rhythms" and "Witch Hunt")

HEADS Remo Clear Ambassadors on both tom sides for some shows.
BASS DRUM ART LP label design of the TV sets 1 and 2 with Rush written around the number. The mike holes were cross-eyed but complimented with a brass ring. L.P.
NOTES Bongos played on "Territories" and "Middletown Dreams" in studio and sampled tribal drums on "Mystic Rhythms". A second kit was built with closed tom interiors that were not painted red.

NEIL One of the small drums I brought from China is an antique that's too fragile to play. So I took it and a few of the other delicate instruments that I own and sampled them—along with many of my other instruments like my temple blocks and glockenspiel. I've built up a huge library of sounds, and they've made their way onto our albums in many of the different patterns I play. (Modern Drummer)

Pieces of Eight (1987)
Hold Your Fire (1987)
A Show of Hands Album (1988)
Presto Album and "Show Don't Tell" Video (1988)

DRUMKIT '87 Ludwig Super Classic with 4-ply maple/poplar shells in Custom white opalescent with pink sparkles (inside and out) by Paintworks. Standard triple-flanged steel hoops and all hardware brass-plated by Percussion Center: 2 14×24 bass drums; 5.5×6 concert tom; 5.5×8 concert tom; 9×6 tom tom; 9×8 tom tom; 9×10 tom tom; 8×12 tom tom; 9×13 tom tom; 12×15 tom tom; 16×18 floor tom.
NOTES 6.5×10 and 8×12 concert toms were also made and used for demos, but retired before recording began. The snares are refinished again as well. The 14×22 Tama gong bass drum is refinished as well and the brass Tama 13″ timbale is kept.
HARDWARE brass-plated. Ludwig Modular stands and holders and Premier stands. Classic arc bass spurs (3 per bass; 2 each on outer). Premier bass drum thumbscrews. Tama Omni-Sphere tom mount on one and the other bass drum w/ another Tama mount. Tama Camco pedals.
BASS DRUM ART LP label design of the red spheres floating with Rush on the side on white. One pair had the mike holes in the center cross-eyed; the other had them on the top corners.
CYMBALS The 20″ Zildjian China Type is temporarily retired as a new smoother 20″ Wuhan is used.

PERCUSSION the glockenspiel is replaced by a K.A.T. malletKAT unit. The temple blocks are gone, too, but are sampled along with the other mallet percussion and a jackhammer sound on "Force Ten".

ELECTRONICS Yamaha KX-76 MIDI controller; Akai S900 samplers (4); Shark triggers; Simmons SDS-5 pads are white-backed.

HEADS Remo Clear Emperor on closed toms (or Clear Evans single ply). Remo Clear Diplomat on bottoms. Remo C.S. Clear Dots on bass and snare. Remo Clear Ambassador on gong bass and concert toms. Evans UNO 58 Glass (one-ply) on tom batters during tour.

NEIL   I found, in a side-by-side test, that the Ludwigs *sounded* better. (What other reason-money? Drum companies don't have enough to buy me!) After the test, Tama assured me they could make a set which sounded "just like the Ludwigs," but that seemed kind of pointless! (Backstage Club Newsletter 1990)

NEIL   Having recorded all the demos on our album with the open [concert] toms, I put up the closed ones when we got into the studio. To carry it even further, I tried both setups one after the other to hear exactly what the difference would be, playing a part that was designed for open toms. To my surprise, the closed ones sounded appreciably better. They had just as much attack as the open ones, but their increased tonality gave them more presence. It seems to me that a well-tuned, well-played closed drum will do anything an open drum will do-and more. Damping is kind of a nasty word to me when applied to toms. I don't use any at all on mine though I used to use little bits of gaffer's tape. There is one good damping tip I picked up from Peter Henderson, for someone who wants to use a bit of damping without affecting the drum's sound too much. If you make a little pad with some tape at the rim, when you hit the drum, the pad will bounce off the head and thus won't interfere with the sound on impact but it still cut off any lingering overtone. (Modern Drummer 1987)

NEIL   I never expected to become a virtuoso on keyboard percussion, but I thought I could contribute to the band sonically. All of those instruments are big. You know, when you start wanting to have a marimba, glockenspiel, timpani, and chimes, it's just an impossibility to get it around you. So when sampling came along, that's when electronics just won me over completely. I used to have my glockenspiel where the KAT is now in my kit. We would mike those bells, and that mic' would pick up only part of the instrument, but it would pick up half the drumkit and most of the bass sound! So using the KAT completely avoids those types of problems. (Modern Drummer 1989)

NEIL   On the song "Time Stand Still" I used temple block sounds. Through the wonder of electronics I was able to manipulate the pitches of the temple blocks, so I got the sound I heard in my head for that part. I have an antique Chinese drum at home that's too fragile to do anything with, but by sampling, I was able to use it on the record ['Tai Shan']. (Modern Drummer 1989)

NEIL   It's just a regular foot pedal really, made by a company called "Shark" which may or may not still be in business. Like a drum pad, it simply triggered a midi impulse into the Akai sampler, which then reproduced a sample of my snare (taken from "Grand Designs," as it happens, as are the tom samples used in the live version of "Closer to the Heart" last tour). (Backstage Club 1991)

NEIL   [For the drum solo which incorporated parts of "Pieces of Eight"] I took the idea from a Count Basie CD that I have. I sampled the horn hits off the CD and triggered them live, but I didn't feel right about using someone else's sounds on our record. I have strict morality about sampling, and it's one reason why I use mostly my samples. So I went into the studio where they have a Synclavier, which is a super-deluxe synthesizer. We analyzed the chording of the Basie samples and reproduced them synthetically. So I got all of the intervals I wanted, and it ended up sounding beautiful. I could then wipe the guilt off my brow because I had gone to the trouble and expense of creating those samples. With Simmons pads. I assigned each one to a different pad, and to a foot switch. I struck the pad and crash cymbal at the same time so the hits came off exactly together. I worked it out so that things were in the right place so that I could do that kind of drum construction I wanted and be in the right place for the brass accents. (Modern Drummer)

NEIL   I really like the resonance of the Evans. (Musician)

NEIL   In the studio, I generally take off the front heads and use quite heavy damping. I'll use those quilted packing blankets placed right against the head. I wonder if I'll get to the point where I'll be able to get the sound I want without any damping. Years ago I muffled everything on the kit-the toms and the snare. Then, as I became better at tuning drums, I stopped using muffling completely on toms and snare drums in the studio. But with the bass drums, I don't know; it's one hell of a big barrel with too much out-of-control transient stuff going on. For live work, I use both heads on the drum. The front head has a hole just large enough to get a mic' inside. For muffling I use a crescent-shaped muffling device that just sits inside the drum and rests against both heads. As for heads on the bass drums I like the clear dots for their durability. And I just use your typical felt beater. It's mundane, I know. [laughs] (Modern Drummer 1989)

Presto Tour (1990)

DRUMKIT same setup (with the same hardware) refinished in a custom metallic plum color by Paintworks (maybe because purple is traditionally thought of as a magical color denoting illusion).

ADDITIONS A matching Ludwig Ensemble 3×13 piccolo snare replaces the satellite kit's Slingerland and the timbale is retired. ddrum pads replace the Simmons. Dauz pad with an Evans Black Gold Hydraulic head.

BASS DRUM ART Album sleeve's hands doing rock paper scissors. Also the mike hole is at the top.

ADDITIONAL SNARES IN STUDIO a Solid Percussion model 3¼×13 cocobolo piccolo (used on most of *Presto*, sampled on "Scars" as a foot trigger). Camco 5×14 (maple finish).

NEIL   Of course, the scissors, paper, stone metaphor comes from the song "Hand Over Fist", but we thought it made a nice picture as well, and wanted to use it somewhere, plus I thought it would be a nice device for the drum heads. As to whether these three symbols represent us—I'll never tell … (Backstage Club 1991)

NEIL   I tried a few piccolo snares, some of the custom-made snares, just trying whatever I could get my hands on. Most piccolos have tremendous definition and a great high-end crack, that they don't have much in the way of a bottom end. The Solid drum that I have is made of cocobolo wood that gives it a resonance that carries into lower frequencies. That must be the fundamental difference, because I tried another piccolo of theirs made of ply maple, and it sounded like a good-sounding piccolo, but not as versatile as the solid-shell cocobolo. I've tried [snares deeper than 5″], but I just don't like the sound. The distance between the heads gives the drum an odd response, at least to me. They feel funny to me. I know they have their uses, but they don't fall into what I'm doing. I'm the same way with tom-toms. I practically had to special order a set that didn't have deep-shelled toms. Everyone thinks that depth equals volume or resonance, or something. It's something that I've experimented with, and have found no basis in fact. I use the standard tom sizes and get a sound that I'm most happy with. (Modern Drummer 1989)

NEIL   Sampling has been a godsend to me, to be able to include sounds in my playing without having to overdub anything. Around an acoustic drumset there are plenty of places to stick a little trigger, and of course there's always room for a footswitch. You can always slip a foot off the hi-hat and send off another sound. I feel it really adds a lot to the character of what I'm doing. (Modern Drummer)

Buddy Rich Scholarship Concert (1991)

DRUMKIT only 9×13, 16×18, 24 bass; cowbells, 10″ splash, 13″ hihats, 16″ crash, 18″ crash, Wuhan china, 22″ ride.

NOTES by this time, Neil was using his Signature line from Pro-Mark, which formerly issued his stick in a digital style lettering on the grip area.

Roll the Bones Album and Tour *(1991)*

DRUMKIT '91 Ludwig Super Classic in Blue Shadow inside and out. Vibrafibing and Brass-plated by Percussion Center: 16×22 bass drum; 5.5×6 custom tom tom; 5.5×8 custom tom tom; 8×10 tom tom; 8×12 tom tom; 9×13 tom tom (over bass); 13×15 left floor tom; 16×16 floor tom.

ADDITIONAL DRUMS Placed back by the Wuhan near the small toms, is a Remo Legato 3×14 piccolo snare (with Remo coated Falams-K Super head); Ludwig Rocker bass spurs; Ludwig Modular tom holder; Ludwig Mini Classic lugs on two smallest toms; Yamaha DF-50 double pedal.

HEADS Remo Ebony Reverse Black Dot head on Dauz pad.

CYMBALS same. The hi hats ordered unlathed. 18″ and 20″ Crash cymbals get sizzles. The fat Wuhan is back!

PERCUSSON L.P. 25-bar chimes with black bar replace the old wooden types.

BASS DRUM ART Dice window and bones falling design; mike hole.

NEIL On the day we began setting up for the writing stage of *Roll the Bones*, I stood in the little studio and watched Larry [Allen] putting my drums together, it occurred to me that I'd been using the same basic set-up for years now, and maybe it was time for a rethink—time to make some changes, take some chances. Just putting the drums in different places might alter my approach to them, push me in some new directions. So we started moving the toms around, putting the floor tom under my left hand, and shifting the others down one position, placing the 15″ where the floor tom used to be, etc. Also, I wanted to try a using a single bass drum with two pedals, to eliminate a big resonating chamber (the other bass drum) which I hardly ever used. I also decided to try a different size: 22″ instead of 24″. (Roll the Bones Tourbook)

NEIL At a later point during the tour, Primus were gone and we were out with Mr. Big. So I went out and got a PureCussion set for myself, because I really enjoyed Herb's. I set myself a course of study. It was getting near the end of the tour. I'd go into the tune-up room and play Max Roach's "The Drum Also Waltzes." (Modern Drummer)

Counterparts Album *(1993)*

DRUMKIT same as previous, but with a Solid Percussion 6.5×14 snare and a Latin Percussion tambourine (heard on "Cold Fire", "Animate", "Double Agent", "Leave that Thing Alone", and mounted over 10″ tom).

NEIL I was going to turn the whole back of my drum set into this hand drum set— triggering snare drum and kick sounds when needed from pedals. But you listen to the songs and they didn't need that … so I had to junk the idea, no matter how much I liked it. (St. Petersburg Times)

Counterparts Tour *(1994)*
Drum Lessons With the Greats 2 *(1995)*

DRUMKIT same refinished in Black Cherry by Paintworks.
ADDITION 14×22 Ludwig Super Classic custom gong bass drum (with the old Tama's gong bass drum hardware) with floor tom brackets lowered and off-center.
HARDWARE Ludwig Rocker tom holder.
BASS DRUM ART album cover (nut and bolt diagram). Satellite bass had the six-pointed star optical illusion.

NEIL Right now, I'm working on playing brushes, which I have no use for in Rush, but it just intrigues me. (Aquarian 1994)

Burning For Buddy I and II *(1994)*

DRUMKIT '94 Ludwig Super Classic in Custom Red Sparkle: 16×22 bass drum; 9×13 tom tom; 16×16 floor tom (traditionally the first modern tom sizes); the still black cherry Slingerland snare.
BASS DRUM ART NP initials in the tradition of the monogram shield big band logos of the 1940s on coated bass heads.

A Work in Progress Video Performance *(1996)*
Test For Echo Album and Tour *(1996)*
Different Stages Album *(1998)*

DRUMKIT '95 Drum Workshop FinishPly set, in custom Blood Red Sparkle (for nostalgic reasons). The shells are 5-ply Maple; for the first time since his first set is not vibrafibed. Brass hardware again and is now an option from companies: 16×22 bass drum; 7×8 custom tom tom (used on tour only); 7×10 custom tom tom; 8×12 tom tom; 9×13 tom tom (over bass); 12×15 floor tom; 16×16 floor tom; 16×18 floor tom (mounted in air); 13×15 floor tom on left; 6×14 Red Sparkle/brass Edge snare; 3×13 piccolo (one with brass and black lugs); 2 14×18 bass drum (back set). The bass hoops have a red sparkle "inlay" with black painted edges.
CYMBALS same.
ADDITIONS 8″ Splash is added on top of cowbells now mounted on left side. 14″ A Custom Hi Hats put on right near 22″ A Custom Ping Ride. The other 8″

Splash is mounted atop the ride and the 16″ crash is over bass still. 13″ Hi Hats have sizzles.

HARDWARE DrumWorkshop: 5500 Delta Hi Hat stand; DW 9210 C-Hat holder; 5002AH Delta double bass pedal; S.T.M. tom mounts; 909 cymbal stackers; 9100 drum throne; 9999 tom/cymbal stand; 9500 snare stands; 9700 cymbal stands (4); 9799 double cymbal stands (2).

PERCUSSION still using malletKAT with Akai samplers, 2 Shark pedals and 8 ddrum pads. Hammer dulcimer used in studio on "Half the World" and "Totem".

HEADS First Neil used stock coated DW heads, then Remo Coated Ambassador with Clear Diplomat on bottoms. FalamSlam bass drum patches. After Work in Progress Neil replaced the polarized image of his face to the Stoneman graphic on front bass; Fractal graphics on 18″ basses.

NOTES Neil's other snares—though not used included a Rogers Dynasonic 5×14; Ludwig Supra-Sensitive 5×14 snare; Goetz Percussion segment shell; Gretsch 5.5×14; Ayotte WoodHoop 5.5×14; Drum Workshop 5×14; White Marine Craviotto; Drum Workshop 5×13 Natural Maple Collectors piccolo snare.

NEIL I still have my arsenal of snare drums, but I didn't feel the need to use them all. My prize drum is an old Rogers *Dyna-sonic*. It was my dream drum when I was a kid, so I *had* to have one! (Modern Drummer)

NEIL For DW, and for this drummer, our methods are tempered by experience, but the enthusiasm and inspiration remain forever young. As the African proverb goes: Happy and wise is the one, who knows how to blend old and young. (DW press ad)

NEIL For the contemporary drummer, the drums themselves are the nouns and verbs, the voices of character and action, while cymbals are the punctuation marks, the modifiers, the shades of narrative and meaning, of mood and texture. For many drummers, the ride cymbal represents the running dialog, the linked phrases, and the accented syllables of rhythmic speech. The 16″ crash represents the comma, the semi-colon, the dash. The 18″ crash makes an exclamation mark, or the definitive full-stop at the end of a sentence, while the 20″ crash is a warm swell, like the cresting of a wave. The 8″ and 10″ splashes offer their subtle comments and accents, and the China Boy ranges from a soft whoosh to an attention-getting smash. The 13″ hihats seem almost able to speak, and they sure can dance. Like all my Zildjians, they not only talk—they sing. (Zildjian "Talking Cymbals" Endorsement)

DISCOGRAPHY & VIDEOGRAPHY 4

Discography

Albums

Year	Album	Producers Composers

1974 **Rush** *Rush*

Side 1
1. Finding My Way (5:03) Lee-Lifeson
2. Need Some Love (2:16) Lee-Lifeson
3. Take a Friend (4:27) Lee-Lifeson
4. Here Again (7:30) Lee-Lifeson

Side 2
5. What You're Doing (4:19) Lee-Lifeson
6. In the Mood (3:36) Lee
7. Before and After (5:33) Lee-Lifeson
8. Working Man (7:07) Lee-Lifeson

Lyrics by John Rutsey

1975 **Fly By Night** *Rush/Terry Brown*

Side 1
1. Anthem (4:10) Lee-Lifeson-Peart
2. Best I Can (3:24) Lee
3. Beneath, Between and Behind (3:00) Lifeson-Peart
4. By-Tor and the Snow Dog (8:57) Lee-Lifeson-Peart
   I.   At the Tobes of Hades
   II. Across the Styx (at :36)
   III. Of the Battle (at 1:11)x
      i)   Challenge and Defiance
      ii) 7/4 War Furor (at 3:52)
      iii) Aftermath (at 4:41)
      iv) Hymn of Triumph (at 6:30)
   IV. Epilogue (at 7:35)

Side 2
5. Fly By Night (3:20) Lee-Peart
6. Making Memories (2:56) Lee-Lifeson-Peart
7. Rivendell (5:00) Lee-Peart
8. In the End (6:51) Lee-Lifeson

Lyrics by Neil Peart

1975 **Caress of Steel** *Rush/Terry Brown*

Side 1
1. Bastille Day (4:36) Lee-Lifeson-Peart
2. I Think I'm Going Bald (3:35) Lee-Lifeson-Peart
3. Lakeside Park (4:07) Lee-Lifeson-Peart
4. The Necromancer (12:36) Lee-Lifeson-Peart
   I.   Into Darkness (4:20)
   II. Under the Shadow (4:25)
   III. Return of the Prince (3:51)

Side 2
5. The Fountain of Lamneth (19:04)
   I.   In the Valley (4:17) Lee-Lifeson-Peart
   II. Didacts and Narpets (1:00) Lee-Lifeson-Peart
   III. No One At the Bridge (4:15) Lee-Lifeson-Peart
   IV. Panacea (3:12) Lee-Peart
   V.   Bacchus Plateau (3:12) Lee-Peart
   VI. The Fountain (3:48) Lee-Lifeson-Peart

Lyrics by Neil Peart

Year	Album	Producers Composers

Year	Album	Producers Composers

1976 2112 — Rush/Terry Brown

Side 1
1. 2112 (19:56)
   - I. Overture (4:32) — Lee-Lifeson-Peart
   - II. The Temples of Syrinx (2:13) — Lee-Lifeson-Peart
   - III. Discovery (3:30) — Lifeson-Peart
   - IV. Presentation (3:40) — Lifeson-Peart
   - V. Oracle: The Dream (2:00) — Lee-Lifeson-Peart
   - VI. Soliloquy (2:23) — Lee-Lifeson-Peart
   - VII. Grand Finale (2:18) — Lee-Lifeson-Peart

Side 2
2. A Passage to Bangkok (3:30) — Lee-Lifeson-Peart
3. The Twilight Zone (3:14) — Lee-Lifeson-Peart
4. Lessons (3:48) — Lifeson
5. Tears (3:29) — Lee
   Guests: Hugh Syme, Mellotron
6. Something For Nothing (3:56) — Lee-Peart

Lyrics by Neil Peart

"Lessons" lyrics by Alex Lifeson

"Tears" lyrics by Geddy Lee

1976 All the World's a Stage — Rush/Terry Brown

LP 1

Side A
1. Bastille Day (4:48)
2. Anthem (4:28)
3. Fly By Night/In the Mood (4:50)
4. Something For Nothing (3:50)

LP 2

Side B
5. Lakeside Park (4:45)
6. 2112 (15:11)
   - I. Overture (4:36)
   - II. The Temples of Syrinx (2:12)
   - III. Presentation (4:25)
   - IV. Soliloquy/V. Grand Finale (4:38)

LP 2

Side C
7. By-Tor and the Snow Dog (11:24)
8. In the End (7:50)

LP 1

Side D
9. Working Man/Finding My Way (13:45) inc. drum solo
10. What You're Doing (5:44) ❶

Recorded at Massey Hall, Toronto, Canada in June 1976 during *2112* tour.

❶ Omitted on CD for space limitations but then released on *Chronicles*; LP and cassette versions have the complete band member voices and door slam sound.

1977 A Farewell To Kings — Rush/Terry Brown

Side 1
1. A Farewell To Kings (5:53) — Lee-Lifeson-Peart
2. Xanadu (11:06) — Lee-Lifeson-Peart

Side 2
3. Closer To the Heart (2:52) — Lee-Lifeson-Peart
4. Cinderella Man (4:20) — Lee
5. Madrigal (2:35) — Lee-Lifeson-Peart
6. Cygnus X-1 (10:27) — Lee-Lifeson-Peart
   Book I: The Voyage

Lyrics by Neil Peart

"Cinderella Man" lyrics by Geddy Lee

1978 Archives

Compilation of first three albums.

1978 Hemispheres — Rush/Terry Brown

Side 1
1. Cygnus X-1 Book II: Hemispheres (18:07) — Lee-Lifeson
   - I. Prelude (4:30)
   - II. Apollo/ III. Dionysus (4:36)
   - IV. Armageddon (2:52)
   - V. Cygnus (5:00)
   - VI. The Sphere (1:09)

Side 2
2. Circumstances (3:42) — Lee-Lifeson
3. The Trees (4:46) — Lee-Lifeson
4. La Villa Strangiato —
   an exercise in self-indulgence
   (instrumental, 9:36 total) — Lee-Lifeson
   - I. Buenas nochas, mein froinds!
   - II. To sleep perchance to dream…(at :27)
   - III. Strangiato theme (at 2:00)
   - IV. A Lerxst in Wonderland (at 3:16)
   - V. Monsters! (at 5:50)
   - VI. The Ghost of the Aragon (at 6:10)
   - VII. Danforth and Pape (at 6:45)
   - VIII. The Waltz of the Shreves (at 7:26)
   - IX. Never turn your back on a Monster! (at 7:52)
   - X. Monsters! (Reprise) (at 8:03)
   - XI. Strangiato theme (Reprise) (at 8:17)
   - XII. A Farewell To Things (at 9:28)

Lyrics by Neil Peart

Year	Album	Producers Composers
1980	**Permanent Waves**	*Rush/Terry Brown*

Side 1
1. The Spirit of Radio (4:54) — Lee-Lifeson
   Guests: Erwig Chapuduah, steel drums
2. Freewill (5:23) — Lee-Lifeson
3. Jacob's Ladder (7:50) — Lee-Lifeson

Side 2
4. Entre Nous (4:37) — Lee-Lifeson
5. Different Strings (3:50) — Lee-Lifeson
   Guests: Hugh Syme, piano
6. Natural Science (9:27) — Lee-Lifeson
   I. Tide Pools
   II. Hyperspace (at 2:20)
   III. Permanent Waves (at 5:08)

Lyrics by Neil Peart, except "Different Strings" lyrics by Geddy Lee

Year	Album	Producers Composers
1981	**Moving Pictures**	*Rush/Terry Brown*

Side 1
1. Tom Sawyer (4:33) — Lee-Lifeson
2. Red Barchetta (6:07) — Lee-Lifeson
3. YYZ -instrumental (4:23) — Lee-Peart
4. Limelight (4:18) — Lee-Lifeson

Side 2
5. The Camera Eye (10:55) — Lee-Lifeson
6. Witch Hunt (4:43) — Lee-Lifeson
   Guests: Hugh Syme, synth
   Part III of Fear Trilogy
7. Vital Signs (4:45) — Lee-Lifeson

Lyrics by Neil Peart

"Tom Sawyer" lyrics by Neil Peart and Pye Dubois

Year	Album	Producers Composers
1981	**Exit ... Stage Left**	*Terry Brown*

Record 1

Side 1
1. The Spirit of Radio (5:15)
2. Red Barchetta (6:45)
3. YYZ — instrumental (7:44) inc. drum solo

Side 2
4. A Passage to Bangkok (3:43) ❶
5. Closer To the Heart (3:06)
6. Beneath, Between and Behind (2:31)
7. Jacob's Ladder (8:39)

Record 2

Side 3
8. Broon's Bane — guitar instrumental (1:35)
9. The Trees (4:30)
10. Xanadu (12:33)

Side 4
11. Freewill (5:31)
12. Tom Sawyer (4:58)
13. La Villa Strangiato — instrumental (9:37)

Sides 1, 3 and 4 recorded at Forum, Montreal, Canada in March 1981 during *Moving Pictures* Tour; Side 2 recorded at Scotland's Apollo Theatre in June 1980 during *Permanent Waves* Tour.

❶ Omitted on first CD for space limitations but then released on *Chronicles*

Year	Album	Producers Composers
1982	**Signals**	*Rush/Terry Brown*

Side 1
1. Subdivisions (5:34) — Lee-Lifeson
2. The Analog Kid (4:47) — Lee-Lifeson
3. Chemistry (4:56) — Lee-Lifeson
4. Digital Man (6:23) — Lee-Lifeson

Side 2
5. The Weapon (6:27) — Lee-Lifeson
   Part II of Fear Trilogy
6. New World Man (3:44) — Lee-Lifeson
7. Losing It (4:53) — Lee-Lifeson
   with Ben Mink, violin
8. Countdown (5:48) — Lee-Lifeson

Lyrics by Neil Peart "Chemistry" lyrics by Lee-Lifeson-Peart

Year	Album	Producers Composers
1984	**Grace Under Pressure**	*Rush/Peter Henderson*

Side 1
1. Distant Early Warning (4:45) — Lee-Lifeson
2. Afterimage (5:00) — Lee-Lifeson
3. Red Sector A (5:08) — Lee-Lifeson
4. The Enemy Within (4:33) — Lee-Lifeson
Part I of Fear Trilogy

Side 2
5. The Body Electric (4:58) — Lee-Lifeson
6. Kid Gloves (4:16) — Lee-Lifeson
7. Red Lenses (4:39) — Lee-Lifeson
8. Between the Wheels (5:36) — Lee-Lifeson

Lyrics by Neil Peart

Year	Album	Producers Composers

| 1985 | **Power Windows** | Peter Collins/Rush
Andy Richards, synth |

Side 1
1. The Big Money (5:36) — Lee-Lifeson
2. Grand Designs (5:05) — Lee-Lifeson
3. Manhattan Project (5:05) — Lee-Lifeson
4. Marathon (6:09) — Lee-Lifeson

Side 2
5. Territories (6:19) — Lee-Lifeson
6. Middletown Dreams (5:17) — Lee-Lifeson
7. Emotion Detector (5:10) — Lee-Lifeson
8. Mystic Rhythms (6:08) — Lee-Lifeson

Lyrics by Neil Peart

| 1987 | **Hold Your Fire** | Peter Collins/Rush |

Side 1
1. Force Ten (4:28) — Lee-Lifeson
2. Time Stand Still (5:07) — Lee-Lifeson
Aimee Mann, *guest vocal*
3. Open Secrets (5:37) — Lee-Lifeson
Aimee Mann, *guest vocal*
4. Second Nature (4:35) — Lee-Lifeson
5. Prime Mover (5:19) — Lee-Lifeson

Side 2
6. Lock and Key (5:08) — Lee-Lifeson
7. Mission (5:15) — Lee-Lifeson
8. Turn the Page (4:14) — Lee-Lifeson
9. Tai Shan (4:14) — Lee-Lifeson
10. High Water (5:32) — Lee-Lifeson

Lyrics by Neil Peart

| 1989 | **A Show of Hands** | Rush |

LP 1

Side 1
1. Intro (0:53)
2. The Big Money (5:52)
3. Subdivisions (5:19)
4. Marathon (6:43)

Side 2
5. Turn the Page (4:46) ❶
6. Manhattan Project (5:00) ❷
7. Mission (5:59) ❸

LP 2

Side 3
8. Distant Early Warning (5:22)

Year	Album	Producers Composers

9. Mystic Rhythms (5:32) ❹
10. Witch Hunt (3:55) ❸
    Part III of Fear Trilogy
11. The Rhythm Method-Drum
    Solo (4:40) — Peart

Side 4
12. Force Ten (4:57) **
13. Time Stand Still (5:10)
14. Red Sector A (5:12)
15. Closer To the Heart (4:53)

Side one and all songs unless noted recorded at National Exhibition Centre, Birmingham, England during *Hold Your Fire* Tour, April 1988.

❶ recorded in New Orleans, LA at UNO Lakefront Arena, January 1988.

❷ recorded in Phoenix, AZ at Veterans Memorial Coliseum, February 1988.

❸ recorded in San Diego, CA at Sports Arena, February 1988.

❹ recorded in E. Rutherford, NJ at Meadowlands Arena during *Power Windows* Tour, April 1986.

| 1989 | **Presto** | Rupert Hine/Rush
Jason Sniderman,
additional keys |

Side 1
1. Show Don't Tell (5:01) — Lee-Lifeson
2. Chain Lightning (4:33) — Lee-Lifeson
3. The Pass (4:51) — Lee-Lifeson
4. War Paint (5:24) — Lee-Lifeson
5. Scars (4:08) — Lee-Lifeson
6. Presto (5:46) — Lee-Lifeson

Side 2
7. Superconductor (4:47) — Lee-Lifeson
8. Anagram (4:00) — Lee-Lifeson
9. Red Tide (4:30) — Lee-Lifeson
10. Hand Over Fist (4:11) — Lee-Lifeson
11. Available Light (5:05) — Lee-Lifeson

Lyrics by Neil Peart

| 1990 | **Chronicles** | |

Record 1

Side A
1. Finding My Way (5:06)
2. Working Man (7:09)
3. Fly By Night (3:19)

Year	Album	Producers Composers

4. Anthem (4:22)
5. Bastille Day (4:37)
6. Lakeside Park (4:07)

Side B
7. 2112 (6:44)
   - I. Overture
   - II. The Temples of Syrinx
8. What You're Doing (live) (5:38)
9. A Farewell To Kings (5:51)
10. Closer To the Heart (2:53)

Record 2

Side C
11. The Trees (4:38)
12. La Villa Strangiato (9:35)
13. Freewill (5:23)
14. The Spirit of Radio (4:57)

Side D
15. Tom Sawyer (4:33)
16. Red Barchetta (6:08)
17. Limelight (4:20)
18. A Passage to Bangkok (live) (3:45)

Record 3

Side E
19. Subdivisions (5:34)
20. New World Man (3:42)
21. Distant Early Warning (4:59)
22. Red Sector A (5:13)
23. The Big Money (5:35)

Side F
24. Manhattan Project (5:07)
25. Force Ten (4:34)
26. Time Stand Still (5:10)
27. Mystic Rhythms (live) (5:42)
28. Show Don't Tell (5:01)

Compiled by Bill Levenson

1991	***Roll the Bones***	*Rupert Hine/Rush*

Side 1
1. Dreamline (4:38) — Lee-Lifeson
2. Bravado (4:35) — Lee-Lifeson
3. Roll the Bones (5:30) — Lee-Lifeson
4. Face Up (3:54) — Lee-Lifeson
5. Where's My Thing? (3:49) — Lee-Lifeson

Side 2
6. The Big Wheel (5:13) — Lee-Lifeson
7. Heresy (5:26) — Lee-Lifeson
8. Ghost of a Chance (5:19) — Lee-Lifeson

Year	Album	Producers Composers

9. Neurotica (4:40) — Lee-Lifeson
10. You Bet Your Life (5:00) — Lee-Lifeson

Lyrics by Neil Peart

1993	***Counterparts***	*Peter Collins/Rush John Webster, additional keys*

Side 1
1. Animate (6:03) — Lee-Lifeson
2. Stick It Out (4:31) — Lee-Lifeson
3. Cut to the Chase (4:49) — Lee-Lifeson
4. Nobody's Hero (4:56) — Lee-Lifeson conducted by Michael Kamen
5. Between Sun and Moon (4:37) — Lee-Lifeson

Side 2
6. Alien Shore (5:48) — Lee-Lifeson
7. The Speed of Love (5:03) — Lee-Lifeson
8. Double Agent (4:53) — Lee-Lifeson
9. Leave That Thing Alone! (4:06) — Lee-Lifeson
10. Cold Fire (4:27) — Lee-Lifeson
11. Everyday Glory (5:11) — Lee-Lifeson

Lyrics by Neil Peart, except "Between Sun and Moon" lyrics by Neil Peart and Pye Dubois.

1996	***Test For Echo***	*Peter Collins/Rush*

Side 1
1. Test For Echo (5:56) — Lee-Lifeson
2. Driven (4:27) — Lee-Lifeson
3. Half the World (3:43) — Lee-Lifeson
4. The Color of Right (4:49) — Lee-Lifeson
5. Time and Motion (5:01) — Lee-Lifeson
6. Totem (4:58) — Lee-Lifeson

Side 2
7. Dog Years (4:55) — Lee-Lifeson
8. Virtuality (5:44) — Lee-Lifeson
9. Limbo (5:29) — Lee-Lifeson
10. Resist (4:24) — Lee-Lifeson
11. Carve Away the Stone (4:05) — Lee-Lifeson

Lyrics by Neil Peart, except "Test For Echo" lyrics by Lee-Lifeson-Peart and Pye Dubois.

1997	***Retrospective I***	

Side 1
1. The Spirit of Radio (4:56)
2. The Trees (4:42)

Year	Album	Producers Composers

3. Something For Nothing (3:58)
4. Freewill (5:22)
5. Xanadu (11:05)
6. Bastille Day (4:37)
7. By-Tor and the Snow Dog (8:37)

Side 2

8. Anthem (4:21)
9. Closer To the Heart (2:52)
10. 2112 — Overture (4:33)
11. 2112 — The Temples of Syrinx (2:12)
12. La Villa Strangiato (9:34)
13. Fly By Night (3:21)
14. Finding My Way (5:06)

1997	**Retrospective II**	

Side 1

1. The Big Money (5:35)
2. Red Barchetta (6:09)
3. Subdivisions (5:33)
4. Time Stand Still (5:09)
5. Mystic Rhythms (5:53)
6. The Analog Kid (4:47)
7. Distant Early Warning (4:57)

Side 2

8. Marathon (6:09)
9. The Body Electric (5:00)
10. Mission (5:16)
11. Limelight (4:19)
12. Red Sector A (5:09)
13. New World Man (3:42)
14. Tom Sawyer (4:33)
15. Force Ten (4:31)

1998	**Different Stages**	Geddy Lee/ Paul Northfield

Set I

1. Dreamline (5:34) (intro music heard under crowd noise)
2. Limelight (4:32)
3. Driven (5:17)
4. Bravado (6:23) ❶
5. Animate (6:29)
6. Show Don't Tell (5:29) ❷
7. The Trees (5:29) ❸
8. Nobody's Hero (5:01)
9. Closer to the Heart (5:13)

10. 2112 ❹
   Overture (4:33)
   The Temples of Syrinx (2:20)
   Discovery (4:18) inc. guitar intro
   Presentation (3:40)
   Oracle: the Dream (1:49)
   Soliloquy (2:08)
   Grand Finale (2:37)

Set II

11. Test For Echo (6:16)
12. The Analog Kid (5:15) ❺
13. Freewill (5:36)
14. Roll the Bones (5:59)
15. Stick It Out (4:42)
16. Resist (4:28) ❻
17. Leave That Thing Alone! — instrumental (4:46) ❻
18. The Rhythm Method 1997 — Drum Solo (8:20)
19. Natural Science (8:06)
20. The Spirit of Radio (5:00)
21. Tom Sawyer (5:19)
22. YYZ — instrumental (5:26)

Note: Japanese CD pressings include "Force Ten". All tracks, unless noted, recorded at World Amphitheater, Chicago, IL, June 1997, during *Test For Echo* Tour:

❶ recorded at Corestates Center in Philadephia, PA, April 1994, during *Counterparts* Tour.

❷ recorded at Arena, Miami, FL, February 1994, during *Counterparts* Tour.

❸ recorded at Starplex Amphitheater, Dallas, TX, May 1997, during *Test For Echo* Tour.

❹ recorded at Great Woods Amphitheater, Mansfield, MA, June 1997, during *Test For Echo Tour.*

❺ recorded at Palace Auburn Hills, Detroit, MI, March 1994, during *Counterparts* Tour.

❻ recorded at Molson Amphitheatre, Toronto, Canada, July 1997, during *Test For Echo* Tour.

Set III

1. Bastille Day (5:08)
2. By-Tor and the Snow Dog (4:59)
3. Xanadu (12:33)
4. A Farewell To Kings (5:54)
5. Something For Nothing (4:01)
6. Cygnus X-1 (10:24)
7. Anthem (4:47)
8. Working Man (4:01)
9. Fly By Night/In the Mood (2:04)
10. Cinderella Man (3:35)

Recorded at Hammersmith Odeon, London, February 20, 1978 during *A Farewell To Kings* Tour. Engineered by Terry Brown.

LP Album Labels

	Album	Label/Catalog No.	Notes
Canada	Rush	Moon MN-100 red logo	
	Rush	Anthem ANR-1-1001	
	Rush	Anthem/Capitol ANR-1-601	
	Fly By Night	Anthem ANR-1-1023	
	Fly By Night	Anthem ANR-1-1002	
	Fly By Night	Anthem/Capitol ANR-1-602	
	Caress of Steel	Anthem ANR-1-603	
	2112	Anthem ANR-1-1004	
	All the World's a Stage	Anthem ANR-1-1005	
	A Farewell To Kings	Anthem ANR-1-1010	
	Archives	Anthem ANR-3-1013	gray or black reissue covers
	Hemispheres	Anthem ANR-1-1014	
	Hemispheres	Anthem SANR-1-1015	red vinyl w/gatefold + poster
	Hemispheres	Anthem PANR-1-1017	picture disc
	Permanent Waves	Anthem ANR-1-1021	Dewey headline
	Moving Pictures	Anthem ANR-1-1030	
	Exit ... Stage Left	Anthem ANR-1-1035	
	Signals	Anthem ANR-1-1038	
	Grace Under Pressure	Anthem ANR-1-1045	
	Power Windows	Anthem ANR-1-1049	
	Hold Your Fire	Anthem ANR-1-1051	cardboard insert
	A Show of Hands	Anthem A1-1055	
	Presto	Anthem ANL-1059	
United States	Rush	Mercury/Phonogram SRM-1-1011	
	Fly By Night	Mercury/Phonogram SRM-1-1023	lyric sleeve
	Caress of Steel	Mercury/Phonogram SRM-1-1046	gatefold
	2112	Mercury/Phonogram SRM-1-1079	gatefold
	All the World's a Stage	Mercury/Phonogram SRM-2-7508	trifold
	A Farewell To Kings	Mercury/Phonogram SRM-1-1184	gatefold, picture sleeve
	Archives	Mercury/Phonogram SRM-3-9200	gatefold; gray cover
	Hemispheres	Mercury/Phonogram SRM-1-3743	gate.; brain lbl w/poster
	Hemispheres	Mercury/Phonogram SRP-1300	picture disc
	Permanent Waves	Mercury/Phonogram SRM-1-4001	wave label
	Moving Pictures	Mercury/PolyGram SRM-1-4013	camera label
	Exit ... Stage Left	Mercury/PolyGram SRM-2-7001	gatefold; logo label
	Signals	Mercury/PolyGram SRM-1-4063	hydrant label
	Grace Under Pressure	Mercury/PolyGram 818-476-1 M-1	P/G label
	Power Windows	Mercury/PolyGram 826-098-1 M-1	TV label
	Hold Your Fire	Mercury/PolyGram 832-464-1 Q-1	spheres label
	A Show of Hands	Mercury/PolyGram 836-346-1	gatefold; ASOH label
	Presto	Atlantic/Anthem 82040-1	

Notes: All were reissued with black Mercury label in 1989 ... reissues had no gatefold (gf); tapes on right have no lyrics until 1984.

	Album	Label/Catalog No.	Notes
United Kingdom	Rush	Mercury/Phonogram 9110-011	PRICE 18
	Fly By Night	Mercury/Phonogram 9100-013	PRICE 19
	Caress of Steel	Mercury/Phonogram 9100-018	PRICE 20
	2112	Mercury/Phonogram 9100-039	PRICE 79
	All the World's a Stage	Mercury/Phonogram 6672-015	PRID 1
	A Farewell To Kings	Mercury/Phonogram 9100-042	PRICE 92
	Archives	Mercury/Phonogram 6641-799	
	Hemispheres	Mercury/Phonogram 9100-059	PRICE 118
	Permanent Waves	Mercury/Phonogram 6337-071	
	Moving Pictures	Mercury/PolyGram 6619-160	
	Rush Through Time	Mercury/PolyGram 9130-001 ❶	
	Exit … Stage Left	Mercury/PolyGram 6337-053	
	Signals	Mercury/PolyGram 6337-243 (In Store Promo pack also issued)	
	Grace Under Pressure	Vertigo/PolyGram VERH12	
	Power Windows	Vertigo/PolyGram VERH31	
	Power Windows	Vertigo/PolyGram VERHP31	P/D
	Hold Your Fire	Vertigo/PolyGram VERH49	
	A Show of Hands	Vertigo/PolyGram 836-346-1	

❶ Fly By Night, Making Memories, Bastille Day, Something For Nothing, Cinderella Man, Anthem; 2112 Overture/Temples of Syrinx, The Twilight Zone, Best I Can, Closer to the Heart, In the End.

The PRICE series was issued in June 1983 except *2112* in January 1985.)

	Album	Label/Catalog No.	Notes
Germany for UK	Presto	Atlantic/WEA 782-040-1	
	Chronicles	Vertigo/PolyGram 838-936-1	3 LPs
	Roll the Bones	Atlantic/WEA 82293-1 WX436	
	Counterparts	Atlantic/WEA 82528-1 CA319	

	Album	Label/Catalog No.
France and Philippines	A Farewell To Kings	9100-042
	Permanent Waves	9100-071
	Moving Pictures	6337-160

West Germany, Netherlands, Colombia

The following numbers correspond to pressings in: Norway, Sweden, Luxembourg, Portugal, Spain, Italy, Australia, Greece, and Israel. *Rush Through Time* was not released except in New Zealand (7141-171); the rest follow these numbers.

Album	Label/Catalog No.
Rush	6338-524
Fly By Night/Rush	6619-040 gatefold
Fly By Night	6338-561
Caress of Steel	6338-600
2112	6338-678
All the World's a Stage	6643-040
A Farewell To Kings	6338-834
Hemispheres	9111-005
Permanent Waves	9111-065
Moving Pictures	6337-160 (Israeli covers read "RUSCH")
Rush Through Time	6337-171
Rush Through Time	9130-001 pic disc
Exit … Stage Left	6619-053
Signals	6337-243
Grace Under Pressure	818-476-1
Power Windows	826-098-1
Hold Your Fire	832-464-1
A Show of Hands	836-346-1
Presto	Atlantic 670-9110

	Album	Label/Catalog No.	Notes
Yugoslavia	A Show of Hands	320048 TRB	
South Africa	Moving Pictures	STAR-5183	
	Grace Under Pressure	STAR-5369 (Trutone)	
	Power Windows	826-098-1	
Russia	Cover is different:		
	Farewell to Kings	AL-3053	
Venezuela	Signals	Mercury 90-038-L	
	Anthology	Mercury 90-043-L ❶	
	Grace Under Pressure	Mercury 90-048-L	
	Power Windows	Mercury 90-078-L	
	Hold Your Fire	Mercury 90-110-L	
	A Show of Hands Vol. I	Mercury 90-127-L with decal	
	A Show of Hands Vol. II	Mercury 90-127-L with decal	
	Presto	Atlantic 25031	

❶ 1984 sampler: 2112 Overture/Temples of Syrinx, Closer to the Heart, The Trees, The Spirit of Radio/Tom Sawyer, Limelight, Subdivisions, The Analog Kid.

	Album	Label/Catalog No.	Notes
Uruguay	Presto	Atlantic 80216 LP	
Ecuador	Signals		
	Grace Under Pressure	70047	
Mexico	Permanent Waves	Mercury LPR-19039	
	Moving Pictures	Mercury LPR-19044	
	Rush Through Time	Mercury LPR-19049	
	Exit … Stage Left	Mercury LPR-19077	
	Signals	Mercury LPR-19060	
	Grace Under Pressure	Mercury LPR-19097	
	Power Windows	Mercury LPR-19132	
	Hold Your Fire	Mercury LPR-19170	
	A Show of Hands	Mercury LPR-19187	
	Presto	Atlantic LPNA-6925	
Brazil, Singapore, Malaysia, and Hong Kong	Rush	Mercury 6338-524	
	Fly By Night	Mercury 6338-661	
	Caress of Steel	Mercury 6338-600	
	2112	Mercury 6338-673	
	All the World's a Stage	Mercury 6643-040	
	A Farewell To Kings	Mercury 6638-834	
	Hemispheres	Mercury 9111-005	
	Permanent Waves	Mercury 9111-065	
	Moving Pictures	Mercury 6337-160	
	Exit … Stage Left	Mercury 6619-053	
	Signals	Mercury 6337-243	
	Grace Under Pressure	Mercury 818-476-1	
	Power Windows	Mercury 826-098-1	
	Hold Your Fire	Mercury 832-464-1	
	A Show of Hands	Mercury 836-346-1	

Album	Label/Catalog No.	Notes
Presto	Atlantic 670-9110	
Chronicles	Mercury 838-936-1	3 LP
Roll the Bones	Atlantic 7609-392	
Counterparts	Atlantic 78258-1	

Argentina

Album	Label/Catalog No.	Notes
2112	6119	lyric insert
A Farewell To Kings	6037	back lyrics
Permanent Waves	9956	
Signals	6089	back lyrics
Grace Under Pressure	27194	back lyrics
Power Windows	27286	back lyrics
Hold Your Fire	29085	back lyrics
A Show of Hands Vol. I	24361 74361	
A Show of Hands Vol. II	24362	
Presto	90216	
Chronicles Vol. I	29294 79294	
Chronicles Vol. II	29300 79300	
Chronicles Vol. III	29305 79305	

Korea

Album	Label/Catalog No.	Notes
2112	SEL-RP-620	omits Starman image
Exit ... Stage Left	SEL-RP-503	
Signals	SEL-RP-626	omits The Weapon
Grace Under Pressure	SEL-RP-626	omits Red Lenses
Power Windows	SEL-RP-696	omits Territories

Taiwan

Album	Label/Catalog No.	Notes
A Farewell To Kings	TD-1984	
Exit ... Stage Left	Yalu YL-4027-28	
Signals	OM-3193	

Japan

Album	Label/Catalog No.	Notes
Rush	Mercury/Nippon Phonogram RJ-6028 (lyrics on back)	
	Mercury/Nippon Phonogram BT-5162 (lyrics insert) reissue	
Fly By Night	Mercury/Nippon Phonogram RJ-7012	
	Mercury/Nippon Phonogram BT-5185 reissue	
Caress of Steel	Mercury/Nippon Phonogram RJ-7066	
	Mercury/Nippon Phonogram BT-5203 reissue	
2112	Mercury/Nippon Phonogram RJ-7098	
	Epic/Sony 25-3P-267 reissue	
All the World's a Stage	Mercury/Nippon Phonogram SFX-10012-3	
A Farewell To Kings	Mercury/Nippon Phonogram RJ-7285	
	Epic/Sony 25-3P-268	
	Epic/Sony 25-8P-5167	
Hemispheres	Mercury/Nippon Phonogram RJ-7531	
	Epic/Sony 25-3P-269	
	Epic/Sony 25-8P-5168	
Permanent Waves	Epic/Sony 25-3P-221	
	Epic/Sony 25-8P-5075	
Moving Pictures	Epic/Sony 25-3P-261	
	Epic/Sony 25-8P-5076	
Exit ... Stage Left	Epic/Sony 36-3P-325-6	
Signals	Epic/Sony 25-3P-378	
Grace Under Pressure	Epic/Sony 25-3P-505	
Power Windows	Epic/Sony 28-3P-679	
Hold Your Fire	Epic/Sony 28-3P-847	

Cassette Album Labels

	Album	Label/Catalog No.	Notes
Canada	Rush	Mercury/Phonogram MN4-1-1011	
	Rush	Anthem 4AN-1-601	
	Fly By Night	Anthem 4AN-1-1002 4AN-1-602	
	Caress of Steel	Anthem 4AN-1-1003 4AN-1-603	
	2112	Anthem 4AN-1-1004	
	All the World's a Stage	Anthem 4AN-1-1025 4AN-1-1005	
	A Farewell To Kings	Anthem 4AN-1-1010	
	Archives	Anthem 4AN-3-1013	black or gray
	Hemispheres	Anthem 4AN-1-1014	
	Permanent Waves	Anthem 4AN-1-1021	Dewey headline
	Moving Pictures	Anthem 4AN-1-1030	ANT-1030
	Moving Pictures (box version)	Anthem 4AN-1-1031	
	Exit … Stage Left	Anthem 4AN-1-1035	ANT-1035
	Signals	Anthem 4AN-1-1038	ANT-1038
	Grace Under Pressure	Anthem 4AN-1-1045	ANT-1045
	Power Windows	Anthem 4AN-1-1049	ANT-1049
	Hold Your Fire	Anthem 4AN-1-1051	VANT-1051
	A Show of Hands	Anthem 4AN-1-1055	ANT-1055
	Presto	Anthem ANT-1059	
	Chronicles	Anthem ANT2-1060	
	Roll the Bones	Anthem ANT-1064	
	Counterparts	Anthem ANT-1067	
	Test For Echo	Anthem ANC-1073	
United States	Rush	Mercury/Phonogram MCR-1-1011	
	Fly By Night	Mercury/Phonogram MCR-1-1023	
	Rush/Fly by Night	Mercury/Phonogram 810-464-4 M-2	
	Caress of Steel	Mercury/Phonogram MR4-1-1046	songs out of order
	2112	Mercury/Phonogram MCR4-1-1079	
	All the World's a Stage	Mercury/Phonogram MCT4-2-7508	
	A Farewell To Kings	Mercury/Phonogram MCR4-1-1184	
	Archives	Mercury/Phonogram MCT4-2-9200	
	Hemispheres	Mercury/Phonogram MCR4-1-3743	
	Permanent Waves	Mercury/Phonogram MCR4-1-4001	
	Moving Pictures	Mercury/PolyGram MCR4-1-4013	
	Exit … Stage Left	Mercury/PolyGram MCR4-1-7001	
	Signals	Mercury/PolyGram MCR4-1-4063	
	(Notes: None have lyrics.)		
United States Reissues	Rush	Mercury/PolyGram 822-541-4 M-1	
	Fly By Night	Mercury/PolyGram 822-542-4 M-1	
	Rush/Fly By Night	Mercury/PolyGram 810-464-4 M-2	
	Caress of Steel	Mercury/PolyGram 822-543-4 M-1	(mixed songs)
	2112	Mercury/PolyGram 822-545-4 M-1	
	All the World's a Stage	Mercury/PolyGram 822-552-4 M-1	
	A Farewell To Kings	Mercury/PolyGram 822-546-4 M-1	
	Archives	Mercury/PolyGram 822-553-4 M-2	(black cover) 2 cassettes
	Hemispheres	Mercury/PolyGram 822-547-4 M-1	
	Moving Pictures	Mercury/PolyGram 822-549-4 M-1	(credits)

Album	Label/Catalog No.	Notes
Exit ... Stage Left	Mercury/PolyGram 822-551-4 M-1	
Signals	Mercury/PolyGram 822-550-4 M-1	
Grace Under Pressure	Mercury/PolyGram 818-476-4 M-1	
Power Windows	Mercury/PolyGram 826-098-4 M-1	
Hold Your Fire	Mercury/PolyGram 832-464-4 Q-1	
A Show of Hands	Mercury/PolyGram 836-346-4	
Presto	Atlantic/Anthem 82040-4	
Chronicles	Mercury/PolyGram 838-936-4	2 Cassettes
Roll the Bones	Atlantic/Anthem 82293-4	
Counterparts	Atlantic/Anthem 82528-4	
Test For Echo	Atlantic/Anthem 82925-4	

United Kingdom, Netherlands, Italy, Germany, New Zealand, Colombia and Brazil

Album	Label/Catalog No.
Rush	Mercury/Phonogram 7142-365
Fly By Night	Mercury/Phonogram 7142-389
Caress of Steel	Mercury/Phonogram 7142-421
2112	Mercury/Phonogram 7142-483
All the World's a Stage	Mercury/Phonogram 7553-047
A Farewell To Kings	Mercury/Phonogram 7142-580
Archives	Mercury/Phonogram 7649-103
Hemispheres	Mercury/Phonogram 7142-647
Permanent Waves	Mercury/Phonogram 7142-720
Moving Pictures	Mercury/PolyGram 7141-160
Rush Through Time	Mercury/PolyGram 7141-171
Exit ... Stage Left	Mercury/PolyGram 7558-053
Signals	Mercury/PolyGram 7143-243
Grace Under Pressure	Mercury/PolyGram 818-476-4
Power Windows	Mercury/PolyGram 826-098-4
Hold Your Fire	Mercury/PolyGram 832-464-4
A Show of Hands	Mercury/PolyGram 836-346-1
Chronicles	Mercury/PolyGram 838-936-4

UK Pressings Differ

Album	Label/Catalog No.
Signals	Mercury/PolyGram 7147-243
Grace Under Pressure	Vertigo/PolyGram VERHC-12
Power Windows	Vertigo/PolyGram VERHC-31
Hold Your Fire	Vertigo/PolyGram VERHC-47

UK Reissues

Album	Label/Catalog No.
Rush	Mercury PRIMC-18
Fly By Night	Mercury PRIMC-19
Caress of Steel	Mercury PRIMC-20
2112	Mercury PRIMC-79
All the World's a Stage	Mercury PRIDC-1
A Farewell To Kings	Mercury PRIMC-92
Hemispheres	Mercury PRIMC-118

Poland

Album	Label/Catalog No.
Fly By Night	885
Caress of Steel	943
Signals	888
Grace Under Pressure	
Power Windows	887
Hold Your Fire	
A Show of Hands	889/890
Roll the Bones	1594
Counterparts	PCW-553

	Album	Label/Catalog No.	Notes
Chile	Power Windows	185125	
	Hold Your Fire	185233	
	Cronicas Vol. I	185394	
	Cronicas Vol. II	185412	
	Presto	195296	
Uruguay	Presto	80216	
Peru	Power Windows	8260984.5	
	Presto	0820404.3	
Venezuela	Signals	90-038-C	
	Anthology	90-043-C	
	Grace Under Pressure	90-048-C	
	Power Windows	90-078-C	
	Hold Your Fire	90-110-C	
	A Show of Hands	90-127-C	
	Presto	25031-C	
Argentina	2112	9985	
	A Farewell To Kings		
	Hemispheres		
	Permanent Waves	9956	
	Moving Pictures		
	Exit … Stage Left		
	Signals	7889	
	Grace Under Pressure	67194	
	Power Windows	67286	
	Hold Your Fire	69085	
	A Show of Hands	74361	
	Presto	90-216-C	
	Chronicles	69294/69300/693005	
Mexico	Moving Pictures	MCR-19044 or MCR 800-048-4	
	Rush Through Time	MCR-19049	
	Exit … Stage Left	2MCR-1905	
	Signals	MCR-19060	
	Grace Under Pressure	MCR-19097	
	Power Windows	MCR-19132	
	Hold Your Fire	MCR-19170	
	A Show of Hands	2MCR-19187	
	Presto		
	Roll the Bones		
	Counterparts		
	Test For Echo	ML-82925-4	

	Album	Label/Catalog No.	Notes
Japan	Moving Pictures		
	Exit ... Stage Left		
	Signals		
	Grace Under Pressure	Anthem/Epic/Sony 25-6P-248	
	Power Windows		
	Hold Your Fire		
	A Show of Hands	Anthem/Epic/Sony 25-6P-5162	
	Different Stages	(no number) promo video style case	
Bali	A Show of Hands	MSC-1103/1104	
	Presto	A-838	
	Chronicles	5284/5285/5286	

CD Album Labels

	Album	Label	Reissue	Reissue
Canada	Rush	ANC-1-1001	WANK-1001	ANMD-1001
	Fly By Night	ANC-1-1002	WANK-1-1002	ANMD-1002
	Caress of Steel	ANC-1-1003	VANK-1003	ANMD-1003
	2112	ANC-1-1004	VANK-1004	ANMD-1004
	All the World's a Stage	A21F-2-1005	WAGK-1005	AND-1005
	A Farewell To Kings	ANC-1-1010	WANK-1010	ANMD-1010
	Hemispheres	ANC-1-1015	WANK-1014	ANMD-1014
	Permanent Waves	ANC-1-1021	VANK-1021	ANMD-1021
	Moving Pictures	ANC-1-1030	VANK-1030	ANMD-1030
	Exit ... Stage Left	A21F-4-1035	WAGK-1035	AND-1035
	Signals	ANC-1-1038	VANK-1038	ANMD-1038
	Grace Under Pressure	ANC-1-1045	VANK-1045	ANMD-1045
	Power Windows	ANC-1-1049	VANK-1049	ANMD-1049
	Hold Your Fire	ANC-1-1051	VANK-1051	ANMD-1051
	A Show of Hands	A2-1055	WAGK-1055	AND-1055
	Presto	ANK-1059		
	Chronicles	AN2K-1060	AND2-1060	
	Roll the Bones	ANK-1064	ANMD-1064	
	Counterparts	ANK-1067	ANMD-1067	
	Test For Echo	ANSD-1073	ANMD-1073	
	Different Stages	AND3-1092		

RUSH Vol. I (Box 123) 3 CDS: 2112/Hemispheres/Signals Anthem W3CD 13512

	Album	Label/Catalog No.
USA/Germany/ Brazil	Rush	Mercury/PolyGram 822-541-2 M-1 no lyrics
	Fly By Night	Mercury/PolyGram 822-542-2 M-1
	Caress of Steel	Mercury/PolyGram 822-543-2 M-1
	2112	Mercury/PolyGram 822-545-2 M-1
	All the World's a Stage	Mercury/PolyGram 822-552-2 M-1 (omits "What You're Doing")
	A Farewell To Kings	Mercury/PolyGram 822-546-2 M-1
	Hemispheres	Mercury/PolyGram 822-547-2 M-1
	Permanent Waves	Mercury/PolyGram 822-548-2 M-1
	Moving Pictures	Mercury/PolyGram 800-048-2
	Exit ... Stage Left	Mercury/PolyGram 822-551-2 M-1 (omits "A Passage"...)

Album	Label/Catalog No.	Notes
Signals	Mercury/PolyGram 810-002-2 (black and white band photos)	
Grace Under Pressure	Mercury/PolyGram 818-476-2 M-1	
Power Windows	Mercury/PolyGram 826-098-2 M-1	
Hold Your Fire	Mercury/PolyGram 832-464-2 Q-1	
A Show of Hands	Mercury/PolyGram 836-346-2	
Presto	Atlantic 82040-2 (longbox)	
Chronicles	Mercury 838-936-2 (longbox) (with 2 previously missing tracks)	
Roll the Bones	Atlantic 82293-2 (longbox)	
Counterparts	Atlantic 82528-2	
Test For Echo	Atlantic 82925-2	
Different Stages	Atlantic 80921-2	

Notes: The first CD to be released was *Moving Pictures* in 1983 followed by *Signals*; *Power Windows* was the first new album to be issued on CD; 1987 saw the rest of the catalog. German limited edition pressings of *Counterparts* and *Test For Echo* came with embossed covers.

Remasters Labels

USA, Germany and Brazil pressings all correspond to the first number; Canada (Anthem) and Japan (Atlantic/eastwest) follow.

Album	USA	Germany	Brazil
Rush	Mercury 314-534-623-2	ANMD 1075	AMCY 2289
Fly By Night	Mercury 314-534-624-2	ANMD 1076	AMCY 2290
Caress of Steel	Mercury 314-534-625-2	ANMD 1077	AMCY 2291
2112	Mercury 314-534-626-2	ANMD 1078	AMCY 2292
All the World's a Stage	Mercury 314-534 627-2	ANMD 1089	AMCY 2289
A Farewell To Kings	Mercury 314-534-628-2	ANMD 1079	AMCY 2293
Hemispheres	Mercury 314-534-629-2	ANMD 1080	AMCY 2294
Permanent Waves	Mercury 314-534-630-2	ANMD 1081	AMCY 2295 ❶
Moving Pictures	Mercury 314-534-631-2	ANMD 1082	AMCY 2296
Exit…Stage Left	Mercury 314-534-632-2	ANMD 1090	AMCY 2290 ❷
Signals	Mercury 314-534-633-2	ANMD 1083	AMCY 2297
Grace Under Pressure	Mercury 314-534-634-2	ANMD 1084	AMCY 2298
Power Windows	Mercury 314-534-635-2	ANMD 1085	AMCY 2299
Hold Your Fire	Mercury 314-534-636-2	ANMD 1086	AMCY 2300
A Show of Hands	Mercury 314-534-637-2	ANMD 1091	AMCY 2291
Retrospective I 1974-1980	Mercury 314-534-909-2	ANSD 1087	AMCY 2287 ❸
Retrospective II 1981-1987	Mercury 314-534-910-2	ANSD 1088	AMCY 2288

Notes: Mercury Records rel. 1974-1980 5-6-97 and the rest 6-3-97; the live releases 7-1-97) all are louder with more equalized sound; CD booklets include all LP graphics/lyrics. Tracks previously omitted on live CDs are intact. Cassettes were also issued: replace the last "−2" with "−4" for those catalog numbers.

❶ Freewill lyric "You cannot have made a choice" is corrected.

❷ Unfortunately the band pics are reversed.

❸ In Brazil, Mercury's Millenium Internacional release of Retrospective I (534-909-2) was issued as Rush #38 in the series.

USA Ultradisc (24KT-plated CDs) Labels

Album	Label/Catalog No.	Notes
Moving Pictures	Mobile Fidelity UDCD-569	
2112	Mobile Fidelity UDCD-590	
Signals	Mobile Fidelity UDCD-614 The Weapon 2nd chorus stanza cut	

	Album	Label/Catalog No.	Notes
Japan	Rush	Atlantic/MMG AMCY 314	
	Fly By Night	Atlantic/MMG AMCY 315	
	Caress of Steel	Atlantic/MMG AMCY 316	
	2112	Epic/Sony 25-8P-5166	
		Atlantic/MMG AMCY 317	
	All the World's a Stage	Atlantic/MMG AMCY 318	
	A Farewell To Kings	Epic/Sony 25-8P-5167	
		Atlantic/MMG AMCY 319	
	Hemispheres	Epic/Sony 25-8P-5168	
		Atlantic/MMG AMCY 320	
	Permanent Waves	Epic/Sony 25-8P-5075	
		Atlantic/MMG AMCY 288	
	Moving Pictures	Epic/Sony 25-8P-5076	
		Atlantic/MMG AMCY 289	
	Exit … Stage Left	Atlantic/MMG AMCY 290	
	Signals	Epic/Sony 25-8P-5169	
		Atlantic/MMG AMCY 291	
	Grace Under Pressure	Epic/Sony 25-8P-5077	
		Atlantic/MMG AMCY 29232-8P-44	
	Power Windows	Epic/Sony 25-8P-5078	
		Atlantic/MMG AMCY 293	
		Mercury/Epic/Sony 32-8P-101	
	Hold Your Fire	Epic/Sony 25-8P-1079	
		Atlantic/MMG AMCY 294	
		Mercury/Epic/Sony 32-8P-228	
	A Show of Hands	Epic/Sony 25-8P-5162	
		Atlantic/MMG AMCY 295	
	Presto	Atlantic/MMG AMCY 4	
	Chronicles	Atlantic/MMG AMCY 327/328	
	Roll the Bones	Atlantic/MMG AMCY 286	
	Counterparts	Atlantic/MMG AMCY 608	
	Test For Echo	Atlantic/eastwest AMCY 995	
	Different Stages	Atlantic/eastwest AMCY 2891-3 ❶	

❶ First pressings include mini tourbooks of *Test for Echo, A Farewell to Kings*. All pressings include "Force Ten".

UK		
	Three Originals (Hemispheres/Moving Pictures/Grace Under Pressure) Mercury PY-801-528	

Eight-Track Cassette Album Labels

Album	Canada	United States
Rush	Moon MN-8-100	Mercury/Phonogram C8-1-1011
	Anthem 8AN-1-1001	Mercury/Phonogram MC8-1-1001
Fly By Night	Anthem 8AN-1-1023	Mercury/Phonogram MC8-1-1023
Caress of Steel	Anthem 8AN-1-1003	Mercury/Phonogram MC8-1-1046
2112	Anthem 8AN-1-1004	Mercury/Phonogram MC8-1-1079
All the World's a Stage	Anthem 8AN-2-1025	Mercury/Phonogram MC8-2-7508
A Farewell To Kings	Anthem 8AN-4-1010	Mercury/Phonogram MC8-1-1184
Archives	Anthem 8AN-3-1013	Mercury/Phonogram MC8-3-9200
Hemispheres	Anthem 8AN-1-1014	Mercury/Phonogram MC8-1-3743
Permanent Waves	Anthem 8AN-1-1021	Mercury/Phonogram MC8-1-4001
Moving Pictures	Anthem 8AN-1-1030	Mercury/PolyGram MC8-1-4013
Exit … Stage Left	Anthem 8AN-4-1035	Mercury/PolyGram MC8-2-7001
Signals	Anthem 8AN-1-1038	Mercury/PolyGram MC8-1-4063

Singles

P/D = Picture Disc

P/S = Picture Sleeves

GEDDY We never try to write a single because we don't know how. And our history proves that out. (Bass Player)

7″ Singles (45RPM)

	A/B Side	Label/Catalog No.	Notes
Canada Stock	Not Fade Away (3:18)/You Can't Fight It (2:52)	Moon MN-001 (1973)	
	Finding My Way (2:55)/Need Some Love	Mercury/Phonogram M-73623	
	In the Mood (3:16)/What You're Doing	Mercury/Phonogram M-73647	
	Fly By Night/Anthem	Mercury/Phonogram M-73681	
	Return of the Prince (2:01)/I Think I'm Going Bald	Mercury/Phonogram M-73728 ❶	
	Lakeside Park/Bastille Day	Mercury/Phonogram M-73737	
	The Twilight Zone (2:41)/Lessons (2:58)	Mercury/Phonogram M-73803	
	Fly By Night/In the Mood(live)//Something For Nothing (live)	Mercury/Phonogram M-73873	
	Making Memories/The Temples of Syrinx (2112 band II)	Anthem ANS-001	first P/S
	Closer To the Heart/Madrigal (or unlisted B-side)	Anthem ANS-004	
	Cinderella Man (3:35)/A Farewell To Kings	Anthem ANS-007	
	Circumstances (2:38)/The Trees	Anthem ANS-009	
	The Spirit of Radio (3:40)/Circumstances (2:58)	Anthem ANS-017	
	Entre Nous (3:45)/Different Strings	Anthem ANS-021	
	Limelight (3:59)/YYZ	Anthem ANS-031	
	Tom Sawyer (3:59)/Witch Hunt	Anthem ANS-034	
	Closer To the Heart (live)/Freewill (live)	Anthem ANS-039 Closer To the Heart (live)/	
	The Trees(live)	Anthem ANS-039 rare Closer To the Heart	
	(live)/Tom Sawyer (live)	Anthem ANS-039 rarer	
	New World Man/Vital Signs (live) 5:12	Anthem ANS-046	P/S
	Subdivisions (4:42)/Countdown	Anthem ANS-048	
	Distant Early Warning/The Enemy Within	Anthem ANS-057	
	The Body Electric (4:16)/Between the Wheels	Anthem ANS-059	P/S
	Red Sector A (4:10)/Red Lenses	Anthem ANS-060	P/S
	The Big Money/Red Sector A (live) 5:25	Anthem ANS-067	P/S
	Mystic Rhythms (5:46)/Emotion Detector	Anthem ANS-069	
	Time Stand Still/High Water	Anthem ANS-075	P/S
	Closer To the Heart (live)/Witch Hunt (live)	Anthem ANS-083	P/S

❶ Some pressings are without voice intro.

Canada Promo	The Spirit of Radio (3:40)/same	Anthem ANS-017PRO	
	The Big Money (4:32)/same	Anthem SPE-029DJ	
	Mystic Rhythms (4:58)/same	Anthem SPE-031DJ	
	Time Stand Still (4:39)/same	Anthem SPE-038DJ	P/S
United States Stock	Finding My Way/Need Some Love	Mercury/Phonogram 73623	
	In the Mood/What You're Doing	Mercury/Phonogram 73647	
	Fly By Night/Anthem	Mercury/Phonogram 73681	
	Return of the Prince/I Think I'm Going Bald	Mercury/Phonogram 73728 (with or w/o Neil intro)	
	Lakeside Park (3:16)/Bastille Day	Mercury/Phonogram 73737	

A/B Side	Label/Catalog No.	Notes
The Twilight Zone (2:41)/Lessons (2:58)	Mercury/Phonogram 73803	
Fly By Night/In the Mood (live)/Something For Nothing (live)	Mercury/Phonogram 73873	
Making Memories/The Temples of Syrinx (2112 band II)	Mercury/Phonogram 73912	
Closer To the Heart/Madrigal	Mercury/Phonogram 73958	
Fly By Night/Anthem	Mercury/Phonogram 73990	
	'78 Archives single	
The Trees/Circumstances	Mercury/Phonogram 74051	
The Spirit of Radio (3:00)/Circumstances	Mercury/Phonogram 76044	
Entre Nous (3:45)/Different Strings	Mercury/PolyGram 76060	
Limelight (4:01)/YYZ	Mercury/PolyGram 76095	
Tom Sawyer (4:07)/Witch Hunt	Mercury/PolyGram 76109	P/S
Closer To the Heart (live 3:06)/Freewill (live)	Mercury/PolyGram 76124	
New World Man/Vital Signs (live 5:12)	Mercury/PolyGram 76179	P/S
Subdivisions/Countdown	Mercury/PolyGram 76196	P/S
The Body Electric (4:18)/Between the Wheels	Mercury/PolyGram 880-050-7	
	(10″ red vinyl)	P/S
The Big Money (4:32)/Red Sector A (live)	Mercury/PolyGram 884-191-7	P/S
Time Stand Still (4:42)/High Water (4:31)	Mercury/PolyGram 888-891-7	P/S

United States Promo

A/B Side	Label/Catalog No.	Notes
Finding My Way (2:55)	Mercury/Phonogram DJ-406 73623	
In the Mood (3:16)	Mercury/Phonogram DJ-417 73647	
Fly By Night	Mercury/Phonogram 73681DJ	
Return of the Prince (3:01)/2:54 edit	Mercury/Phonogram 73728DJ	
Lakeside Park	Mercury/Phonogram 73737DJ	
The Twilight Zone	Mercury/Phonogram 73803DJ	
Fly By Night/In the Mood (live)	Mercury/Phonogram 73873DJ	
Closer To the Heart	Mercury/Phonogram 73958DJ	
Fly By Night	Mercury/Phonogram DJ-553 73990	
	'78 Archives single	
The Trees	Mercury/Phonogram 74051DJ	
The Spirit of Radio (3:54)/3:00 edit	Mercury/Phonogram 76044 DJ	
Entre Nous (3:45)	Mercury/Phonogram 76060 DJ	
Limelight (4:01)	Mercury/PolyGram 76095 DJ	
Tom Sawyer (4:07)	Mercury/PolyGram 76109 DJ	
Closer to the Heart (live 3:06)	Mercury/PolyGram 76124 DJ	
New World Man	Mercury/PolyGram 76179 DJ	P/S
Subdivisions/4:23 edit	Mercury/PolyGram 76196 DJ	
The Body Electric (4:18)	Mercury/PolyGram 880-050-7 DJ	
Red Sector A (4:10)	Mercury/PolyGram PRO 319-7 red vinyl	
The Big Money (5:35)/4:32	Mercury/PolyGram PRO 383-7	
Time Stand Still (5:09)/4:42	Mercury/PolyGram 888-891-7 DJ	

United Kingdom Stock

A/B Side	Label/Catalog No.	Notes
Closer To the Heart/Bastille Day, The Temples of Syrinx	Mercury/Phonogram RUSH7	
The Spirit of Radio (3:00)/The Trees	Mercury/Phonogram RADIO7	
Vital Signs/In the Mood	Mercury/PolyGram VITAL7	
Tom Sawyer (live)/A Passage To Bangkok (live)	Mercury/PolyGram EXIT7	
Closer To the Heart (live, 3:07)/The Trees (live, 4:30)	Mercury/PolyGram RUSH1	P/D
New World Man/Vital Signs (live 5:12)	Mercury/PolyGram RUSH8	
Subdivisions/Red Barchetta	Mercury/PolyGram RUSH9	P/S
Subdivisions/Red Barchetta	Mercury/PolyGram RUSHP9	P/D
Subdivisions(edit)/Red Barchetta (live)	Mercury/PolyGram RUSHD9	
Countdown/New World Man	Vertigo/PolyGram RUSH10	
Countdown/New World Man	Vertigo/PolyGram RUSHP10	
	shuttle shaped	P/D

	A/B Side	Label/Catalog No.	Notes
	The Body Electric/The Analog Kid	Vertigo/PolyGram RUSH11	
	The Big Money/Territories	Vertigo/PolyGram RUSH12	
	The Big Money/Territories, Closer to the Heart, The Spirit of Radio	Vertigo/PolyGram RUSHD12	gatefold sleeve
	The Big Money/Middletown Dreams	Vertigo/PolyGram RUSHG12	gatefold sleeve
	Time Stand Still/Force Ten	Vertigo/PolyGram RUSH13	
	Time Stand Still/Force Ten	Vertigo/PolyGram RUSHD13	die-cut sleeve
	Prime Mover/Tai Shan	Vertigo/PolyGram RUSH14	
	Prime Mover/Distant Early Warning (live)	Vertigo/PolyGram RUSHR14	white vinyl
	The Spirit of Radio (2:57)/Closer to the Heart (2:52)	Old Gold OG9767 1988	reissue
	Ghost of a Chance/Dreamline	Atlantic 87491-7 A7491	
	Roll the Bones/Show Don't Tell	Atlantic 87524-7 A7564	
	Roll the Bones/The Pass, It's a Rap Pt. 1: Alex Speaks	Atlantic 85899-7 A7524TE	
	(Note: All with picture sleeves.)		
United Kingdom Promo	Vital Signs (4:00)/blank	Mercury/PolyGram VITAL 7DJ	
	The Body Electric (edit)/same	Mercury/PolyGram RUSDJ11	
	The Big Money (edit)/Territories	Mercury/PolyGram RUSDJ12	
	Time Stand Still (edit)/Force Ten	Mercury/PolyGram RUSDJ13	
	Prime Mover/Tai Shan	Mercury/PolyGram RUSHDJ14	P/S
	Roll the Bones (4:39)/blank	Atlantic/WEA SAM 974	P/S
West Germany	The Spirit of Radio (3:00)/Circumstances	Mercury/Phonogram 6167-895	P/S
	Roll the Bones/Show Don't Tell	Atlantic/WEA 87524-7	P/S
	Roll the Bones/Tom Sawyer (live)	Atlantic/WEA 87558-7	P/S
Ireland	Closer To the Heart/Bastille Day, The Temples of Syrinx	Mercury/Phonogram RUSH7	
	Closer To the Heart/The Trees	Mercury/Phonogram RUSH1	
	Vital Signs/In the Mood	Mercury/PolyGram VITAL7	
	Countdown/New World Man	Mercury/PolyGram RUSH10	
	The Big Money/Territories	Vertigo/PolyGram RUSH12	
Netherlands Stock	Fly By Night/Best I Can	Mercury/Phonogram 6167-497 (first 45 with P/S)	P/S
	The Trees/Circumstances	Mercury/Phonogram 6167-814	P/S
	The Spirit of Radio (3:00)/Circumstances	Mercury/Phonogram 6167-895	P/S
	New World Man/Vital Signs (live)	Mercury/PolyGram 6167-227	P/S
	The Big Money/Red Sector A (live)	Vertigo/PolyGram 884-191-7	P/S
	Time Stand Still/Force Ten	Vertigo/PolyGram 888-941-7	P/S
Netherlands Promo	Force Ten/blank	Mercury/PolyGram 888-882-7	
Spain	The Spirit of Radio/Different Strings	Mercury/Phonogram 6832-196	P/S
	Vital Signs/Limelight	Mercury/PolyGram 6170-089 (Vital "Sings")	P/S
	New World Man/Vital Signs (live)	Mercury/PolyGram 6170-227	P/S
	Distant Early Warning/Between the Wheels	Mercury/PolyGram 880-249-7	P/S
Australia	Fly By Night/Anthem	Mercury/Phonogram 6167-172	
	Fly By Night/In the Mood (live)//Something For Nothing(live)	Mercury/Phonogram 6167-497	
	Closer To the Heart/Madrigal	Mercury/Phonogram 6167-588	

A/B Side	Label/Catalog No.	Notes
The Spirit of Radio (3:00)/Circumstances	Mercury/Phonogram 6167-895	
New World Man/Vital Signs (live)	Mercury/PolyGram 6170-227	
Time Stand Still/High Water	Mercury/PolyGram 888-891-7	
The Pass/Presto	Atlantic 7-87986	

New Zealand

Closer To the Heart/Madrigal	Mercury/Phonogram 6167-588	
The Spirit of Radio (3:00)/Circumstances	Mercury/Phonogram 6167-895	

Japan Promo

Closer To the Heart/Madrigal	Mercury/Nippon Phonogram SFL-2233	P/S
Afterimage/The Body Electric	Epic/Sony 07-5P-284	P/S
The Big Money/Red Sector A	Epic/Sony 07-5P-386	P/S
Mystic Rhythms/Emotion Detector	Epic/Sony 07-5P-401	P/S

France
(Jukebox Special
Edition promos)

The Trees/Circumstances	Mercury/Phonogram 6837-526	P/S
Subdivisions/New World Man	Mercury/PolyGram 6837-775	P/S
Bravado/Roll the Bones (4:28)	Atlantic 15156	P/S

Mexico

In the Mood	
New World Man	S/N 286

Peru

New World Man	6170227.4

Ecuador

Show Don't Tell	Atlantic PR-3082-2 45-73083

Guatemala

Time Stand Still/Force Ten	Mercury/PolyGram 888-941-7

Russia

(1995 Flexidiscs by AKOH all prefixed by A60) promos w/pic sleeves (vinyl chart B=blue C=clear R=red G=Green Y=Yellow BR=Brown):

Finding My Way	2224	(B)				
Before and After	2225	(B)	(C)	(R)	(BR)	
In the End	3168	(C)	(R)	(BR)		
Twilight Zone	3169	(C)	(BR)	(B)		
Making Memories	3182	(C)	(Y)	(G)		
Neurotica	3327	(C)	(Y)	(BR)		
Cygnus	3389	(B)	(C)	(BR)		
The Trees	3394	(B)	(C)	(Y)		
On Stage Vol. 1	3411	(G)	(C	(R)		Tom Sawyer live
Xanadu	4121	(C)	(G)	(B)		
Lock and Key	4122	(R)	(Y)	(C)		
The Spirit of Radio	4147	(C)	(Y)	(B)		
High Water	4221	(C)	(G)	(BR)		
Second Nature	4222	(C)	(B)	(R)		
Tai Shan	4223	(C)	(R)	(Y)		
On Stage Vol. 2	4321	(C)	(Y)	(G)		Stick It Out
On Stage Vol. 3	4322	(C)	(BR)	(B)		Nobody's Hero
On Stage Vol. 4	4517	(G)	(B)	(C)		Xanadu
Armageddon	4522	(G)	(B)	(C)		
La Villa Strangiato	4523	(R)	(Y)	(C)	(G)	
Fly By Night	433	(G)	(B)			33rpm
Distant Early Warning	434	(R)	(Y)	(G)		33rpm
Making Memories	435	(G)	(R)	(C)		33rpm

12″ Singles and Special Editions (78RPM)

Single	Record Label	Notes
Canada		
Hemispheres interview disc	Anthem SPE-001	rec. 12/28/78
Hemispheres	Anthem SPE-002	
Live in St. Louis	Anthem SPE-003	1980 concert ❶
Moving Pictures Radio Special	Anthem SPE-007	interview
A Passage To Bangkok (live)/Freewill (live)	Anthem SPE-009	Special Edition Live
The Rush Special	Anthem SPE-2-009	2 LP interview
New World Man/Vital Signs (live) 5:12	Anthem SPE-011	
Signals Radio Special	Anthem SPE-012	
The Weapon (4:18)/Digital Man	Anthem SPE-014	Count Floyd intro
Distant Early Warning	Anthem SPE-019	
Grace Under Pressure interview	Anthem SPE-021	
The Body Electric (4:16/4:58)	Anthem SPE-022	
Red Sector A (4:10)/Red Lenses	Anthem SPE-023	
The Big Money	Anthem SPE-028	
Mystic Rhythms	Anthem SPE-030	
The Big Money/Red Sector A (live)	Anthem SPE-031	
Marathon (6:10)	Anthem SPE-032	
Time Stand Still	Anthem SPE-037	
Time Stand Still/High Water	Anthem SPE-038	
Lock and Key	Anthem SPE-039	
Mission (live) 5:44	Anthem SPE-050	

❶ 2112, The Spirit of Radio, Beneath, Between and Behind, Natural Science, By-Tor and the Snow Dog/ Xanadu, Working Man/Finding My Way/Anthem/Bastille Day/In the Mood/Drum Solo, La Villa Strangiato.

United States Promo

Mercury In-Store Play Special (with Anthem and Fly By Night, other bands) MK-8 (1975)

Everything Your Listeners Ever Wanted to Hear By Rush... But You Were Afraid to Play ❶ MK-32

Single	Record Label	Notes
The Trees/Prelude, Circumstances	Mercury/Phonogram MK-75	P/S
The Spirit of Radio/The Trees, Working Man	Mercury/Phonogram MK-125	
Entre Nous/3:45 edit	Mercury/Phonogram MK-137	P/S
Rush N' Roulette ❷	Mercury/PolyGram MK-185 (1981)	P/S
A Passage To Bangkok/Freewill	Mercury/PolyGram MK-188	P/S
New World Man/Vital Signs (live)	Mercury/PolyGram MK-216	clear vinyl
Distant Early Warning/Between the Wheels	Mercury/PolyGram PRO 276-1	
The Body Electric	Mercury/PolyGram PRO 290-1	
Red Sector A (4:10)/The Enemy Within	Mercury/PolyGram PRO 320-1	red vinyl
The Big Money	Mercury/PolyGram PRO 382-1	
Mystic Rhythms	Mercury/PolyGram PRO 400-1	
Force Ten	Mercury/PolyGram PRO 532-1	
Marathon (live) 6:32	Mercury/PolyGram PRO-689-1	

❶ 1976 sampler — Fly By Night, Making Memories, Bastille Day, Something For Nothing, Lakeside Park, Anthem; 2112 pts. I and II, The Twilight Zone, Best I Can, Bacchus Plateau, In the End.

❷ 6 *Exit... Stage Left* promo sampler — Tom Sawyer, Red Barchetta, The Trees, A Passage To Bangkok, Closer To the Heart, Freewill. Mastered by Ray Hagerty at Sound Wave Recording Studios.

	Single	Record Label	Notes
United Kingdom (P/S on all)	Closer To the Heart, Bastille Day/The Temples of Syrinx, Anthem	Mercury/Phonogram RUSH12	
	The Spirit of Radio/The Trees, Working Man	Mercury/Phonogram RADIO12	
	Vital Signs/In the Mood, A Passage To Bangkok, Circumstances	Mercury/PolyGram VITAL12	
	Tom Sawyer (live)/A Passage To Bangkok (live), Red Barchetta (live)	Mercury/PolyGram EXIT12	
	New World Man/Vital Signs (live), Freewill (live)	Mercury/PolyGram RUSH812	
	Subdivisions/Red Barchetta, Jacob's Ladder (live)	Mercury/PolyGram RUSH912	
	Countdown/New World Man, The Spirit of Radio (live), interview	Mercury/PolyGram RUSH1012	
	The Body Electric/The Analog Kid, Distant Early Warning	Vertigo/PolyGram RUSH1110 10″	red or blk vinyl
	The Body Electric/The Analog Kid, Distant Early Warning	Vertigo/PolyGram RUSH1112	
	The Big Money/Territories, Red Sector A (live)	Vertigo/PolyGram RUSH1212	
	Time Stand Still, Force Ten/The Enemy Within (live), Witch Hunt (live)	Vertigo/PolyGram RUSH1312	
	Time Stand Still/Force Ten, The Enemy Within (live)	Vertigo/PolyGram RUSHP1312	pic disc
	Prime Mover, Tai Shan/Distant Early Warning (live), New World Man (live)	Vertigo/PolyGram RUSHR1412 metallic cover	
	Prime Mover/Tai Shan, Open Secrets	Vertigo/PolyGram RUSH1412	
	(**Notes:** Live tracks on last four singles from Grace Under Pressure Tour 9-21-84)		
United Kingdom Promo	Time Stand Still, Force Ten/The Enemy Within (live), Witch Hunt (live)	Vertigo/PolyGram RUSH1312DJ	
	Prime Mover, Tai Shan/Distant Early Warning (live), New World Man (live)	Vertigo/PolyGram RUSH1412DJ	
	Roll the Bones, Face Up/Dreamline	Atlantic SAM 869	
	Stick It Out, Cold Fire/Nobody's Hero, Double Agent	Atlantic SAM 1263	
West Germany	Roll the Bones/Tom Sawyer (live), The Spirit of Radio (live) ❶	Atlantic 85929-1 OLB	P/S
	❶ Live tracks culled from *Exit … Stage Left.*		
Netherlands	Subdivisions/New World Man, The Spirit of Radio (live)	Mercury/PolyGram 812-005-1	P/S
Sweden	"Rock On" Rush/Max Webster	Phillips/PolyGram 199 275 (1977)	
Japan	REO Speedwagon/Rush	Mercury/PolyGram QY-3P-90028 (1981)	P/S
New Zealand	Subdivisions/New World Man, The Spirit of Radio (live)	Mercury/PolyGram 812-005-1	
	The Big Money (edit)/Territories, Red Sector A (live)	Vertigo/PolyGram 884-240-1	
	Time Stand Still, Force Ten/The Enemy Within (live), Witch Hunt (live)	Vertigo/PolyGram 888-941-1	

Cassette Singles

Canada	Show Don't Tell/Red Tide, Force Ten (live)	Anthem ANCS-001	
	The Pass/Presto	Anthem ANCS-002	
	Roll the Bones, Face Up/(same)	Anthem ANCS-003	

United States	The Pass/Presto	Atlantic/Anthem 4-87986
	Ghost of a Chance/Where's My Thing?	Atlantic/Anthem 4-87498 also has interview
	Nobody's Hero/Stick It Out	Atlantic/Anthem 4-87267
UK Promo	A Selection of Songs from Chronicles	Vertigo/PolyGram no #
Tapes	Ghost of a Chance, Dreamline/Red Tide, Chain Lightning	Atlantic WEA no #
Australia	The Pass/Presto	Atlantic/Anthem 94-87986

CD Promo Singles and Special Editions

	Single	**Record Label**	**Notes**
Canada	Marathon (live) 6:32	Anthem PRO-1	P/S
	Show Don't Tell (4:47)	Anthem PRO-CD-3	no
	fade-up intro		
	Show Don't Tell/4:17 edit	Anthem PRO-4	
	The Pass	Anthem PRO-5	
	The Pass/4:04 edit	Anthem PRO-6	P/D
	Superconductor	Anthem PRO-7	
	Dreamline	Anthem PRO-8	
	Roll the Bones	Anthem PRO-9	P/D
	Roll the Bones Radio Special	Anthem PRO-10	71min interview
	Half the World (3:42 edit)	Anthem PRCD-17	
		100 copies before withdrawn	
	Different Stages sampler	Anthem PRCD-18	9 trks ❶

    ❶ Limelight, Driven, Closer To The Heart, Freewill, Roll The Bones, Tom Sawyer, Bastille Day, A Farewell To Kings, Working Man.

	Single	**Record Label**	**Notes**
United States	Time Stand Still (5:07)/4:42 edit	Mercury/PolyGram CDP-05	
	Show Don't Tell	Atlantic/Anthem PRCD 3082-2	
	Show Don't Tell (5:01 LP/4:17 edit)	Atlantic/Anthem PRCD 3125-2	
	The Pass	Atlantic/Anthem PRCD 3165-2	
	The Pass (5:01 LP/4:17 edit)	Atlantic/Anthem PRCD 3175-2	
	Profiled!	Atlantic/Anthem PRCD 3200-2	
		55min interview	
	Superconductor	Atlantic/Anthem PRCD 3331-2	
	Dreamline	Atlantic/Anthem PRCD 4120-2	
	Where's My Thing?	Atlantic/Anthem PRCD 4126-2	P/D
	only 200 pressed		
	Roll the Bones	Atlantic/Anthem PRCD 4260-2	P/D
	Ghost of a Chance (5:19 LP/4:25 edit)	Atlantic/Anthem PRCD 4458-2	P/D
	Bravado (3:49 edit)	Atlantic/Anthem PRCD 4580-2	P/D
	Stick It Out	Atlantic/Anthem PRCD 5314-2	
	Nobody's Hero	Atlantic/Anthem PRCD 5430-2	
	Double Agent	Atlantic/Anthem PRCD 5497-2	
	Nobody's Hero (LP/4:29 master edit)	Atlantic/Anthem PRCD 5497-2	
	Test For Echo	Atlantic/Anthem PRCD 6853-2	P/D
	Test For Echo (5:19 LP/4:25 edit)	Atlantic/Anthem PRCD 6885-2	P/D
	Half the World	Atlantic/Anthem PRCD 6930-2	
	Driven	Atlantic/Anthem PRCD 8009-2	
	Virtuality (5:44 LP/4:50 edit)	Atlantic/Anthem PRCD 8139-2	

	Different Stages promo sampler	Atlantic/Anthem PRCD 8681-2
	The Spirit of Radio/2112 (live)	Atlantic/Anthem PRCD 8690-2
	Closer To the Heart (live)/edit	Atlantic/Anthem PRCD 8804-2

United Kingdom

The Big Money, Territories, Red Sector A (live), Closer To the Heart	Vertigo RUSCD12
Time Stand Still, Force Ten, The Enemy Within (live), Witch Hunt (live)	Vertigo RUSCD13
Prime Mover, Tai Shan, Distant Early Warning (live), New World Man (live)	Vertigo RUSCD14
Roll the Bones, Anagram, It's a Rap Pt. 2: Geddy Speaks	Atlantic 85900-2
Roll the Bones, Where's My Thing?, Superconductor, It's a Rap Pt. 3: Neil Speaks	Atlantic 85901-2

(**Notes:** The Roll the Bones discs were limited edition hologram discs.)

West Germany
(for United Kingdom)

The Big Money, Territories, Red Sector A (live), Closer To the Heart (video track + 2 audio only)	Vertigo 080-084-2 (PAL)
The Big Money, Territories, Red Sector A (live), Closer To the Heart (video track + 2 audio only)	Mercury 070-717-2 (NTSC)
Time Stand Still, Force Ten, The Enemy Within (live), Witch Hunt (live)	Vertigo RUSCD13 Mercury/PolyGram 888-941-2
Prime Mover, Tai Shan, Distant Early Warning (live), New World Man (live)	Mercury/PolyGram 870-108-2
Roll the Bones (3:37 edit), Neurotica, Heresy	Atlantic PM-1098 promo P/S
Ghost of a Chance (3:31 edit), Where's My Thing?, Ghost of a Chance (LP)	Atlantic PM-1119 promo P/S
Ghost of a Chance, Dreamline, Chain Lightning, Red Tide	Atlantic 85874-2 ❶
Roll the Bones, Tom Sawyer (live), The Spirit of Radio (live)	Atlantic 85929-2 ❷

❶ Pressed on blue or silver discs

❷ Live tracks culled from *Exit … Stage Left.*

Related Discography

Solo and Side Projects

Victor (1-10-96)

Produced and written by Alex, who performs on mandola, bass and programmed synthesizers. Victor is the group name as well: vocalist Edwin of I Mother Earth, bassist Les Claypool of Primus, Bill Bell of Tom Cochrane Band, drummer Blake Manning. Some synthesizer programming by Adrian Zivojinovich on "Victor".

1. Don't Care (4:04) Lifeson
2. Promise (5:44) Bell/Lifeson
3. Start Today (3:48) Lifeson (vocal by Dalbello)
4. Mr. X—instrumental (2:21) Lifeson
5. At the End (6:07) Lifeson-Zivojinovich
6. Sending Out a Warning (4:11) Bell/Lifeson
7. Shut Up Shuttin' Up (4:02) Bell-Lifeson (guest voices by Alex, Charlene Zivojinovich, Esther)
8. Strip and Go Naked (3:57) Bell-Lifeson
9. The Big Dance (4:14) Lifeson-Zivojinovich (bass by Claypool)
10. Victor (6:25) From the collected works of W.H. Auden (spoken word by Lifeson)
11. I Am the Spirit (5:31) Bell-Lifeson

CD/C	Atlantic/Anthem 82852-2/-4
Canada CD/C	Anthem ANSD-1072/ANC-1072
Japan CD	Atlantic/eastwest AMCY 911
CD Promo Single: Don't Care	Atlantic PRCD-6550
CD Promo Single: Promise (4:30 edit)	Atlantic PRCD-6551
CD Promo Single: I Am the Spirit (5:31)/4:36 edit	Atlantic PRCD-6686

Notes: "Strip and Go Naked" is found on the sampler 'Guitar World Presents: Guitars That Rule the World Part 2: Smell the Fuzz/The Superstar Guitar Album' (Metal Blade D 108065) released in 1997.

The Dexters: Hip To the Tip, Live at the Orbit Room (1995)

Alex plays with the Orbit Room house band on "Born Under a Bad Sign" and "1967 Again".

Canada CD	Alma ACD-1002 (enhanced features)

Burning For Buddy: A Tribute to the Music of Buddy Rich (10-4-94)

Neil produced this tribute to the drumming world's most celebrated innovators besides playing on Duke Ellington's "Cotton Tail" and percussion with Kenny Aronoff on a cover of Average White Band's "Pick Up the Pieces", while 20 other drummers appear on other songs. Guest drummers: Bill Bruford, Simon Phillips, Matt Sorum, Max Roach, Dave Weckl, Ed Shaughnessy, Steve Gadd, Marvin "Smitty" Smith, Omar Hakim, Billy Cobham, Rod Morganstein, Steve Ferrone, Steve Smith.

US CD/C	Atlantic/Anthem 82699-2/-4
Japan CD	Atlantic/eastwest AMCY 775
CD Promo Single: Pick Up the Pieces/Beulah Witch	Atlantic PRCD-5879

Burning For Buddy: A Tribute to the Music of Buddy Rich, Volume II (7-20-97)

Neil produces again with the same players with another performance of Count Basie's "One O'Clock Jump".

US CD/C	Atlantic/Anthem 83010-2/-4

Geddy Lee: My Favourite Headache (11-14-00)

Produced by Geddy Lee, David Leonard and Ben Mink. Songs written by Geddy and
Ben Mink. Guest drummers Matt Cameron and Jeremy Taggert.

1. My Favourite Headache (3:33)
2. The Present Tense (3:25)
3. Window To the World (3:01)
4. Working At Perfekt (4:59)
5. Runaway Train (4:31)
6. The Angels' Share (4:34)
7. Moving To Bohemia (4:25)
8. Home On the Strange (3:47)
9. Slipping (5:05)
10. Still (4:29)
11. Grace To Grace (4:57)

US CD/C	Atlantic 83384-2/-4
	(also issued on 24kt gold disc)
Canada Advance CD	Universal/Anthem UMCF 4241-2

Canada CD sampler: *Selections From … My Favourite Headache* ("My Favourite Headache", plus 2 minute
excerpts of "The Present Tense", "Window To The World", "Working At Perfekt", "Runaway Train", "Slipping",
and "Grace To Grace").

Canada CD	Anthem 668251094-2
Japan CD	Atlantic/eastwest AMCY 7206
US CD Promo Singles My Favorite Headache	Atlantic PRCD-300343
Grace To Grace	Atlantic PRCD-300391
Home on the Strange/interview	Atlantic PRCD-300520

Guest Performances

Max Webster: *Universal Juveniles* (1980)

Rush performs alongside Max Webster on the track "Battle Scar".

US LP	Mercury/Phonogram SRM-1-3855
Canada LP	Anthem ANR-1-1027 and ANR-1-1627
	(reissue)
Netherlands LP	Mercury/Phonogram 6337-144
Canada CD	Anthem ANK-1027 or WANK-1027
US 12″ Single: Battle Scar (5:48)/Blue Liquor Shine	Mercury/Phonogram MK-159
UK 7″ Single: Battle Scar (5:48)/April in Toledo (3:40)	Mercury/Phonogram MER-59 P/S

Also found on these CD releases:
Max Webster — Diamonds
The Best of Max Webster (Anthem ANK-1058 and WAGK-1058) 1989

Bob and Doug McKenzie: *Great White North* (1981)

Geddy Lee sings the chorus to "Take Off". He also speaks at the beginning and ending.

Canada LP		Anthem ANR-1-1036	
US LP		Mercury/PolyGram SRM-1-4034	
Canada CD		AA-1036 or ABBD-1036	
7″ Canada Single:	Take Off (2:49)	Anthem ANS-041	
7″ Canada Single:	Take Off (2:42)/12 Days of Christmas	Anthem ANS-050	
7″ US Single:	Take Off (2:42)/Elron McKenzie (2:28)	Mercury/PolyGram 76134	
		Mercury/PolyGram 76134 DJ US Promo	P/S
7″ UK Single:	Take Off (2:42)/Elron McKenzie (2:28)	Mercury/PolyGram HOSER1	P/S
12″ US Single:	Take Off (2:42)/Elron McKenzie (2:28)	Mercury/PolyGram MK-184	

Also found on these CD samplers:
Contact: Canadian Hockey Hall of Fame (Canada Promo)
Wild and Crazy Tunes (Priority)

As well as these LPs:
Dr. Demento Vol. 5: The 1980's US (ST-12278)

Marie-Lynn Hammond: *Vignettes* (1983)

Geddy Lee on bass for "Over Queen Charlotte Sound" and "All the Horses Running".

LP	Black Tie BTR-1002
CD (1999)	Vignettes Media VM7881-2

Platinum Blonde: *Alien Shores* (1985)

Alex Lifeson performs the guitar solos on "Crying Over You" and "Holy Water."

LP	Columbia PCC-80105
Canada CD	Epic EK-40147
Canada	Epic BFE-40147
UK	Epic EPC-26658
7″ Canada Single: Crying Over You (3:35)/ It Ain't Love Anyway (3:08)	Epic C4-7085 P/S
7″ Canada Single: Crying Over You (3:59 Radical Mix)/ Somebody (4:03)	Epic C4-7127 P/S
12″ Canada Single: (Radical Mix)/(Dub Ver. Instrabeat Mix)	Crying Over You Columbia 12CXP-7115

Notes: Both 45 picture sleeves feature Alex.

Also found on these samplers:
Hits in Overdrive (Canada compilation LP)
The Best of Platinum Blonde Live (Canada CD)

Ken Ramm (1985)

Neil Peart plays.

Unreleased.

Jeff Berlin and Vox Humana: *Champion* (1985)

Neil Peart on a drum duet with Steve Smith (Journey) on "Marabi" and "Champion (of the World)".

Canada LP	Passport Jazz PJ-88004-A
Canada CD	Passport Jazz PJCD-88004
Jap. LP	Passport/Victor VLJ-1029
Jap. CD	Passport/Victor VDJ-1029

Notes: Track also found on Jeff Berlin's "Crossroads".

"Pieces of Eight" (1987)

An original percussion piece (Neil Peart's first and only sound supplement thus far) which would later feature the marimba solo part that would be incorporated into his live drum solo. As a side note, the Drum Giveaway Contest Winners' solos were issued as a soundsheet as well in the February 1988 *Modern Drummer* (Eva-Tone Flexidisc 1032951XS). They are in order from Grand Prize to Third Prize.

Released in May 1987 Modern Drummer	Eva-Tone Flexidisc soundsheet 1018551XS

"Beyond Borders" (1987)

Alex with Triumph's Rik Emmett; Ed Bickert; Liona Boyd.

Released in July 1987 Guitar Player	Eva-Tone Flexidisc soundsheet 1023711AXS

The Big Picture: Dream On the Horizon
A Tribute to the Olympic Spirit (1988)

Alex Lifeson on guitar on "Hands of Man".

Canada LP	Chartwell WSC-331
7" Canada Single: Hands of Man/inst. ver.	Chartwell WSC-453

Climb: *Take a Chance* (1988)

Geddy's voice is heard on track four of his friend Warren Cromartie's project.

Japan LP	Insideout/Toshiba EMI RP32-5730
Japan CD	Insideout/Toshiba EMI CP32-5730
Japan Cassette	Insideout/Toshiba EMI ZP32-5730

Greenway: *Serious Business* (1988)

Alex solo on "In the Danger Zone".

US LP/CD/cass.:	Atlantic 81827-1/2/4
7" US Single: In the Danger Zone	Atlantic 7-89118 Promo
7" US Single: In the Danger Zone/Playing To Win	Atlantic 7-89118 P/S

Gowan: *Lost Brotherhood* (1990)

Alex Lifeson performs on 8 of the 10 tracks.

US CD/cassette:	Atlantic 82117-2/4
US CD Promo Single: Lost Brotherhood	Atlantic PRCD-3736-2
US cassette Single: All the Lovers in the World/Fire It Up	Atlantic 74-87873
Canada CD/cassette:	Columbia CT80160
Canada cassette Single: All the Lovers in the World/Fire It Up	Columbia C4T3140
Canada cassette Single: Lost Brotherhood/Message From Heaven	Columbia C4T3142

Standing in the Shadows of Motown:
The Life and Music of Legendary Bassist James Jamerson (1990)

by Allen Slutsky (Dr. Licks series book and audio tape/CD)Hal Leonard Corp. ISBN: 0881888826

Geddy Lee on bass on "Get Ready".

Mendelson Joe: *Women Are the Only Hope* (1991)

Geddy Lee on bass throughout.

(independent, unreleased commercially)

Rheostatics: *Whale Music* (1992)

Neil Peart plays drums and/or percussion on "Guns", "Rain Rain Rain" and "Palomar".

US CD	Sire 9 45564-2

Tom Cochrane: *Ragged Ass Road* (1995)

Alex Lifeson plays on "Will of the Gun", "Crawl" and solo on "Just Scream".

Canada CD	EMI CDP 7243 8 32951 2 8
US CD	Capitol CDP 7243 8 32951 2 8

I Mother Earth: *Scenery and Fish* (1996)

Alex Lifeson plays on "Like a Girl".

US CD	Capitol 064948
Canada CD	EMI 724383291908

Merry Axemas: A Guitar Christmas (1997)

Alex plays all instruments including keyboard and guitar on "Little Drummer Boy".

US CD	Epic EK-67775
Japan CD	Sony SRCS 8509

Euphoria (1999)

Geddy Lee co-produced with Garry Hughes and Ken Ramm as well as plays bass and keys with guitarist Ramm, The Art of Noise's Anne Dudley, jazz artist Ray Babbington and dance pop singer Juliet Roberts. Geddy also co-wrote "The Road".

CD	Six Degrees 1015-2

I Mother Earth: *Blue Green Orange* (1999)

Geddy Lee on bass on "Good For Sule".

CD	Mercury 809496-2

Rocket Science (1999)

EP co-produced by Geddy for his nephew Rob Higgins; vocals on "Space Suit".

Music Inspired by South Park: Bigger, Longer, Uncut (1999)

Geddy Lee sings with Alex Lifeson on guitars on "O Canada" with South Park characters Terrance and Phillip. Matt Stone on drums.

CD	Atlantic 83199-2

Three Doors Down

Alex plays on "Dangerous Game", "Dead Love", "Wasted Me" (unavailable on CD to date).

Gene Roddenbury's Andromeda TV series (2000)

Alex Lifeson performs "March of the High Guard" (unavailable on CD to date).

Albums Produced by Rush Members

Wireless: *No Static* (1979)
Produced by Geddy Lee.

Canada LP	Anthem ANR-1-1025

Boys Brigade (1983)
Produced by Geddy Lee.

Canada LP	Anthem ANR-1-1040
US LP	Capitol ST-12278
Canada 7" Single: The Passion of Love/Exodus	Anthem ANS-053 P/S
Canada 7" Single: Melody/Africa	Anthem ANS-056 P/S
Canada 12" Single: Interview with Boys and Geddy	Anthem SPE-018
Canada 12" Single: Melody/same	Anthem SPRO-9066 Promo
UK 12" Single: Maxi Single	Capitol 12CL234 P/S

Note: Track also found on original motion picture soundtrack to *Heavenly Bodies* (Private Bodies SZ-39930) released 1985.

Clean Slate (1988)
Produced by Alex Lifeson.

Canada EP	Anthem ANR-1-5002 5 tracks

7" Single-Survivor/Losin' You	Anthem ANS-047
7" Single-Survivor (live)/A Million Ways	Anthem SPE-047
12" Single-Survivor/same	Anthem SPE-044

Lifer (2001)

Produced by Alex Lifeson.

CD:	Republic/Universal 14-124-2
CD promo single_Boring	Republic/Universal UNIR 20509-2

Benefit Albums

We Are the World (1985)

Geddy Lee sings with Canadian Artists Against Hunger (Northern Lights)

US LP	Columbia USA-40043
Canada LP	Columbia BEN-40043
US CD	Mercury/PolyGram 824-822-2

7" Canada Single: Tears Are Not Enough (3:56)/4:53
instrumental ver.   Columbia 7BEN-7073 P/S

Hear N' Aid (1986)

US LP	Mercury/PolyGram 826-044-M-1
LP	Mercury/ Nippon Phonogram AIDL-1 826-
044-1	

Includes *Distant Early Warning live* from P/G video.

After the Hurricane (1989)

US CD (F221750DIDX5999); also in a gold edition.
Includes *Time Stand Still.*

Rock Aid Armenia: *Smoke On the Water* (1989)

7" UK Single/Paranoid	Harp Beat ARMEN 001	P/S
7" UK Single Mega Rock Mix on both sides	Harp Beat ARMEN 002	P/S
12" UK Single/Paranoid	Harp Beat ARMENT 001	P/S
12" UK Single: Mayhem Mix/orig. extended ver.	Harp Beat ARMENT 002	P/S
12" UK Mega Rock Remix/Paranoid	Harp Beat ARMENTR 001	P/S
UK/France CD	Harp Beat ARMENCD 001	
Japan CD	BMG/Victor BVCZ-3 AID CD001	

Notes: Track can be found on these CD samplers:
Pop Dreams and Rock Tracks: The Earthquake Album (1992)
Rock Aide Armenia's Smoke On the Water (also with "The Spirit of Radio")

The Earth Day Album (1993)

US CD:	Marketworks/EMI E226594

Includes *Red Tide.*

The Kumbaya Album (1994)

"Nobody's Hero".

Canada CD:	Sony Music EK-80206

The Kumbaya Album (1995)

Alex with others on "All Along the Watchtower".

Canada CD:	WEA CD-11719

Rush Videography

Promo Videos

1975 Fly By Night
1975 Anthem
1977 A Farewell To Kings
1977 Closer To the Heart
1977 Xanadu
1978 Circumstances
1978 The Trees
1978 La Villa Strangiato
1981 Limelight ❶
1981 Tom Sawyer ❶
1981 Vital Signs ❶
1982 Limelight (live '81)
1982 Tom Sawyer (live '81) ❷
1982 Red Barchetta (live '81)
1982 Closer To the Heart (live '81)
1982 Freewill (live '81)
1982 Subdivisions
1983 Countdown
1984 Distant Early Warning
1984 The Body Electric
1984 The Enemy Within
1984 Afterimage ❸
1985 Red Sector A (live '84)
1985 The Big Money ❹
1986 Mystic Rhythms
1987 Time Stand Still
1987 Lock and Key
1989 Marathon (live '88) (solo cut)
1989 Mission (live '88)
1989 Show Don't Tell ❺
1990 The Pass
1990 Superconductor
1991 Roll the Bones
1993 Stick It Out ❻
1994 Nobody's Hero ❼
1996 Half the World
1997 Driven ❽
1998 Closer To the Heart (live '97) ❾

1970s promos were never aired on MTV but were subsequently aired on MuchMusic. They are different versions than the studio counterparts.

❶ These videos were shot in Le Studio. Some versions are only performance, others commonly are the final versions with '70s promo live video footage in the case of "Limelight" and snowy outer studio footage as in "Tom Sawyer".

❷ This live clip exists in a few variations: one with polarization effects, one without, and others with concert crowd shots before the song.

❸ Released straight to home video.

❹ Released in shortened MTV version with the full-length version on home video of Grace Under Pressure Tour.

❺ Aired with conceptual parts and without.

❻ Aired with additional street scenes in Canada.

❼ Only aired in Canada and Europe.

❽ Only aired in Canada, Europe, and MTV2.

❾ Some versions have edited jam sections. Not aired on MTV. Only shown in Canada, Europe, and VH-1.

Home Video

Concerts and Video Compilations

Exit ... Stage Left (1981)

Directed by Martin Kahan (uncredited). Produced by Grant Lough. Filmed at the Montreal Forum, March 1981. 60 minutes. Voices of Alex, Geddy, and Neil are from a July 1981 *Off the Record* interview disc.

The Camera Eye (intro)
Limelight
Tom Sawyer
The Trees
Xanadu
Red Barchetta
Freewill
Closer To the Heart
YYZ/drum solo (excerpt)
Medley: By-Tor and the Snow Dog/In the End/In the Mood/ 2112 Finale
YYZ (over credits)

USA:
BETA: RCA/Columbia Pictures Home Video BE-91125
VHS: RCA /Columbia Pictures Pictures Home Video VH-91125
VHS: RCA/Columbia Pictures Home Video-Musicvision 60285 (Discontinued in 1991)
LD: Pioneer Artists PA-83-035 (later pressings in digital stereo)
CED Videodisc: RCA SelectaVision 12127 ❶

❶ Write-up on back describes the recording trucks, as well as mentioning Rush's new LP *Signals*. Note the medley is listed out of order and incorrectly includes "Working Man".

UK:
PAL: Spectrum/PolyGram PMV-7915582
PAL: Channel Five Video CFV-05072
PAL LD: Spectrum 791-558-1

Japan:
BETA: RCA/Victor BE-91125
VHS: RCA/Victor 91125; Video Arts VAVJ-274
LD: Pioneer SM058-3021; Video Arts VALJ-2087; Video Arts
       VALJ-3274 DVD: Columbia COBY-90123; released 7-20-00

Through the Camera Eye (1985)

45 minutes.

Distant Early Warning
Vital Signs
The Body Electric
Subdivisions
Afterimage
Tom Sawyer (live)
The Enemy Within
Countdown
YYZ (over credits)

USA

VHS: RCA/Columbia Pictures Home Video-Musicvision 60466
       (Disc. in 1991)
LD: Pioneer Artists/PMV PA-85-112

UK

PAL: Spectrum SPC-00132
PAL: Embassy Video EV-5602
PAL: Channel Five Video CFV-06332 (released 1987)

Japan

VHS: Video Arts VAVJ-273
LD: Pioneer SM058-0068; Video Arts VALJ-3273

Grace Under Pressure Tour (1986)

Directed by David Mallet. Filmed at Toronto Maple Leaf
Gardens, September 1984. 70 minutes.

Three Stooges Intro
The Spirit of Radio
The Enemy Within
The Weapon
Witch Hunt
New World Man
Distant Early Warning
Red Sector A
Closer To the Heart
Medley: YYZ/2112-Temples of Syrinx/Tom Sawyer
Medley: Vital Signs/Finding My Way/In the Mood
Afterimage (over end credits)
The Big Money (full-length video)

US:
VHS: RCA/Columbia Pictures Home Video-Musicvision 60607
       (Disc. in 1991)
LD: PolyGram Video CDV 080 103-1

UK:
PAL: Channel Five Video CFV-07352 (Does not have "The Big
       Money" video)

Japan
VHS: Toshiba VTS-M152VH
LD: Video Arts VALJ-2181

A Show of Hands (1989)

Directed by Larry Jordan. Filmed at Birmingham National
Exhibition Centre, England, April 1988. 95 minutes.

Three Stooges Intro
The Big Money
Marathon
Turn the Page
Prime Mover
Manhattan Project
Closer To the Heart
Red Sector A
Force Ten
Lock and Key ❶
Mission
Territories
YYZ>The Rhythm Method-Drum Solo
The Spirit of Radio
Tom Sawyer
Medley: 2112: I. Overture II. Temples of Syrinx/La Villa
Strangiato/In the Mood.

❶ Although every ASOH laserdisc jacket has it listed, *Lock and
   Key* was exclusively included on first run pressings of the US
   laserdiscs, distinguishable by a lavender label on the disc. The
   track was removed from all VHS versions.

US:
VHS: PMV (PolyGram Music Video) 041-760-3 (Disc. in 1999)
LD: PMV (PolyGram Music Video) CDV 082 575-1 ❶

UK:
PAL: Channel Five Video CFV-07812

Japan
VHS: Video Arts VAH-0105
LD: Video Arts VAL-3105

Chronicles: The Video Collection (1990)

Compiled by Bill Levenson. 63 minutes.

Closer To the Heart
The Trees
Limelight
Tom Sawyer (live)
Red Barchetta (live)

Subdivisions
Distant Early Warning
Red Sector A (live)
The Big Money
Mystic Rhythms
Time Stand Still
Lock and Key
Closer To the Heart (end credits)

US:

VHS: PMV (PolyGram/Anthem Music Video) 082-765-3
Released 11-4-90
LD: PMV (PolyGram Music Video) CDV 082 765-1 ❶
Released 6-92
DVD: Universal/Mercury 827659 rel. 9-25 ❷

❶ Does not contain Red Sector A.

❷ Includes The Enemy Within and Afterimage

UK:

PAL: Channel Five Video CFM-2764

Japan:

VHS: Video Arts VAVJ-272
LD: Video Arts VALJ-2088
DVD: Columbia COBY-90108; released 3/18/00

Different Stages

Directed by Don Allan. Filmed at Toronto Molson Amphitheatre, July 1997. Unreleased as of 2000.

CDV (Compact Disc Video) Singles

The Big Money (1988) Vertigo/PolyGram CDV 080 084-2 (PAL format)
The Big Money video (5:05) + audio tracks Red Sector A (live), Marathon

The Big Money (1988) Mercury/PolyGram CDV 422 870 717-2 (NTSC format)
The Big Money video (4:52) + audio tracks Red Sector A (live), Marathon. Printed in UK.

Samplers

Incident at Channel Q (1985)

US

VHS: RCA/Columbia Pictures Video-Musicvision 60577
LD: Pioneer Artists/PMV PA-87-186

A small-town Canadian youth tries to keep a pirate radio station playing Scorpions, KISS, Iron Maiden, Rainbow, Deep Purple, etc. This is part movie, part video compilation. Rush's "The Body Electric" is first up. Val Azzoli-produced.

PolyGram Records
Rush Promo Sampler (no number) 1986

Tom Sawyer (studio), Limelight (studio), Subdivisions, Distant Early Warning, Red Sector A (live), The Big Money, Mystic Rhythms, and Marathon.

Rock Classics (PolyGram Music Video 083103-3) 1991
Sampler including Tom Sawyer (live) from Exit … Stage Left.

Guest Appearance/Related Videos

1983   Boys Brigade: Melody (Geddy produced)
1985   Northern Lights:Tears Are Not Enough (two versions) (Geddy sings)
1985   Platinum Blonde: Crying Over You (Alex solo heard)
1988   Greenway: In the Danger Zone (Alex appearance)
1989   Rock Aid Armenia: Smoke On the Water + (Alex appearance)
1990   Gowan: Lost Brotherhood + (Alex solo/appearance)
1996   Victor: Promise

Tears Are Not Enough: Northern Lights (1985)

Documentary about the benefit track; Geddy sings and speaks.

Canada/USA:
VHS: Key Video

Japan:
VHS: 67141-98 BETA: 67142-98 LD: 70020-78

Hard 'N Heavy Vol. 5 (MPI Video MP1680) 1993

Includes "Smoke On the Water".

Buddy Rich Memorial Scholarship Concert (11-91)

Taped at the Ritz, NYC, 4-8-91
Vol. 3 (73m) DCI Video VH081 Neil on 1 track
Vol. 4 (60m) DCI Video VH082 Neil on 2 trks

The Making of Burning For Buddy

(11-96 for 1 and 2; 11/97 for 3 and 4)

Part 1 (81m) DCI Video VH0206 Neil talks, plays "Cotton Tail"
Part 2 (89m) DCI Video VH0207 Neil talks
Part 3 (61m) DCI Video VH0354 Neil talks, plays "One O'Clock Jump"
Part 4 (68m) DCI Video VH0355 Neil talks

Tower of Song:
The Epic Story of Canada and Its Music (2001)

Includes a few words from Geddy Lee and footage from "Tom Sawyer" from Exit… Stage Left DVD:Image Entertainment ID9695CDDVD. 92 minutes.

Musical Instruction Videos

Neil Peart — A Work in Progress (11-96)

VHS: DCI Video VH0293 (2 tape set, 110m each, with poster
        and booklet)
Jap VHS:Yamaha Music Trading LDCIVH293

The only instructional video from a Rush member thus far.
Includes "Momo's Dance Party". Excerpts appear on the *Drum
Workshop: American Dream II* promo videotape.

Other

Geddy Lee — My Favourite Headache (electronic presskit)

VHS: Anthem (12 minute interview tape)

GEDDY I guess *2112, Moving Pictures, Permanent Waves, Roll the Bones,* I think that's some of our best work. Some of our dicey work is *Caress of Steel, Grace Under Pressure,* although times have been kinder to that record than I imagined. (Seconds 1994)

NEIL You get colored by playing them live. I tend to be more excited to hear the songs that we don't play live. *Hold Your Fire* is one of my recent faves. There's a mood about that album and a strength in the songs that if I were outside of it all as a Rush fan, I think I would rate that album very highly. There are bits of all of them that I like, and it always tends to be a diminishing rating system. Each one I like less than the one after it. (Seconds 1994)

R<small>USH HAS ALWAYS BEEN COMMITTED TO TOURING</small> to support their recordings and to keep close contact with their fans.

NEIL I think it's important to tour. Even when touring's not a commercial necessity, it's still important musically. Because, like anything else, if you stop doing it for awhile, you tend to get complacent and your abilities atrophy. Traveling is important—in terms of getting input and staying in touch with what's happening in the world. (Circus 1980)

The band prefers arena shows over outdoor festival concerts, such as Woodstock, Monsters of Rock, Rock in Rio, etc.

NEIL Well, it seems that our name is announced as a rumour every year and only then do the organisers come to us and ask if we'd be interested. The plain truth is that we'd never consider playing such an event. I've been in the audience at stadium shows and they're awful. They're also a big rip-off, with no humanity about them. It's like a mass, a mob and all they do is provide the opportunity for a lot of people to make a lot of money. Theatres are great, but only if you wanna turn around and say, "I know that 12000 people wanna see us, but the band only wants to play for 3000 kids." Who are you serving with that attitude? Who are you doing it for? All the people who won't be able to see you? For those people in the industry or with contacts to get tickets? No, we know where we are at our best and that's in arenas, where we intend to stay! (Metal Hammer 1988)

Rush was special guest to bands listed until 1977 when they headlined.

NEIL We were lucky to have come up through the ranks slowly. We saw a lot of other bands headlining, and saw how they handled fame with all its temptations. I certainly got to see how dangerous it is for an unstable person to deal with the whole situation. I've seen many of them just crumble underneath it. So strong character is pretty much an irreplaceable quality to have in this business. That is something that doesn't always go with a very creative personality. (Modern Drummer)

GEDDY We don't go kill ourselves to go and play Europe and Japan every time. We go to those places very sporadically. Even though there's demand, we can't fit it into our lives and that has a toll to pay on our total image. We recognize the importance of having a life outside of the band—sometimes that takes precedence over promotion. We've had to slow down a bit. We're not 25, we just can't keep doing that. It amazes me when some of these guys—like Bryan Adams who go on the road for 3 or 4 years. (Bassics 1997)

1973

| October | 27 | Toronto, ON | Victory Burlesque Theatre (guest for The New York Dolls) |
| December | 9 | Binghamton, NY | Men's Gym (guest for The Sons of Champlin; Papa John Creach) |

Rush Tour 1974 (with John Rutsey on drums)

May	18	East Lansing, MI	North Side Drive-In (guest for Dr. John; with Skyhook; Liverpool)
June	6	Salt Lake City, UT	Terrace Ballroom (guest for KISS)
	7	Boise, ID	Western Idaho Fairgrounds (guest for KISS)
	27	Toronto, ON	Centennial Hall (guest for Symphonic Slam)
	28	Cleveland, OH	Allen Theater (guest for ZZ Top; with Locomotive GT)
July	1	Toronto, ON	Seneca Theater-Minkler Auditorium (guest for Nazareth)
	2	Toronto, ON	Colonial Tavern20 MZ Bennett (Summer Dance)
	25	London, ON	Centennial Hall (guest for KISS; with Ronny Leyton)

Rush North American Tour 1974 (with Neil)

August	16	Pittsburgh, PA	Civic Arena (Neil debut) (guest for Uriah Heep; with Manfred Mann's Earth Band)
	17	Comstock, MI	Thunderchicken (guest for KISS)
	18	Hammond, IN	Parthenon Theater (guest for KISS)
	19	Lincoln, NE	Pershing Memorial Auditorium
October	23	London, ON	University of Western Ontario
	24	Toronto, ON	Massey Hall
	25	Kingston, ON	Grant Hall, Queen's University
	28	Roslyn, NY	My Father's Place
	29	Roslyn, NY	My Father's Place
	31	Ottawa, ON	Civic Centre
November	1	Montreal, PQ	Forum
	3	Columbus, OH	Agora Ballroom
	4	Upper Darby, PA	Tower Theater
	5	New York City, NY	Felt Forum
	7	Schaumburg, IL	Beginnings
	9	Detroit, MI	Michigan Palace (guest for KISS)
	10	St. Louis, MO	Ambassador Theater
	12	Milwaukee, WI	Riverside Theater
	14	Columbus, OH	Veterans Memorial Auditorium
	15	Chicago, IL	Aragon Ballroom
	20	Toronto, ON	Convocation Hall
	22	San Diego, CA	Tuesday Ballroom
	23	Los Angeles, CA	Shrine Auditorium
	27	Los Angeles, CA	Whiskey A-Go Go (guest Butts Band)
	28	Ventura, CA	Ventura Theater

December	5	New York City, NY	Electric Ladyland Studios (guest for Uriah Heep)
	16	Cleveland, OH	Agora Ballroom (guest for Don Preston)
	17	Cleveland, OH	Agora Ballroom (guest for Don Preston)
	20	Detroit, MI	Michigan Palace
	25	Cleveland, OH	Agora Ballroom (guest for Law)

Fly By Night North American Tour 1975

February	14	Toronto, ON	Seneca College Theatre
	15	Owen Sound, ON	Roxy Theater
	16	Barrie, ON	
	17	London, ON	
	18	Kingston, ON	
	20	Indianapolis, IN	Convention Center
	25	La Porte TX	Sylvan Beach Pavilion (guest for Steve Long Group)
	31	Atlanta, GA	Electric Ballroom
March	5	Atlanta, GA	Electric Ballroom
	6	Atlanta, GA	Electric Ballroom
	7	Atlanta, GA	Electric Ballroom
	8	Atlanta, GA	Electric Ballroom
	11	Newark, DE	Stone Ballroom
	19	North Hampton, PA	Roxy Theater (guest for KISS)
	28	Toledo, OH	Sports Arena (guest for KISS)
April	7	Cleveland, OH	Agora Ballroom (guest for Sky King)
	8	Akron, OH	Civic Theater (guest for KISS; with The Kidds)
	9	Erie, PA	Erie County Fieldhouse (guest for KISS; with Vitale's Madmen)
	13	Detroit, MI	Michigan Palace (guest for KISS)
	15	Pittsburgh, PA	Warner Theater
	17	Burlington, IA	Burlington Auditorium
	19	Palantine, IL	Fremd High School Auditorium
	21	Buffalo, NY	Veterans Memorial Auditorium
	22	Indianapolis, IN	Convention Center
	24	Louisville, KY	Freedom Hall (guest for KISS; The Kidds)
	25	Charlotte, NC	Park Center (guest for KISS)
	26	Fayetteville, NC	Cumberland Auditorium (guest for KISS)
	27	Richmond, VA	Coliseum (guest for KISS)
	29	Lansing, MI	Metro Theater (guest for KISS)
May	3	Philadelphia, PA	Tower Theater (guest for KISS)
	4	Bedford, OH	Chanel High School Auditorium (guest Sweetleaf)
	6	Milwaukee, WI	Riverside Theater (guest for KISS)
	8	Lockport, IL	Louis University (guest for KISS)
	9	Ada, OH	Northern Ohio University (guest for KISS; with James Gang)
	10	Largo, MD	Capital Center (guest for KISS)
	11	Boston, MA	Orpheum Theater (guest for KISS)
	15	Cleveland, OH	Agora Ballroom (guest for KISS)
	16	Detroit, MI	Cobo Hall Arena (guest for KISS)
	17	Johnston, PA	Cambria County War Memorial Arena (guest for KISS)

22	Yakima, WA	Capital Theater (guest for KISS)
23	Medford, OR	Medford Armory (guest for KISS)
24	Portland, OR	Paramount Theater (guest for KISS)
25	Seattle, WA	Paramount Northwest (guest for KISS)
26	Portland, OR	Paramount Theater (guest for KISS)
27	Spokane, WA	Gonzaga University (guest for KISS)
29	Las Vegas, NV	Sahara Hotel (guest for KISS)
30	Sacramento,CA	Memorial Auditorium (guest for KISS)
31	Long Beach, CA	Arena (guest for KISS)
June 1	San Francisco, CA	The Winterland (guest for KISS; with The Tubes)
2	San Francisco, CA	The Winterland (guest for KISS; with The Tubes)
6	Fresno, CA	Warner Theater (guest for KISS)
7	San Diego, CA	Civic Theater (guest for KISS)
13	Windsor, ON	Cleary Auditorium
18	Regina, SK	Trianon Ballroom
19	Winnipeg, MB	Convention Centre
20	Thunder Bay, ON	Arena
21	Saulte Ste. Marie, ON	Arena
22	Dundas, ON	Arena
23	Lakefield, ON	Arena
25	Toronto, ON	Massey Hall
26	Kitchener, ON	Waterloo Lutheran University Theatre
27	London, ON	Centennial Hall (guest Symphonic Slam)
28	Bala, ON	Kee to Bala
29	Port Dover, ON	Summer Gardens

Caress of Steel North American Tour 1975 – 76 (Down the Tubes Tour)

November 7	Akron, OH	Civic Theater (guest for Ted Nugent)
8	Cleveland, OH	Allen Theater (guest for Ted Nugent; with The Artful Dodger)
	Arlington Heights, IL	Hershey High School Auditorium
15	Rockford, IL	The Armory (guest for KISS)
16	Flint, MI	I.M. Auditorium (guest for KISS)
17	Flint, MI	I.M. Auditorium (guest for KISS)
18	Port Huron, MI	McMorran Arena (guest for KISS)
19	Traverse City, MI	Glacier Arena (guest for KISS)
21	Terre Haute, IN	Indiana State University (guest for KISS)
22	Chicago, IL	International Amphitheater (guest for KISS)
23	Evansville, IN	Roberts Stadium (guest for KISS; with Mott the Hoople)
26	Huntsburg, VA	Memorial Fieldhouse (guest for KISS; with Mott the Hoople)
27	Fayetteville, NC	Cumberland Auditorium (guest for KISS)
28	Asheville, NC	Civic Center (guest for KISS)29 Charlotte, NC Park Center (guest for KISS)
30	Largo, MD	Capital Center (guest for KISS)
December 2	Columbus, GA	Municipal Auditorium (guest for KISS)
3	Dothan, AL	Farm Arena (guest for KISS)
5	Atlanta, GA	Omni (guest for KISS)
6	Jacksonville, FL	Coliseum (guest for KISS)

	12	Syracuse, NY	Onondaga County War Memorial Arena (guest for KISS)
	14	Boston, MA	Orpheum Theater (guest for KISS)
	15	Toledo, OH	Sports Arena (guest for Lynyrd Skynyrd; with Leslie West)
	18	Waterbury, CT	Palace (guest for KISS)
	19	Binghamton, NY	Arena (guest for KISS)
	20	Pittsburgh, PA	Civic Arena (guest for KISS; with Mott the Hoople)
	21	Richmond, VA	Mosque (guest for KISS; with Mott the Hoople)
January 1976	10	Toronto, ON	Massey Hall (guest Joe Mendelsson)

2112 North American Tour 1976

March	5	Mount Prospect, IL	Randhurst Arena (guest Kansas; with Starcastle)
	15	Hollywood, CA	Starwood Amphitheatre
	16	Hollywood, CA	Starwood Amphitheatre
	17	Hollywood, CA	Starwood Amphitheatre
	18	Hollywood, CA	Starwood Amphitheatre
	25	Medford, OR	The Armory (guest for Styx; with Sutherland Brothers; Quiver)
	28	Seattle, WA	Paramount Theater (guest for Styx)
	30	Guelph, ON	Memorial Gardens (guest Max Webster now on)
April	1	Ottawa, ON	Civic Centre
	2	Cornwall, ON	Civic Complex
	3	Kingston, ON	Jock Harty Arena
	4	Petersborough, ON	Memorial Centre
	6	Fredericton, NB	Aitken University Centre
	7	Moncton, NB	J. Louis Levesque Arena
	8	Halifax, NS	Metro Centre
	17	Pekin, IL	Memorial Arena (guest for Thin Lizzy; with Starcastle)
May	25	Ft. Wayne, IN	Memorial Coliseum (guest for Aerosmith; with Stu Daye)
	29	St. Paul, MN	Civic Center Arena (guest for Blue Oyster Cult; REO Speedwagon)
	30	Springfield, IL	Nelson Center (with Roller; Smokehouse; Fat Tuesday)
June	11	Toronto, ON	Massey Hall (guest Max Webster) recorded for ATWAS album
	12	Toronto, ON	Massey Hall (guest Max Webster) recorded for ATWAS album
	13	Toronto, ON	Massey Hall (guest Max Webster) recorded for ATWAS album
	16	Evansville, IN	Roberts Stadium (guest for Aerosmith)
July	23	Greensboro, NC	Memorial Hall
	27	Jackson, MS	University Hall
	29	Montgomery, AL	Civic Center
	30	Columbus, GA	Municipal Auditorium
August	1	Huntsville, AL	Von Braun Civic Center
	27	Normal, IL	Union Auditorium (Illinois State University) (guest Head East)

All the World's a Stage North American Tour 1976–77

September	18 Syracuse, NY	War Memorial Auditorium (guest for Blue Oyster Cult; with Angel)
	19 Harrisburg, PA	Forum Theater (guest Angel)
	20 Allentown, PA	Agricultural Hall (guest Angel)
	22 Rochester, NY	Dome Auditorium (guest for Blue Oyster Cult; with Angel)
	28 Moncton, NB	J. Louis Levesque Arena
	29 Charlottetown, PEI	Simmons Sports Center
October	1 Sydney, NS	Forum
	3 St. John's, NB	Lord Beaverbrook Rink
	4 Halifax, NS	Forum
	8 North Bay, ON	Memorial Gardens
	9 Sudbury, ON	Arena
	10 Ottawa, ON	Civic Centre
	11 Kingston, ON	Memorial Centre
	25 Seattle, WA	Paramount Theater (guest Tommy Bolin)
	26 Seattle, WA	Paramount Theater (guest Tommy Bolin)
	30 Seattle, WA	Paramount Theater (guest Tommy Bolin)
Novem ber	3 Roseburg, OR	Douglas Hall Fairgrounds (guest Tommy Bolin)
	14 Davenport, IA	RKO Orpheum Theatre
	24 Sacramento, CA	Memorial Auditorium (guest for Ted Nugent; with Be-Bop Deluxe)
	26 San Francisco, CA	The Winterland (guest for Ted Nugent; with Be-Bop Deluxe)
	27 San Francisco, CA	The Winterland (guest for Ted Nugent; with Be-Bop Deluxe)
	28 Fresno, CA	Selland Arena (guest for Ted Nugent until the 15th)
December	1 Los Angeles, CA	Great Western Forum (guest for Ted Nugent)
	4 Denver, CO	Auditorium Arena
	15 Montreal, QC	Forum (guest for Aerosmith)
	16 Chicago, IL	Auditorium
	20 Clarksville, TN	Dunn Center (Austin Peay State University) (guest for Lynyrd Skynyrd)
	30 Hamilton, ON	
	31 Toronto, ON	Maple Leaf Gardens Concert Bowl (guests Chilliwack, Wireless)
January 1977	3 Toronto, ON	Maple Leaf Gardens Concert Bowl (guests Chilliwack, Wireless)
	14 Oklahoma City, OK	Fairgrounds (guest for Ted Nugent, The Artful Dodger now)
	15 Kansas City, MO	Municipal Auditorium
	16 Tulsa, OK	Pavilion
	18 El Paso, TX	Coliseum
	19 Lubbock, TX	Coliseum
	20 Odessa, TX	Ector County Coliseum
	21 Abilene, TX	Taylor County Coliseum
	22 Amarillo, TX	Civic Auditorium
	27 Columbus, OH	Veterans Memorial Auditorium (guest Starcastle, Max Webster until the 30th)
	29 Evansville, IN	Robertsville Stadium30 South Bend, INMorris Civic Center

February	9	Saginaw, MI	Civic Center (guest The Runaways)
	10	Detroit, MI	Cobo Hall Arena (guest The Runaways)
	11	Port Huron, MI	Memorial Arena
	12	Davenport, IA	RKO Orpheum Theatre
	13	St. Louis, MO	Kiel Auditorium (guest T.Rex, Max Webster)
	15	Detroit, MI	Cobo Hall Arena
	26	Fayetteville, NC	Cumberland County Memorial Arena (guest for Blue Oyster Cult; REO Speedwagon)
March	26	San Diego, CA	Sports Arena
	30	San Francisco, CA	Winterland Ballroom
April	4	Cincinnati, OH	Riverfront Coliseum (guest Starcastle; opening for Boston)
	8	Toledo, OH	Sports Arena (guest Angel, Max Webster)
	9	Dayton, OH	Hara Arena (guest Rick Derringer, Max Webster)
	14	Ft. Wayne, IN	Allen County Memorial Coliseum (guest Starcastle)
	15	Cleveland, OH	Public Hall (guest Rick Derringer, Max Webster)
	17	Washington, DC	Lisner Auditorium
	21	Poughkeepsie, NY	Mid-Hudson Civic Center (guest Max Webster)
	22	Binghamton, NY	Broome County Arena (guest Max Webster)
	23	Syracuse, NY	War Memorial Auditorium (guest Angel; Max Webster)
	24	Albany, NY	Palace Theater (guest Angel; Max Webster)
May	4	Omaha, NE	Music Hall (guest Angel, Max Webster)
	6	St. Paul, MN	Civic Center Arena (guest Styx, Starcastle)
	8	Duluth, MN	Arena (guest Styx)
	15	Springfield, IL	Nelson Center (guest Cheap Trick; Max Webster)
	18	Marquette, MI	Lakeview Arena
	20	Chicago, IL	Aragon Ballroom
	21	Chicago, IL	Aragon Ballroom
	22	Port Huron, MI	McMorran Arena

All the World's a Stage World Tour 1977
(United Kingdom/Europe)

June	1	Sheffield	City Hall
	2	Manchester	Free Trade Hall
	3	Birmingham	Odeon
	4	London	Hammersmith Odeon (guest Stray)
	8	Stockholm, Sweden	Gjta Lejon
	11	Newcastle	City Hall
	12	Glasgow, Scotland	Apollo Theatre
	13	Liverpool	The Empire

A Farewell to Kings North American Tour 1977–78
(Drive Til You Die Tour)

August	17	Davenport, IA	Orpheum Theater
	20	Houston, TX	Music Hall
	23	Toronto, ON	Canadian National Exhibition (guest Max Webster)
September	6	Thunder Bay, ON	Fort William Gardens (guest Max Webster through 15th)
	7	Winnipeg, MB	Arena
	8	Regina, SK	Agridome
	9	Edmonton, AB	Kinsmen's Fieldhouse
	10	Saskatoon, SK	Arena
	11	Calgary, AB	Stampede Corral
	13	Vancouver, BC	Pacific National Exhibition Coliseum
	14	Victoria, BC	Memorial Coliseum
	16	Spokane, WA	Coliseum (guest UFO; Max Webster now on)
	17	Seattle, WA	Center Coliseum
	18	Pullman, WA	Beasley Performing Arts Coliseum (Washington State University)
	19	Portland, OR	Coliseum
	20	Portland, OR	Coliseum
	21	Portland, OR	Coliseum
	22	Roseburg, OR	Douglas Hall Fairgrounds
	23	Medford, OR	Armory
	24	San Francisco, CA	Winterland
	26	Bakersfield, CA	Civic Center
	27	Reno, NV	Fairgrounds
	28	Fresno, CA	Selland Arena
	29	Stockton, CA	Memorial Civic Auditorium
	30	San Diego, CA	Sports Arena
October	1	Santa Monica, CA	Civic Auditorium (guest UFO, no Max Webster)
	2	Santa Monica, CA	Civic Auditorium (guest UFO, no Max Webster)
	3	Hollywood, CA	Starwood Amphitheater
	4	Mesa, AZ	Mesa Amphitheater
	5	Phoenix, AZ	Veterans Memorial Coliseum
	7	Salt Lake City, UT	Terrace Ballroom (cancelled due to illness)
	8	Denver, CO	Auditorium Arena
	10	Amarillo, TX	Civic Center
	11	El Paso, TX	County Coliseum
	12	Odessa, TX	Ector County Coliseum
	13	Lubbock, TX	Coliseum
	14	Tulsa, OK	Assembly Center
	15	Oklahoma City, OK	Myriad Convention Center
	16	Abilene, TX	Expo Center
	17	Austin, TX	Municipal Auditorium
	20	Houston, TX	The Music Hall
	21	Dallas, TX	Will Rodgers Auditorium
	22	San Antonio, TX	Hemisphere Arena
	23	San Antonio, TX	Hemisphere Arena

	24	Corpus Cristi, TX	Coliseum
	25	Beaumont, TX	Civic Center
	27	Little Rock, AR	Barton Coliseum
	28	Shreveport, LA	Hirsch Memorial Coliseum
	29	New Orleans, LA	Municipal Auditorium
	30	Mobile, AL	Dixon Myers Hall
	31	Columbus, GA	Convention Center
November	1	Dothan, AL	Civic Center
	10	Buffalo, NY	Memorial Auditorium
	11	Buffalo, NY	Memorial Auditorium
	12	New York City, NY	Palladium (guest Max Webster; UFO)
	13	Baltimore, MD	Civic Center (guest Cheap Trick; UFO)
	15	Fitchburg, MA	Wallace Civic Center
	16	Poughkeepsie, NY	Civic Center
	17	Albany, NY	Palace Theater
	19	Rochester, NY	War Memorial Auditorium
	20	Bridgeport, CT	Klein Memorial Auditorium
	23	Pittsburgh, PA	Stanley Theater
	25	Passaic, NJ	Capitol Theater (guest Cheap Trick)
	26	Philadelphia, PA	Tower Theater (guest Tom Petty and the Heartbreakers)
December	2	Fitchburg, MA	Theater (guest Lynx)
	3	Washington, DC	Warner Theater (guest City Boy)
	7	Milwaukee, WI	Auditorium
	9	Lakeland, FL	Civic Center
	10	Hollywood, FL	Sportatorium
	11	Jacksonville, FL	Veterans Memorial Coliseum
	13	Knoxville, TN	Civic Auditorium
	14	Wheeling, WV	Civic Center
	15	Detroit, MI	Cobo Hall Arena
	16	Cleveland, OH	Richfield Coliseum
	17	Toledo, OH	Centennial Hall
	18	Kalamazoo, MI	Wing Stadium
	29	Toronto, ON	Maple Leaf Gardens
	30	Toronto, ON	Maple Leaf Gardens
January 1978	3	Columbus, OH	Ohio Center
	4	Columbus, OH	Ohio Center
	5	Indianapolis, IN	Market Square Arena
	6	Chicago, IL	Aragon Ballroom (guest April Wine)
	7	Chicago, IL	Aragon Ballroom (guest April Wine)
	8	Chicago, IL	Aragon Ballroom (guest April Wine)
	14	New Haven, CT	Veterans Coliseum (guest Blue Oyster Cult)
	18	St. Louis, MO	Checkerdome (guest April Wine)
	19	Louisville, KY	Gardens (guest Starcastle, April Wine)
	21	Saginaw, MI	Civic Center (guest Pat Travers Band now until end)
	26	Milwaukee, WI	Auditorium
	28	Stevens Point, WI	Splash Fieldhouse
	29	Madison, WI	Dane County Memorial Coliseum
	30	Davenport, IA	RKO Orpheum Theater
	31	Hammond, IN	Civic Center

A Farewell to Kings World Tour 1978 (guest Tyla Gang)

February	12	Birmingham	Odeon
	13	Leicester	DeMontfort Hall
	14	Newcastle	City Hall
	15	Newcastle	City Hall
	16	Glasgow, Scotland	Apollo Theatre
	17	Glasgow, Scotland	Apollo Theatre
	19	London	Hammersmith Odeon
	20	London	Hammersmith Odeon
	22	Sheffield	City Hall
	23	Manchester	Apollo Theatre
	24	Manchester	Apollo Theatre
	25	Liverpool	Empire
	26	Bristol	Colston Hall
	27	Southampton	Gaumont

Archives Tour 1978

March	15	Knoxville, TN	Coliseum (guest The Babys, Pat Travers Band)
	17	Johnson City, TN	Freedom Hall (guest The Babys, Pat Travers Band)
	19	Norfolk, VA	Auditorium (guest The Babys)
	21	Chattanooga, TN	Memorial Auditorium (guest The Babys)
	22	Birmingham, AL	Boutwell Auditorium
	24	Tampa, FL	Curtis Hixon Hall (guest Pat Travers Band, Head East)
	25	Hollywood, FL	Sportatorium
May	10	Niagara Falls, NY	Convention Center
	11	Fort Wayne, IN	Allen County Memorial Arena
	12	Cincinnati, OH	Riverfront Coliseum
	13	Nashville, TN	Municipal Auditorium (guest Uriah Heep till the end)
	16	Denver, CO	Auditorium Arena
	17	Salt Lake City, UT	Salt Palace Center
	18	Boise, ID	Idaho State University Pavilion
	26	Sioux City, IA	Municipal Auditorium
	27	Waterloo, IA	McElroy Auditorium
	28	East Troy, WI	Alpine Valley Amphitheater

Tour of the Hemispheres 1978–79

October	14	Kingston, ON	Memorial Centre
	15	Guelph, ON	War Memorial Hall (University of Guelph)
	17	North Bay, ON	Memorial Gardens
	18	Sudbury, ON	Arena
	20	Thunder Bay, ON	Fort William Gardens
	21	Winnipeg, MB	Arena
	22	Brandon, MB	Keystone Centre
	24	Regina, SK	Agridome
	25	Saskatoon, SK	Arena

	27	Edmonton, AB	Northlands Coliseum
	28	Calgary, AB	Stampede Corral
	29	Lethbridge, AB	Sportsplex
	31	Kamloops, BC	K.X.A. Auditorium
November	2	Nanaimo, BC	Beban Park Arena
	3	Victoria, BC	Memorial Arena
	4	Vancouver, BC	Pacific National Exhibition Coliseum
	6	Portland, OR	Coliseum (guest Pat Travers Band until Dec.)
	7	Seattle, WA	Coliseum
	8	Spokane, WA	Coliseum
	9	Reno, NV	Centennial Coliseum
	11	Vancouver, BC	Pacific Coliseum
	13	San Diego, CA	Sports Arena
	14	Long Beach, CA	Arena
	15	Fresno, CA	Varnors Theater
	16	Oakland, CA	Coliseum
	18	San Bernardino, CA	Swing Auditorium
	20	Tucson, AZ	Community Center
	21	Phoenix, AZ	Veterans Memorial Coliseum
	30	Indianapolis, IN	Market Square Arena
December	1	Dayton, OH	Hara Arena (guest UFO until 7th)
	2	Detroit, MI	Cobo Hall Arena
	5	Davenport, IA	Palmer College
	7	Milwaukee, WI	Auditorium (guest Golden Earring until 21st)
	8	Green Bay, WI	Brown County Arena
	9	St. Paul, MN	Civic Center
	10	Omaha, NE	Civic Auditorium
	12	Chicago, IL	International Amphitheater
	13	St. Louis, MO	Checkerdome
	14	Chicago, IL	International Amphitheater
	15	Chicago, IL	International Amphitheater
	16	Chicago, IL	International Amphitheater
	21	Ottawa, ON	Civic Centre (guest Wireless until 21st)
	26	Montreal, PQ	Forum
	27	Montreal, PQ	Forum
	29	Toronto, ON	Maple Leaf Gardens
	30	Toronto, ON	Maple Leaf Gardens
	31	Toronto, ON	Maple Leaf Gardens
January 1979	3	Columbus, OH	Ohio Center
	4	Columbus, OH	Ohio Center
	6	Chicago, IL	International Amphitheater
	7	Chicago, IL	International Amphitheater
	8	Chicago, IL	International Amphitheater
	11	Boston, MA	Gardens
	12	Philadelphia, PA	Spectrum
	13/14	New York City, NY	Palladium
	16	Allentown, PA	Fairgrounds
	17	Passaic, NJ	Capitol Centre

	19	Pittsburgh, PA	Civic Arena
	20	Baltimore, MD	Civic Center (guest Stillwater)
	21	Philadelphia, PA	Spectrum (guest Blondie)
	23	Syracuse, NY	War Memorial Auditorium
	24	Buffalo, NY	Memorial Auditorium
	26	Cincinnati, OH	Electric Factory (guest Starz until Feb. 19th)
	27	Huntsville, AL	Von Braun Civic Center
	28	Memphis, TN	Mid-South Coliseum
	30	Louisville, KY	Gardens (guest Toto)
	31	Bloomington, IN	Indiana University Auditorium (guest Boyzz)
February	1	Columbus, OH	St. John's Arena (guest April Wine)
	2	Saginaw, MI	Civic Center (guest April Wine)
	3	Columbus, OH	St. John's Arena (guest April Wine)
	19	Fayetteville, NC	Cumberland County Memorial Coliseum (guest Head East until 25th)
	20	Knoxville, TN	Coliseum
	23	Shreveport, LA	Coliseum
	24	Oklahoma City, OK	Fairgrounds Pavilion
	25	Austin, TX	Palmer Auditorium (guest April Wine until 12th)
	27	Corpus Christi, TX	Coliseum
March	1	Houston, TX	Sam Houston Coliseum
	2	Dallas, TX	Memorial Auditorium
	3	San Antonio, TX	Arena
	4	Beaumont, TX	Civic Center
	6	New Orleans, LA	Municipal Auditorium
	8	Mobile, AL	Expo Hall
	9	Jacksonville, FL	Civic Auditorium (guest UFO until 20th)
	10	Tampa, FL	Curtis Hixon Hall
	11	Tampa, FL	Curtis Hixon Hall
	13	Birmingham, AL	Boutwell Auditorium
	14	Pittsburgh, PA	Stanley Theatre
	16	Nashville, TN	Municipal Auditorium
	17	Johnson City, TN	Freedom Hall
	18	Wheeling, WV	Civic Center (guest Sad Café)
	19	Chattanooga, TN	Memorial Auditorium
	27	Salt Lake City, UT	Salt Palace Center
	28	Denver, CO	Auditorium Arena (guest Wireless)
	29	Lincoln, NE	Pershing Memorial Auditorium (guest Kickin')
	30	Topeka, KS	Municipal Auditorium (guest Gran Max)
April	3	Poughkeepsie, NY	Civic Center (guest Falcon Eddy)
	4	Rochester, NY	War Memorial Auditorium (guest The Madcats)
	6	Uniondale, NY	Nassau Coliseum (guest The Good Rats)
	7	New Haven, CT	Veterans Coliseum (guest The Good Rats)
	10	Salem, VA	Civic Center
	11	Hampton, VA	Civic Center (guest Blackfoot)
	12	Pittsburgh, PA	Civic Arena
	13	Atlanta, GA	Fox Theater
	14	Greensboro, NC	Coliseum (guest Molly Hatchet)
	15	Providence, RI	Civic Center (guest The Good Rats)

World Tour of the Hemispheres 1979 (guest Max Webster)

April	23	Newcastle, Eng.	City Hall
	24	Newcastle, Eng.	City Hall
	25	Glasgow, Scot.	Apollo Theatre
	26	Glasgow, Scot	Apollo Theatre
	27	Glasgow, Scot.	Apollo Theatre
	28	Edinburgh, Scot.	Odeon
	29	Manchester, Eng.	Apollo Theatre
	30	Manchester, Eng.	Apollo Theatre
May	1	Liverpool	Empire
	2	Liverpool	Empire
	4	London	Hammersmith Odeon
	5	London	Hammersmith Odeon
	6	London	Hammersmith Odeon
	7	London	Hammersmith Odeon
	9	Coventry	Theatre
	10	Birmingham	Odeon
	11	Birmingham	Odeon
	13	Southampton	Gaumont Theatre
	14	Bristol	Colston Hall
	15	Bristol	Colston Hall
	17	Paris, France	Stadium (canceled—fire set at venue a few days before)
	18	Poperinge-Maekeblijde	(Belg.) Nr. Kortrijt
	22	Oslo, Norway	Chateau Neuf
	23	Gotenburg, Swed.	Concert House
	25	Stockholm, Swed.	Tivoli Gardens
	27	Nuremburg, Ger.	Stadthalle
	28	Frankfurt, Ger.	Musikhalle
	29	Hamburg, Ger.	Musikhalle
	31	Mannheim	Rosengarten
June	1	Zurich, Swit.	Volkshaus
	2	Munchen, Ger.	Circus Krone
	4	Galeen, Holland	Pink Pop Festival

Warm Up Tour 1979

August	17	Davenport, IA	Palmer College
	18	Dubuque, IA	Civic Arena
	19	Chicago, IL	Comisky Park (Chicago Jam II)
	21	Charleston, WV	Civic Center
	22	Largo, MD	Capital Centre (guest Nantucket Band)
	24	Hamilton, ON	Ivor Wynne Stadium (guest Streetheart)
	26	Dallas, TX	Cotton Bowl (A Farewell to a Texas Summer)
	27/28	Detroit, MI	Joe Louis Arena
	29	Lansing, MI	Civic Center (guest New England)
	30	Saginaw, MI	Civic Center
	31	Dayton, OH	Hara Arena (no guest)

September	1	Dayton, OH	Hara Arena (no guest)
	2	Toronto, ON	Varsity Stadium FM
	5	Lexington, KY	Rupp Arena
	7	Cedar Rapids, IA	Five Seasons Theater (guest Pat Travers Band until 13th)
	8	East Troy, WI	Alpine Valley Amphitheater
	9	Mt. Pleasant, MI	Central Michigan University
	10	Detroit, MI	Pine Knob Music Theatre
	12	Allentown, PA	Fairgrounds
	21/22	Stafford, Eng.	Bingley Hall (guest Wild Horses)

Permanent Waves North American Tour 1980

January	12	Detroit, MI	Cobo Hall Arena (guest Max Webster now)
	20/21	Montreal, PQ	Forum 23 Albany, NY Palace Theater
	24	Rochester, NY	War Memorial Auditorium
	27	Binghamton, NY	Broome County Arena
	29	Birmingham, AL	Boutwell Auditorium
	30	Atlanta, GA	Omni
February	1	Atlanta, GA	Omni
	2	Ft. Worth, TX	Tarrant County Convention Center
	3	San Antonio, TX	Convention Center Arena
	6	Corpus Christi, TX	Coliseum
	7	Houston, TX	Sam Houston Coliseum8 Beaumont, TXCivic Center
	9	Tulsa, OK	Assembly Center
	10	Wichita, KS	Coliseum
	13/14	St. Louis, MO	Kiel Auditorium
	15	Evansville, IN	Roberts Stadium
	16	Louisville, KY	Gardens
	18	Cleveland, OH	Richfield Coliseum
	20	Fort Worth, TX	Tarrant County Convention Center
	27	Kansas City, MO	Kemper Arena (guest Roadmaster now)
March	1	Denver, CO	McNichols Arena
	2	Albuquerque, NM	Tingley Coliseum
	3	Tucson, AZ	Community Center
	?	Phoenix, AZ	Veterans Memorial Coliseum
	6	San Diego, CA	Sports Arena (guest .38 Special until 21st)
	7	San Bernardino, CA	Swing Auditorium
	9	Long Beach, CA	Arena
	10	Los Angeles, CA	Great Western Forum
	11	Los Angeles, CA	Great Western Forum
	12	Los Angeles, CA	Great Western Forum
	13	Sacramento, CA	(canceled)
	14	San Francisco, CA	Cow Palace
	15	San Francisco, CA	Cow Palace
	16	Eugene, OR	McArthur Court
	18	Seattle, WA	Center Coliseum
	19	Seattle, WA	Center Coliseum
	20	Portland, OR	Memorial Coliseum

	21	Spokane, WA	Coliseum
	23	Edmonton, AB	Northlands Coliseum (guest Saga until April 3)
	24	Calgary, AB	Max Bell Arena
	25	Calgary, AB	Max Bell Arena
	27	Victoria, BC	Memorial Arena
	28	Nanaimo, BC	Beban Park Arena
	29	Vancouver, BC	Pacific National Exhibition Coliseum (no guest)
	31	Regina, SK	Agridome
April	1	Winnipeg, MB	Arena
	3	Chicago, IL	International Amphitheater (no guest)
	4	Chicago, IL	International Amphitheater (no guest)
	5	Chicago, IL	International Amphitheater (no guest)
	6	Chicago, IL	International Amphitheater (no guest)
	16	Detroit, MI	Joe Louis Arena
	17	Milwaukee, WI	Auditorium (guest .38 Special until May)
	18	Milwaukee, WI	Auditorium
	19	Milwaukee, WI	Auditorium
	20	Madison, WI	Dane County Memorial Coliseum
	22	Green Bay, WI	Brown County Arena
	23	Kalamazoo, MI	Wing Stadium
	24	Toledo, OH	Sports Arena
	27	Indianapolis, IN	Market Square Arena
	29	Columbus, OH	St. Johns Arena (Ohio State University)
May	8	New York City, NY	Palladium (no guest)
	9	New York City, NY	Palladium (no guest)
	10	New York City, NY	Palladium (no guest)
	13	Hershey, PA	Hershey Park Arena (guest Laurie and the Sighs)
	14	Pittsburgh, PA	Civic Arena (guest Laurie and the Sighs)
	16	Providence, RI	Civic Center (guest The Fools)
	17	South Yarmouth, MA	Cape Cod Coliseum
	18	Portland, ME	(canceled to illness)
	20	New Haven, CT	Veterans Memorial Coliseum
	21	Buffalo, NY	Memorial Auditorium
	22	Utica, NY	Memorial Auditorium
	23	Uniondale, NY	Nassau Coliseum (guest The Fools)

Permanent Waves World Tour 1980

June	1	Southampton	Gaumont Theatre
	2	Southampton	Gaumont Theatre
	4	London	Hammersmith Odeon
	5	London	Hammersmith Odeon
	6	London	Hammersmith Odeon
	7	London	Hammersmith Odeon
	8	London	Hammersmith Odeon
	10	Glasgow, Scot.	Apollo Theatre
	11	Glasgow, Scot.	Apollo Theatre
	12	Newcastle	City Hall

13	Newcastle	City Hall
15	Leeds	Queen Hall
16	Deeside	Chester Deeside Leisure Court Centre
17	Manchester	Apollo Theatre
18	Manchester	Apollo Theatre
19	Manchester	Apollo Theatre
20	Birmingham	Odeon
21	Leicester	De Montfort Hall
22	Brighton	Conference Centre

Warm-up Tour 1980 (with guest Saxon)

September	11	Hampton, VA	Coliseum
	12	Charlotte, NC	Coliseum
	13	Charleston, WV	Civic Center
	14	Nashville, TN	Municipal Auditorium
	16	Baton Rouge, LA	Centroplex
	18	Ft. Myers, FL	Lee County Arena
	19	Hollywood, FL	Sportatorium
	20	Lakeland, FL	Civic Center Arena
	23	Cincinnati, OH	Riverfront Coliseum
	25	Philadelphia, PA	Spectrum
	26	Largo, MD	Capital Center
	27	Cape Cod, MA	Coliseum
	28	Springfield, MA	Civic Center
	30	Allentown, PA	Fairgrounds
October	1	Portland, ME	Cumberland County Civic Center

Moving Pictures North American Tour 1981

February	20	Kalamazoo, MI	Wing Stadium (guest Max Webster)
	21	Dubuque, IA	Civic Arena
	22	Davenport, IA	Palmer College Auditorium
	24	La Crosse, WI	Center
	26	Chicago, IL	International Amphitheater
	27	Chicago, IL	International Amphitheater
	28	Chicago, IL	International Amphitheater
March	1	Chicago, IL	International Amphitheater
	2	Milwaukee, WI	Mecca Arena
	4	St. Louis, MO	Checkerdome
	5	St. Louis, MO	Checkerdome
	7	Louisville, KY	Gardens
	8	Dayton, OH	Hara Arena
	10	Evansville, IN	Roberts Stadium
	11	Indianapolis, IN	Market Square Arena
	13	Detroit, MI	Cobo Hall Arena
	14	Detroit, MI	Cobo Hall Arena

	15	Detroit, MI	Cobo Hall Arena
	21	London, ON	Gardens (guest FM)
	23/24	Toronto, ON	Maple Leaf Gardens
	27	Montreal, PQ	Forum (guest Max Webster) (Exit … Stage Left show)
	28	Ottawa, ON	Civic Center (guest FM)
April	3	Tucson, AZ	Community Center (guest Max Webster until)
	4	Phoenix, AZ	Veterans Memorial Coliseum
	5	Albuquerque, NM	Tingley Coliseum
	7	New Orleans, LA	Municipal Auditorium
	8	Houston, TX	Sam Houston Coliseum
	10	Dallas, TX	Reunion Arena
	11	San Antonio, TX	Convention Center
	12	Ft. Worth, TX	Tarrant County Convention Center
	14	Little Rock, AR	Barton Coliseum
	16	Jackson, MS	Coliseum
	17	Memphis, TN	Mid-South Coliseum
	18	Mobile, AL	Municipal Auditorium
	19	Lake Charles, LA	Civic Center
	21	Shreveport, LA	Coliseum
	22	Oklahoma City, OK	Myriad Convention Center (no guest)
	23	Kansas City, MO	Kemper Arena (no guest)
	24	Kansas City, MO	Kemper Arena (no guest)
May	6	Pittsburgh, PA	Civic Arena (guest FM)
	7	Cleveland, OH	Richfield Coliseum (guest FM)
	8	Cleveland, OH	Richfield Coliseum (guest FM)
	9	Buffalo, NY	Memorial Auditorium
	12	Rochester, NY	War Memorial Auditorium (guest Saga)
	13	Syracuse, NY	War Memorial Auditorium (guest FM now through June 15th)
	15	Philadelphia, PA	Spectrum
	16	Largo, MD	Capital Center
	17	Largo, MD	Capital Center
	18	New York City, NY	Madison Square Garden
	20	Uniondale, NY	Nassau Coliseum
	22	Providence, RI	Civic Center
	23	Boston, MA	Gardens
	24	Glen Falls, NY	Civic Center
	26	New Haven, CT	Veterans Memorial Coliseum
	27	Springfield, MA	Nelson Center
June	1	Denver, CO	McNichols Arena
	3	Salt Lake City, UT	Salt Palace Center
	5	Oakland, CA	Coliseum
	6	Oakland, CA	Coliseum
	7	Fresno, CA	Selland Arena
	9	San Diego, CA	Sports Arena
	10	Los Angeles, CA	Great Western Forum
	11	Los Angeles, CA	Great Western Forum
	12	Anaheim, CA	ConventionCenter
	14	Long Beach, CA	Arena

	15	Las Vegas, NV	Alladin Theater (no guest)
	16	Reno, NV	Centennial Coliseum
	18	Seattle, WA	Center Coliseum
	19	Seattle, WA	Center Coliseum
	20	Portland, OR	Memorial Coliseum
	21	Spokane, WA	Coliseum
	23	Vancouver, BC	Pacific National Exhibition Coliseum (guest Goddo)
	25	Edmonton, AB	Coliseum (guest Goddo)
July	2	Bloomington, MN	Met Center
(with guest Joe	3	Bloomington, MN	Met Center
Perry Project)	4	East Troy, WI	Alpine Valley Amphitheater
	5	East Troy, WI	Alpine Valley Amphitheater

Exit ... Stage Left World Tour 1981

October	29	Stafford	Bingley Hall
	30	Stafford	Bingley Hall
	31	Brighton	Conference Centre
November	2	Brighton	Conference Centre
	4	London	Wembley Arena
	5	London	Wembley Arena
	6	London	Wembley Arena
	8	Edinburgh, Scot.	Royal Highland Arts Exhibition Centre
	9	Stafford	Bingley Hall
	11	Hamburg, W. Ger.	Congress Centrum
	12	Nuremberg, Ger.	Hammerleinehalle
	14	Rotterdam, Neth.	Sportpalais de Ahoy
	18	Stuttgart, Ger.	Eissporthalle Boblingen
	19	Stuttgart, Ger.	Eissporthalle Boblingen
	21	Essen, Ger.	Grugenhalle (guest Girlschool)

Exit ... Stage Left North American Tour 81 (with guest Riot)

November	28	Hollywood, FL	Sportatorium
	29	Jacksonville, FL	Veterans Memorial Coliseum
December	1	Birmingham, AL	Jefferson Civic Center
	2	Nashville, TN	Municipal Auditorium
	4	Charlotte, NC	Coliseum
	5	Fayetteville, NC	Cumberland County Coliseum
	6	Greensboro, NC	Coliseum
	8	Knoxville, TN	Coliseum
	9	Atlanta, GA	Omni
	11	Greenville, SC	Memorial Auditorium
	12	Johnson City, TN	Freedom Hall
	13	Roanoke, VA	Civic Center
	15	Norfolk, VA	Scope Arena

18	Hartford, CT	Civic Center
20	Hartford, CT	Civic Center
21	East Rutherford, NJ	Brendan Byrne Arena
22	East Rutherford, NJ	Brendan Byrne Arena

Spring Training Tour 1982 (Tour of the Nadars)

April 1982	1	Little Rock, AR	Barton Coliseum (guest Riggs)
	2	Jackson, MS	Civic Auditorium (guest Riggs)
	3	Monroe, LA	Civic Center (guest Riggs)
	6	Lake Charles, LA	Civic Center (guest Riggs)
	7	Memphis, TN	Mid-South Coliseum (Rory Gallagher)
	8	Shreveport, LA	Coliseum (guest Krokus until end)
	9	Baton Rouge, LA	Centroplex
	10	Tallahassee, FL	Leon County Civic Center
	11	Lakeland, FL	Civic Center
	12	St. Petersburg, FL	Bayfront Center
	14	Savannah, GA	(canceled)

Signals New World (North American) Tour 1982–83

September	3	Green Bay, WI	Brown County Arena (guest Rory Gallagher through 17th)
	4	La Crosse, WI	Center
	5	Dubuque, IA	Five Flags Center
	7	Sioux Falls, SD	Arena
	8	Des Moines, NE	Civic Arena
	9	Omaha, NE	Veterans Memorial Auditorium
	11	Rapid City, SD	Rushmore Plaza Civic Center
	12	Bismarke, ND	Civic Center
	14	Billings, MT	Shrine Auditorium
	15	Casper, WY	Events Center
	17	Denver, CO	McNichols Arena
	19	Pocatello, ID	Idaho State University Minidome
	20	Boise, ID	Idaho State University Pavilion
	21	Salt Lake City, UT	Salt Palace Center
	30	Vancouver, BC	Pacific National Exhibition Coliseum (guest Wrabit until 3rd)
October	2	Calgary, AB	Stampede Corral
	3	Edmonton, AB	Northlands Coliseum (guest White Wolf)
	5	Winnipeg, MB	Arena
	7	Duluth, MN	Arena (guest Rory Gallagher until Nov. 15th)
	9	Milwaukee, WI	Mecca Arena
	10	Madison, WI	Dane County Arena
	12	St. Louis, MO	Checkerdome
	13	Champagne, IL	Assembly Hall (Univ. of Illinois)
	15	St. Louis, MO	Checkerdome
	16	Kansas City, MO	Kemper Arena
	17	Wichita, KS	Kansas Coliseum

	19	Memphis, TN	Mid-South Coliseum
	20	Nashville, TN	Municipal Auditorium
	30	Lexington, KY	Rupp Arena
	31	Evansville, IN	Roberts Stadium
November	1	Indianapolis, IN	Market Square Arena
	3	Cleveland, OH	Richfield Coliseum
	4	Columbus, OH	Ohio Center
	5	South Bend, IN	Morris Civic Center
	7	Detroit, MI	Joe Louis Arena
	8	Detroit, MI	Joe Louis Arena
	9	Dayton, OH	University of Dayton Auditorium
	11	Kalamazoo, MI	Wing Stadium
	12	Toledo, OH	Sports Arena
	14	Dayton, OH	University of Dayton Arena
	15	Toronto, ON	Maple Leaf Gardens (guest The Payolas)
	17	Toronto, ON	Maple Leaf Gardens (guest The Payolas)
	18	Toronto, ON	Maple Leaf Gardens (guest The Payolas)
	19	Chicago, IL	Rosemont Horizon
	20	Chicago, IL	Rosemont Horizon
	21	Chicago, IL	Rosemont Horizon
	29	Largo, MD	Capital Center
	30	Hampton, VA	Coliseum (Y & T)
December	2	New York City, NY	Madison Square Garden
	3	New York City, NY	Madison Square Garden
	5	Providence, RI	Civic Center (guest Rory Gallagher again)
	6	Boston, MA	Gardens
	8	Uniondale, NY	Nassau Coliseum
	9	Uniondale, NY	Nassau Coliseum
	11	New Haven, CT	Veterans Coliseum
	13	Philadelphia, PA	Spectrum
	14	Philadelphia, PA	Spectrum
	15	Worcester, MA	Centrum
February	14	Long Beach, CA	Arena (guest Golden Earring now)
	15	Long Beach, CA	Arena (guest Golden Earring now)
	17	Los Angeles, CA	Great Western Forum
	18	Los Angeles, CA	Great Western Forum
	21	San Diego, CA	Sports Arena
	23	Phoenix, AZ	Veterans Memorial Coliseum
	24	Tucson, AZ	Community Center
	26	Las Cruces, NM	Pan American Center
	28	Dallas, TX	Reunion Arena
March	1	Dallas, TX	Reunion Arena
	2	San Antonio, TX	Convention Center Arena
	4	Oklahoma City, OK	Myriad Convention Center
	7	Houston, TX	Summit Arena
	17	Hollywood, FL	Sportatorium (guest John Butcher Axis now)
	20	Lakeland, FL	Civic Center
	24	Tampa, FL	Curtis Hixon Hall

	25	Charlotte, NC	Coliseum
	26	Columbia, SC	University of South Carolina
	27	Greensboro, SC	Coliseum
	28	Atlanta, GA	Omni
	29	Charleston, WV	Civic Center
	30	Cincinnati, OH	Riverfront Coliseum
April	1	Hartford, CT	Civic Center
	2	Syracuse, NY	Carrierdome
	4	Pittsburgh, PA	Civic Arena
	5	Buffalo, NY	Memorial Auditorium
	7	Quebec City, PQ	Le Colisee
	8/9	Montreal, PQ	Forum

Signals World Tour 1983

May	3	Rotterdam, Neth.	Sportpalais de Ahoy (guest Vandenburg)
	6	Stuttgart, Ger.	Schleyerhalle (guest Nazareth until end)
	7	Frankfurt, Ger.	Festhalle
	8	Hamburg, Ger.	Congress Centrum
	10	Dusseldorf, Ger.	Philipshalle
	11	Heidelberg, Ger.	Rheine-Neckarhalle
	12	Bruselles, Belgium	Forest National
	14	Birmingham	National Exhibition Centre
	15	Birmingham	National Exhibition Centre
	17	London	Wembley Arena
	18	London	Wembley Arena
	20	London	Wembley Arena
	21	London	Wembley Arena
	22	Birmingham	National Exhibition Centre
	23	Rotterdam, Neth.	Sportpalais de Ahoy
	24	Edinburgh, Scot.	Royal Highlands Arts Exhibition Centre
	25	Edinburgh, Scot.	Royal Highlands Arts Exhibition Centre

Radio City Music Hall (guest Marillion) 1983

September	18	New York City, NY	Radio City Music Hall
	19	New York City, NY	Radio City Music Hall
	21	New York City, NY	Radio City Music Hall
	22	New York City, NY	Radio City Music Hall
	23	New York City, NY	Radio City Music Hall

Grace Under Pressure North American Tour 1984

May	8	Albuquerque, NM	Tingley Coliseum (guest Gary Moore now on)
	10	Las Vegas, NV	Thomas and Mack Arena
	12	Reno, NV	Lawlor Events Center

	14	Salt Lake City, UT	Salt Palace Center
	15	Boise, ID	Idaho State University Pavilion
	17	Portland, OR	Memorial Coliseum
	18	Tacoma, WA	Tacoma Dome
	19	Vancouver, BC	Pacific National Coliseum
	25	San Francisco, CA	Cow Palace
	26	San Francisco, CA	Cow Palace
	28	San Diego, CA	Sports Arena
	29	Los Angeles, CA	Great Western Forum
	30	Los Angeles, CA	Great Western Forum
June	1	Hollywood, CA	Guitar Institute of Technology (appearance only)
	2	Irvine, CA	Irvine Meadows Amphitheater
	3	Tucson, AZ	Community Convention Center
	4	Phoenix, AZ	Veterans Memorial Coliseum
	5	Las Cruces, NM	Pan American Center
	6	Odessa, TX	Ector County Coliseum
	8	Houston, TX	Astrodome (Texxas World Music Festival)
	10	Dallas, TX	Cotton Bowl (Texxas World Music Festival)
	12	Little Rock, AR	Barton Coliseum
	13	Tulsa, OK	Convention Center
	15	Wichita, KS	Kansas Coliseum
	16	Kansas City, MO	Kemper Arena
	25	Milwaukee, WI	Mecca Arena
	26	Bloomington, MN	Met Center
	27	Bloomington, MN	Met Center
	29	Chicago, IL	Rosemont Horizon
	30	Chicago, IL	Rosemont Horizon
July	2	St. Louis, MO	Checkerdome
	3	Indianapolis, IN	Market Square Arena (guest Pat Travers Band)
	5	Cleveland, OH	Richfield Coliseum (guest Gary Moore)
	6	Cleveland, OH	Richfield Coliseum (guest Gary Moore)
	7	Columbus, OH	Ohio Center (guest Pat Travers Band)
	8	Pittsburgh, PA	Civic Arena (guest Pat Travers Band)
	9	Detroit, MI	Joe Louis Arena (guest Pat Travers Band)
	12	Buffalo, NY	Memorial Auditorium (guest Red Rider)
	14	Montreal, PQ	Forum (guest The Tenants)
	15	Montreal, PQ	Forum (guest The Tenants)
	16	Quebec City, PQ	Le Colisee (guest The Tenants)
September	14	Portland, ME	Cumberland County Civic Center (guest Fastway now)
	15	Glen Falls, NY	Civic Center
	17	New York City, NY	Madison Square Garden
	18	Lake Placid, NY	Olympic Center
	21	Toronto, ON	Maple Leaf Gardens (guest Red Rider) (recorded for home video)
	22	Toronto, ON	Maple Leaf Gardens (guest Red Rider) (recorded for home video)
	24	New Haven, CT	(canceled due to illness; rescheduled)
	25	Providence, RI	Civic Center

	27	Largo, MD	Capital Centre (guest Helix)
	28	New Haven, CT	Coliseum
	29	East Rutherford, NJ	Brendan Byrne Arena (guest Fastway)
	30	Uniondale, NY	Nassau Coliseum
October	2	Worcester, MA	Centrum
	3	Worcester, MA	Centrum
	6	Dayton, OH	University of Dayton Arena
	7	Columbus, OH	Ohio Center
	18	Toledo, OH	Sports Arena
	19	Saginaw, MI	Civic Center
	21	Lexington, KY	Rupp Arena
	23	Memphis, TN	Mid-South Coliseum
	24	Jackson, MS	Civic Auditorium
	26	Biloxi, MS	Gulf Coast Coliseum
	27	New Orleans, LA	University of New Orleans Lakefront Arena
	29	Nashville, TN	Municipal Auditorium
	30	Atlanta, GA	Omni
November	1	Charleston, WV	Civic Center (guest Y & T)
	2	Johnson City, TN	Freedom Hall
	3	Hampton, VA	Coliseum
	5	Philadelphia, PA	Spectrum
	7	Providence, RI	Civic Center
	9	New Haven, CT	Civic Center (guest Y & T)

Grace Under Pressure World Tour 1984

November	16	Nagoya, Japan	Seto-shi Bunka Center (no guest)
	18	Fukuoka, Japan	Sun Palace Hall (no guest)
	20	Osaka, Japan	Furitsu Taikukaikan (no guest)
	21	Tokyo, Japan	Budokan Hall (no guest)
	24	Honolulu, HI	NBC Arena (guest Strict-Neine)
	25	Honolulu, HI	NBC Arena (guest Strict-Neine)

Spring Training Tour 1985

March	10	Lakeland, FL	Civic Center
	11	Lakeland, FL	Civic Center
	12	Lakeland, FL	Civic Center
	14	Ft. Myers, FL	Lee County Arena
	15	Hollywood, FL	Sportatorium

Power Windows North American Tour 1985 – 86

December	4	Portland, ME	Cumberland County Civic Center
	5	Providence, RI	Civic Center
	7	New Haven, CT	Civic Center (guest Steve Morse Band now)
	8	Hartford, CT	Civic Center

	10	Rochester, NY	Civic Center
	12	Worcester, MA	Centrum
	13	Worcester, MA	Centrum
	15	Richmond, VA	Coliseum
	16	Largo, MD	Capital Center
	18	Pittsburgh, PA	Civic Arena
	19	Cleveland, OH	Richfield Coliseum
January 1986	9	Pensacola, FL	Civic Center
	10	Lafayette, LA	Cajundome
	12	Dallas, TX	Reunion Arena
	13	Dallas, TX	Reunion Arena
	15	Houston, TX	Summit Arena
	16	Houston, TX	Summit Arena
	19	San Antonio, TX	Convention Center
	30	San Francisco, CA	Cow Palace
	31	Oakland, CA	Alameda County Coliseum
February	2	Las Vegas, NV	Thomas and Mack Arena
	3	San Diego, CA	Sports Arena (power fails twice)
	5	Los Angeles, CA	Great Western Forum
	6	Los Angeles, CA	Great Western Forum
	7	Los Angeles, CA	Great Western Forum (day of Neil's P.I.T. clinic)
	8	Phoenix, AZ	Veterans Memorial Coliseum
	10	Tucson, AZ	Community Center
	12	Albuquerque, NM	Tingley Coliseum
	14	Denver, CO	McNichols Arena
	27	Buffalo, NY	Memorial Auditorium (guest Marillion)
	28	Hamilton, ON	Viktor K. Copps Coliseum
March	1	Ottawa, ON	Civic Arena (guest FM w/Nash)
	3	Quebec City, PQ	Le Colisee
	4	Montreal, PQ	Forum (Marillion again)
	6	Toronto, ON	Maple Leaf Gardens (guest FM)
	7	Toronto, ON	Maple Leaf Gardens (guest FM)
	20	Indianapolis, IN	Market Square Arena (guest Marillion again until 4/12)
	21	Chicago, IL	Rosemont Horizon
	22	Chicago, IL	Rosemont Horizon
	24	Milwaukee, WI	Mecca Arena
	25	Bloomington, MN	Met Center
	28	Detroit, MI	Joe Louis Arena
	29	Cincinnati, OH	Riverfront Coliseum
	31	East Rutherford, NJ	Meadowlands Arena
April	1	East Rutherford, NJ	Meadowlands Arena
	3	Springfield, MA	Civic Center
	4	Uniondale, NY	Nassau Coliseum
	5	Uniondale, NY	Nassau Coliseum
	13	Binghamton, NY	Broome County Arena (guest Blue Oyster Cult through 25th)
	14	Philadelphia, PA	Spectrum
	16	Philadelphia, PA	Spectrum
	17	Baltimore, MD	Civic Center

	19	Richmond, VA	Coliseum
	20	Charlotte, NC	Coliseum
	22	Greensboro, NC	Coliseum
	23	Augusta, GA	Civic Center
	25	Atlanta, GA	Omni
	26	Birmingham, AL	Jefferson Civic Center
	28	St. Louis, MO	Arena (no guest)
	29	Kansas City, MO	Kemper Arena
May	1	Oklahoma City, OK	Myriad Convention Center
	2	Wichita, KS	Kansas Coliseum
	11	Winnipeg, MB	Arena
	12	Salt Lake City, UT	Salt Palace Center (guest The Fabulous Thunderbirds now)
	14	Calgary, AB	Olympic Saddledome (guest Kick-Axe until 18th)
	15	Edmonton, AB	Northlands Coliseum
	17	Vancouver, BC	Pacific National Exhibition Coliseum
	19	Portland, OR	Memorial Coliseum (guest The Fabulous Thunderbirds)
	21	Seattle, WA	Center Coliseum
	24	Sacramento, CA	Cal Expo
	25	Costa Mesa, CA	Pacific Amphitheatre
	26	Costa Mesa, CA	Pacific Amphitheatre

Hold Your Fire North American Tour 1987–88

October	29	St. John's, NF	Lord Beaverbrook Rink (guest Chalk Circle now)
	30	St. John's, NF	Lord Beaverbrook Rink (guest Chalk Circle now)
November	1	Sydney, NS	Forum
	2	Halifax, NS	Forum
	4	Moncton, NB	Joe Louis Levesque Arena
	6	Providence, RI	Civic Center
	7	Providence, RI	Civic Center
	9	Springfield, MA	Civic Center
	10	Utica, NY	Memorial Auditorium
	12	Troy, NY	RPI Fieldhouse
	13	Binghamton, NY	Broome County Arena (guest MSG now)
	14	Buffalo, NY	Memorial Auditorium
	15	Philadelphia, PA	Spectrum
	16	Hartford, CT	Civic Center
	25	Atlanta, GA	Omni
	27	Charlotte, NC	Coliseum 28 Hampton, VAColiseum
	30	Largo, MD	Capital Center
December	2	Worcester, MA	Centrum
	3	Worcester, MA	Centrum
	5	New Haven, CT	Veterans Coliseum
	7	East Rutherford, NJ	Meadowlands Arena (guest Tommy Shaw now)
	9	Uniondale, NY	Nassau Coliseum
	11	New York City, NY	Madison Square Garden
	13	Philadelphia, PA	Spectrum
	14	Philadelphia, PA	Spectrum

	16 Pittsburgh, PA	Civic Arena
	17 Cleveland, OH	Richfield Coliseum
January 1988	13 Jackson, MS	Civic Auditorium
	14 Richmond, VA	Coliseum
	15 Raleigh, NC	Reynolds Coliseum
	16 Nashville, TN	Municipal Auditorium
	17 Birmingham, AL	Jefferson Civic Center
	19 Dallas, TX	Reunion Arena
	20 Dallas, TX	Reunion Arena
	21 San Antonio, TX	Convention Center
	23 Oklahoma City, OK	Myriad Convention Center
	24 Shreveport, LA	Coliseum
	25 Little Rock, AR	Barton Coliseum
	26 Little Rock, AR	Barton Coliseum
	27 New Orleans, LA	University of New Orleans Lakefront Arena
	29 Houston, TX	Summit Arena
	30 Austin, TX	Frank Erwin Special Events Center
February	1 Phoenix, AZ	Veterans Memorial Coliseum
	3 San Diego, CA	Sports Arena
	4 Los Angeles, CA	Great Western Forum
	5 Los Angeles, CA	Great Western Forum
	12 Memphis, TN	Mid-South Coliseum
	13 Hollywood, FL	Sportatorium
	15 Lakeland, FL	Civic Center
	16 St. Petersburg, FL	Bayfront Center (canceled due to poor ticket sales)
	18 Jacksonville, FL	Veterans Memorial Coliseum
	19 Pensacola, FL	Civic Center
	21 Memphis, TN	Mid-South Coliseum
	22 St. Louis, MO	Arena
	23 Cincinnati, OH	Riverfront Coliseum24 Cincinnati, OHRiverfront Coliseum
	25 Chicago, IL	Rosemont Horizon26 Chicago, ILRosemont Horizon
	28 Peoria, IL	Civic Center
March	1 St. Louis, MO	Arena
	2 Indianapolis, IN	Market Square Arena
	4 Detroit, IL	Joe Louis Arena (no guest)
	7 Toronto, ON	Maple Leaf Gardens (guest Chalk Circle again until April)
	8 Toronto, ON	Maple Leaf Gardens
	10 Montreal, PQ	Forum
	11 Quebec City, PQ	Le Colisee
	28 Edmonton, AB	Coliseum
	29 Calgary, AB	Olympic Saddledome
	31 Vancouver, BC	Pacific National Exhibition Coliseum
April	2 Omaha, NE	Civic Auditorium
	4 Bloomington, MN	Met Center (guest The Rainmakers)
	5 Milwaukee, WI	Mecca Arena
	7 Kansas City, MO	Kemper Arena
	9 Louisville, KY	Gardens
	10 Dayton, OH	Hara Arena (no guest)

Hold Your Fire World Tour 1988

April	21	Birmingham	National Exhibition Centre (recorded for home video)
	23	Birmingham	National Exhibition Centre (recorded for home video)
	24	Birmingham	National Exhibition Centre (recorded for home video)
	26	Glasgow, Scot.	Scottish Exhibition Centre
	28	London	Wembley Arena
	29	London	Wembley Arena
	30	London	Wembley Arena
May	2	Rotterdam, Netherlands	Sportpalais de Ahoy
	4	Frankfurt, Ger.	Festhalle
	5	Stuttgart, Ger.	Hans Martin Schleyerhalle (guest Wishbone Ash)

Presto North American Tour 1990

February	17	Greenville, SC	Memorial Auditorium (guest Mr. Big)
	18	Jacksonville, FL	Veterans Memorial Coliseum
	19	Jacksonville, FL	Veterans Memorial Coliseum
	20	St. Petersburg, FL	Bayfront Center
	22	Miami, FL	Arena
	23	Orlando, FL	Arena
	25	New Orleans, LA	University of New Orleans Lakefront Arena
	26	Houston, TX	Summit Arena
	28	San Antonio, TX	Convention Center
March	1	Dallas, TX	Reunion Arena
	3	Kansas City, MO	Kemper Arena
	5	St. Louis, MO	Arena
	6	Cincinnati, OH	Riverfront Coliseum
	8	Detroit, MI	Palace Auburn Hills
	9	Detroit, MI	Palace Auburn Hills
	20	Edmonton, AB	Northlands Coliseum
	21	Calgary, AB	Olympic Saddledome
	23	Vancouver, BC	Pacific National Exhibition Coliseum
	24	Portland, OR	Memorial Coliseum
	26	Seattle, WA	Center Coliseum
	28	Sacramento, CA	Arco Arena
	30	Oakland, CA	Alameda County Coliseum
	31	Oakland, CA	Alameda County Coliseum
April	2	Los Angeles, CA	Great Western Forum
	3	Los Angeles, CA	Great Western Forum
	5	San Diego, CA	Sports Arena
	7	Costa Mesa, CA	Pacific Amphitheater
	8	Phoenix, AZ	Veterans Memorial Coliseum
	19	Rochester, NY	(canceled due to illness)
	20	East Rutherford, NJ	Meadowlands Arena
	22	Uniondale, NY	Nassau Coliseum
	24	Philadelphia, PA	Spectrum

	25	East Rutherford, NJ	Meadowlands Arena
	27	Philadelphia, PA	Spectrum
	28	Rochester, NY	War Memorial Auditorium
May	1	Atlanta, GA	Omni
	2	Charlotte, NC	Coliseum
	4	Richmond, VA	Coliseum
	5	Largo, MD	Capital Centre
	7	Providence, RI	Civic Center
	8	Hartford, CT	Civic Center
	10	Worcester, MA	Centrum
	11	Worcester, MA	Centrum
	13	Quebec City, QC	Le Colisee (guest Voivod begin)
	14	Montreal, PQ	Forum
	16	Toronto, ON	Maple Leaf Gardens
	17	Toronto, ON	Maple Leaf Gardens
June	1	Old Orchard Beach, ME	(canceled)
	2	Albany, NY	Knickerbocker Arena
	4	Baltimore, MD	Civic Center
	5	Hampton, VA	Hampton Coliseum (guest Mr. Big again)
	7	Pittsburgh, PA	Civic Arena
	8	Cleveland, OH	Richfield Coliseum
	10	Cuyahoga Falls, OH	Blossom Music Center
	11	Cincinnati, OH	Riverbend Music Center
	13	Columbus, OH	Cooper Stadium
	14	Noblesville, IN	Deer Creek Music Theater
	16	East Troy, WI	Alpine Valley Music Theater
	17	East Troy, WI	Alpine Valley Music Theater
	19	Bloomington, MN	Met Center
	20	Omaha, NE	Civic Auditorium
	22	Englewood, CO	Fiddlers Green Amphitheater
	24	Salt Lake City, UT	Salt Palace Center
	26	Sacramento, CA	Cal Expo
	27	Mountain View, CA	Shoreline Amphitheater
	29	Irvine, CA	Irvine Meadows Amphitheater

Roll the Bones North American Tour 1991–92

October	25	Hamilton, ON	Viktor K. Copps Coliseum (guest Andy Curran)
	26	Rochester, NY	War Memorial Auditorium (guest Eric Johnson now)
	28	Pittsburgh, PA	Civic Arena
	29	Cincinnati, OH	Riverfront Coliseum
	31	Indianapolis, IN	Market Square Arena
November	1	Chicago, IL	Rosemont Horizon
	3	Minneapolis, MN	Target Center
	4	Omaha, NE	Civic Auditorium
	6	Topeka, KS	Expo Center
	7	St. Louis, MO	Arena

	9	Normal, IL	Redbird Arena
	10	Milwaukee, WI	Bradley Center
	13	Detroit, MI	Palace Auburn Hills
	14	Detroit, MI	Palace Auburn Hills
	16	Toledo, OH	John F. Savage Hall (University of Toledo)
	17/18	Cleveland, OH	Richfield Coliseum
	26	Ottawa, ON	Civic Arena
	28	Quebec City, PQ	Le Colisee
	29	Montreal, PQ	Forum
December	1	Philadelphia, PA	Spectrum (guest Vinnie Moore until 16th)
	3	Philadelphia, PA	Spectrum
	4	Largo, MD	Capital Centre
	6/7	New York City, NY	Madison Square Garden
	9	Providence, RI	Civic Center
	10	Worcester, MA	Centrum
	12	Albany, NY	Knickerbocker Arena
	13	Hartford, CT	Civic Center
	15	Buffalo, NY	Memorial Auditorium
	16	Toronto, ON	Maple Leaf Gardens (guest The Tragically Hip)
January 1992	18	Las Cruces, NM	Pan American Center (guest Primus now)
	20	San Diego, CA	Sports Arena
	22	Los Angeles, CA	Great Western Forum
	23	Los Angeles, CA	Great Western Forum
	25	Fresno, CA	Selland Arena
	27	Sacramento, CA	Arco Arena
	29/30	Oakland, CA	Alameda County Coliseum
February	2	Vancouver, BC	Pacific National Exhibition Coliseum
	4	Seattle, WA	Center Coliseum
	5	Portland, ME	Memorial Coliseum
	15	San Antonio, TX	Convention Center Arena (at Hemisfair Park)
	16	Dallas, TX	Reunion Arena 18 Houston, TX Summit Arena
	20	Austin, TX	Frank Erwin Special Events Center
	22	Shreveport, LA	(canceled)
	23	New Orleans, LA	University of New Orleans Lakefront Arena
	25	Pensacola, FL	Civic Center
	26	Jacksonville, FL	Veterans Memorial Coliseum
	28	Miami, FL	Arena
	29	St. Petersburg, FL	Suncoast Dome
March	2	Orlando, FL	Arena
	4	Atlanta, GA	Omni
	5	Columbia, SC	University of South Carolina
	7	Chapel Hill, NC	Dean E. Smith Center
	8	Hampton, VA	Coliseum
	10	Richmond, VA	Coliseum
	12	Binghamton, NY	Broome County Arena
	14	New Haven, CT	Coliseum
	15	Uniondale, NY	Nassau Coliseum

Roll the Bones World Tour 1992 (with guest Primus)

April	10	Sheffield	Arena
	12	Birmingham	National Exhibition Centre
	13	Birmingham	National Exhibition Centre
	15	Glasgow, Scotland	Scottish Exhibition Centre
	17	London	Wembley Arena
	18	London	Wembley Arena
	21	Hannover, Ger.	Musikhalle
	23	Koln, Ger.	Eissporthalle
	24	Frankfurt, Ger.	Festhalle
	27	Berlin, Ger.	Eissporthalle
	28	Nuremberg, Ger.	Frankenhalle
	29	Stuttgart, Ger.	Hans Martin Schleyerhalle
May	1	Paris, France	Le Zenith
	3	Rotterdam, Holland	Sportpalais de Ahoy

(US third leg; guest Mr. Big until end)

	21	Memphis, TN	Mid-South Coliseum
	23	Kansas City, MO	Kemper Arena
	24	Wichita, KS	Kansas Coliseum
	25	Oklahoma City, OK	Myriad Convention Center
	27	Englewood, CO	Fiddlers Green Amphitheater
	29	Salt Lake City, UT	Delta Center
	31	Mountain View, CA	Shoreline Amphitheater
June	1	Reno, NV	Lawlor Events Arena
	3	Irvine, CA	Irvine Meadows Amphitheater
	4	Irvine, CA	Irvine Meadows Amphitheater
	6	Las Vegas, NV	Thomas and Mack Arena
	7	Phoenix, AZ	Desert Sky Pavilion
	9	Albuquerque, NM	Tingley Coliseum
	10	Lubbock, TX	Coliseum
	12	St. Louis, MO	Riverport Amphitheater
	13	Memphis, TN	Starwood Amphitheater
	14	Charlotte, NC	Blockbuster Pavilion
	16	Columbia, MD	Merriwether Post Pavilion
	17	Mansfield, MA	Great Woods Amphitheater
	19	East Rutherford, NJ	Meadowlands Arena
	20	Wantaugh, NY	Jones Beach Amphitheater
	21	Burgettstown, PA	Starlake Amphitheater
	23	Dayton, OH	Ervin J. Nutter Center
	24	Noblesville, IN	Deer Creek Music Theater
	26	Clarkston, MI	Pine Knob Music Theater
	27	East Troy, WI	Alpine Valley Music Theater
	28	Chicago, IL	World Music Theater Tinley Park

Counterparts North American Tour 1994

January	22	Pensacola, FL	Civic Center (guest Candlebox)
	23	New Orleans, LA	University of New Orleans Lakefront Arena
	25	Austin, TX	Frank Erwin Special Events Center
	26	Houston, TX	Summit Arena
	28	Dallas, TX	Reunion Arena
	29	San Antonio, TX	Convention Center
	31	Las Cruces, NM	Pan American Center
February	1	Phoenix, AZ	Veterans Memorial Coliseum
	3	Los Angeles, CA	Great Western Forum
	5	Anaheim, CA	Arrowhead Pond
	7	San Diego, CA	Sports Arena
	8	Fresno, CA	Selland Arena (guest The Melvins now)
	10	Sacramento, CA	Arco Arena
	11	San Francisco, CA	Cow Palace
	12	San Jose, CA	Arena
	23	Murfreesboro, TN	Murphy Athletic Center (guest Candlebox now)
	24	Atlanta, GA	Omni
	25	Charlotte, NC	Blockbuster Pavilion
	27	Miami, FL	Arena
March	1	Orlando, FL	Arena
	2	Jacksonville, FL	Veterans Memorial Coliseum
	4	St. Petersburg, FL	Thunderdome
	6	Chapel Hill, NC	Dean E. Smith Center
	8	New York City, NY	Madison Square Garden
	9	New York City, NY	Madison Square Garden
	11	Worcester, MA	Centrum
	12	Worcester, MA	Centrum
	22	Detroit, MI	Palace Auburn Hills (guest Primus until April 18th)
	23	Columbus, OH	Richfield Coliseum
	25	Cincinnati, OH	Riverfront Coliseum
	26	Indianapolis, IN	Market Square Arena
	27	Detroit, MI	Palace Auburn Hills
	29	Chicago, IL	Rosemont Horizon
	30	Chicago, IL	Rosemont Horizon
April	1	Peoria, IL	Civic Center
	2	Madison, WI	Dane County Coliseum
	4	St. Louis, MO	Riverport Amphitheater
	5	Kansas City, MO	Kemper Arena
	7	Milwaukee, WI	Bradley Center
	8	Minneapolis, MN	Target Center
	9	Moline, IL	The Mark
	18	Buffalo, NY	Memorial Auditorium (guest Candlebox until May 5th)
	20	Pittsburgh, PA	Civic Arena
	22	East Rutherford, NJ	Brendan Byrne Arena
	23	Uniondale, NY	Nassau Coliseum
	24	Hartford, CT	Civic Center

	26	Landover, MD	USAir Arena
	27	Hampton, VA	Coliseum (canceled to illness)
	28	Philadelphia, PA	Spectrum
	29	Philadelphia, PA	Spectrum
May	1	Providence, RI	Civic Center
	3	Albany, NY	Knickerbocker Arena
	4	Rochester, NY	War Memorial Auditorium
	5	Quebec City, QC	Le Colisee
	6	Montreal, PQ	Forum (guest The Doughboys)
	7	Toronto, ON	Maple Leaf Gardens (guest I Mother Earth)

Test For Echo North American Tour 1996 – 97 (An Evening With RUSH) no guests

October	19	Albany, NY	Knickerbocker Arena
	20	Buffalo, NY	Marine Midland Arena
	22	Dayton, OH	Ervin J. Nutter Center
	23	Grand Rapids, MI	Van Andel Arena
	25	Detroit, MI	Palace Auburn Hills
	26	Rockford, IL	MetroCentre
	28	Chicago, IL	United Center
	29	Minneapolis, MN	Target Center
	31	St. Louis, MO	Kiel Center
November	1	Milwaukee, WI	Bradley Center
	3	Pittsburgh, PA	Civic Arena
	4	Cleveland, OH	Gund Arena
	6	Philadelphia, PA	CoreStates Center
	7	Landover, MD	USAir Arena
	9	Boston, MA	FleetCenter
	10	Hartford, CT	Civic Center
	20	San Jose, CA	Arena
	21	Sacramento, CA	Arco Arena
	23	San Diego, CA	Sports Arena
	24	Las Vegas, NV	Thomas and Mack Arena
	26	Los Angeles, CA	Great Western Forum
	27	Los Angeles, CA	Great Western Forum
	29	Phoenix, AZ	America West Arena
	30	El Paso, TX	UTEP Special Events Center
December	2	San Antonio, TX	Alamodome
	3	Dallas, TX	Reunion Arena
	5	Houston, TX	Summit Arena
	6	New Orleans, LA	University of New Orleans Lakefront Arena
	8	West Palm Beach, FL	Coral Sky Amphitheater
	9	Tampa, FL	Ice Palace Arena
	11	Atlanta, GA	Omni
	12	Charlotte, NC	Coliseum
	14	Uniondale, NY	Nassau Coliseum

	15	East Rutherford, NJ	Continental Arena
	17	Toronto, ON	Maple Leaf Gardens
	18	Toronto, ON	Club Phoenix (secret show sponsored by Molson Beer)
	19	Ottawa, ON	Civic Arena
	20	Montreal, PQ	Forum
	26	Toronto, ON	Lee's Palace (Labour of Love Festival) cancelled
May 1997	1	Pensacola, FL	Civic Center (canceled)
	7	Phoenix, AZ	Desert Sky Pavilion
	8	San Diego, CA	GTE Summer Pops Bowl Amphitheater
	10	Devore, CA	Glen Helen Blockbuster Pavilion
	11	Mountain View, CA	Shoreline Amphitheater
	14	Portland, OR	Rose Garden
	16	Vancouver, BC	General Motors Place
	17	George, WA	The Gorge
	19	Boise, ID	Idaho State University Pavilion
	20	Salt Lake City, UT	Delta Center
	22	Englewood, CO	Fiddlers Green Amphitheater
	24	Dallas, TX	Starplex Amphitheater
	25	Houston, TX	Woodlands Pavilion
June	4	Cincinnati, OH	Riverbend Music Center
	5	Nashville, TN	Starwood Amphitheater
	7	Bonner Springs, KS	Sandstone Amphitheater
	8	St. Louis, MO	Riverport Amphitheater
	10	Noblesville, IN	Deer Creek Music Theater
	11	Burgettstown, PA	Starlake Amphitheater
	13	Milwaukee, WI	Marcus Amphitheater
	14	Chicago, IL	The World Music Center
	16	Columbus, OH	Polaris Amphitheater
	17	Detroit, MI	Pine Knob Music Theater
	19	Holmdel, NJ	PNC Bank Arts Center
	20	Bristow, VA	Nissan Pavilion
	22	Camden, NJ	Blockbuster-Sony Entertainment Center
	23	Mansfield, MA	Great Woods Amphitheater
	25	Wantaugh, NY	Jones Beach Amphitheater
	26	Darien Lake, NJ	Darien Performing Arts Center
	28	Montreal, PQ	Molson Centre
	30	Toronto, ON	Molson Amphitheatre
July	2	Toronto, ON	Molson Amphitheatre
	3	Quebec City, PQ	Le Colisee
	4	Ottawa, ON	Corel Centre

Setlists

Choosing a setlist for a career spanning two and a half decades is no easy feat. Rush's live performances have been praised for their precision but criticized for being 'too perfect', lacking 'spontaneity.'

GEDDY That's the scenario we're going through right now; figuring out what songs we're going to play on this tour; how many songs from the new album we can squeeze in; how much new material our fans want to hear; how much old material we want to play. It's a long involved process. We start sending each other wish lists by fax—"I like these songs", "I like these songs." We're hoping on this tour we might be able to play a bit longer than we normally do and squeeze some more songs in." (T4E Premiere)

ALEX We're so regimented in all our parts, and we depend on each other for cues for the next parts. If somebody does one thing different, it could screw up somebody else's part. So we just stay away from that. (Guitar Player 1986)

NEIL I'm a bit on the adventurous side live. I'll try something out. I'll take a chance. Most of the time I'm playing above my ability, so I'm taking a risk. I think every-day is really a practice … playing within a framework of music every night you have enough familiarity you feel comfortable to experiment. If the song starts to grow a bit stale, I find one nice little fill which will refresh the whole song. (Modern Drummer)

NEIL Some of the songs that we're playing now are five, six, seven, eight and nine years old. You have to bring something fresh to them every year. And you have to play that with true conviction every night. We've dropped songs that were very popular and people expected us to play forever. There comes a day when we have to say, "We have nothing to say with this song anymore. We can't play it with conviction." Otherwise, it becomes like a joke—like we're taking advantage of people or we're pandering to them. We can't do that, so we drop the song. And we take a lot of flak for it. People say, "Well, why didn't they play more old songs?" It's because we can't do that honestly. We can't play "Fly By Night" or "Working Man" anymore with any conviction. We get that pressure, sometimes, directed right at us. "Why didn't you play that song?" Because we can't honestly play it for you anymore. If we played it, it would be a lie. And you don't want us to lie to you. We don't lie to our audience on any level. When we make our records or play in concert, that same set of standards comes to the stage with us. We're not there to play a role. (Modern Drummer 1984)

Tour dates are noted by month, day, year.

🎤 = new song for tour

▶ = medley segue

▮ = abbreviated song

Rush Tour 1974

8/14/74

Finding My Way
In the Mood
Working Man ▶
Drum Solo ▶
Working Man

8/26/74

Finding My Way
Best I Can 🎤
Need Some Love
In the End 🎤
Fancy Dancer 🎤
In the Mood
Bad Boy 🎤 (remake of Larry Williams 1959 hit later covered by Beatles)
Guitar SoloHere Again
Working Man ▶
Drum Solo ▶
Working Man
Encore:
What You're Doing

10/4/74

Finding My Way
Best I Can 🎤
What You're Doing
Working Man ▶
Drum Solo ▶
Working Man

11/17/74

Finding My Way
Best I Can 🎤
Anthem 🎤
In the Mood
Here Again
Bad Boy 🎤
Working Man ▶
Drum Solo ▶
Working Man

11/27/74

Finding My Way
Fancy Dancer
In the Mood
In The End
What You're Doing
Bad Boy

Note: "In the Mood" was stopped to fix a broken bass drum head as Alex proceeded to play a country-styled jingle used in subsequent tours and most recently on the 1994 Tour before "Cold Fire".

12/5/74

Finding My Way
Best I Can 🎤
In the Mood
Anthem 🎤
Need Some Love
Fly By Night 🎤
Here Again
Bad Boy 🎤
Working Man ▶
Drum Solo
Working Man

Fly By Night Tour 1975

Supporting Set:

What You're Doing
Anthem 🎤
Beneath, Between and Behind 🎤
In the End 🎤
Fly By Night 🎤
Working Man ▶
Drum Solo ▶
In the Mood

Headlining Set:

What You're Doing
Best I Can 🎤
Anthem 🎤
Beneath, Between and Behind 🎤
In the End 🎤
Fly By Night 🎤
By-Tor and the Snow Dog 🎤
Working Man ▮▶
Drum Solo ▶

In the Mood ▣ ▶
Need Some Love ▣
Encore:
Finding My Way

6/25/75

Finding My Way
Best I Can ⬍
Anthem ⬍
Beneath, Between and Behind
In the End
Fly By Night ⬍
By-Tor and the Snow Dog ⬍
In the Mood ▶
Need Some Love ▶
Working Man ▶
Drum Solo
Working Man
Encore:
What You're Doing

Caress of Steel Tour 1975
(Down the Tubes Tour)

Finding My Way
Best I Can (replaced by Anthem on 12/75)
I Think I'm Going Bald ⬍
Beneath, Between and Behind
Lakeside Park ⬍
Anthem (replaced by Fly By Night on 12/75)
Bastille Day ⬍
By-Tor and the Snow Dog
The Necromancer ⬍
Fly by Night (replaced by In the End on 12/75)
Working Man ▶
Drum Solo ▶
In the Mood

November 15, 1975 Setlist:

Bastille Day
Anthem
Lakeside Park
The Necromancer
By-Tor and the Snow Dog
Working Man/Drum Solo
In the Mood

2112 Tour 1976

Bastille Day
Anthem
Lakeside Park
2112 (abbrev. Discovery, no 'Oracle') ⬍
Fly By Night ▶
In the Mood
Something For Nothing ⬍
By-Tor and the Snow Dog
Working Man ▶
Finding My Way ▶
Drum Solo ▶
Working Man
Encore:
What You're Doing

NEIL

In 1976, we were still opening most shows, and our set was usually about forty minutes long. Thus, even from the beginning we played an abbreviated version, even leaving out "Discovery" as well I think, and then later we tended just to play "Overture" and "The Temples of Syrinx" to allow time for other songs. (Backstage Club Newsletter 1990)

All the World's a Stage Tour 1976–77

Skip Gildersleeve intros the band on All the World's a Stage. Same setlist as *2112* but with "Best I Can" as encore.

Supporting Sets:

Anthem
2112 (minus Oracle)
Working Man
Finding My Way ▶
Drum Solo
Fly By Night ▶
In The Mood

Bastille Day
Anthem
2112 (minus Oracle)

Lakeside Park
Working Man
Finding My Way ▶
Drum Solo

Headlining Set:

Bastille Day
Anthem
Lakeside Park
2112 (minus Oracle)
Fly By Night
In The Mood
Something For Nothing
Instrumental
In The End
By-Tor and the Snow Dog
Working Man ▶
Finding My Way ▶
Drum Solo
Encore:
Best I Can

12/31/76

Bastille Day
Anthem
Lakeside Park
2112
The Twilight Zone ♀
Something For Nothing
Best I Can
By-Tor and the Snow Dog
The Necromancer
    (Under the Shadow-ab. instr./Return of the Prince)
In the End
Working Man ▶
Finding My Way ▢ ▶
Drum Solo
Encore:
Fly By Night ▶
In the Mood

6/2/77

Bastille Day
Anthem
Lakeside Park
2112
Xanadu ♀
By-Tor and the Snow Dog ▶
The Necromancer (Return of the Prince)
Working Man ▶

Finding My Way ▢ ▶
Drum Solo
Encore:
Fly By Night ▢ ▶
In the Mood ▢ ▶
What You're Doing

A Farewell To Kings Tour 1977 – 78

Intro: unknown
Bastille Day
Lakeside Park
By-Tor and the Snow Dog ▢ ▶
Xanadu ♀
A Farewell To Kings ♀
Something For Nothing
Cygnus X-1 ♀
Anthem
Closer To the Heart
2112 (ab. Discovery minus Oracle)
Working Man ▢ ▶
Fly By Night ▢ ▶
In the Mood ▢ ▶
Drum Solo
Encore:
Cinderella Man ♀

Tour of the Hemispheres 1978 – 79

Intro: unknown
Anthem
A Passage To Bangkok ♀
By-Tor and the Snow Dog ▢ ▶
The Trees ♀
Xanadu
Something For Nothing
Cygnus X-1
Hemispheres ♀ (with ab. Apollo/Dionysus)
Closer To the Heart
Circumstances ♀ (dropped 4/23/79)
A Farewell To Kings
The Twilight Zone ♀ (or La Villa Strangiato ♀)
2112 (ab. Discovery; except Oracle: The Dream)
Working Man ▶
Bastille Day ▶
In the Mood ▶ ▢
Drum Solo
Encore:
Cinderella Man

Warm-Up Tour 1979

2112 (Overture/The Temples of Syrinx)
A Passage To Bangkok
By-Tor and the Snow Dog ▯ ▶
Xanadu
The Spirit of Radio 🎤
The Trees
Cygnus X-1 ▶
Hemispheres (with ab. Apollo/Dionysus)
Closer To the Heart
Freewill 🎤
Working Man ▯ ▶
Finding My Way (intro) ▶
Bastille Day ▯ ▶
In the Mood ▯ ▶
Drum Solo
Encore:
La Villa Strangiato

GEDDY

OK Kids! It's time for Doctor Braino!
(introducing the drum solo)

Permanent Waves Tour 1980

2112 (Overture/ Temples of Syrinx)
Freewill 🎤
By-Tor and the Snow Dog ▯ ▶
Xanadu
The Spirit of Radio 🎤
Natural Science 🎤
A Passage To Bangkok
Spanish classical guitar intro 🎤
The Trees
Cygnus X-1
Hemispheres (with ab. Apollo/Dionysus) ▶
Closer To the Heart ▯ ▶
Beneath, Between and Behind ▯
Jacob's Ladder 🎤
Working Man (reggae ver.) ▶
Finding My Way (intro) ▶
Anthem ▯ ▶
Bastille Day ▯ ▶
Drum Solo
Encore:
La Villa Strangiato (electric guitar intro)

"This is an old Russian song ..." (intro to
"Working Man")

Warm-up Tour 1980

2112 (Overture/The Temples of Syrinx)
Freewill
By-Tor and the Snow Dog ▯ ▶
Xanadu
Limelight 🎤 (different intro, faster)
Broon's Bane (classical guitar intro)
The Trees
Hemispheres (Prelude)
The Spirit of Radio
Closer To the Heart ▶
Beneath, Between and Behind ▯
Tom Sawyer 🎤 (different second verse, faster)
Jacob's Ladder
Natural Science
Working Man (reggae ver./ ▯) ▶
Finding My Way (intro) ▶
Anthem ▯ ▶
Bastille Day ▯ ▶
In the Mood ▯ ▶
Drum Solo
Encore:
La Villa Strangiato

Moving Pictures Tour 1981

2112 (Overture/The Temples of Syrinx)
Freewill
Limelight 🎤
Hemispheres (Prelude) ▶
Beneath, Between and Behind ▯
The Camera Eye 🎤
YYZ 🎤 ▶
Drum Solo ▶
YYZ 🎤
Broon's Bane (classical guitar intro)
The Trees
Xanadu
The Spirit of Radio
Red Barchetta 🎤
Closer To the Heart
Tom Sawyer 🎤

Vital Signs 🎤
Natural Science
Working Man (reggae ver.) ▶
Hemispheres (Armageddon) (ab. instrumental) ▶
By-Tor and the Snow Dog 🔲 ▶
In the End 🔲 ▶
In the Mood 🔲 ▶
2112 (Grand Finale)
Encore:
La Villa Strangiato (with classical guitar intro)

GEDDY

"This is a little Spanish song …" (introducing "Closer to the Heart")

The country jingle used in 1974 resurfaced on certain dates before "YYZ". The lyrics changed in some shows from this tour on with "Tom Sawyer". "Catch the spirit/catch the fish" was started after roadies threw fish onstage during the song.

Exit … Stage Left Tour 1981

Same as Moving Pictures Tour but "Subdivisions" 🎤 followed "Beneath, Between and Behind".

Tour of the Nadars 1982

Same as Exit … Stage Left Tour set but "The Analog Kid" 🎤 follows "The Trees".

Signals/ New World Tour 1982

Intro: Three Stooges
The Spirit of Radio ▶
Tom Sawyer
Freewill
Digital Man 🎤
Subdivisions 🎤
Vital Signs
The Camera Eye
Closer To the Heart
Chemistry 🎤 (dropped 5/3/83)
The Analog Kid 🎤
Broon's Bane

The Trees
Red Barchetta
The Weapon 🎤
New World Man 🎤
Limelight
Countdown 🎤
Encore:
2112 (Overture/The Temples of Syrinx) ▶
Xanadu 🔲 ▶
La Villa Strangiato 🔲 ▶
In the Mood 🔲
YYZ ▶
Drum Solo ▶
YYZ

Note: Midway through the tour, Count Floyd (Joe Flaherty) from SCTV in 3-D intros "The Weapon" while a Get Smart TV show excerpt intros "New World Man". Lyrics in "Spirit" were changed sometimes to "one likes to believe in the freedom of baseball"; in "2112" sometimes changed to "we are the plumbers who have come to fix your sinks" for comic effect. Film footage simulating the *Moving Pictures* album appears before "Tom Sawyer".

Radio City Music Hall

Intro: Three Stooges
Tom Sawyer
Freewill
Digital Man
Kid Gloves 🎤
Subdivisions
Vital Signs
Red Sector A 🎤
Closer to the Heart
Chemistry
The Body Electric 🎤
Broon's Bane
The Trees
Red Barchetta
The Weapon
New World Man
Limelight
Countdown

Grace Under Pressure Tour 1984

Intro: The Three Stooges
The Spirit of Radio
Subdivisions
The Body Electric 🎤
The Enemy Within 🎤
The Weapon
Witch Hunt+ 🎤 (first time live)
New World Man
Between the Wheels 🎤
Red Barchetta
Distant Early Warning 🎤
Red Sector A 🎤
Closer To the Heart
Afterimage 🎤 (dropped 9/14;
    replaced by Kid Gloves 🎤-dropped 11/9)
YYZ ▯ ▶Drum Solo moved later
2112 (The Temples of Syrinx) ▶
Tom Sawyer
Encore:
Red Lenses 🎤 ▶
Drum Solo ▶
Red Lenses 🎤
Vital Signs ▶
Finding My Way ▶
In the Mood

The early versions of the Grace songs have different structures, solos and sometimes lyrics — for example, "one humanoid escapee/one robot on the run."

Spring Tour 1985

Same as previous tour except "The Big Money" followed "Witch Hunt"; "Middletown Dreams" followed "Closer to the Heart"; followed by "YYZ" with "Drum Solo" medley ▶ "2112" ▶ "Tom Sawyer". "Red Lenses" was the final song and the encore was the "Vital Signs" medley.

Power Windows Tour 1985–86

Intro: The Three Stooges
The Spirit of Radio
Limelight
The Big Money 🎤
New World Man
Subdivisions

Manhattan Project 🎤
    (Middletown Dreams followed on 2nd set;
    after 2/14)
Red Sector A
Closer To the Heart
Middletown Dreams 🎤
Witch Hunt (dropped 2/26/86)
Marathon 🎤
The Trees (dropped 4/13/86; replaced by Mystic Rhythms)
Distant Early Warning
Territories 🎤
The Weapon (dropped 12/8/85)
YYZ ▯ ▶
Drum Solo ▶
Red Lenses ▯
Encore:
Tom Sawyer
2112 (Overture/The Temples of Syrinx) ▶
    (more was played on 4/3/86)
Grand Designs ▶
In the Mood ▯

Hold Your Fire Tour 1987–88

Intro: The Three Stooges
The Big Money
Subdivisions
Limelight
Marathon
Turn the Page 🎤
Prime Mover 🎤
Manhattan Project
Closer To the Heart
Red Sector A
Force Ten
Time Stand Still 🎤
Red Barchetta
Distant Early Warning
Lock and Key 🎤
Mission 🎤
Territories
YYZ ▯ ▶
The Rhythm Method (Drum Solo) ▶
Red Lenses ▯ ▶
The Spirit of Radio
Tom Sawyer

R · U · S · H

Encore:
2112 (Overture/The Temples of Syrinx) ▶
La Villa Strangiato ▶ ▯
In the Mood ▯

Alex began clowning around even more this tour—he even started 'singing'. In the case of "2112", he started replying into the mike: after Geddy would sing, "We are the priests of the Temples of Syrinx," Alex would answer, "It's a tough job ya know! … What do our computers do … Where is Syrinx anyway?" The band also threw in parts from Cheech and Chong's rock band beats in the film *Up in Smoke* to close "The Big Money". Occasionally the "Pipeline" jazzy bass ending would be thrown in at the end of the later shows.

Presto Tour 1990

Intro: A Show of Hands
Force Ten
Freewill ▯ ▶
Distant Early Warning
Time Stand Still
Subdivisions
Marathon
Red Barchetta
Superconductor ♀
The Pass ♀
Closer To the Heart
Manhattan Project
Xanadu+ ▯ ▶
YYZ ▯ ▶
The Rhythm Method (Drum solo)
Scars ♀
War Paint ♀
Mission
Tom Sawyer (inflated rabbits)
Encore:
The Big Money ▶ (replaced by The Spirit of Radio on 4/3/90)
2112 (Overture) ▯ ▶
La Villa Strangiato ▯ ▶
In the Mood ▯ ▶
Pipeline (jazz bass)

NEIL

Early in the Presto tour we found that "Radio" was feeling a bit stale, so we put it aside for awhile. Then later we brought it back to alternate with "Big Mahoney", and eventually stayed with "Radio" as the better encore-opener. (Backstage Club '91)

Hired Playboy bunnies would come out on stage to wipe sweat off Alex and Geddy and kiss them. Giant inflatable rabbits made their debut (these would be used for the following two tours).

Roll the Bones Tour 1991–92

Intro: A Show of Hands
Force Ten
Limelight
Freewill ▯ ▶
Distant Early Warning
    (replaced by Red Sector A for Euro dates/third leg)
Time Stand Still
Dreamline ♀
Bravado ♀
Roll the Bones ♀
Show Don't Tell
The Big Money
Ghost of a Chance ♀
    (added after the first month or so)
Subdivisions
    (replaced by Vital Signs on Euro dates/third leg)
The Pass
    (replaced by The Analog Kid on Euro dates/third leg)
The Trees (added on third leg)
Where's My Thing? ♀
The Rhythm Method (Drum Solo)
Closer To the Heart
Xanadu ▯ ▶
Superconductor
Tom Sawyer
Encore:
The Spirit of Radio ▶
2112 (Overture/The Temples of Syrinx) ▶
Finding My Way ▯ ▶

La Villa Strangiato ▶Anthem 🔲 ▶
Red Barchetta 🔲 ▶
The Spirit of Radio (Reprise) ▶
Cygnus X-1 (teaser added near start of third leg)

Counterparts Tour 1994

Intro: Thus Spoke Zarathustra (Richard Strauss)
Dreamline
The Spirit of Radio
The Analog Kid
Cold Fire 🎤
Time Stand Still
Nobody's Hero 🎤
Roll the Bones
Animate 🎤
Stick It Out 🎤 (fireworks)
Double Agent 🎤 (flame jets)
Limelight
Bravado (added 4/20/94)
Mystic Rhythms
Closer To the Heart
Show Don't Tell
Leave That Thing Alone! 🎤
Mystic Rhythms
The Rhythm Method (Drum Solo)
The Trees
Xanadu 🔲 ▶
Hemispheres(Prelude) ▶+
Tom Sawyer
Encore:
Force Ten (absent 4/24)
YYZ

GEDDY

This is a little country song … (introducing
'Cold Fire' with the country/western jam in the
background)

During the jam part of "Closer", Alex on every gig
would speak to the audience on the microphone.
Introducing himself as everyone from Fabio to Alec
Baldwin, Geddy as Ted Nugent, Spike Lee, and Buddy
Hackett and Neil as Karen Carpenter. Alex would also
talk about the state they were playing in. The intro
cartoon to "Leave" has the inflatable rabbit being shot

and deflated. Geddy often perched his Mystery
Science Theater 3000 TV show lunchbox atop his
synthesizer.

Test For Echo Tour 1996

Intro: Thus Spoke Zarathustra (Richard Strauss)
Dreamline
The Big Money ▶
Wipeout!
Driven 🎤
Half the World 🎤
Red Barchetta
Animate
Limbo 🎤
The Trees
Red Sector A
Virtuality 🎤
Nobody's Hero
Closer To the Heart
2112 (all seven parts and an extended guitar
    intro on Discovery) 🎤

Intermission: 50's drive-in cartoons "Let's All Go to
the Lobby and Have Ourselves a Snack"

Trailers for: Hell's Belles, Werewolves On Wheels, Free
Grass, Selvaggi. Music heard included "At the End" by
Victor and "Momo's Dance Party" by Neil Peart (from
"A Work in Progress" end titles).

Test For Echo 🎤
Subdivisions
Freewill
Roll the Bones
Resist 🎤 (absent 10/23,26,29/96 and 11/1,4,7/96)
Leave That Thing Alone!
The Rhythm Method (Drum Solo)
Natural Science+
Force Ten
Time and Motion (absent 10/22,25,28,31/96 and 11/6/
96; dropped 11/9/96)
The Spirit of Radio
Tom Sawyer
Encore:
YYZ
Cygnus X-1 teaser
(**Note:** Resist and Time and Motion were played the
first two dates of the tour.)

GEDDY

This is a song about Scotland … (introducing 'Resist')

Alex employed a Pamela Anderson lifesize cardboard standee and Geddy a refrigerator with magnets representing each of the States.

12/18 Secret Show

Intro: Thus Spoke Zarathustra (Richard Strauss)
The Big Money ▶
Wipeout!
Driven ⚲
Half the World ⚲
Red Barchetta
Animate
Virtuality ⚲
Nobody's Hero
Closer to the Heart
Test For Echo ⚲
Subdivisions
Freewill
Roll the Bones
Resist ⚲
Leave That Thing Alone!
The Spirit of Radio
Tom Sawyer

Encore:
Force Ten
YYZ
Cygnus X-1 (teaser)

May 7 on:
Intro: Thus Spoke Zarathustra (Richard Strauss)
Dreamline
Limelight
Stick It Out
Driven
Half the World
Red Barchetta
Animate
Limbo
The Trees
Virtuality
Nobody's Hero
Closer To the Heart
2112
Intermission
Test For Echo
Freewill
Red Sector A
Roll the Bones
Resist
Leave That Thing Alone!
The Rhythm Method - Drum Solo
Natural Science
Force Ten
The Spirit of Radio
Tom Sawyer
Encore:
YYZ

BIBLIOGRAPHY 6

WHILE RUSH MEMBERS HAVE BEEN INTERVIEWED EXTENSIVELY in the media and their recordings and concerts have been reviewed far and wide, the band has always been reserved in their comments and humble in the face of criticism, positive or negative. The band has always put making music ahead of making sound bites.

NEIL   We're more interested in the work than the press in a general sense. I enjoy doing interviews because I like to talk about what I'm doing, but we don't go out of our way to go to every radio station in town, and we don't go out of our way to get in print everywhere we can. I think that's a limiting factor—we won't inconvenience ourselves for the sake of getting some press. It has to be done as a secondary priority. (Circus 1980)

NEIL   I won't do an interview for a promotional reason. I do them because I like to get my ideas out. Sometimes I can talk about something in an interview and realize that I was totally wrong. And I'll have had the opportunity to air those thoughts out which most people don't. You don't have conversations with your friends about metaphysics, the fundamentals of music, and the fundamentals of yourself really. When I do an interview I look for an ideal. I'm looking for an interview that's going to be stimulating, and I'll get right into it. Just sit for hours and relate. That's an ideal, like an ideal show. It doesn't happen very often. (Modern Drummer 1980)

Magazines

This is not a complete list of the articles and interviews pertaining to the band, but a list of the literature I reference in this book.

Aquarian Weekly   1994 (3/9): Interview (Neil): "To Be Totally Obsessed — That's the Only Way," Ula Gehret.

Bass and Drums   1992 (No. 2-3): Cover, Geddy.

Bassics   1997 (Vol. VI, No. 12): Cover, Geddy; Interview: "You Can't Hurry Change," Philip Dawdy.1998 (Fall): Review: *Different Stages*.

Bassist   1999 (1): Cover, Geddy.

Bass Frontiers   1996 (11-12): Cover, Geddy; Interview: "Geddy Lee and Rush Test For Echo," Christopher Buttner.

Bass Player   1988 (11-12) Debut Issue: Cover, Geddy; Interview: "Bass Is Still the Key," Robin Tolleson.
1990 (Summer): Review: *Presto*.
1990 (Fall): Geddy in "Ask the Experts" column.
1991 (9-10): Geddy wins Readers Poll.
1992 (2): Review: *Roll the Bones*.
1992 (6): Interview: "The Roll the Bones Interview" (with Geddy Lee).
    Poll results: Geddy in 1st.
1993 (12): Cover, Geddy; Interview: "Geddy Lee Still Going", Karl Coryat.
2000 (12): Review: *My Favorite Headache*.
2001 (1): Cover, Geddy; Interview: "No Rush," Chris Jisi.

Beetle (Canada)   1974 (12): Interview.

Billboard   1974 (10/19): Article: Rush Hot on Circuit
1980 (1/1): Article: "Rush Won't Rush Into Style Fads of the Moment," Cary Darling.
1984 (6/21): Review: *Grace Under Pressure*.
1989 (1/21): Review: *A Show of Hands*.
1989 (11/25): Review: *Presto*.
1991 (9/14): Review: *Roll the Bones*.
1991 (9/21): Article: Rush Rolls in Highest Ever #3 With *Roll the Bones*.
1993 (10/30): Article: Rushing Back to the Limelight — Power Trio Returns With *Counterparts*.
1993 (11/6): Article: Rush's *Counterparts* Mark Group's Highest Debut Ever.
1996 (8/3): Article: "Rush Aims For New Generation: After 3-Year Break, Trio Regroups For New Atlantic Set".
1996 (9/21): Review: *Test For Echo*.
1996 (10/26): Article: Daniels Manages *Grace Under Pressure* — Rush Manager Maintains Rock Focus.
1998 (11/7): Article
2000 (10/28): Article

The Canadian Composer (Canada)

>1981 (5): Interview: "Geddy Lee/Rush", Greg Quill.
>
>1986 (4): Interview: (Neil): "Surviving with Rush: Drummer-lyricist Neil Peart Looks Forward."

Canadian Musician (Canada)

>1979 (3): Notice: tour dates; debut issue.
>
>1979 (5-6): Cover, Alex; "Rush", Mad Stone.
>
>1981 (11-12): Cover, Rush; "Rush", Greg Quill.
>
>1985 (11): Interview: "On the Road With Rush", Jim Norris.
>
>1985 (12): Cover, Rush; Interview (Geddy): "Baroque Cosmologies in the Past: The Boys Focus On the 'Perfect Song', Perry Stern.
>
>1988 (2): Cover, Rush
>
>1988 (12): Rush cover (and others)
>
>1989 (2): Cover, Rush; Interview: "Rush A Show of Hands," Bill Reynolds.
>
>1989 (4): Cover, Rush(Neil) 10th anniv. issue
>
>1990 (4): Cover, Rush; Interview: "Presto Change-O," Nick Krewen.
>
>1991 (10): Cover, Rush; "Straight From the Heart," Frank Schulte.
>
>1994 (2): Cover, Rush.
>
>1996 (12): Cover, Rush; Interview: "Rush Put Themselves To the Test (and End Up Even Closer To the Heart)," Paul Myers.
>
>2000 (9-10): Cover, Geddy; Interview (Geddy) "Rush Man Flies Solo."

Car Stereo Review

>1994 (1-2): Interview (Alex): "Smart Alex: A Day in the Lifeson."

Cheap Thrills   1976 (1): Cover, Geddy.

Circus   1976 (4/27): Interview (Geddy/Neil): 'Rush Goes Into Future Shock: Music Will Not Exist In 2112'," Dan Nooger.

>1976 (11/25): Interview (Neil): "Rush Release: Canada's Power Trio Is Switched On Live," Anastasia Pantsios.
>
>1977 (2/14): Interview (Geddy/Neil): "A Canadian Rush — The Metal Marvels That Took the Rock World By Surprise," Debra Frost.
>
>1977 (3/17): Interview (Geddy/Neil): "Rush and Foghat — Two Top Live Acts Team Up for One Night of Electrified Pleasure," Richard Hogan.
>
>1977 (10/27): Interview (Geddy): "Rush Tapes, Part 2: Geddy Lee, From Immigrants' Son to Rush's Lead Singer," Scott Cohen Frost.
>
>1979 (2/27): Interview (Geddy, roadies): "A Day in a Rush Roadie's Life," David Fricke.
>
>1980 (4/1): Cover, Rush; Interview: "Battered by Old & New Waves, Rush Keeps Their Boat Afloat by Rocking It", David Fricke.
>
>1981 (8/31): Article: "Stage Pass: Rush Wrap Up Five Month Tour," Steve Weitzman.
>
>1981 (12/30): Article: "Vital Signs from Rush," Richard Hogan.
>
>1982 (2/28): Review: *Exit Stage Left.*
>
>1982 (3/31): Interview (Alex) (Alex 'centerfold') : "Lifeson Arrives Center Stage with Rush."
>
>1982 (11/30): Cover, Rush; "Rush's Simpler Signals," Phillip Bashe; Review: *Signals.*
>
>1984 (2): Interview (Geddy): "The Three Musketeers: Legendary Trio Complete New Album and Prepare for International Tour," Kerry Doole.
>
>1984 (7/31): "Rush: Aging With Grace," Michael Smolen.
>
>1984 (12/31): "Rush Fight Atrophy With Musical Exercise," Lisa Robinson.

1986 (1/31): Review: *Power Windows*.
1986 (2/28): Interview (Geddy): "Rush: A Power Rock Tradition," Dan Dale.
1986 (6/30): "Rush's Mystic Rhythms Pulse in Canada," Richard Hogan.
1987 (10/31): Review: *Hold Your Fire*.
1988 (1/31): Interview (Alex): "Rush Open Fire," Paul Gallotta.
1989 (2/28): Review: *A Show of Hands*.
1990 (1/31): Review: *Presto*.
1992 (1/31): Review: *Roll the Bones*.
1992 (4/30): Interview (Alex): "Rush Relives 18 Years of Widescreen Rock," Dan Hedges.

Creem
1981 (6): Interview (Neil/Alex): "Rush But Why Are They In Such a Hurry?" J. Kordosh.
1983 Interview (Hugh Syme): "From Brain Waves to Tidal Waves: The Story Behind Rush's Album Covers," Jeffrey Morgan.
1984 (8): Review: *Grace Under Pressure*.
1986 (9): Interview (Geddy): "It's Those Wacky Guys In Rush," Daniel Brogan; concert review.
1990 (6): Review: *Presto*.

Cycle World Canada
1996 (4): Article: "Chasing Some Midnight Rays," Neil Peart.

The Entertainment Profile (Canada)
1999 (2): Interview (Geddy): "Retro Rush."

EQ
1997 (7) #7: Cover, Geddy; "Rush's Live MIDI Secrets Revealed," Jack Secret.

Faces Rocks
1988 (5): Interview (Geddy): "What Makes Rush Inherently Unhip?" Bob Mack.

Guitar Player
1980 (6): Cover, Alex; "Rush's Kinetic Lead Guitarist," Jim Schwartz; "Hi-Tech Bassist and Synthesist with Rush"; Interview: Geddy, Tom Mulhern.
1984 (10): Article: Alex.
1986 (4): Cover, Geddy; Interview: "Geddy Lee of Rush: Rock's Leading Bassist," Tom Mulhern; Interview: "Alex Lifeson of Rush: The Evolving Art of Rock Guitar," Jas Obrecht.
1987 (7): Cover, Alex with others; Interview: "Canadian Guitars Summit," Jim Ferguson; "Beyond Borders" soundsheet.
1987 (10): Review: *Hold Your Fire*.
1991 (11): Cover, Interview: Geddy, Alex; "Rush Redefined," Andy Widders-Ellis.
1993 (12): Article: "Profile: Alex Lifeson: Rush Strips Down," Andy Widders-Ellis.

Guitar: The Magazine
1992 (Vol. 2): Article: Alex Lifeson: Guitar Techniques.

Guitar: For the Practicing Musician
1984 (7): Cover/Interview, Alex.
1984 (9): Review: *Grace Under Pressure*.
1987 (6): Interview: Geddy; Transcription: "New World Man".
1988 (1): Review: *Hold Your Fire*.
1988 (Summer): "The Acoustic Classics Issue" (Alex talks).
1988 (8): Article: "Alex Lifeson: Classical Precision: Blues Touch."

1989 (6): Review: *A Show of Hands.*

1989 (Winter): "Singing Bass"; Transcription: "Tom Sawyer".

1990 (6): Transcription: "Presto".

1990 (11): 2112 retrospective.

1991 (5): Cover, Alex with others in Hall of Fame; "The Art of Preparation"; Transcription: "Freewill".

1991 (12): Cover with others, Geddy; Interview with Geddy: "It's a Groove Thing", John Stix, Transcription: "La Villa Strangiato".

1992 (2): Review: *Roll the Bones.*

1993 (11): Interview: "The Listening Room: Geddy Lee and Alex Lifeson of Rush," John Stix.

1994 (2): Cover, Alex; Interview: "Rush: Alex Lifeson's Attitude Adjustment," John Chappell; Review: *Counterparts*; Transcription: "Cold Fire".

1994 (5): Interview: "Makin' Trax: Alex Lifeson," John Chappell.

1996 (11): Cover, Rush; Interview: "Rush Hour: Lifeson and Lee Test Their Metal with a Heavy Echo," Mike Mettler; Transcription: "Test For Echo".

1997 (7): Transcription: "Driven".

1997 (11): Transcription: "Fly By Night".

Guitar School

1990 (5): Cover, Geddy/Alex; "Magic Men" Interview: Geddy/Alex; Transcriptions: "Show Don't Tell", "Free Will".

1992 (1): Transcription: "Dreamline".

1992 (11): Interview: "The Pit" with Geddy and Mr Big.

1993 (5): Transcription: "Limelight".

1993 (9): Article: "Rush Chronicles-Wolf Marshall's Rock History: Strange Days-Wolf Marshall Chronicles the Growth of Rush's Electric Style With and Examination of La Villa Strangiato, the Trio's Magnum Opus."

1994 (3): Cover, Interview: Geddy, Alex, Article: "Alex Lifeson and Geddy Lee Return to Their Roots with Nineteenth Album, Counterparts: Back To the Future," Matt Resnicoff; Geddy bass clinic; Transcription: "Closer To the Heart".

1996 (10): Article: "Analyzing Two Decades of Rush's Unparalleled Prog-Rock Prowess: Grace Under Pressure;" Interview: Alex and Geddy, Andy Aledort.

1997 (4): Transcription: "2112 I/II".

Guitar Shop

1994 (Summer): Debut issue, Cover, Alex (small pic); Interview: "Back To the Stack: Alex Lifeson Discovers the Joy of Crankin' It Up," Pete Prown.

1996 (2): Interview: "Solo Signals-Alex Lifeson Does It Alone with Victor," Mike Mettler.

1996 (10): Notice: Alex guitar tip.

1996 (12): Interview: "On the Spot: Geddy Lee of Rush," Pete Prown.

1999 (3): Interview (Alex): "The Different Stages of Rush: Guitarist Alex Lifeson Reveals The Secrets Behind a 25-Year Legacy", Jeffrey L. Perlah; Interview (Geddy): "Getting Closer To The Heart of Rush … with Geddy Lee," Jeffrey L. Perlah.

Guitar World

1981 (11): Cover, Alex., Interview: "Alex Lifeson: Is He Too Good For Heavy Metal?", John Swenson

1988 (4): Cover, Alex and Geddy; Interview: "Lifeson, Lee Together."

1989 (4): Interview: "Rock Masters: Rock Bass" (Geddy talks, Signature ad).

1990 (3): Interview: "Rush in Revolution," Alex/Geddy, Bill Milkowski.

1991 (12) : Interview: "Flesh and Bones," Alex/Geddy, Mike Mettler.

1992 (6): Interview: "First Bass Men," Geddy and Primus' Les Claypool.

1993 (5): Transcription: "The Spirit of Radio".

1993 (12): Review: *Counterparts.*

1994 (2): "Closer To the Heart: Guitarist Alex Lifeson and Bassist Geddy Lee Revisit Their Stripped Down, Power Trio Roots on Counterparts, the Strongest Rush Release in Years," Andy Aledort; "Anthems: Guitar World Chronicles 20 years of Rush's Greatest Riffs," Troy Stetina; Transcription: Stick It Out."

1996 (12): Interview (Geddy/Alex): "Living in the Limelight — Geddy Lee, Alex Lifeson and Neil Peart Look Back at Rush's Long, Illustrious Career, Pt.1," Chris Gill; Interview Pt. 2 (Alex): "Time And Motion", Chris Gill; Pt. 3, "A Peart Response" by Neil; Transcription: "Tom Sawyer".

1997 (Summer) Guitar Legends special issue; Transcription: "YYZ".

1998 (12): Review: *Different Stages.*

2001 (01): Interview (Geddy): "No Rush — Profile: Geddy Lee," Allan Paul.

Guitarist   1996 (12): Interview (Alex): "Echo Soundings," Tim Slater.

Harmonix (Maryland's Veneman Music magazine)

1983 (2): Interview: "Interview With Alex Lifeson," Ted Veneman.

Hit Parader   1981 (10): Interview (Geddy): "Rush: Band of Outsiders," Andy Secher.

1984 (Winter): Guitar Gods Issue: "Alex Lifeson Rushing Ahead."

1984 (2): Interview (Geddy): "Rush: The Three Musketeers."

1985 (12): Interview (Neil and Alex): "Rush: Mind Over Metal," Peter Ross.

1988 (Summer): Article: 20 Years of Heavy Metal 1968 – 1988 "70s Rush: Masters of Sophisticated Metal Celebrate Their 15th Anniversary."

1992 (3): Interview (Geddy): "Rush: Bad To the Bones," Andy Secher.

1994 (10): Interview (Alex/Geddy): "Caught in the Act," Dave Arroca.

1994 (11): Interview (Neil): "Gearing Up, Tech Talk: Rush's Neil Peart," Annie Leighton.

Hitmen   1984 (12): Cover, Neil (with others).

hUH?   1996 (9): Interview (Geddy/Alex): "Rush Never Sleeps," Paul Semel.

International Musician and Recording World

1983 (1): Cover, Alex; Interview (Alex and Neil): "Rush N' Roll."

1984 (7): Cover; Interview (Geddy): "Art For Art's Sake."

1985 (12): Cover, Rush.

1988 (1): Interview (Alex): "Lifeson Times," Bass.

Kerrrang!   1982 (9/23-10/6): Cover, Alex; "A Rush of Old Age."

1983 (5/19-6/2): Cover, Alex; Article: "Rush-New World Men or Bots?", Malcolm Dome; exclusive Ross Halfin photos.

1983 (6/17-30): Interview: "Spirit of Peart: Part One of a Major Interview with Neil Peart of Rush," Dave Dickson.

1983 (7/17-30): Concert review.

1984 (4/5-18): "Pressure Points," album review by Geoff Barton, pullout of P/G cover

1984 (5/3-16): Rush cover.

1984 (6/28-7/11): Concert review.

1985: Interview (Alex): "Pane and Pleasure…," Mark Putterford.

1987 (10/17): Cover, Alex; Interview (Alex): "Lifeson Times," Mark Putterford.

1988 (4/30): Interview (Geddy): "Mayhem Don't All Rush…"

1988 (5/7): Concert review.
1988 (5/21): Interview (Neil): "Prime Groover," Chris Watts.
1989 (2/4): Interview (Neil): "You Need Hands," Neil Jeffries.
1989 (11/18): Review: *Presto.*
1989 (11/25): Interview (Alex): "The Meaning of Lifeson," Phil Wilding.
1990 (3/24): Concert review.
1990 (7/14): Cover, Alex/Geddy; Band Interview: "Excuse Me, Do You Happen To Know Where Rush Are Playing Tonight?" Paul Henderson.
1990 (9/15): Review: *Chronicles.*
1991 (8/31): Review: *Roll the Bones.*
1991 (9/21): Cover, Geddy/Alex; Interview: "The Dicemen Cometh," Paul Henderson.
1992 (3/7): "Touring Pictures."
1992 (4/18): Cover, Alex; Interview (Geddy/Alex): "Roll Models," Paul Elliott.
1993 (10/16): Review: *Counterparts.*
1993 (11/27): Interview (Geddy): "The Bum's Rush!" Paul Elliott.
1994 (3/8): Concert review.
1995 (2/18): "Technical Ecstacy," Malcolm Dome.
1996 (8/31): Review: *Test For Echo.*

Keyboard 1984 (9): Cover, Geddy; Interview with Geddy; Greg Armbruster; "On the Road With Rush: Tony Geranios: Synthesizer Technician."
1989 (3): "Rush to Perfection on A Show of Hands," Robert L. Doershuk.

Liberty 1997 (9): Interview (Neil): "A Rebel and a Drummer," Scott Bullock.

Lighting Design 1997 (3): Interview (Howard Ungerleider): "A Rush of Excitement."

LOUD 1991 (Winter) Issue 8, Vol. 5: Interview (Geddy): "Rush Rolling Along."

M.E.A.T. 1993 (11-12): Cover, Alex; Interview: "Alex Lifeson Reveals Counterparts."

Macleans (Canada)

1978 (1/23): Cover, Alex, Geddy; Interview (Geddy/Alex): "To Hell With Bob Dylan, Meet Rush — They're in It for the Money," Roy MacGregor.
1991 (9/30): Interview (Geddy/Alex): "Rock and Roll Royalty," Nicholas Jennings.
1995 (4/3): Article: "Into Africa," Neil Peart.

Making Music 1991 (10): Cover, Rush; Article: "Rush and Revolution."

Metal Attack (France)

1984 (6): Interview (Geddy): "Rush: Precision Sous Tension."

Metal Forces 1989 (12): Review: *Presto.*
1991 (10): Interview (Geddy): "Shake, Rattle and Roll."
1992 Interview (Alex): "The King's Call," Jerry Ewing.

Metal Hammer (UK)

1987 (10): Review: *Hold Your Fire.*
1987 (10/29): Interview (Alex): "Hold Your Fire, It's Rush," Kirk Blows.
1988 (4/25): Cover, Alex; Interview (Neil): "Rush All Fired Up," Malcolm Dome.
1988 (5/23): Concert review.
1989 (2/6): Interview (Neil): "Rush Show Their Hands," Chris Welch.
1989 (4/3): Rush Fan Magazine.
1989 (11/13-26): Review: *Presto.*
1989 (11/27-12/10): Interview (Alex): "The Next Chapter," Gotz Kuhemund.
1991 (10): Interview (Geddy): "Rush and Roulette," Howard Johnson.
1992 (2): Concert review.
1992 (5): Concert review.
1993 (11): Interview (Alex): "In the Rush Hour," Jerry Ewing; Review: *Counterparts.*

Modern Drummer

1980 (4-5): Cover, Neil; Interview by Cheech Iero.
1982 (5): Ask a Pro; Drumset giveaway.
1982 (10): Drumset giveaway results.
1982 (12): Article: "Notes On the Making of Moving Pictures Part 1," Neil Peart.
1983 (1): Article: "Notes On the Making of Moving Pictures Part 2," Neil Peart.
1983 (2): Article: Response From Neil on Riot; "Notes on the Making of Moving Pictures Part 3," Neil Peart.
1983 (4): Transcription: "New World Man".
1983 (12): Article: "The Art of Soloing," Neil Peart.
1984 (4): Cover, Neil; Interview (Neil), Scott K. Fish.
1986 (1): Interview (Neil), Scott K. Fish.
1986 (10): Article: Neil's thoughts on fitness.
1987 (2): Article: "A Real Job," Neil Peart.
1987 (3): Ask a Pro; Article: "Another Drumset Giveaway," Neil Peart.
1987 (5): Article: "The Quest For New Drums," Neil Peart; "Pieces of Eight" sound sheet.
1987 (10): Article: "Here's To the Winners," Neil Peart (drumset giveaway results).
1987 (12) Article: "Thoughts on Tom Tuning," Neil Peart.
1988 (2): Drumset contest winners (with sound sheet of their performances).
1988 (8): Article: "Creating the Drum Part," Neil Peart.
1989 (1): Ludwig ad; Zildjian mike ad.
1989 (12): Cover, Neil; Interview (Neil), William F. Miller.
1992 (1): Transcription: "Where's My Thing?".
1994 (2): Cover, Neil; Interview: "Neil Peart: In Search of the Right Feel," William F. Miller.
1995 (2) Cover, Neil and Buddy Rich; "On the Making of Burning for Buddy," Neil Peart.
1995 (11) Article: "Starting Over," Neil Peart.
1996 (8) Neil's letter on internet/fanmail.
1996 (11) Article/Interview: "The Reinvention of Neil Peart," William F. Miller; DW giveaway.
1997 (3): Transcription: "Lakeside Park".

Musician

1986 (1): Review: *Power Windows.*
1988 (6): Interview (Neil): "Neal [sic] Peart Headdy Metal," Chip Stern.
1990 (4): Interview (Geddy): "Screwing Up Pop — On Purpose."

The Music Paper

       1990 (3): Article: "Presto! Here's Rush."

       1991 (12): Interview: "Rush: Three Is Never a Crowd," Lisa Fantino.

       1994 (2): Cover, Rush; Interview (Geddy): "The Dawn of a New Direction."

Music Technology

       1988 (2): Cover, Rush; "Fire in the Hold."

Network (Canada)

       1989 (1-2): Cover, Geddy; Interview (Geddy): "Aging Gracefully," Wilder Penfield III.

       1993 (11): Cover, Geddy; Band Interview: "The Godfathers of Cyber-tech Go Organic," Perry Stern.

       1996 (11): Cover, Rush; Interview (Geddy): "Rush Returns to Guitar Roots for Aggressive New Album," Perry Stern.

Only Music   1987 (12) Interview (Geddy): "Rush: The Premiere Progressive Rock Trio," Lance Laskosky.

Parachutist   1993 (1): Article: "Rush: Roll the Bones Skydiving Team."

People   1989 (4/24): Review: *A Show of Hands* video.

       1990 (1/22): Review: *Presto.*

Professional Sound

       1994 (Summer): Cover, Rush.

Raw   1989 (2/8-21): Interview (Neil): "Closer to the Peart."

       1989 (11/15-28): Review: *Presto.*

       1989 (11/29-12/12) Interview (Alex): "Makin' Magic," Phil Alexander.

       1992 (5/13-26): Interview (Geddy): "Rush: Uneven? For Sure …"

       1993 (10/13-26): Review: *Counterparts.*

       1993 (10/27-11/9): Interview (Geddy): "Rush: A Farewell To Bings?!" Howard Johnson.

Record Collector (UK)

       1990 (12): Article: "Rush, Canada's Premiere Hard Rockers Remain a Cult in Britain, As Steve Adams Explains."

Rip   1990 (9): Interview (Neil): "Presto Chango."

       1994 (2): Interview (Geddy): "Rush: Trip Out!" Troy Augusto.

       1994 (4): Interview (Geddy): "Rush: Feed Your Head," Michael Moses.

Rolling Stone   1981 (5-28): Interview (Geddy): "Rush: Power To the People," David Fricke.

       1996 (12/28): Interview (Geddy), Jancee Dunn.

RPM Weekly (Canada)

       1978 (12/9): Cover, Rush; Article: "Rush: into the Global Village," J.J. Linden.

       1982 (10/23): Interview: "Rush Has All the Right Signals," Peter Martin.

       1990 (12/15): Article: "Double Honors For Rush At Toronto Music Awards."

Seconds	1994 #25: Interview (Geddy/Neil): "Rush: Astronomicon — Canadian Space Rock Cosmonauts Confront the Grunge Generation," Steven Blush.
Spin	1990 (4): Review: *Presto.*
	1992 (3): Interview (Neil): "Confessions of a Rush Fan," Bob Mack.
Sound Attitude	1991 (11): Cover, Geddy; Interview (Geddy), Kevin Michaels.
Sounds (UK)	1977 (2/5): Article: "Caress of Steel — Poor Man's Zeppelin? Or Underrated Scions of Sword and Sorcery Rock? Geoff Barton States the Case for Rush."
	1980 (4/5): Interview (Neil): "The Moustache That Conquered the World," Sylvie Simmons.
	1981 (3/14): Interview (Geddy): "Permanent Raves," John Gill.
	1982 (12/18): Article, Interview (Geddy): "Adrenalin Rush," Pete Makowski.
	1983 (1): Fan Library (all Rush issue, 48pp.).
	1985 (10/19): Review: *Power Windows.*
	1988 (5/7): Interview (Geddy): "Another Round of … Rush N Roulette," Mr. Spencer.
	1989 (1): Review: *A Show of Hands.*
	1989 (12/2): Review: *Presto.*
Fanzines	**The Spirit of Rush** (UK): 55+ issues (1987–99)
	Rush Backstage Club: 17 issues (1981–96)
	Tom Sawyer's Treasure: 3 issues (1993–94)

Recorded Interviews

Note: This is not a listing of all recordings, just a few that are known to exist and that may have aided in the research of this book. See also CD and 12″ special editions for additional interviews that were part of the Anthem, Mercury, or Atlantic label releases. Each entry notes the year, followed by the month and day, where this information is available.

LP and CD

BBC Rock Hour (LP)

1981 (8/2) #231: The Rush Special w/Alex, 53 min.
1982 #308: Rush/Bob and Doug McKenzie
1983 (3/22) :#421: Second Annual Tribute to the Great White North (Rush/Bob and Doug)

In the Studio with host Redbeard (The Album Network): 60 min. CD or tape

1989 (1/2) #163: Moving Pictures (Geddy/Alex)
1991 (8/5) #163 show repeated
1996 (4/22): Power Windows/Hold Your Fire (Alex) CD
1996 (9/2) #428: Counterparts/Victor (Alex) CD
1999 (4/19) #565: Signals/Grace Under Pressure (Neil) CD

Jim Ladd Innerview (LP unless specified)

1978: Neil 50m
1980 (5/25) (15-5): Neil, 60 min.
1981 (2/1) (15-5): repeat
1981 (5/18) (18-4): repeat
1981 (9/23) (17-7): Neil interview
1981 (12/27): repeat of above
1983 (2/17-18): Geddy 85m (24½)
1983 (4/11): same as above 2 LP
1984 (7/23): Neil 50 min. (29-3)
1986 (1/1): Neil 45 min. (36-1)

King Biscuit Flower Hour (Direct Broadcasting)

1981 (10/18): Rush/Ian Hunter, 2 LP, 3 tracks
1983 (9/4): The Best of the Biscuit: Rush/Squeeze, 2 LP, same tracks as above
1986 (8/3) #639: Grace Under Pressure concert (all the rest of the CDs used this performance)
1987 (12/20): CD (withdrawn by band)
1990 (12/10): Compilation CD
1991 (3/11): CD
1993 (11/29): CD
1993 (12/5): CD
1995 (1/9): CD
1998 (11/30-12/6): CD

Legends of Rock (NBC)

1987 (5/11-24) 4 LP NBC (87-19) 110 min.
1988 (6/27-7/3) 2 LP

Live Cuts (CD)   1989 (1/22)
1989 (5/4)
1989 (7/31)

Live From Central Park (TBS Syndication)

#TBS-CP-15 (same as 1981 King Biscuit Flower Hour performance)

Metalshop (1 LP, all with Geddy unless noted)

1986 (4/25)
1987 (10/23)
1989 (1/13)
1989 (2/10): Marathon-live
1989 (2/24)
1989 (12/1): Show Don't Tell
1989 (12/8)
1990 (5/11): War Paint
1991 (2/8): Fly by Night
1991 (3/1): Presentation

(2 LP with other bands)
1989 (1/13)
1989 (12/8) Feature Interview: Rush
1990 (2/23) (Making Memories)
1990 (4/20)
1990 (6/22) (Closer…)
1991 (10/4)
1992 (3/27)
1992 (3/30)
1993 (9/3)
1993 (10/22): Alex

Off the Record with Mary Turner (60m 2 LP)

1981 (7/13): all 3 members interview, 54 min.
1982 (3/29): Geddy and Neil, 10 min.1982 (11/1) #82-44: Geddy, 56 min.
1984 (8/27) #84-36: Neil, 60 min.
1984 (12/10) #84-51: repeat of above
1986 (1/20) #86-04: Geddy, Alex, 56 min.
1987 (11/2) #87-45
1988 (2/8) #88-07: Geddy, 49 min.
1989 (3/13) #89-12: Geddy, 53 min.
1989 (5/8): Off The Record Special
1989 (12/25) #89-53: Geddy, 50 min.
1992 (3/9) #92-11: Neil, 52 min., 2 LP
1992 (6/29) #92-27: CD repeat of above
1993 (12/6) #93-50: CD repeat of above
1994 (4/4) #94-15: CD repeat of above
1997 (4/7) #97-15: OTR Classic CD
1997 (5/19) #97-21: OTR Special: Rush/Sponge
1998 (12/5-6) #98-49: OTR Special: Rush/Cake

PFM Guest DJ (3 LPs)

1984 (7/9): Greg Kihn/Geddy Lee WNEW FM, 35 min.

Rock Stars (Radio Today)

1989 (12/11-24) #034: Geddy with host John Sebastian, 2 CDs, 110 min.

Rolling Stone　　1981: Canadian Rock (Rolling Stone Prod. RSMP3281-X) 2 LP
1983 (1/30): (issued 1989) Continuous History of Rock and Roll (60 min. CD)
band interviews

Scott Muni's World of Rock (Direct Broadcasting)

1989 (1/7) #28: Geddy + 6 tracks, 40 min.

The Source (NBC) 3 LP unless noted

1980 (3/28-30): St. Louis live show, 2 LP
1982 (3/19): The Rush Special
1983 (2/27)
1983 (12/12): The Rush Christmas Countdown (#83-53)

1984 (6/10): Total Access Pass Profile: Rush (#84-21), 120 min., 2 LP
1986 (5/23): Rush: Profile '86 (#86-05), 60 min.

Supergroups In Concert (3 LP's live)

1983 (10/8): Rush/Black Sabbath (from Exit Stage Left recording)

Up Close (Media America)

1990 (2/13): 2 CD, 118 min.
1991 (10/9): 2 CD
1994 (1/17): 3 CD, 86 min.
1998 (11/7-14): 2 CD

Westwood One Radio (60 min. tape)

1984
1989
1990 (12/10): 2 CD
1992 (11): Neil interview

Radio Call-In Shows

Rockline (Global Satellite Network)
1984 (5/21): Geddy, 90 min.
1985 (11/18): Geddy, 80 min.
1987 (10/5): Geddy, 70 min.
1989 (2/6): Geddy, Alex 68 min.
1989 (12/4): Geddy, 73 min.
1990 (4/30): Geddy, Alex, 69 min.
1991 (12/2): Neil, 78 min.
1992 (5/18): Geddy, 89 min.
1994 (1/24): Geddy, Alex, 79 min.
1994 (11/21): Neil (Burning For Buddy), 77 min.
1996 (1/15): Alex, 77 min.
1996 (9/23): Geddy, Alex, 89 min.
1999 (1/20): Geddy, Alex, 90 min.
2000 (11/29): Geddy

Interview CDs

1988: Tribute to Sam Sniderman (Geddy speaks and Rush song)
1991 (7/4): The Spirit of Rush Holiday Radio Special (Global Satellite Network), 3 CDs, 150 min. ❶ 200 made
1992 (4/20) Rock and the Environment (Neil), 2 CD

❶ **Disc 1** Fly By Night, In The Mood, Working Man, Temples Of Syrinx, Sweet Memories, What Your Doing, Closer To The Heart, La Villa Strangiato, The Trees.

Disc 2 Spirit Of Radio, Freewill, Limelight, Tom Sawyer, Red Barchetta, New World Man, Subdivisions, Distant Early Warning, Red Sector A, The Body Electric.

Disc 3 The Big Money, Territories, Manhattan Project, Time Stand Still, Mission, Mystic Rhythms, The Pass, Show Don't Tell.

7″ Amnesty Interview Discs

No # : Hold Your Fire
No # : A Show of Hands cover

United Kingdom 12″ Interview Picture Discs

1982 Chris Tetley Interview with Alex (Geddy/Al cover)Rock Sagas CT1026
1987 (9) Baktabak Interviews: Alex (Baktabak BAK 2083) 31 min.

United Kingdom CD Interviews

1992 The Story of the Kings (Sept. 1987 Alex interview reissue) Bakatabak CBAK 4055
1996 Rush The Interviews Volume 2: Geddy Lee (June 1993 int.) Baktabak CBAK 4064

Miscellaneous Interviews Not Formally Released

1977 (6/11): Newcastle, "Keep On Truckin' 46 min.
1991 (11/10): 103 WLZR Milwaukee, 2 min.
1991 (11/10) 103 WLZR Milwaukee (DJ at Bradley Center) 2 min.
1993 (9/26): Counterparts advance broadcast DC101, 25 min.
1994 (2): 103 WLZR Milwaukee, 2 min.

Alex and Neil: 1994: Chronicles with Keith Elshaw, 90 min.

Geddy and Alex: 1979 (9/10): WABX Detroit, 24 min.
1979 (9/10): WRIF Detroit, 13 min.
1980 (6/21): 10 min.
1981 (3/24): Toronto, ON radio, 4 min.
1981 (5/19): The Robert Klein Show #35 23m aired 6/21/81
1988 (11/11): Toronto Music Awards, 15 min.
1990 (9/15): Malibu Music and Tennis Festival Malibu, CA, 25 min.
1997 (10/12): Q107 Toronto
1998 (12/3): Q107 Toronto

Geddy and Neil: 1990 (2): S.W. Lowdown (Seattle), 4 min.

Geddy: 1977 (8): CHUM-FM Toronto "AFTK World Premiere" 18 min.
1978 (11/24-25): Earth News Radio, 5 min.
1979 (4/29): Newcastle Metro Radio, 13 min.
1979 (5/28): Offenbach, Germany, 46 min.
1980 (6/21): Radio One, London, England, 15 min.
1980 (12/21): Billboard Report, 5 min.
1981 (2/11): CHUM-FM Toronto (with Terry Brown) 36m
1981 (2/11): CHUM-FM Toronto, 50 min.
1984 (5/3): CHUM-FM Toronto, 15 min.
1984 (6/29): WLSF Chicago, 5 min.
1985: KERRANG! party, 5 min.
1985 (10/17): Q107 Toronto, 10 min.
1986 (5/12): Rock Chronicles, 5 min.
1987 (9): WNEW New York, 30 min.
1987 (9): Q107 Toronto 30m

1987 (9/22): WNEW New York City, 46 min.

1987 (11/14): WPHD Buffalo, 90 min.

1987 (11/22): Rock Today, 7 min.

1989 (1/8): The World of Rock, 50 min.

1989 (3/6): High Voltage, 5 min.

1989 (12): Streetcorner Q107, Toronto, 50 min.

1990 (1/13): The World of Rock, 40 min.

1990 (2/28): KSHE St. Louis/ Fever Prod., 18 min.

1990 (6/8): WMMS Cleveland, 7 min.

1990 (6/26): Backstage, Sacramento, 15 min.

1990 (6/27): KOME Oakland, 10 min.

1991 (8/19): Frank Lancaster interview

1991 (9/2): WNEW New York, 50 min.

1991 (12/9): WHJY Backstage, Providence 7m

1992 (1/27): Rock Today

1993 (10/6): Munich, Germany, 37 min.

1994 (1/22): Pensacola, FL

1994 (2): WLZR Milwaukee 1m

1994 (2/5): KLOS-FM Anaheim, CA 5 min.

1994 (2/11): San Francisco, CA1997 (2/27): Q107 Toronto 15 min.

1999 (1/25): Rocktropolis "Rock and the Environment"

2000 (11/13): Opie & Anthony show New York, 102.7 WNEW-FM

2000 (11/24): HTZ-FM, St. Catherines, ON, 50 min.

2000 (11/29): Christopher Rude, 96 Rock

2000 (11/30): Mike and Brian show, KLOS-FM Anaheim

Alex: 1978 (2/17) Glasgow, Scotland, 22 min.1980 (6/19) Radio Piccadilly, Manchester, England, 10 min.

1981 (11/19) Stuttgart, Germany, 10 min.

1984 (10/2) WAAF, Worcester, MA, 10 min.

1985 (10/21) Capitol Radio, 40 min.

1985 (11) Power Hour England, 5 min.

1986 (1/30) "Stonetrack", San Francisco, 10 min.

1987 (9/18) In Holland, 10 min.

1987 (9) Power Hour England, 10 min.

1987 (9) Radio City England, 15 min.

1987 (9) Piccadilly Radio England, 25 min.

1987 (9) BBC Liverpool, 25 min.

1987 (12/15) WDVE-FM Pittsburgh, 15m

1988 (1/20) Q102-FM Dallas TX, 65 min.

1988 (4/26) Glasgow, Scotland, 20 min.

1988 (4/28) Radio 210 (Reading, Eng.), 32 min.

1988 (8/27) WMMR Philadelphia B-Man (John Rutsey also phoned), 25 min.

1989 (12) Streetcorner Q107, 20 min.

1990 (2/28) KSHE St. Louis, 35 min.

1990 (3/24) KGON Portland, OR, 2 min.

1990 (3/30) KOME Oakland, 5 min.

1990 (11/20) Q107-FM Toronto, 15 min.

1991 (12/16) Q107 Backstage, Toronto (w/Tragically Hip), 19 min.

1994 (5/3) Albany "The Spirit of Rush", 35 min.

1994 (5/6) Montreal
1998 (11/27) HTZ-FM, St. Catharines, ON, 25 min.

Neil:

1978 Rock Around the World, 15 min.
1978 (1/30) Davenport, IA 10 min.
1979 Backstage Special w/Jimmy Roach, 40 min.
1979 BBC, 15 min.
1979 Manchester, England, 40 min.
1980 (2/17) WABX Detroit, 20 min.
1983 (5/24) Radio Clyde Glasgow, Scot., 50 min.
1984 (5) KTXQ Dallas, 105 min.
1984 (10/2) KGB101 San Diego
1984 Private Interview, 35 min.
1986 (1/12) KZEW Dallas, 5 min.
1987 (12/9) Uniondale, NY, 10 min.
1991 (4/8) Buddy Rich Memorial Scholarship Concert, 23 min.
1992 (1/28) Q107 Toronto, "One on One", 30 min.
1992 (2) KISW Seattle "Rock and the Environment", 9 min.
1994 (10/13) Q107, Toronto, 30 min.
1996 (11/6) Morningside (CBC radio), 20 min.
1997 (4) Q107 Toronto, 20 min.

Telephone Interviews

Geddy:

1980 (2) Scene Magazine in Clevelend (Geddy from Toronto), 40 min.
1983 (2/26) CHOM-FM Montreal, 10 min.
1984 (11/2) WMMR Philadelphia, with B-Man, 7 min.
1987 (11/14) WPHD Buffalo, 34 min.
1994 (1/21) WTKX Pensacola, 10 min.
1997 (3/31) Budweiser Sports Forum, 16 min.
1997 (6) WYSP, Philadelphia, 5 min.

Alex:

1990 (2/28) KSHE St. Louis, 18 min.

Neil:

1991 (12/9) Q107 Toronto, "One On One", 55 min.

Radio Specials

1982 (9) Signals, 54 min.
1984 (4) Grace Under Pressure, 54 min.
1991 (8/27) Roll the Bones, Geddy, Alex (host Dan Near), 71 min.
1993 (10/14) Counterparts, Geddy, Alex (host Steve Warden), 100 min.
1996 (1/10) Victor, Alex (host Steve Warden), 60 min.
1996 (9) Test For Echo, Geddy, Alex, Neil (host Jo Robinson), 85 min.
1996 (9/5) Test For Echo, Geddy, Alex (host Steve Warden), 85 min.
1998 (11/4) Different Stages, Geddy, Alex, 120 min., 2 CDs
2000 (11/12) Geddy Lee: My Favourite Headache (host Jim Ladd), 75 min.

Radio Spots

1998 (2) R.A.D.D. (Rockers Against Drunken Driving): Geddy promo spot

Television Interviews

A list of notable (but not every one of) Rush's TV appearances.

US TV Appearances

1982: HBO Intermission: Heart of Gold: Geddy speaks on Canadian Rock, Donald Sutherland
   narrates.
1983 (2): MTV News: Alex in San Diego/ "Countdown" 5 minute highlight of a 25 minute
   interview.
1984 (5): MTV News (Geddy)
1985: Nick Rocks (Nickelodeon) Rush plugs show spot
1985: MTV Studios (Geddy on Power Windows)
1987: Showbiz Today (Geddy in Steinberger story)
1989 (11/14): MTV Studios (Geddy)
1989 (12): MTV Now Hear This (Geddy holiday wish)
1992 (6): ABC-TV In Concert — Rush profiled
1993 (7/13): 64th Annual All-Stars Major League Baseball Game (Baltimore) Geddy sings
   Canadian anthem
1994 (11/3): Politically Incorrect with Bill Maher (HBO) (Neil)
2000 (11/18): VH1 Rockshow (Geddy)

Muchmusic Appearances

1987 (11): In the Spotlight: Rush Hour (Hold Your Fire)
1989 (1): In the Spotlight: Rush Hour (same as above but with A Show of Hands preview
   at end)
1990: In the Spotlight: Presto
1991: In the Spotlight: Roll the Bones
1991: Roll the Bones video shoot (11m interview with video actor, director and Neil)
1991 (12/10): Geddy/Alex interview (Detroit '91 live clips)
1992: Geddy interviewed
1992 (5): Alex in Canadian Air Force
1993 (9/5): Kumbaya Festival-Alex
1993 (10): Intimate and Interactive-A Concert of Politics (Neil interviews Prime Minister
   (Lib.) Jean Chretien)
1993: In the Spotlight: Counterparts
1994 (9/4): Kumbaya Festival-Alex (Pye Dubois reads "Between Sun and Moon" poem too)
   1994: Burning For Buddy Special
1995 (9/2): Kumbaya Festival-Alex (with the "Boomers")
1996 (9/17): Muchmusic Awards (Geddy presents award)
1996: The New Music (Geddy at seaquarium with concert footage from New Orleans)
1996: Big Life (Geddy)

Canadian TV Appearances

1974: Boogie — Rush
1979 (6-4): Pink Pop Festival (La Villa Strangiato 7 min. excerpt and interview)
1979 (8): Ivor Wynn Stadium concert clips of Jacob's Ladder and The Spirit of Radio, and
   Geddy interview (2 min.)

R · U · S · H

1979: Digging Through the Vaults (Ray Danniels) 3m
    Reaired with '79 footage, Subdivisions and Countdown bits in 1982.
1980: CityTV live bits from 5-80 Buffalo Memorial Auditorium (3 mins of 2112 Temples of Syrinx)
1980: CityTV (11 min. soundcheck and interview)
1981: Geddy at CHUM-FM
1981: 1980 in Canadian Rock (Buffalo '80 live footage)
1985: Northern Lights (83 min.) Geddy
1990 (1): Rock and Reading (1 min. Geddy interview)
1990 (1): Rock and Reading (3 min. Neil interview)
1990 (5/14): Musique Plus (10 min. interview)
1990 Hot Licks-The Space Between the Notes (Alex 9m)
1990 Andrew MacNaughtan (6 min.; Geddy interviewed also)
1991 (11): Musique Plus (Geddy interview)
1992 (4/24): 4m interview with Alex backstage at Wembley
1996 (9): Live With Pamela Wallin (Neil)
1997 (4/22): Life Network-Live On Life with John Oakley (Neil)
1998 (5/5): Life Network-Life With Erica Ehm (Justin Lifeson)
1999 (5/14): Pamela Wallin and Co. (Geddy, Salman Rushdie, Rheostatics)
2000 (11/10): CBC Newsworld "On the Arts" (Geddy)
2000 (11/10): Open Mike with Mike Bullard (Geddy)

Juno Awards

1980 (4): Gary McCracken (Max Webster drummer) and Alex present award
1981 (4): Alex presents award
1994 (3/20): Hall of Fame
1999 (3/7): Geddy presents award

Other Taped Awards

1983: LaBatt Music Express (Band accepts award on videotape)
1984: Labatt Rock Express Awards (Geddy accepts award as best live group) 2 min.
1990 (11/20): CARAS Artists of the Decade (all members) of the 136 min. show only 16 min. is Rush
1990 (12/5): 4th Toronto Music Awards (Geddy and Neil win awards; band accepts)
1993: Greater Toronto Music Awards (Rush's parents interviewed)
1993 (5/9): Harvard Lampoon (Cambridge, MA) Musicians of the Millenium Ceremony
1997 (2/26): Royal Order of Canada proceedings (Rideau Hall, Ottawa, ON)
1999 (5/27): Canadian Walk of Fame (Roy Thompson Hall)

Foreign or Untelevised Appearances

1984 (11/27): Japanese interview with Geddy and Alex (5m)
1985 (10/22): Old Grey Whistle Test (Alex) 5m
1985: German show Power haus (Kerrang! party with Geddy)
1990 (9): Malibu Tennis Fest-Geddy, Alex playing with Kansas and Mr. Big
1991 (11/26): Electric Press Kit (concert footage)
1992 (4/23): Koln, Germany (5m backstage interview with Alex)
1992: Rock Hard (Alex/Primus interview)

1985: The Making of The Big Money (7m) animation only
1987: The Making of Time Stand Still
1991: The Making of Roll the Bones (4m) animation only

TV Spots

1981 Moving Pictures
1982 Signals
1982 Signals New World Tour
1984 Grace Under Pressure
1984 Muchmusic Channel (Geddy)
1985 Power Windows
1987 Hold Your Fire
1988 A Show of Hands
1989 Presto (Camelot Music)
1990 Chronicles
1991 Roll the Bones
1992 Tower Records (Grammy Nominees-Roll the Bones video shown)
1992 Canadian public service announcement with Geddy and "Ghost of a Chance"
1993 Counterparts
1996 Test For Echo (Camelot Music)
1998 Different Stages
2000 Nissan Maxima commercial (Tom Sawyer)

Night Flight (USA)

1981 – 85: Exit … Stage Left concert
1985: Grace Under Pressure videos and concert
1985: Take Off to Canada Rock ("The Big Money")
1985: Power Windows album special

MTV Saturday Night Concert

1982 (2/13): Exit … Stage Left
1986 (4/19): Grace Under Pressure Tour (re-aired 12/19/87)

Miscellaneous Showings

1974 (12/6) Don Kirschner Rock Concert: taped 10/9/74 - re-aired concert; Christmas 1977
    with other videos and in 1978 with Hemispheres videos.
1991 (6): Global Jam — "The Spirit of Radio" and "Tom Sawyer" from A Show of Hands
1998 (5/16) VH1 Pop Up Video — #81-Canadian Invasion (Limelight; Northern Lights)

Rush References in Books

The Defenders #45 (Mar. 1977, Marvel)

dedicated to Rush with 2112 references
2112 (1992, Dark Horse Comics)

Cinematic References

Movies With Rush Tracks

Gas (Paramount, 1981)

In this Canadian comedy we hear "Limelight".

Incident at Channel Q (PMV, 1985)

This film, financed by Val Azzoli, did see a theatrical release. "The Body Electric" is the first video played in the title channel. "The Camera Eye" is featured in the chase scene and a character wearing miscellaneous Rush shirts is featured.

The Body Electric (1985)

Animated feature aired on TV and simulcast on radio.

Small Soldiers (Universal, 1998)

In this kids' action movie, a "Tom Sawyer" remix is heard in the scene where the character played by Kristen Dunst is talking on the phone in her room.

Whatever (Sony Pictures Classics, 1998)

"Tom Sawyer" is on the soundtrack album to this indie and is played loudly up to the solo in the party scene set in 1981.

The Waterboy (Touchstone, 1998)

"Tom Sawyer" is on the soundtrack to this Adam Sandler blockbuster and is looped in the final football game sequence.

Strange Frequency (VH1, 2000)

"Tom Sawyer" again is used in a sequence.

Movies With Rush Images

Over the Edge (Orion, 1979)

Guy in Rush t-shirt.

The Last American Virgin (Cannon, 1982)

Rush largely written on a student's folder when he comes down stairs in school.

Strange Brew (MGM, 1983)

Lakeside Park sign; Moving Pictures' Parliament Building.

A Nightmare On Elm Street (New Line, 1984)

Grace Under Pressure poster above Johnny Depp's character's bed.

The Gate (New Century Ent., 1987)

A live 1981 poster in the metalhead character's room. Canadian movie … that explains it.

Orgazmo (October Films, 1998)
Photographer says "Smile and say Geddy Lee." Someone asks, "Who's that?" and he says, "The best bass player in the world."

S.L.C. Punk! (Sony Pictures Classics, 1999)
Salt Lake City punks in the early '80s reveal they listened to Rush before discovering punk. Note the Freaks and Geeks character of Nick (the Peartite) is in the cast.

EDTV (Universal, 1999)
Matthew McCanaughey's title character wears a Starman shirt, an understandable reference, as Ron Howard has been interested in a Rush soundtrack.

Star Trek Creator (1999 CDROM Multimedia)
USS Syrinx and USS Lamneth are both names of ships.

Gregory's Girl (Samuel Goldwyn, 1999)

Movies That Inspired Rush

The Last Mile (Astor Pictures, 1932)
"Lock and Key".

Mr. Deeds Goes To Town (Columbia, 1936)
Frank Capra film that inspired "Cinderella Man".

Dr. Strangelove Or How I Learned To Stop Worrying and Love the Bomb (Columbia, 1964)
This Stanley Kubrick picture inspired the "Distant Early Warning" video concept.

2001: A Space Odyssey (MGM, 1968)
Also a Kubrick film, Rush has used the familiar opening theme (Thus Spake Zarathustra) in concerts and cartoon images in the Manhattan Project rear projection screenand in TFE insert.

Eraserhead (Columbia, 1977)
David Lynch fantasy drama. A poster for it hung in Le Studio in the '80s and Geddy often wore a promo button.

The Turning Point (1982)
For the dancer in "Losing It".

Blue Velvet (D.E.G., 1986)
Another David Lynch movie, contains the line "Now it's dark," which was used in RTB liner notes.

Books

Lyric Books

The Words and the Pictures Vol. I (1979)
Issued as a tour program on the 1979 Warmup Tours. Reproductions of Neil's handwritten original lyric sheets. Foreward by Geoff Barton.

The Words and the Pictures Vol. II (1979)
Covers Permanent Waves lyrics too.

Songbooks
(all from Warner Bros. Music Publishing)

Hemispheres	VF0670 UK AM28424
Permanent Waves	VF0746
Moving Pictures	VF0872
Exit … Stage Left	VF0945
Deluxe Anthology	VF0901 (1982) ❶ 39 trks
Signals	VF1011
Complete	VF1063 (all LPs to Signals, inc. "Thrice-Told Tales" intro by Neil) '83
Grace Under Pressure	VF1135
Power Windows	VF1263
Complete Vol. I	VF1284 ('74 – '78) 1985
Complete Vol. II	VF1285 ('80 – '85) 1985
Hold Your Fire	VF1424
Retrospective	VF1475 (1988) ❷ 38 trks
A Show of Hands	VF1522
Presto	VF1622
Chronicles	VF1682
Roll the Bones	GF0486
Anthology	GF1872 ❸ 164pp (rel. 10/92)
Counterparts	VF2087
Test For Echo	PG9658

❶ Anthem, Bastille Day, By-Tor & The Snow Dog, Cinderella Man, Closer To The Heart, Different Strings, Entre Nous, A Farewell To Kings, Finding My Way, Fly By Night, Freewill, Hemispheres, Jacob's Ladder, La Villa Strangiato, Lakeside Park, Limelight, Madrigal, Natural Science, No One At The Bridge, Red Barchetta, Something For Nothing, The Spirit Of Radio, Tom Sawyer, The Trees, 2112 (minus Discovery and Oracle), The Twilight Zone, Working Man, Xanadu.

❷ Between The Wheels, The Big Money, Broon's Bane, By-Tor & The Snow Dog, The Camera Eye, Closer To The Heart, Different Strings, Distant Early Warning, Emotion Detector, The Enemy Within, Finding My Way, Fly By Night, Freewill, In the End, In The Mood, La Villa Strangiato, Lakeside Park, Lessons, Limelight, Lock & Key, Losing It, Middletown Dreams, Mission, Mystic Rhythms, Natural Science, The Necromancer, New World Man, Red Barchetta, Something For Nothing, Spirit Of Radio, Subdivisions, Time Stand Still, Tom Sawyer, The Trees, Vital Signs, Working Man, Xanadu.

● Between The Wheels, The Big Money, The Big Wheel, The Body Electric, Broon's Bane, The Camera Eye, Closer To The Heart, The Enemy Within, Fly By Night, Jacob's Ladder, Limelight, Madrigal, New World Man, Different Strings, Distant Early Warning, Emotion Detector, Free Will, Mystic Rhythms, No One At The Bridge, Presto, Red Barchetta, Red Sector A, Roll The Bones, The Spirit Of Radio, Something For Nothing, Tom Sawyer The Trees, Xanadu, YYZ.

"Classic Rush" Series:

Grace Under Pressure	GF0472 (1992)
Moving Pictures	GF0494(1992)
Presto	GF(1992) "Selections From…" (8 trks only)
Permanent Waves	GF0614 (1994)
Counterparts	GF0631 (1996) "Selections From…" (8 trks only)

Super Tab "Classic Rush" Series:

Anthology	GF0518
Guitar Anthology	PG9530 (1995) ●
Bass Anthology	0138B (1999) ●

● A Passage To Bangkok, Closer To The Heart, Cold Fire, Distant Early Warning, Dreamline, Freewill, Red Sector A, Roll The Bones, Spirit Of Radio, The Trees, Tom Sawyer, YYZ, Xanadu, La Villa Strangiato, Limelight, New World Man, Red Barchetta, Show Don't Tell, Stick It Out, Working Man

● Closer to the Heart, Cold Fire, Distant Early Warning, Dreamline, Free Will, La Villa Strangiato, Limelight, New World Man, Presto, Red Barchetta, Roll the Bones, Show Don't Tell, The Spirit of Radio, Test for Echo, Tom Sawyer, The Trees, 2112: Overture/Temples of Syrinx, Working Man, YYZ, Xanadu.

Miscellaneous Musical Transcription Books

Drum Lessons With the Greats Vol. 2
by John Xepoleas.New York: Warner Bros. Publications, 1995, ISBN: 1576232557.

Neil is first of 6 drummers to demonstrate fills for "YYZ", "Show Don't Tell", "Roll the Bones" and all of "Leave That Thing Alone!"; he does not speak. Includes 2 CDs.

Drum Techniques of Rush	DF0010 (1985) ●
Drum Superstar Series: More Rush	DF0029 (1989) ●
Guitar Techniques of Rush	GF0269 (1986)
Guitar Superstar Series: Rush	GF0290
Bass Superstar Series: Rush	IF0198 (1986)
The Music of Rush Made Easy For Guitar	GF0217 (2 diff. covers)
The Best of Rush	VF1201 10 trks
The Best of Rush For Guitar	GF0357
The Best of Yes and Rush For Guitar (Dual Dynamite Series)	GF0484
The Essential Progressive Rock Guitar	GF9608
Looking For Drummer: Rush (1 tape)	
Star Jam Series: Neil Peart Style (2 tapes)	
Starlicks Guitar Lesson: Alex Lifeson Style (2 tapes)	

❶ Limelight, Subdivisions

❷ The Analog Kid, A Farewell to Kings, Manhattan Project, Marathon, Red Sector A, Vital Signs, 2112.

Sheet Music

2112: Overture/Temples of Syrinx
Closer To the Heart
The Trees
The Spirit of Radio
Tom Sawyer
YYZ
Red Barchetta
Limelight
New World Man
Distant Early Warning
The Big Money
Presto
Dreamline
Roll the Bones
Where's My Thing?
Stick It Out

Tourbooks
(with text by Neil)

United States

A Farewell to Kings (purple cover)	Thrice Told Tales: A Rush Primer
Tour of the Hemispheres	
Permanent Waves	Personal Waves
Moving Pictures	A Rush Newsreel
Signals	Stories From Signals
Grace Under Pressure	Pressure Release
Power Windows	Looking Through Power Windows
Hold Your Fire	Fireworks
Presto	Scissors Paper Stone
Roll the Bones ❶	Row the Boats
Counterparts	Wilderness of Mirrors
Test For Echo ❷	
An Evening With Rush (VIP Programme)	

❶ Some versions picture *Chronicles* in discography section.

❷ Some editions misprinted an Alex Lifeson picture twice on page 5. Summer 1997 tour versions had "Retrospective" covers in discography section. Tourbooks were from 1980 to 1984 had 16 pages, from 1985 to present 28 pages.

United Kingdom

2112
A Farewell To Kings (white cover)
Tour of the Hemispheres (with Max Webster ad)
Moving Pictures

Japan

Grace Under Pressure (35 pp)

Tour Riders

Hold Your Fire
Presto

Published Non-Fiction

The Golden Lion by Neil Peart
Privately published, 1987, 100 numbered copies.

The African Drum by Neil Peart
Privately published, 1988, 100 numbered copies.

Radiance Over the Rockies by Neil Peart
Toronto: Cumberland Press, 1988.

The Masked Rider: Cycling in West Africa by Neil Peart
Lawrencetown Beach, NS: Pottersfield Press, 1996, ISBN 1895900026.

Published Fiction

"Drumbeats" by Neil Peart and Kevin J. Anderson, in **Shock Rock II,** ed. by Jeff Gelb.
New York: Pocket Books, 1994, ISBN 0671870882.

Biographies

Rush by Brian Harrigan
New York & London: Omnibus Press, 1982, 88 pp, ISBN: 0860019349.
Harrigan wrote for *Melody Maker* in the 1970s, and the pictures are largely from that era.

Rush: Success Under Pressure by Steve Gett
Port Chester, NY: Cherry Lane Books ("Rock Read" Series), 1984, 48 pp, ISBN: 0895242303.
Many color pictures, aimed at intermediate (teen) readers.

Rush: Visions The Official Biography by Bill Banasiewicz.

New York & London: Omnibus Press, 1988, 96 pp, ISBN: 0711911622.

The only authorized biography thus far; pictures were used liberally from Geddy's scrapbooks. In later years the band would not endorse the book. US/UK versions differ in a few pictures.

Program Books with Rush Coverage

12/90 4th Annual Toronto Music Awards, Canada
3/94 Juno Awards, Canada

Comic Books

Rock and Roll Comics #49 (July 1992)
Unauthorized bio with notorious mistakes like Geddy's real name erroneously listed as Gary Leibovitch.

Revolutionary #1 (April 1994 Canadian version)
Same as above, slightly different cover.

Instrument Books

Bass Heroes: Styles, Stories & Secrets of 30 Great Bass Players/from the Pages of Guitar Player Magazine by Tom Milhern (ed.)
San Francisco: Miller Freeman, 1993, 201 pp, ISBN: 0879302747.

Rickenbacker: History of the Rickenbacker Guitar by Richard R. Smith
Milwaukee, WI: Hal Leonard Corp., 1988, 256pp, ISBN: 0931759153.

The PRS Guitar Book: A Compete History of Paul Reed Smith Guitars
by Dave Burrlock, Tim Wheeler.
San Francisco, CA: Backbeat Books, 1999, 126 pp, ISBN: 0879305932.

A-Z of Rock Guitarists by Chris Charlesworth.
New York, NY: Proteus Publishing Co., 1983, 128 pp, ISBN: 086276081X.

A-Z of Rock Drummers by Harry Shapiro.
New York, NY: Proteus Publishing Co., 1983, 128 pp, ISBN: 0553057758.

The Best of Modern Drummer (Rock)
The Best of Modern Drummer Vol. II

Modern Drummer Publications (excerpts from Neil interviews).

History of the Ludwig Drum Company by William and Paul Schmidt.
Fullerton, CA: Centerstream, 1995, 178 pp, ISBN: 0931759498.

Star Sets: Drum Kits of the Great Drummers by Jon Cohan.
Milwaukee, WI: Hal Leonard Corp., 1995, 160 pp, ISBN: 0793534895.

The Drum Book by Geoff Nicholls.
San Francisco, CA: Miller Freeman, 1997, 108 pp, ISBN: 0879304766.

Lyric Analysis Books

Mystic Rhythms: The Philosophical Vision of Rush by Robert and Carol Price.
San Bernadino, CA: Borgo Press, 1998, 160 pp, ISBN: 0809508001; rpt 1999, Wildside Press,
ISBN: 1587151022

Volume One of Woodstock Series' Popular Music of Today.
Excellent analysis of Rush themes like power, self-reliance, individuality, etc. Two covers
pressed, a greenish textbook style cover and on the reprint, a guitar silhouette design.

Miscellaneous Books with Rush References

Skinny Legs and All by Tom Robbins.
New York: Bantam, 1990, 432 pp, ISBN: 0553057758.
Neil offers praise inside this novel.

Mondo Canuck: A Canadian Pop Culture Odyssey by Geoff Pevere.
Toronto: Prentice Hall Canada, 1996.

Tributes

Primus (bootlegs from 1989)
The Spirit of Radio

Primus: *Frizzle Fry* (Caroline 1619) 1990
YYZ

Primus: *Suck On This* (Caroline 1620) 1990
YYZ intro on John the Fisherman.

Solomon Grundy
"Spirit of Radio" unreleased

Barenaked Ladies: *Gordon* (Sire 26956) 1992
"Grade 9" features parts of Xanadu and Tom Sawyer.

Skid Row: *B-Sides Ourselves* (Atlantic 82431-2) 1992
What You're Doing.

Groove Daddys: *Sunburn* (Alert) 1995
Subdivisions

Working Man, A Tribute to Rush (Magna Carta MA-9010-2) 1996

13 tracks mixed by Terry Brown.

"Working Man": Sebastian Bach (vocals), Jake E. Lee (guitar), Mike Portnoy (drums), Billy Sheehan (bass), Brendt Allman (rhythm guitar).
BY-TOR AND THE SNOW DOG: (same performers except James La Brie on vocals).
"The Analog Kid": Jack Russell (vocals), Michael Romeo (guitar), Miek Pinnella (keyboards), Mike Portnoy (drums), Billy Sheehan (bass), Brendt Allman (rhythm guitar).

"The Trees": Mike Baker (vocals), Brendt Allman (lead and rhythm guitars), Chris Ingels (piano), Mike Portnoy (drums), Billy Sheehan (bass), Gary Wehrkamp (keyboards).
"La Villa Strangiato": Steve Morse (classical guitar/main solo), Mike Portnoy (drums), Billy Sheehan (bass), Brendt Allman (rhythm guitar), James Murphy (ending guitar solo and keyboards), David Townson (rhythm guitar).
"Mission": Eric Martin (vocals, Brad Keiser (drums), Robert Berry (lead guitar, bass, rhythm guitar), Stu Hamm (bass).
"Jacob's Ladder": Sebastian Bach (vocals), John Petrucci (guitars), Matt Guillory (keyboards), Mike Portnoy (drums), Billy Sheehan (bass), Brendt Allman (rhythm guitar).
"Closer to the Heart": Performed by Fates Warning.
"Natural Science": Devin Townsend (vocals), Matt Guillory (keyboards), Deen Castronovo (drums), James Murphy (lead and rhythm guitars), Stu Hamm (bass), David Townson (ending guitar solo).
YYZ: James Murphy (lead and rhythm guitar), Matt Guillory (keyboards), Deen Castronovo (drums), Stu Hamm (bass).
"Red Barchetta": James LaBrie (vocals), Steve Morse (lead guitar), Richard Chycki (rhythm guitars), Sean Malone (bass), Sean Reinert (drums), James Murphy (rhythm guitar/keyboards), David Townson (rhythm guitar).
"Freewill": Gregoor van der Loo (lead vocals), Marcel Coenen (lead guitar), Trent Gardner (keyboards), Jeff Brockman (drums), Carl Cadden-James (bass).

Catharine Wheel: Like Cats and Dogs (1996)
The Spirit of Radio ghost track.

Jaymz Bee and the Royal Jelly Orchestra:
Cocktail-Shakin' and Stirred (BMG 35815) 1997

Closer to the Heart

Yngwie Malmsteen: *Inspiration*
(Foundation 720907-1401-2) 1996

Anthem

Silver Sun: *Too Much, Too Little, Too Late*
EP (Polydor 569 915-2) UK, 1998

Xanadu

Dream Theater FanClub CD (1998)

Tears (an acoustic studio version and live performances). The band has also performed Different Strings live.

Death Organ: *Universal Stripsearch*
(Ad Perpetuum) 1997

Tom Sawyer

Liquid Gang: *Fantastic Pirate Satellite*
EP (Gotham 0032) 1998

Working Man

Greg Howe: *Ascend* (Shrapnel 1128) 1998

La Villa Strangiato

Paul Roraback: *Mother of All Tribute Albums*
(1998)

2112 Overture

Rage: 13 (Victor) 1999

Tom Sawyer

Rachel Barton: *Stringendo: Storming the Citadel*
(Cacophony) 1999

The Spirit of Radio

Red Star: A Tribute to Rush (Dwell DWEL-021) 1999

ANTHEM: Engrave Speed Death
WORKING MAN: Killing Field (version minus the inst. jam)
BASTILLE DAY: Shallows of the Mundane
SUBDIVISIONS: Hostile Intent
WHAT YOU'RE DOING: Hate Theory
TEARS: Capital 2

A PASSAGE TO BANGKOK: Scary German Guy
TOM SAWYER: Disarray
THE TEMPLES OF SYRINX: Blood Coven
FREEWILL: Mythiasin
RED BARCHETTA: Prototype
THE SPIRIT OF RADIO: Premonition

Smashing Pumpkins

Limelight (acoustic) 1999 (not released)

Rage Against the Machine

Rosetta Stone: Unerotica, Spirit of Radio. (Cleopatra CLP09042) 2000

Working Man 2000 (not released/finished)

Sampled Recordings

Young Black Teenagers: *Dead Enz Kidz Doin' Lifetime Bidz* (Elektra) 1994

"Time To Make the Donuts" samples Tom Sawyer. Rush is thanked also.

Remixes

Small Soldiers Soundtrack
(Dreamworks DRMD-50051) 1998

DJ Z-Trip remixes Tom Sawyer.

Small Soldiers sampler promo US CD PRO-CD 5101 1998. 2 edits of TS + Cult

Beastie Boys

Hello Nasty Tour '98 bootlegs. Shows in Canada opened with Tom Sawyer.

Artists Who Thank Rush On Their Liner Notes

Max Webster: *High Class in Borrowed Shoes*
("messieurs Lifeson, Lee and Peart") 1979

Wireless: *Positively Human, Relatively Sane*
("Geddy Lee") 1979

Metallica: *Master of Puppets* ("Geddy, Alex and Neil of Rush") 1986

Jeff Berlin: *Pump It* (track dedicated to Rush) 1986

Mr. Big: *Lean Into It* ("Rush and crewmates") 1991

Mr. Big: *Bump Ahead* ("Rush, Ray Danniels and Crew") 1993

Candlebox: *Lucy* ("Rush") 1995

Pavement: *Brighten the Corners* (Geddy mentioned in lyrics to "Stereo") 1996: "What about the voice of Geddy Lee?/How did it get so high?/I wonder if he speaks like an ordinary guy/ ('I know him and he does')/Well, you're my fact-checkin' cuz."

Ben Folds Five: The Biography of Reinhold Messner ("Geddy Lee") 1999

Rush Collectibles

(**Note**: wallets, patches, bumper stickers, decals, etc. are too varied/numerous and couldn't be listed.)

Metal Pins/Jewelry

Starman pin (AFTK logo, pewter)
Starman necklace (AFTK logo-no man, pewter)
Star with Hemispheres logo
Starman necklace (Hem. Logo, pewter)
Starman gold necklace (Mercury licensed)
Roll the Bones
Rush-Limbo dog tag necklace

Enamel Pins

Starman (various styles, too numerous)
Rush (round 1980 Bi-Rite pin)
Fly By Night (round 1980 Bi-Rite pin)
Caress of Steel (round 1980 Bi-Rite Pin)
2112 (round 1980 Bi-Rite pin)
A Farewell to Kings
Hemispheres (live)
Hemispheres (Starman/logo)
Permanent Waves
Moving Pictures
Exit … Stage Left (black with logo)

Exit … Stage Left (double image of Starman)
Signals
Grace Under Pressure
Power Windows (square LP art)
Hold Your Fire (square LP art)
A Show of Hands (square LP art)
Presto (square LP art)
Roll the Bones (square LP art)
Roll the Bones (boy skeleton)
Chronicles (logo with band pics)
Counterparts (square LP art)
Test For Echo (square LP art)

Hats

Rush (first logo)
2112 (issued 2000 by Backstage Club on red or
    black hats)
Hemispheres (issued in 2000 by Backstage Club)
Moving Pictures (white logo)
Exit Stage Left era painters hat (drawing)
Signals (dog and hydrant)
Grace Under Pressure (1984 written on sides)
Hold Your Fire (issued 2000 by Backstage Club)
Roll the Bones
Counterparts (nut/bolt on back)
Counterparts (large logo)
Test For Echo (stoneman on back)

Calendars

Tama/Ibanez 1984 (Neil with Red Kit)
Ready To Rock 1985 (Geddy on set of The Enemy
Within video for August)
Tama Drums Calendar 1984 (Neil w/red set on
    barge pic)
Roll the Bones (pinwheel promo calendar from
    Anthem), 1992
Kumbaya Festival 1994 (Alex)

Door Signs

Hold Your Fire (Dressing Room, Hospitality,
    Production Office, Tuning Room)
Presto (Tuning Room: Do Not Disturb)
Roll the Bones (Hospitality, Tuning Room)
Counterparts (Dressing Room, Drysdale and Drysdale,
    Hospitality, Tuning Room)
Door wall hanging (2´×6´): Through the Camera Eye

Posters

LP/CD Cover and Inside Artwork

A Farewell To Kings

#P-7880, drawing of Rush on top, horizontal, 6 albums on bottom

Hemispheres

25×35, vertical

Permanent Waves

20×26.5, "Now Available," red/black
25×38 Gold Logo, horizontal
Cover + other LPs, 22×37

Moving Pictures

24×34
Cover + 6 other LPs, 24×36

Exit ... Stage Left

Mercury/PolyGram #MP415, 19×33.5

Signals

38×54
Anthem promo, vertical, 3 other LPs on red 24×36

Grace Under Pressure

Promo, horizontal, 24×34
Promo, vertical, with previous 4 LPs, MP #576, 24×34
24×24
Promo, horizontal, 24×34
20×29

Grace Under Pressure Tour

RCA/Columbia Video promo, vertical, 12×18.5

Power Windows

(M5664) Now In Stock, horizontal
(M5665) 24×24
Promo, cover + 4 other LPs, (#MP672), 24×36, vertical

Hold Your Fire

(S8324641) black logo, 9×20, horizontal
24×36
(CB8324641) 24×24 w/grey strip
Juggler 25×35

Cover + all other CDs on brick wall (Netherlands) 24×35

A Show of Hands

(AI-1055) 24×30.5
Promo, vertical, inset pic of LP, CD, tape, video and laserdisc, 24×36

Presto

Atlantic promo, vertical, 24×36 (cover w/rabbit in hat on bottom)

Chronicles

24×24

Roll the Bones

24×24
Boy skeleton 22×34
Boy w/dice window 24×34

Counterparts

"Counterpoints", Rush On Tour, gold small poster (advance title)
In Stores Oct. 19 16×36
20×30 w/ small lock stock barrel pic at bottom

Test For Echo

Promo, horizontal, "In Stores Sept. 10," 1996, 18×36
Same as above, but with no store info and in dim sky variation (as on tourbook), 18×36

Retrospective I/II

Mercury promo, vertical, double-sided, 24×36

Different Stages

Anthem promo, vertical, 18×36, grey sky/crowd image from booklet cover

Geddy Lee: My Favorite Headache

Anthem promo, vertical, double-sided, 12×24

Live Shot Posters

Hemispheres

Tour of the Hemispheres 20×30 (smoky), horizontal, #BT483, Switzerland
Rock On, #RO 053, horizontal, printed in Holland

'77 Stage shot 24×33 (B243 BIG-O), England
LP live poster insert-11.5×23
Dutch LP poster-same (9111 005)
1979 Alex with black Stratocaster with band (Pace International 31/P3196), 25×38 horizontal, printed in Scotland
1979 22×34, Live Circles, horizontal, BiRite

Permanent Waves

'80 Stage shot 18.5×30.5
Rock On, #RO 014, horizontal, printed in Holland
B313, horizontal, London
207-874-6630

Moving Pictures

(RU 01) 15×21
Q107 FM, vertical

Exit ... Stage Left

Mountain Dew Exclusive, 17×22, vertical (sold at Dairy Queen, 7-11)
1982 Stage shot, (6 inset photos) #15-215, Bi-Rite
1984 #1352, Holland, horizontal

Signals

None produced.

Grace Under Pressure

'82 live shot of Geddy and Alex; P/G in corner, 24×36
Artemis #8076, 24×36, vertical, split live shots (black/red/blue),
'82 Stage shot (RU 02), 20×29 horizontal

Power Windows

Six square live shots, 24×36
Artemis #8116, 24×33, three live shots

Hold Your Fire

Funky #3152, 24×35, 3 squares on grey
Artemis #8169, 24×36, vertical, 3 squares on red with spheres

Presto

Tour exclusive, 24×36, current 1990 live shots

Roll the Bones

Commercial, Anthem #7158, 22×34, horizontal, '90 shots from tourbook

Tour exclusive, 24×36, vertical, 3 square photos w/LP cover on top

Counterparts

None produced.

Test For Echo

Tour exclusive, 24×36, vertical, with 1994 shots

Portrait Posters

1976 2112 portrait, group posed
1977 42×54, square pics, some live shots, Rush in makeup
1977 A Farewell To Kings-16×24, vertical, Alex in throne, Neil and Geddy standing behind in color, AFTK Rush logo on bottom
1980 '78 era group portrait on red background; live shots on bottom (Pace Minerva 47/8010) 25×38, vertical, printed in Scotland
1981 Moving Pictures-LP cover and band portraits from LP insert on bottom, (#MP364), vertical
1982 Signals-Anthem promo, horizontal, digitized portraits from inside cover 24×36
1984 Grace Under Pressure-Cat Productions, 22×32, horizontal, LP Karsh portrait in color
1984 Through the Camera Eye, digitized portraits, 18×24
1985 Power Windows-Band posed, vertical, (like on Music Express magazine)
1994 Anthem promo, Juno Awards Hall of Fame, 18×24, vertical (1991 era posed w/5 album covers)

Other Posters

1980 Hemispheres Starman on black velvet 23×35

Magazine Posters

Geddy (Faces) 11×15
Alex (Circus) 11×16
Rush (Metal Hammer) 11×16
Rush (Kerrang 10/82) 11×17
Rush (Break Out) 12×17
Geddy and Alex (Guitar 2/86) 16×21
Rush (UK Metal Fury poster magazine #3) 24×33
Rush (UK Metal Fury poster magazine #15) 24×33

Store Displays

Grace Under Pressure
13×20
3D
Power Windows 3D
Hold Your Fire 3D 2 pc
A Show of Hands
Presto
Roll the Bones 3D 2 pc
Counterparts 3D 2 pc
Victor
Geddy Lee

Endorsement Posters

Alex:

1987 Gallien-Krueger, vertical, (Alex standing) 18×24
1987 Gallien Krueger, vertical, (Alex sitting) 18×24
1994 Paul Reed Smith Guitars (Alex) 22×24
1996 Paul Reed Smith Guitars (Alex with short hair) 22×24

Neil:

1980 Zildjian Cymbals (with Steve Gadd, Freddie White, etc)
1980 Tama Drums, 20×28
1981 Zildjian Cymbals (with rosewood kit)
1984 Zildjian Cymbals, vertical, live shot with electronic kit
1986 Zildjian Cymbals, 17×22, horizontal, different views with red kit
1987 Ludwig Drums, vertical, 17×22, white kit
1990 Wuhan (Neil on tour)
1990 Ludwig Drums, 18×24, vertical, plum kit
1991 Ludwig Drums, 18×24, vertical, blue kit
1994 Ludwig Drums, 18×24, vertical, black kit
1996 DW Drums, 16×21, vertical, red sparkle kit
1996 Zildjian Cymbals, 18×27, horizontal, "Talking Cymbals" live shot, #ZM0110
1996 Zildjian Cymbals vinyl banner of above
1997 Pro-Mark (Neil and others), horizontal, #B797-1

Promo Posters 12×15

All the World's a Stage Tour through current tour
1978 Juno Awards Winner
Archives through current album

Hemispheres lightning bolts w/Starman
Presto Atlantic Debut
Superconductor (tourdates)
Welcome Back Rush to ATI
Roll the Bones Dreamline Kickoff
Dreamline #1 Debut
Roll the Bones Recession Proof Rock

Concert Handbills/Mini Posters

Rush/Styx 3/25/76 at Medford Armory
Rush/Tommy Bolin 11/3/76 Douglas Hall Fairgrounds
Rush/Starcastle 4/14/77 Memorial Coliseum Ft. Wayne
Rush/UFO/Max Webster 9/22/77 Douglas Hall Fairgrounds
Rush/Nazareth 5/6-11/79 diff. Euro dates 46 ? × 33 (blue/purplish logo)
Rush at Memorial Coliseum 4/25/80 in Ft. Wayne 17×22½ (blue Starman and wavelengths)
Rush/Max Webster 3/8/81 Hara Arena 11×17
Rush Hour '81, Rush/Girlschool 11/17/81, horizontal
Rush/Nazareth, 5/10/83, Dusseldorf
European Tour '83 (Kings and Pictures collage art with Starman) 24×34
Rush 5/10/84 Thomas and Mack Arena 14×22
Rush 7/14-15/84 Montreal Forum 12×20
Rush/Steve Morse 12/18/85 Civic Arena 11×17
WDVE grey/black 21×35 of above
World Tour '88, HYF cover w/3 b & w portraits bottom, 24×34
Rush 2/19/88 Pensacola Civic Center
Hold Your Fire UK Tour 4/88, vertical, Juggler on white w/red logo
Rush On Tour — Roll the Bones 20×30 (dark greyish), horizontal
Rush/Primus at Sheffield Arena (3 in black) 40×60
Rush at the Forum 4/2-3/92 13×18
Rush/Mr. Big at Fiddlers Green Amphitheater 11×17
Rush/Mr. Big 1992 On Tour 15 ? ×36 (grp posed)
Rush/Candlebox at Providence Civic Center 1994
Rush 3/11-12/94 Centrum
Rush 4/24/94 Hartford Civic Center
An Evening With Rush 1996
UNO Lakefront/New Orleans (bat) 1996
Test For Echo at Fiddlers Green Amphitheater 5/22/97

Tapestries

Hemispheres logo and portrait in white on red 39×54
    (unofficial)
Starman 22.5× 22.5 in black/red with blue star
Starman 44×44 in black/white or white/blue/red
Starman 45×48
Signals 22.5×22.5
Signals 45×48 olive
Grace Under Pressure 22.5×22.5
Grace Under Pressure 45×48
"The Enemy Within" video shot 44×44
Hold Your Fire (white)

Banners

Grace Under Pressure
Power Windows
Hold Your Fire 21×31 red
Hold Your Fire 5×39 black/yellow
Presto
Roll the Bones (skulls/logos) 14×14

Miscellaneous

Chu-Bops Mini Album Sleeves with Gum: Permanent
    Waves #7
("Spirit of Radio" lyrics), Moving Pictures #37 ("Vital
    Signs" lyrics)
Moving Pictures Lighter
Mirror: Starman 12.5×12.5
Grace Under Pressure
Rockardz (1981)
Book Cover: Rock'n School Products Inc. 13.5×22
    (1982)
Folders: Moving Pictures; Signals
Spiral notebook: Moving Pictures; Signals
Metal poster/sign: Exit … Stage Left
Hold Your Fire balloon
Presto pencil (two styles-black w/rabbit in hat on top;
    white w/rabbit in hat on top)
Roll the Bones 8.5×33 promo scroll-Row the Boats
Roll the Bones jar of dice
Anthem Christmas ornaments: Hold Your Fire (red
    with lettering), Presto rabbit in hat
ERTL Rock and Roll Road Haulers Rush tour truck
    (red) 1997 (other two in series were for Cheap
    Trick and Van Halen)
Waste basket
Frisbee

Satin headband- red 2112 style Rush logo with white
    Starmen on each side

Related Miscellaneous

1977 Guitar World Magazine, Alex's ES-355, 11×15
1982 Neil Peart (circa '80 from Tama ad) lithograph by
    Joey Coya
1984 Tama Drums 3′×6′ silk tapestry of Neil on barge
    with red kit
1992 History of Rock and Roll lithograph (Presto
    portrait drawings with other bands)
11/5/94 Burning For Buddy Giveaway at Manny's
    Music, 12×17
1997 Guitars That Rule the World Vol. 2: Smell the
    Fuzz (Alex pic), 13×19
1998 R.A.D.D. (Rockers Against Drunk Driving), Take
    the Lead, (Driven video shoot) 27×19
2000 Soul In the City (Alex picture)
2000 Sunrise Records, St. Catharine's ON 11/24/00
    Geddy In-Store Signing

Clothing

Shirts

Rush (white)
Fly By Night (black/cover art)
2112 cover art

A Farewell To Kings

Starman and logo
Crowned skull
Navy blue-star man and crown below
white Starman jersey

Hemispheres (black)

Starman (globe back designs)
Collage (gold 2112 style logo, band live, Starman,
    crowned skulls)
white Jersey
jersey-yellow sleeves, crowned skull and star, Archives
    circle pics
Polar fleece jacket (issued 2000 by Backstage Club)
Turtleneck (issued 2000 by Backstage Club)

Permanent Waves

Black with cover girl and wavelength
Bingley Hall UK Tour
white sleeves-Tour 1980 (Crowned skull front, Starman back)
collage (Tour 1980, HEMISPHERES brain, band live on sides)
white jersey (blue sleeves, pot leaves, drawing of band on front)
grey Jersey (faces on back)

Moving Pictures

Cover (clapstick back)
"Rainbow" style
grey jersey (cover with clapstick on back)
Muscle shirt
Tanktop
Sweater

Exit ... Stage Left

cover (black)
grey Jersey
grey jersey (Moving Pictures pic on front/AFTK live LP circle pics on back and 2112 style font over Starman)
European Tour '81
European jersey (green sleeves)

Signals

cover (black or olive with back cover on back)
white collage
white Jersey
Sold Out in Texas jersey
green jersey ('He's a rebel and a runner' back)
Muscle shirt
tanktop
sweatshirt

Grace Under Pressure

cover (white)
black (logo on pastel colors)
c-clamp picture (white)
jersey
muscle shirt (white-cover; P/G back)
muscle shirt (black-P/G front; glow in dark)

Power Windows

cover (black with title on back)
cover (grey w/tourdates on back)
boy with binoculars with window over him (white)
band pics
Big Money video
jersey-binocular boy (black sleeves)-tourdates back
window in sky and remote (white)
muscle shirt

Hold Your Fire

cover (red)
spheres (black)
vertical red Rush logo (white)
juggler (white)
juggler w/label pic, songs on back (white)
intersecting red Rush logo (black)
1974 Rush logo, collage (white)
tanktop
Sweater

A Show of Hands

cover (white)
cover (black)
Sweater (white)

Presto

cover (white w/hands on back)
cover (black)
paper/scissors/rock under logo/logo on back (white)
Tic tac toe board (black)
Rabbit in hat (grey)
Tanktop
Sweater

Chronicles

T-shirt-white

Roll the Bones

cover (white)
cover (black-songs on back)
skull w/skeletal starman on back (white)
collage (white)
Pushead-drawn skull jack in the box (black)
skull pocket design w/colorful logo on back (black)
Pushead-drawn skullboy skeleton kicking (black)
cover w/black/yellow dice back (white)
Rush front/Primus back

Pushead/Rap Lyrics on back
Photos from CD insert of Rush (white) w/wishbones
All-over print of skull of dice
Tanktop (black cover)
Tanktop (black skeleton boy)
Sweater (white)
Sweater (blk Pushead)

Counterparts

Cover (Navy blue)
Cover w/sink diagram back (blue)
Adam and Eve w/Slave to the Hormone on back
    (white)
Album portrait (white)
Monkeys (white)
Tortoise and hare w/Time and tide back (black)
Lock stock barrel-cattle w/phrases on back (black)
Pushead (black)
Tanktop (grey)
Jams
Turtleneck (navy w/embroidered pocket nut/bolt)
Hooded longsleeve (white Adam and Eve)

Test For Echo

cover (white)
cover w/songs on back (white) promo
Stoneman on pocket w/mariner's map on back
    (white)
Wolf photo w/Test For Echo on back (black)
Wolf photo w/dates on back (bootleg)
Child photos (tan)
Half the World photo (black)
1974 logo w/Stoneman (white)
If You Want Something Done Right….(frnt)/…Just
    Forget It (back) (black)
Kiddie shirt (black w/Stoneman)
Tye dye-Pink fractal front (CD image in jewel case)
Tye dye-Blueish fractal (CD itself)
Ski vest (Stoneman)
Test For Echo turtleneck (black w/embroidered
    pocket logo and Stoneman)
Polar fleece jacket (issued 2000 by Backstage Club)

Different Stages

Black t-shirt (red logo/toys on right)

Miscellaneous Shirts

Geddy Lee: My Favourite Headache (black, Gordian
    Knot on front, small CD cover on back) 2001
Geddy Lee: My Favourite Headache (blue, CD art)
Geddy Lee: My Favourite Headache (black, three
    Geddy photos, voodoo pins on back)
Neil Peart shirt (art by Joey Coya, 1982) sold by Casino
    Percussion
Starman (Blk w/red Farewell to Kings style Rush logo)
Starman (Blk w/red 2112 style logo)
Starman (Blk w/comic book style block letter logo)
Starman (Tye-dye w/2112 style logo)
Starman ("Complete" book style design; Special
    Edition Oct. 1, 1992)
Starman (1998, black, red PeWaves logo)
Comic Book cover art (blk)
National Midnight Star
The Spirit of Rush
Rush Backstage Club T-shirt (80s)

Satin Jackets

Exit … Stage Left
World Tour '83 (Starman on back with AFTK logo)
Presto
Chronicles
Roll the Bones
Counterparts
Test For Echo
Different Stages

Bandanas and Scarves

Presto bandana
Presto bandana
Roll the Bones bandana
Roll the Bones bandana
Counterparts bandana
Counterparts bandana
Counterparts gypsy scarf

Album Ads

75 Caress of Steel (The More You Hear It, the More
    You Hear In It)
76 2112 small ad
77 A Farewell to Kings small ad
77 A Farewell to Kings (caricature) 12×15

78 Hemispheres
78 Hemispheres (gold)
80 Permanent Waves
81 Moving Pictures
81 Rush Through Time (German ad)
81 Exit … Stage Left (live shot) Anthem
81 Exit … Stage Left (theatre)
82 Canada Dry (albums in glass)
82 Signals
82 Signals (Platinum and Still Pouring) 12×15
84 Grace Under Pressure
85 Grace Under Pressure Tour video
85 Power Windows (Look No Further…)
    Music Express ad
85 Power Windows (Rush is in Sight…)
85 Power Windows
87 Hold Your Fire
89 A Show of Hands
89 Presto
89 Presto (small; tourdates)
89 Presto (tourdates) 12×15
90 Chronicles
91 Roll the Bones (Dreamline kickoff) 12×15
91 Roll the Bones
91 Roll the Bones (On Tour with live shots)
93 "Stick It Out" (tortoise/hare)
93 Counterparts
93 Counterparts (limited edition-How Many Times
    Do We Have To Say It?)
94 "Cold Fire" (u and i game)
96 Victor
96 Test For Echo
97 Retrospective
97 Retrospective (smaller)
98 Different Stages 12×15
98 Different Stages (smaller)

Instrument Catalogs

80–90 Zildjian Set-Up Guide (Neil)
80 Tama Drums (Neil)
82 Tama Drums (Neil)
84 Tama Drums (Neil)
88 Carvin Guitars (Alex)
96 Drum Workshop (Neil)

Equipment Endorsement Ads

Neil

80 VibraFibe
80 Zildjian

80 Tama
80 Tama Drums: rosewood kit
83 Tama Drums: red kit for Artstar sets
85 Evans Heads: Neil's name mentioned
86 Wuhan Cymbals: Neil's name mentioned
86 Zildjian
87 Zildjian
87 Ludwig (white)
88 Zildjian ZM10 microphone ad
89 Ludwig/Musser salute to Neil for winning MD poll
89 Solid Percussion snare ad
90 Ludwig Drums: plum kit
90 Wuhan
91 Pro-Mark Autograph drumsticks small ad
91 Pro-Mark Autograph drumsticks (sticks on photo)
91 Ludwig Drums: blue kit
92 Zildjian: Hall of Fame (Neil '85 pic)
94 Ludwig Drums: black kit
95 Zildjian Time #18 (Neil cover)
96 Drum Workshop: "Something Old, Something
    New" by Neil
96 Pro-Mark Sticks: Rush and Get a Pair
96 Zildjian Cymbals: "Talking Cymbals" by Neil
97 Pro-Mark Sticks: 40th Anniv. ad (w/others)
97 Zildjian Cymbals: (w/others)
3/98 Guitar Center "Rhythm Notes"
01 Modern Drummer 25th ad

Alex:

80 ProStar strings
80 Alvarez (with Jon Anderson of Yes)
85 Dean Markley
85 Fender
87 Gallien-Krueger: Alex
87 Signature: Alex
91 Gallien-Krueger: Alex with pics of others
91 Paul Reed Smith
94 Paul Reed Smith
96 Paul Reed Smith: short hair

Geddy:

84 Roto-Sound Super Wound 606 bass strings (ad also
    came in red)
87 Steinberger basses
87 Roto-Sound Funkmaster bass strings
91 Roto-Sound bass strings: Geddy with other artists'
    pics
95 Musicians Institute of Technology (Geddy and Alex
    seen in)
99 Emagic software

Band:
91 Muchmusic (quote and picture)

Roadie Passes

Fly By Night
Guest (cover art)

2112
All Access (cover art)

A Farewell To Kings
All Access (puppet strings picture from back cover)

Archives
All Access (cover art)

Hemispheres 1/19/79 Civic Arena Backstage
(brown/white or pink/black)
Road Crew (cover art)

Permanent Waves
All Access (cover art)

Moving Pictures
5/7/81 Richfield Coliseum
World Tour '81 Guest (white, pink or orange)

Signals
New World Tour '82 – '83
Total Access (white or black)

Grace Under Pressure (blue/gray)
World Tour '84 – '85: Total Access (red/white or
purple/gray)

Power Windows
Tour '85 – '86 Total Access
V.I.P.

Neil Peart Seminar
5/5/86 All Access

Hold Your Fire
'87 – '88 Total Access (juggler)
V.I.P. (cover)
Aftershow (Rockin' Constructivists from ASOH
cover art)

Presto
V.I.P. (cover)
Total Access

Roll the Bones
Total Access
V.I.P. (cover or wishbones)

Counterparts
V.I.P. (cover art or nut/bolt photos)
All Areas

Backstage Passes

All the World's a Stage

A Farewell To Kings
Crowned skull

Hemispheres
1/19/79 Civic Arena (pink/white or pink/black) gold
seal
1/26/79 Electric Factory Backstage (orange or blue/
black)
3/14/79 WDVE-DKE Pittsburgh (blue/black or blue/
pink)
? at the Stanley
? 93 QFM Milwaukee

Moving Pictures
2/81 The Loop Presents Rush (WLUP 98 FM Chicago)
2/81 95.5 WMET Celebrates the New Album by Rush
2/26-28/81 and 3/1/81 WMET 95.5 Chicago
3/2/81 93 QFM Milwaukee
4/11/81 San Antonio Convention Center 99.5
4/16/81 Mid-South Coliseum Memphis Rock 103
5/7/81 Belkin Productions Presents Rush at the
Richfield Coliseum
5/11/81 The Arena 99 WAAL FM
5/18/81 Madison Square Garden (WPLJ 95.5)

5/24/81 Providence Civic Center (WAAF 107 FM)
7/4/81 Alpine Valley Music Theater (FM 98)

Signals

9/8/82 Civic Arena Omaha Z92 FM
9/17/82 McNichols Arena Denver 96 KPKE
11/3/82 Party Pass
4/2/83 Carrierdome Syracuse 95X WAQX (gold seal)
New World Tour '82 – '83 Guest (pink or orange) gold seal

Grace Under Pressure

Yellow/blue
Red/gray

Power Windows

12/15/85 Richmond Coliseum (WRXL 102)
12/18/85 Civic Arena Pittsburgh WDVE((red/black or blue/black)
'85 – '86 Aftershow Promoter
'85 – '86 3/25/86 Guest

Hold Your Fire

Round ball
Triangle shape
Juggler (gold seal)
cover art

Presto

Guest (cover)
Guest (round in blue or red)
Access All Areas (pink, blue, or red)
Photo Rabbit in hat shape (green or red)

Roll the Bones

WFOOD Welcomes Rush
Aftershow
Aftershow (round)
Guest (round)
Access All Areas (wishbones or cover)
Photo Dice shape (2 versions)

Counterparts

Guest (round, sink design in gray or red)
Guest (round, gameboard in blue or red)
All Areas (blue, gray, or red)
WFYV Rock 105 Welcomes Rush
Aftershow (octagon shape in blue or red)

Test For Echo

Press Pre-Concert
Press Echo Review
Press After Concert